T0144131

Zen of Cloud
Learning Cloud Computing by Examples

Second Edition

Zen of Cloud
Learning Cloud Computing by Examples

Second Edition

Haishi Bai

CRC Press
Taylor & Francis Group
Boca Raton London New York

CRC Press is an imprint of the
Taylor & Francis Group, an **informa** business

Comic Strips by Sabrina Bai and Cover Painting by Jing Zhao. Used with Permission.

CRC Press
Taylor & Francis Group
6000 Broken Sound Parkway NW, Suite 300
Boca Raton, FL 33487-2742

© 2019 by Taylor & Francis Group, LLC
CRC Press is an imprint of Taylor & Francis Group, an Informa business

No claim to original U.S. Government works

Printed on acid-free paper

International Standard Book Number-13: 978-1-138-33260-7 (Hardback)

Visit the Taylor & Francis Web site at
http://www.taylorandfrancis.com

and the CRC Press Web site at
http://www.crcpress.com

Contents

Preface

I wrote the first edition of *Zen of Cloud* in 2014, right after Windows Azure was renamed Microsoft Azure. The new name sent an important signal—Microsoft's cloud platform was not only about Windows technologies. Instead, it was an open platform that embraced all workloads. Four years later, Linux-based workloads have taken over 42% of Azure cores. And that number is still rising.

The openness of Azure has given me a terrific opportunity to look at the cloud landscape with a broader vision. Somewhat ironically, I worked on non-Microsoft technologies much more than before I had joined Microsoft. Now, after four years of accumulation, I think I'm ready to write an updated version to share my learnings.

This book will be quite different from the first edition, which focused exclusively on Microsoft Azure technologies. This book takes a completely different approach—it focuses on workloads instead of technologies. At the end, what you care about is how you can operate you own workloads with high service qualities. Coincidentally, Azure (or any other cloud platform) doesn't care much about which technologies you choose, because at the end, what Azure cares about is compute consumption. As long as you can run your workloads with high efficiency, Azure is more than happy to help you achieve more regardless of which technologies or frameworks you use.

So this book is all about workloads. I'll discuss various scenarios and help you to navigate through various possible paths. I'll still cover a lot on Azure, but I'll discuss other platforms and technologies as well. The grand goal of this book is to help you to maintain clarity as you take on your journey to the cloud. The book will explain "hows," but it focuses more on "whys." And I hope you'll enjoy reading the book as much as I enjoyed writing it.

Organization of the Book

The first two chapters of the book cover fundamental ideas of the cloud. I recommend you read these two chapters if you are new to cloud computing. Otherwise, you can skip ahead and pick the chapters of your interests. Except for the first two chapters, all the chapters are pretty much independent from each other, so you can read them in any order.

Each chapter in this book contains a mixture of special sections, including *theories*, *patterns*, *tutorials*, *hands-on labs*, *patterns*, *warnings*, *best practices* and *random information*. A unique icon marks each of these sections. Skipping any of these sections should not affect your ability to continue reading the rest of the book. So you can use these icons to tailor your reading experience. For example, if you learn best with hands-on practice, you can follow through all tutorials and hands-on labs; if you are interested mostly in architecture and design patterns, you can spend more time with the design pattern sections; and if you want to geek out on a subject, the theory sections are your best friends.

Tutorials. Tutorials focus on simple scenarios. They guide you to get something up and running quickly.

Hands-on labs. Hands-on labs walk you through end-to-end implementations of typical scenarios.

Theories. These sections drill into technical and mathematical details of a specific topic. If you are new to the topic and want to understand its underlying mechanism, you should read these sections.

Patterns. These sections provide background information on design patterns used in text. If you are interested in a pattern, you should read the corresponding section to understand the key ideas and concepts behind the pattern.

Warnings. These notes provide warnings and reminders of common pitfalls.

Best practices. These are useful tips that help you to be at the top of your game.

Random information. These are small pieces of random information that provide interesting detours from the text. They provide some fun facts and background information for the geeks.

Supplements

Cloud is changing fast, so the tutorials and labs are likely to change. The book comes with a companion GitHub repository at https://github.com/Haishi2016/ZoC.git, where you can find updated tutorials, samples, and labs.

About the Author

 **Haishi Bai** is a Principal Software Engineer at Microsoft Azure. He wrote his first program when he was 12, and, ever since, the world has been all about software and services. In his 20 years of professional life, he's been engaged in various areas ranging from finance to public safety, and he's taken on different roles such as architect, development lead, and project manager. He's also a passionate educator who loves to share his knowledge. He's the author of 8 cloud computing books (including this one). He also runs a technical blog at http://blog.haishibai.com that focuses on cloud technologies. The site attracts over 60,000 views monthly. His Twitter handle is @HaishiBai2010. He's also a volunteer teacher of TEAL, which aims at bringing computer science education to all schools.

Chapter 1

The Journey to Cloud

Understanding Cloud

A few years back, I worked for a startup in Santa Clara, California, that was literally located in the CEO's garage when I joined. I still remember one morning, as I came to the "office," I found the garage door wide open and all our servers were gone. I called my boss and found out that the whole company had been evicted that morning because the neighbor had filed a complaint because we were too noisy.

Availability

I couldn't blame the neighbor. What the company did was to detect and report on gunshot incidents in near real time (seconds between a gun is fired and 911 is dispatched). To test our detection system, we needed to make a lot of popping sounds, which surely could be quite annoying. Before the company could find a real office, we were working from home. The code server was down (because it was unplugged), so we were asked to be "very, very careful" not to lose our work. Fortunately, our Exchange server was still running because it was "hosted." That was my first real-life experience with comparing a hosted environment and a self-managed environment:

A hosted environment was more available because it was unlikely to be evicted.

As a matter of fact, the Exchange host had protections against not only evictions, but also failures such as power outages, intrusions, floods, cooling failures, server failures, network failures, viruses, hackers, and many other threats that might have taken down the servers. Keeping the server running was the host's core business, so the host made every effort to build up protections against all imaginable failures. As a service consumer, all we needed to do was subscribe to the service without taking on any of the management complexities.

The service host didn't have perfect servers that would never fail. They probably had "commodity" (a.k.a. cheap) servers to keep the cost down. How did the service host provide high available services with ordinary servers? The service host had an important advantage—it had many servers. When a server failed, the host could start another server to replace the broken one rather quickly. On the contrary, for a company that ran its own servers, if a broken server was to be replaced, a new server had to be purchased, installed, and configured, which could take days or even months. So with the same hardware quality, the service host could provide higher availability because it had *redundant resources* to replace failed ones.

By How Much Does Redundancy Improve Availability?

Availability is generally expressed as a percentage. For example, the availability level of your subscribed service from Microsoft Azure can be shown in the following formula:

$$\text{Availability} = \frac{Total\ time - unavailable\ time}{Total\ time} \times 100\%$$

The formula should be self-explanatory. As the formula shows, a machine with higher availability is less likely to fail. Assume you have two identical servers that both have 90% of availability. If they are configured as backups for each other, they can jointly provide 99% of availability. This is because the availability of the system A_s can be calculated as:

$$A_s = 1 - \left(probability\ of\ both\ machines\ fail \right) = 1 - 10\% \times 10\% = 0.99$$

Similarly, adding a machine with availability A_m to a system with availability A_s yields a new availability A_s':

$$A_s' = A_s + A_m \left(1 - A_s \right)$$

The above formula tells us two things: 1) when you add a new server, the overall availably of the system does increase; 2) as you add more servers to the system, the availability gain of adding a new server exponentially decreases. For example, if all machines have an availability of 90%, adding a new server to a system that consists of at least two servers is to add another "9" after the decimal places—three servers give you 99.9%, four servers give you 99.99%, and so on.

Before I move off the topic, I need to mention that availability calculations can be based on different time intervals such as month or year. A yearly availability commitment is weaker than a monthly commitment because it allows more variations month-by-month, which means you may have a bad month with much lower availability during a given year. Most cloud services promise monthly availabilities.

Scalability

My wife has been a loyal Apple user. She upgrades her iPhone every other major generation. So over the years, she only used her iPhone with odd version numbers (and I'm so grateful Apple skipped version 9!) With each iPhone, she takes lots of pictures—selfies, cats, places we go, and various foods before they are consumed.

My wife appreciates cloud from a different angle—she uses iCloud. She likes the fact that you can get seemingly infinite storage space on iCloud so that she can keep all her pictures, all the way back to the first picture she took with her first iPhone. In 2018, when you sign up for iCloud, you get 5GB of storage for free, and you can pay for a subscription with up to 2TB of storage. While the number is moderately impressive for a single user, when you multiply that with millions of users, you reach a quite impressive number.

Does App really have that much disk space? First, they don't. Apple uses cloud providers such as Azure and AWS to provide storages for them. Second, they don't need as much. When you subscribe to a storage account, you are unlikely to fill it up very quickly. This means iCloud only needs to allocate enough resources for the pictures you uploaded, not for the whole subscribed capacity. In other words, iCloud has a huge pool of storage resources, and it can re-purpose these resources for different users, creating the illusion of *elasticity* for each individual user. I call it an illusion because your resources on cloud aren't magically growing or shrinking. You are simply allocated more resources from the cloud's resource pool. Imagine all storage accounts are filled up and the iCloud is at its capacity; there won't be any elasticity to expand any of the accounts.

I should pause a little to briefly talk about *overselling*. Allocating fewer resources than you subscribe to is not necessarily overselling. If your ability to consume the fully subscribed capacity is guaranteed without service degradation, this is a legit optimization technique by a cloud provider to reduce cost.

The beauty of scalability to a consumer resides not only in how easily you can acquire new resources, but also in how quickly you can release unwanted resources. As we become more and more used to hosted resources on cloud, it might be increasingly hard to appreciate the ease of giving up resources. When I was in California, I had an old desktop tower that I wanted to discard or recycle. I called a few places to offer donating my desktop, which had a quite decent spec and wasn't very old. None of them wanted to take it. Eventually I found a place that would take it, but I had to drive over there to drop off my desktop and pay a $75 processing fee. Although my experience isn't universal, it still shows the challenges in managing physical resources, even just to get rid of them.

Security

Imagine you have 1 million dollars. And you are given two options: put the money into a plastic bag and tape it behind the water tank of your toilet; or make an impressive deposit to a bank and earn yourself a VIP status. I don't know about you, but I think the second option is obviously a more favorable choice. A bank is much more secured than a bathroom—just look at how much trouble the bad guys needed to go through to break into the Federal Reserve in *Die Hard with a Vengeance*! To break into a bathroom, on the other hand, all one needs to do is to kick in the door. And if something bad like a fire happens, you can probably kiss your money in the bathroom goodbye (that sounds a little weird, I know). On the contrary, even if a bank caught on a fire, you'll have means to recover your money.

However, when it comes to data, this analogy isn't always obvious to people. People like to keep their data "close," even if that means it's actually more vulnerable to theft and damage in most cases. Does your data center have layered access point controls? Is your data center equipped with biological scanners and metal detectors? Is your data center equipped with generators backed by an on-site oil reserve? These security measures are pretty common to cloud data centers; but they are too hard to be implemented and too expensive to be maintained by regular data centers.

Even if you were the real life Iron Man and could afford all these, cloud still has some advantages over your own data centers. First, cloud platforms have data centers across the globe. They can replicate your data to data center facilities that are far from each other, protecting your data from the most devastating disasters such as floods, earthquakes, and alien invasions. Second, cloud platform data centers contain a lot of data. Even if a hacker can break into the data center, it's would be quite hard for him to fish out your data from the ocean of data in those data centers. Finally, nowadays, many clouds offer encryption-at-rest, which keeps data encrypted while saved on disk. Even if a hacker grabbed the disk out of a data center, he or she would have an extremely hard time cracking the data open.

Agility

One day in 2000 while I was working for a financial software company at San Francisco, one of my colleagues came over to my cubicle and showed me a site called Google. "You can find anything on the Internet," he claimed. "Who would search the Internet when all interesting contents are curated and presented by beautiful web portals such as Yahoo!" I thought at the time. Seventeen years later, my life can't function without a search engine. Due to the nature of my work, I use many different programming languages, OSes, and frameworks. It's impossible for me to remember all the nifty syntax details of them. And I don't need to. All I need to do is to pull up a browser, do a search, and the answer is right there. This unprecedented ability to acquire information is very significant. Google alone performs over 5 billion queries per day. One has to ask, "Who's been answering those questions before?" I believe it's fair to say that Google's contribution is not just to the computer industry, but also to the entire civilization. For this reason alone, Google will always be one of my most respected companies on this planet.

Computer science has made several civilization-scope contributions in the past decades: Microsoft's personal PC, Google's search engine, Apple's mobile device, and Amazon's cloud. And I believe the most important contribution made by cloud is *agility*. Cloud allows new ideas to be incubated, tested, and productionized with unprecedented agility. Have an excellent idea for a web service? Get a free cloud subscription, deploy your application, and your business is open to the whole world within minutes, without any upfront investment. The idea doesn't work? You can walk away with no strings attached. The idea works and is taking over the world? You can scale out to hundreds of servers easily. This kind of agility benefits not only start-ups, but also innovation teams within established enterprises to try out new ideas to improve their services.

Airbnb is a company that has grown up almost entirely on cloud. Initially, the creators of Airbnb were simply trying to make a little profit by turning their living room into a bed and breakfast. As the idea grew, their demands on compute resources drastically increased. Before the cloud era, they would have had to raise millions of dollars to build up their infrastructures alone. And to support a global-scale business, the investments on servers alone would have been huge. With cloud, they could bootstrap their business with a few tens of thousands of dollars and continue on to disrupt the entire hotel business.

Of course, cloud is not a magic potion that makes everything work. A successful business is certainly still built on passion, devotion, ingeniousness, and some luck. However, cloud does take a tremendous burden off the creators' shoulders, allowing them to explore new possibilities with unprecedented agility, reduced risk, and unlimited potential to go big.

Scaling Out, Scaling In, Scaling Up, Scaling Down?

In the above text, I carefully used "scale out" when I talked about acquiring new compute power by adding more servers. Sometimes, acquiring more compute power is called "scaling up" regardless of how the compute resources are scaled. Throughout this book, I'll use more precise terms to distinguish between two fundamentally different ways to scale compute resources—horizontal scale and vertical scale.

Horizontal scaling adds more compute powers by adding more servers. Vertical scaling adds more compute power by making existing servers more powerful. Scaling up is often used in an on-premises data center through hardware upgrades. Horizontal scaling is often used by cloud that joins more virtual machines together to handle increasing workloads.

Horizontal scaling uses *scaling out* and *scaling in* to refer to compute resource increases and decreases. Vertical scaling uses *scaling up* and *scaling down* to refer to server capacity increases and decreases. Although *scaling up* and *scaling down* are often used in place of *scaling out* and *scaling in* within the context of cloud, this book follows a strict usage of these terms to avoid possible confusions.

Modeling Cloud

It is an old and dingy hotel room. Thunder is rolling outside the window. Morpheus is holding two pills in front of Neo. "Take the blue pill and the story ends. You wake up in your bed and you believe whatever you want to believe. You take the red pill and you stay in Wonderland and I show you how deep the rabbit hole goes," he says.

The movie reference may be unclear now, but I guarantee it will rush back to you when you try to deploy your first application to cloud, especially if you hire a cloud consultant (who hasn't read this book). "IaaS or PaaS?" the consultant will ask. Or, in a fancier way, "Do you want to lift-and-shift, or do you want to write a cloud-native application from the ground up?"

The *-aaS Model

When you read cloud literature, you will certainly see three terms: Infrastructure as a Service (IaaS), Platform as a Service (PaaS), and Software as a Service (SaaS). These three terms form a high level model of how cloud is organized (Figure 1.1). They also represent three different entry points to cloud.

Infrastructure as Service (IaaS) is the lowest abstraction layer on top of the actual data center hardware. It exposes resources such as virtual machines, virtual networks, load balancers, and IP addresses. IaaS brings on-premises concepts to cloud so that you can model your applications in the same way as in an on-premises environment. In other words, if you have an existing

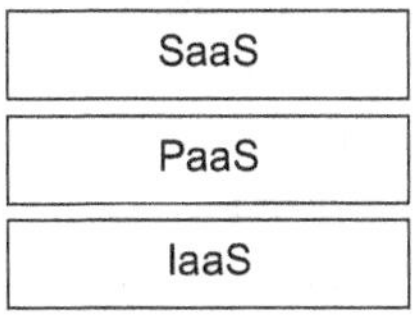

SaaS
PaaS
IaaS

Figure 1.1 IaaS–PaaS–SaaS cloud model

on-premises application, you can simply "lift" it from your on-premises data center and "shift" it to cloud—this is where shift-and-lift came from.

Shift-and-lift sounds easy and logical. However, there are some pitfalls, some of which may be quite dangerous and can break your projects on cloud. We'll discuss these pitfalls later in this chapter.

Platform as a Service (PaaS) hides infrastructural concepts and provides programming and hosting frameworks on top of which you design and deploy your applications. A PaaS platform can be very opinionated. It may mandate specific design patterns, programming frameworks, deployment topologies, and workflows. The constrained scope allows PaaS to provider deeper optimization and additional productivity features. Furthermore, the PaaS offerings on cloud are designed specifically for the cloud platforms. If you follow their guidance to design and host your applications, you can avoid the IaaS pitfalls, and you can better leverage cloud features to gain more returns. You'll learn about a few PaaS options throughout this book.

Software as a Service (SaaS) refers to software running as hosted services. SaaS provides a very simple way to consume software features. You don't need to download, install, and configure any software packages. Instead, you simply subscribe to a hosted service and consume the service through common communication protocols such as HTTP and TCP. There are many SaaS offerings on the Internet, offering many features that we rely on in our everyday lives—Office 365, Salesforce, YouTube, Twitter, XBOX Live, and many others.

Once your own applications are deployed on cloud, they potentially become SaaS as well. So from a service author's perspective, SaaS is the result; PaaS and IaaS are two options for approaching cloud (hence the red pill, blue pill analogy).

Picking between IaaS and PaaS seems straightforward—if you have an existing on-premises application, use IaaS to lift-and-shift. If you are starting new on cloud, use PaaS to enjoy the productivity of the PaaS. Unfortunately, things are not that straightforward. Many on-premises applications are not designed for a cloud environment. The applications might be easily "lifted and shifted," but they'll expose various problems when being continuously operated on cloud. You may find you'll have to redesign and rewrite parts of your applications to make them really thrive on cloud. On the other hand, learning a new PaaS system and writing everything new from the ground up could be a significant investment.

This dilemma is what I see as the biggest problem when you think of cloud using the *-aaS model. This is precisely why I've designed a different model—the CRM model—to describe cloud.

The CMR Model

The *-aaS model is based on different abstraction levels over the cloud hardware, so it's centered on cloud internal structure. The CMR model is a workload-centric model that focuses on how a user's workload is deployed and hosted on cloud.

The CMR model, or the Control-Mesh-Resource model views the cloud as a huge compute resource pool, on top of which user applications roam around. Instead of approaching cloud through either IaaS or PaaS, you approach cloud through a unified *control plane*. The control plane takes your workloads and projects them on top of a *compute plane*, which comprises various compute resources such as CPU, RAM, and disks. Workloads on the compute plane take the form of *service meshes*. A service mesh defines an isolated networking environment for an application. A service mesh can be scaled and moved on the compute plane as needed. Figure 1.2 shows a high-level view of the CMR view.

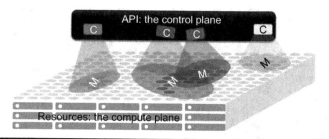

Figure 1.2   CMR cloud model

The easiest way to understand CMR is to imagine having a rack of projectors. When you need to deploy an application, you load a deck of slides in one of the projectors and project the application onto a huge screen (the compute plane). You can zoom in and zoom out as you wish (for scaling), and you can pan your projector around to move the projection to anywhere you want (for failovers, upgrades, etc.) The CMR model is my own creation and it's designed for describing *micro services*. Concepts and principals of CMR model will become clearer as the book progresses.

Approaching Cloud

Now it's time to get some hands-on experiences with cloud. In the following walkthrough, you'll create a free Azure subscription and provision a couple of compute resources. Getting an account on other cloud platforms follows a very similar process.

Tutorial: Creating and Using an Azure Subscription

 In this tutorial, you'll create a free Azure subscription. Then, you'll provision a Windows virtual machine as well as a Linux virtual machine.

Part I: Create an Azure Subscription

1. Before you can create an Azure subscription, you need a Microsoft account, which you can apply for free. If you were using AWS, you need to create a new AWS account. Similarly, if you use Google Compute Engine, you need to have a Google account. To create a new Microsoft account, navigate to https://signup.live.com and follow the wizard to create a free Microsoft account.
2. To sign up Azure, navigate to https://signup.azure.com. Sign in using your Microsoft account.
3. Follow the wizard to complete the sign-up process. In addition to the Microsoft account, you need a cell phone for identity verification, and a credit card for payment verification. Please note your credit card will not be charged unless you explicitly convert your free account to a paid offer.
4. Once your subscription is created, you can navigate to Microsoft Azure Management Portal at https://portal.zure.com to start using your Azure subscription.

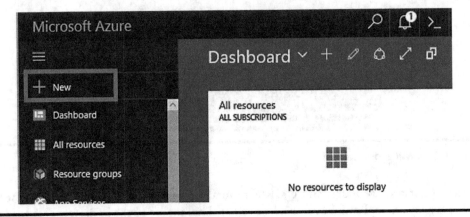

Figure 1.3   New resource link on Azure portal

Part II: Create a Windows VM

1. To create a new virtual machine, click on the **+New** link at the upper-left corner of the portal, as shown in Figure 1.3.
2. On the **New** screen, click on the **Windows Server 2016 VM** entry, as shown in Figure 1.4. If you don't see the entry, you can search for "Windows Server 2016" in the search box and click on the found entry.
3. In the creation wizard, enter basic information for your virtual machine, including machine name, administrator name, and password. Please note that you need to create a *resource group* to hold your virtual machine. Every entity you provision on Azure is called a *resource*. And you can put one or multiple resources into a *resource group*. A resource must belong to a single resource group. After entering all information, click on the **OK** button to continue, as shown in Figure 1.5.

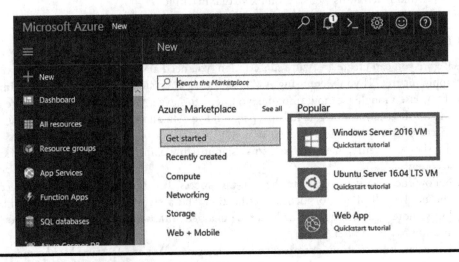

Figure 1.4   Creating Windows Server 2016 VM

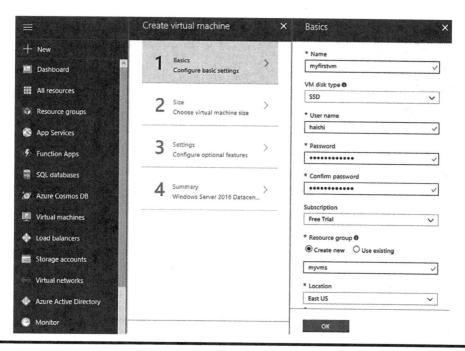

Figure 1.5   Entering basic VM information

4. Next, you can choose from various virtual machine sizes. Microsoft Azure provides several series of virtual machines with different memory and CPU core capacities. For this tutorial, you can use the **DS1_V2 Standard** size, which offers 1 virtual CPU, 3.5 GB of memory and up to 4 data disks. Click on the **DS_V2 Standard** tile and click on the **Select** button to continue, as shown in Figure 1.6.

Figure 1.6   Selecting VM size

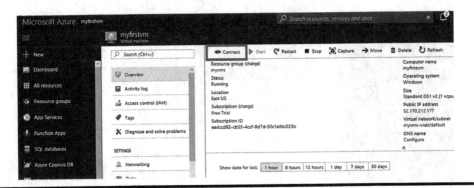

Figure 1.7 VM overview page

5. On the *Settings* screen, accept all default settings and click on the **OK** button to continue. There are several things on the setting screen that are worth noticing: 1) a virtual network in automatically created; 2) a subnet is automatically created; 3) a public IP address is automatically allocated; 4) a network security group (NSG) is automatically created. We'll discuss networking in more details in upcoming sections. For now, accepting all defaults should work just fine.

6. At last, on the *Summary* screen, click on the **Create** button to create the virtual machine. At the time of writing, the VM creation wizard has been updated. To enable remote RDP access, you'll need to make sure port 3389 is enabled in the Inbound Port Rules section before you can use RDP to connect to the machine.

7. Machine creation takes a few minutes. Once the machine is created, the machine's overview page will automatically open, as shown in Figure 1.7. If the page doesn't open automatically, you can bring it up from the portal home. To return to the portal home, click on the *Microsoft Azure* text at the upper left corner of the screen. A virtual machine tile should have been added to the portal home page. Clicking on the tile brings you to the same page as shown in Figure 1.7.

8. Click on the **Connect** link (see Figure 1.7). Open the downloaded RDP file and log in to the virtual machine using your administrator credential. You should see the remote desktop of the machine, as shown in Figure 1.8.

VMs are charged by the actual time they are kept running. To save cost, you should shut down your VMs when you are not using them. Azure also provides an auto-shutdown feature that you can configure on the VM's overview page. You can schedule a VM to be shutdown at specific time, and configure a notification hook to notify you 15 minutes before that happens.

Part III: Create a Linux VM

Creating a Linux VM follows the same steps. The only difference is that at step two, you need to select a Linux image such as *Ubuntu Server 16.04 LTS*. Then follow the same wizard to complete the provisioning process. You need to enable port 22 for SSH in this case.

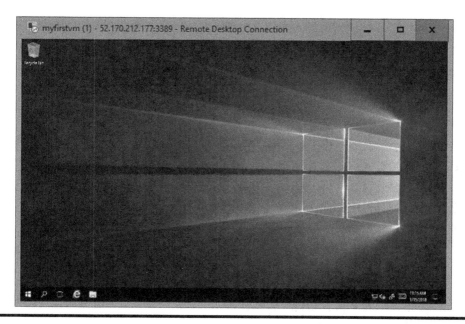

Figure 1.8   VM remote desktop

If you want to put the Linux VM on the same virtual network as the Windows VM, you need to make a few different choices:

1. You should choose to reuse the same resource group instead of creating a new one.
2. On the Settings page, instead of creating a new virtual network, you should pick the one that was created when the Windows VM was provisioned.

Once the machine is provisioned, you can use a SSH terminal such as Putty to connect to the Linux VM just like how you'd connect to any other remote Linux machines.

How do you Reach a Virtual Machine Hosted on Cloud?

When you provision a virtual machine, Azure picks an appropriate hosting machine from its hundreds of thousands of physical servers. Then it leverages Hyper-V to create a new virtual machine for you (other cloud platforms use other virtualization techniques such as VMware). The virtual machine has a virtualized network interface card (NIC), which is attached with a private IP. A virtual machine is placed on an automatically created virtual network, and the private IP is used by the virtual machine to communicate with other virtual machines on the same virtual network.

Azure allocates a public IP address from a public IP pool it owns, and assigns the IP address to your virtual machine. This allows you to access your virtual machine from a remote session over the Internet. Available public IP addresses on the Internet are limited resources, so you are only allowed to allocate a certain number of public IP addresses per subscription. You can also associate a DNS name to the public IP address so that you can access your machine using a

DNS name with a fixed postfix of *<location>.cloudapp.azure.com*, such as *mymachine.westus2.cloudapp.azure.com*.

If you don't associate a public IP with your virtual machine, you can't directly reach the machine from the Internet. Instead, you need to connect to one of the other machines on the same network that does have a public IP address, and then use that machine as a "jump box" to access your machine through its private IP address.

Cloud Networks

When you access a VM on Azure, you are likely to be connected via a "regular" Internet—that is, through a rented connection through your Internet Service Provider (ISP). Traffic among Azure data centers stays on Microsoft's Global WAN and doesn't flow over to the Internet. To support the traffic, Microsoft owns and runs one of the largest WAN backbones in the world. Microsoft spends lots of capital (a.k.a. money) on laying out the global network infrastructure. For example, the MAREA cable is a 6,600 KM (that is about 4,101 miles) submarine cable between Virginia Beach, Virginia USA, and Bilbao, Spain. It has eight fiber pairs providing 160 Tbps bandwidth across Atlantic—that's a lot of bandwidth to stream your funny cat videos! Other cloud platforms do similar things. So nowadays, there are multiple cross-continent connections running across major oceans of the Earth. Having multiple connections is good for everybody, because, as you've learned earlier, redundancy improves availability.

In 2008, there were a series of submarine cable disruptions with multiple submarine cables cut within a short time window. There were many conspiracy theories explaining why this had happened, but it could have just been coincidental. Special boats lay cables across the seabed. They take wheels of thousands of kilometers of cable and basically drop the cable onto the ocean floor as they go. These cables work under harsh conditions—low temperature, high pressure, and high salinity. And they may get caught by dragging ship anchors. So they do break.

As do most cloud platforms, Azure manages its compute resources by regions. A region usually maps to a geographic boundary, such as *US East*, *Japan West*, and *Germany Northeast*. Traffic going in and out a region goes through a pair of Regional Network Gateways (RNGs) through 100 Gbps network optics. The pair connects to all data centers in the region, providing redundant routes to the Azure backbone. Figure 1.9 illustrates how an Azure network looks, from the global backbone to a host on a data center rack.

Software Defined Network (SDN)

Computer networks are constructed with many different types of hardware and software, with control logics, which design packet routes and policies, and data logics, which handle actual packet routing, scattered in different hardware and software implementations from different vendors. This has been very problematic for data center managers because they must program the network devices piece by piece, using closed and proprietary configuration interfaces provided by different vendors. The complexity is amplified to a devastating mess on cloud. Furthermore, cloud requires a shared infrastructure to simultaneously serve multiple customers, which requires overlaying different network configurations for customers over the same physical infrastructure.

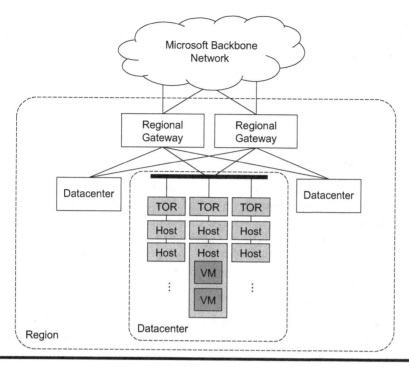

Figure 1.9   Azure network architecture

To handle these challenges, cloud vendors turn to Software Defined Networks (SDN). SDN separates *control plane*, which decides how to handle traffic, and *data plane*, where actual data packets flow based on decisions made by the control plane. The control plan offers a well-defined Application Programming Interface (API) that consolidates management interfaces across all network device types. One prominent example of such an API is OpenFlow, which has gained broad support in the industry. In early 2018, the Open Networking Foundation (ONF) acquired a set of next-generation SDN interfaces named Stratum as an open source project.

SDN makes networks programmable. On the same physical network infrastructure, you can program different routing rules and middlebox behaviors (such as firewalls and proxies) for different customers (or "tenants").

> ⓘ SDN and network virtualization are two technologies that have been developing in parallel. Nowadays, network virtualization relies heavily on SDN. However, other virtualization techniques exist such as overlay networks and network slicing. This book doesn't distinguish between the two because they work toward the common goal of programmable networks.

Deploying Workloads

Now you've got a couple of VMs; they can talk to each other (assuming you've placed them on the same virtual network); and you can access these VMs through public IP addresses. From here, operating the VMs isn't much different from operating a VM on your on-premises data centers. For Windows VMs, you can simply copy and paste files onto the machine using RDP client; for

Linux VMs, you can use tools such as WinSCP to transfer files between your Windows PC and the remote Linux server. Or, you can use any Internet-based file transferring mechanisms to transfer your files to the remote VMs.

While this is fine for testing and development purposes, you, never want to manually deploy your workloads. Instead, you want to use some sort of automation techniques that can help you to deploy your workloads. And you do this not because you are lazy. Rather, you do this for an utterly important characteristic in workload management—consistency.

Consistent Software Deployments

I'm a big fun of the How It's Made documentary on the Discovery Channel. I especially enjoy watching how fully automated production lines churn out all kinds of products with cunningly designed machineries. It seems that almost everything can be produced in mass production, from haggis to gingerbread houses, from mozzarella cheese to apple pies (okay, I admit it—I watch a lot of episodes on producing food. But don't let me misguide you—there are lots of episodes on producing other things like cars and washing machines).

The products made by these automated product lines demonstrate incredible consistency. At every step of the production defective products are rejected from the product line and only the ones that match up perfectly with the spec can be shipped. Consistency is the key to delivering a satisfactory customer experience. When you dig into an apple pie from your favorite brand, you get the same, expected taste every single time. There are no surprises—what you get is exactly what you expected, no matter where and when you buy it.

Software industry desires such consistency as well. However, it faces a unique challenge—for other industries, consistency is reinforced during production in controlled environments; for software, consistency needs to be reinforced during usage on customer sites. This is a very challenging problem because one can never predict how customer environments are configured.

About 10 years ago, I was once tasked to create an installation package for the company's flagship product. I decided to use InstallShield, which was a popular solution for creating software installers. I bought the product, put the DVD (for younger readers - it looks like a Blue-ray disk, but with lower capacity) in the DVD drive on my PC and launched the installer to install InstallShield itself. The installation failed with a "file not found" error. It turned out that the installer had expected the DVD drive on drive letter D, while my DVD had drive letter E. This little story shows that even for guys who make installers for a living, getting everything right for all possible system configurations is a hard (and quite tedious) job.

Even if a software can install and configure itself perfectly, some incompatible software may be later deployed to the same machine and break its dependencies. To handle such situations, people came up with the idea of Desired State Configuration (DSC), which monitors the machine state and runs corrective actions to bring the machine back to the desired state. There are many DSC systems nowadays, such as PowerShell DSC, Chef, and Puppet. They all allow you to declaratively define desired states of your machines and use on-machine agents to periodically reconcile a machine's current state with the desired state.

Some other people took a more extreme approach—a machine is reimaged to a brand-new OS installation before the software is applied. The software occupies the whole machine, and it's never updated. To update the software, you need to start from a fresh OS installation and install the new software version. Recent literature calls this *Immutable Infrastructure* (II).

Reimaging and holding onto an entire machine is quite expensive. Then in 2013 a small software company called Docker came around and took over the world. Docker popularized the idea of creating a concise, lightweight virtual environment for running software. This additional level of isolation is called a container. Containers are lightweight. You can launch hundreds of containers on a single machine. And all of them run in their isolated environments without interfering with each other. Containers provide such an elegant and efficient solution to consistent software deployment that it quickly became a very popular technique for software deployment. We'll spend more time on containers in Chapter 3.

Just to be clear—Docker didn't invent workload isolation. Isolation techniques have long existed in Linux systems such as *cgroups* (which can be traced back to 2006, when Google engineer Rohit Seth added to the Linux kernel the feature that grouped processes together under a common resource control), *namespaces* (which was added to Linux kernel in 2002), and *Copy-on-Write* (CoW) file systems. Windows has similar isolation constructs such as *job objects*.

Since all the challenges of consistent software deployment seem to root from variations in client machines, can we bring software back to a well-controlled environment like the mainframe machines in 1960s and allow users to use the software without ever modifying it? This is precisely the ideal behind Software as a Service (SaaS). With SaaS, software is installed and maintained in controlled server environments by a service provider. Instead of buying a software license, customers subscribe to the service without needing to install or configure anything. This is really a win-win situation. On one hand, the service provider can provide consistent services to all customers without the trouble of figuring out millions of possible configurations on user machines. On the other hand, the customer can start to consume a new service right away without making a long-term commitment.

SaaS sounds like a great idea. However, that's not the end of the story. Modern software products are complex. They often comprise many interacting services that collectively deliver a set of features. Consistent deployment of such products requires consistent deployment not only of the individual components, but also of the configurations that link them together. Instead of configuring software piece by piece and server by server, cloud platforms such as Azure provide templating languages that capture entire application infrastructures in declarative models. Some popular models include AWS's CloudFormation, Azure's ARM Template, and a cloud-agnostic model called Terraform developed by HashiCorp.

The preceding templating languages aren't designed for deploying workloads. Instead, their primary goal is to capture infrastructure as code. In other words, these templating languages are (compute) resource oriented instead of workload oriented. In such templating languages, workloads are simply described as black box payloads that are deployed on some resources. They don't provide native support for describing application behaviors in great details. In the next chapter, we'll take a much closer look at how you fully describe and deploy an application.

(i) I've been asked many times if I am related to HashiCorp because my name is Haishi, which looks quite like Hashi. Unfortunately, I'm not affiliated with HashiCorp in any way. I'm not sure what Hashi means. It could be the Japanese word Hashi (箸), which means chopsticks. Or, it could be short for a Japanese puzzle called Hashiwokakero (橋をかけろ). Haishi, on the other hand, is a combination of two Chinese characters, ocean (海) and stone (石). So my name can be interpreted as either an ocean of stones, or a stone rising from the ocean—basically a small island. Both my older sisters are named after sea birds. My mother ingenious idea was to name me as a landing pad for them when they get tired.

Hands-On Lab: Deploying a Web Application

In this hands-on lab, you'll deploy a WordPress application described by an Azure Resource Manager (ARM) template. An ARM template is a JSON file that fully describes an Azure resource group. It describes all resources in the resource group in great detail so that these resources can be consistently deployed. In this lab, you'll deploy a Hello World WordPress application.

Part I: Deploy the Infrastructure

An ARM template is quite verbose. Instead of writing one from scratch, you'll use a prebuilt template from Azure Quickstart Templates (https://azure.microsoft.com/en-us/resources/templates/).

1. Navigate to https://azure.microsoft.com/en-us/resources/templates/wordpress-app-service-mysql-inapp/. This page contains an ARM template that provisions a WordPress application.
2. Azure provides a "Deploy to Azure" feature that allows you to embed a button on your website and configure the button to directly launch an ARM template deployment process. Click on the **Deploy to Azure** button on the page, as shown in Figure 1.10.
3. Clicking on the button takes you to Azure Management Portal. An automatically generated UI will guide you to enter necessary parameters. In this case, you just need to enter a name for a new resource group. Check the I **agree to the terms and conditions stated above** checkbox and click the **Purchase** button to deploy the template, as shown in Figure 1.11.
4. It takes a few minutes to deploy the template. Once the template is deployed, click on the **Go to resource group** button in the notification area to navigate to the deployed resource group, as shown in Figure 1.12. Alternatively, you can click on the **Resource groups** link to the left of the portal home page and click on the resource group name to navigate to the resource group.
5. The resource group contains two resources: an App Service plan (hosting plan for your web applications) and an App Service (the hosted web application), as shown in Figure 1.13. Click on the **App Service** resource.
6. On the overview page of the App Service resource, click on the **Browse** link or the website's **URL** link to browse to the default web service, as shown in Figure 1.14.

Once the default WordPress page shows up, you can finish the WordPress configuration and start to create your sites.

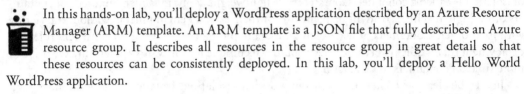

Figure 1.10   Deploy to Azure button on a template page

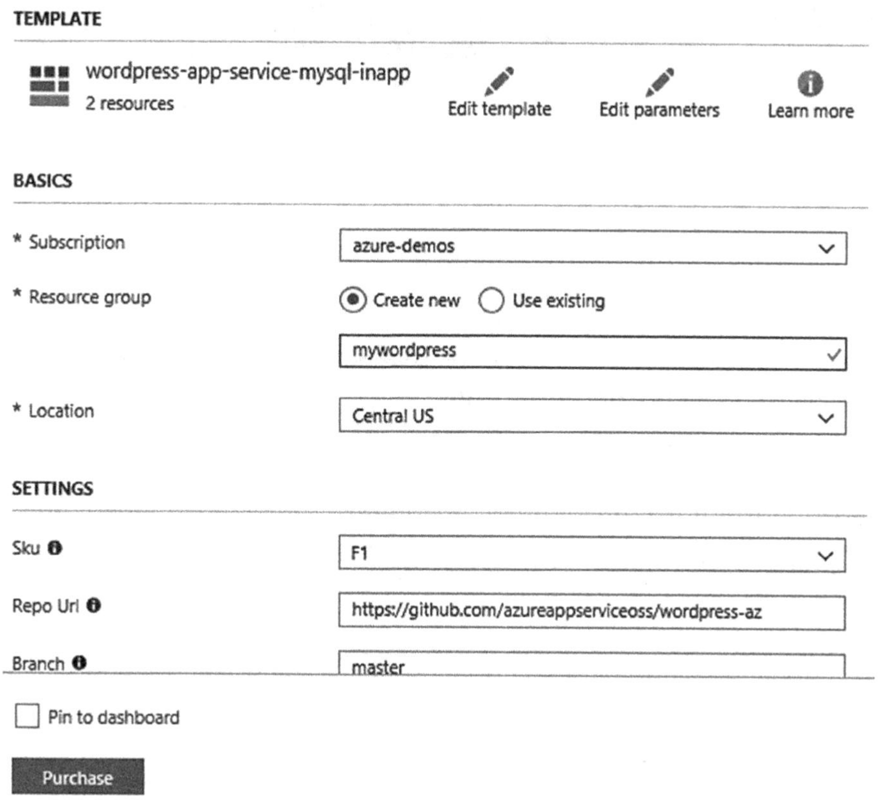

TEMPLATE
wordpress-app-service-mysql-inapp
2 resources
Edit template
Edit parameters
Learn more
BASICS
* Subscription
azure-demos
* Resource group
Create new
Use existing
mywordpress
* Location
Central US
SETTINGS
Sku
F1
Repo Url
https://github.com/azureappserviceoss/wordpress-az
Branch
master
Pin to dashboard
Purchase

Figure 1.11 Deploy an ARM template on Azure Management Portal

hbai@microsoft.com
MICROSOFT
Notifications
Dismiss: Informational Completed All
Deployment succeeded
11:33 PM
Deployment 'Microsoft.Template' to resource group 'webwithdb' was successful.
Go to resource group
Pin to dashboard

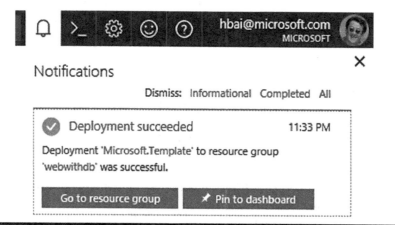

Figure 1.12 Deployment success notification

Figure 1.13   Resource list of a resource group

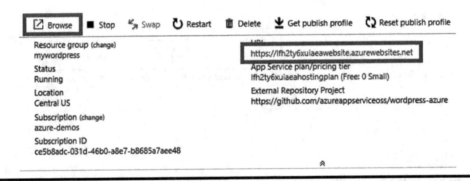

Figure 1.14   Links to the deployed website

Part II: Understanding the Template

What just happened? You just created a new Azure resource group, deployed a new web application hosting plan, and then added a new web application to your plan. All these are described by the ARM template. In this part of the lab, you'll take a closer look at the template.

1. Go back to the template's web page and click the **Browse on GitHub** button (see Figure 1.10). This takes you to the template's GitHub page, where you can find an **azuredeploy.json** file and an **azuredeploy.parameters.json** file. The first file is the main template, and the second template supplies values to parameters defined in the main template. Click on **azuredeploy.json** to open it.

2. An ARM template consists of several top level elements, including *parameters, variables,* and *resources.* The *resources* element defines all resources in the template. Azure ARM uses an extensible architecture in which a Resource Provider (RP) manages every resource type. A RP takes calls from ARM and performs resource lifetime management actions such as provisioning a resource, updating a resource, and deleting a resource. For example, **Microsoft. Web/Site** is a resource type that describes a website. A resource can have children resources.

In the case of the website resource, it has a **sourcecontrols** child resource and a **config** child resource, as shown in the following code snippet:

```json
"resources": [
  {
    "type": "sourcecontrols",
    "name": "web",
    "apiVersion": "2016-08-01",
    "properties": {
      "RepoUrl": "[parameters('repoUrl')]",
      "branch": "[parameters('branch')]",
      "IsManualIntegration": true
    },
    "dependsOn": [
      "[resourceId('Microsoft.Web/Sites', variables('siteName'))]"
    ]
  },
  {
    "type": "config",
    "name": "web",
    "apiVersion": "2014-06-01",
    "properties": {
      "phpVersion": "7.0"
    },
    "dependsOn": [
      "[concat('Microsoft.Web/sites/', variables('siteName'))]"
    ]
  }
]
```

The **sourcecontrol** resource allows you to link to an existing GitHub repository and trigger a new deployment when the specified branch is updated. This is a streamlined but simplified Continuous Deployment (CD) configuration. To implement a proper CI/CD pipeline, you want to use systems such as Visual Studio Team Services (VSTS) and Jenkins.

3. Navigate back to the resource group's overview page. Click on the **1 Succeeded** link at the top of the page (see Figure 1.13) to see the deployment history of the resource group.
4. Click on the first entry in the list and then click the Template link to the left of the deployment page, as shown in Figure 1.15.
5. Click on the **Deploy** link (see Figure 1.15). Then, on the custom deployment page (see Figure 1.11), click on the **Edit template** link. Next, you'll edit the template to add a new Azure Storage account to the resource group. The Azure Storage account allows you to save non-relational data such as tables, queues, blobs, and files on cloud.
6. On the *Edit template* page, click the **Add resource** link. Then select the **Storage account** resource type, enter a name for the new storage account, and click the OK button to add the resource to the resource group, as shown in Figure 1.16.

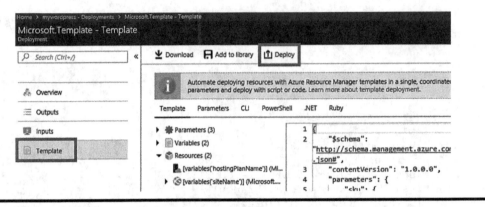

Figure 1.15 Template page of a resource group deployment

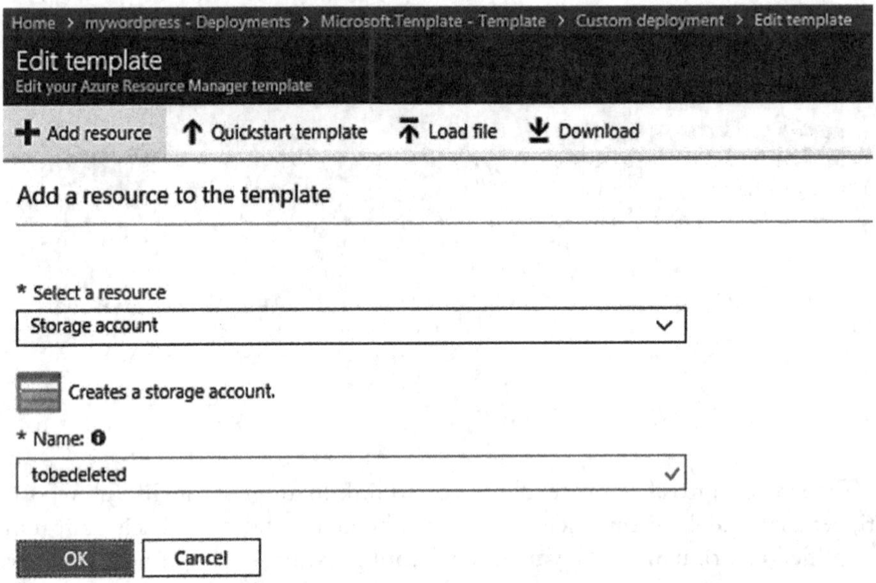

Home > mywordpress - Deployments > Microsoft.Template - Template > Custom deployment > Edit template

Edit template
Edit your Azure Resource Manager template

╋ Add resource   ↑ Quickstart template   ↥ Load file   ↧ Download

Add a resource to the template

* Select a resource

| Storage account | ∨ |

Creates a storage account.

* Name: ❶

| tobedeleted | ✓ |

| OK | | Cancel |

Figure 1.16 Adding a storage account to an ARM template

Once the resource is added to the template, you can click on it to see its JSON definition, as shown in the following code snippet:

```
{

    "name": "[variables('tobedeletedName')]",
    "type": "Microsoft.Storage/storageAccounts",
    "location": "[resourceGroup().location]",
    "apiVersion": "2015-06-15",
```

```
  "dependsOn": [],
  "tags": {
    "displayName": "tobedeleted"
  },
  "properties": {
    "accountType": "[parameters('tobedeletedType')]"
  }
}
```

A resource definition contains a name, a resource type, a location, an API version, and a collection of properties, dependencies, and tags. It takes quite some editing to craft a proper resource definition. The most efficient way is to find a similar scenario in an Azure Quickstart Template site, copy the resource definitions you need, and make necessary modifications for your project.

7. Click the **Save** button to save your changes. Then back on the custom deployment page, select the resource group to which you previously deployed the resource group, and click the **Purchase** button to update your resource group. This triggers a resource group upgrade. ARM compares the new resource template with the existing one and takes necessary actions to bring the resource group to the new resource template.

Continuous Delivery

When I was in college back in 1993, the primary means of software distribution among students were floppy disks. The most common disks were 5.25 inches, and there were smaller, 3.25 inch disks with a whopping capacity of 1.44MB (which is enough to save half of a picture I take with my current cellphone). I was writing simple video games such as poker and horseracing games. The games circulated in computer labs by students copying the disks from one to another. I often got requests for new features. And I would update the code, make a new disk, and hand the disk to the requestor. Interestingly, larger firms like Microsoft were doing essentially the same thing, but at a larger scale—Windows 3.1 came on 6 floppy disks, and Windows 95 came on 22 disks. Then, as software sizes increased, they were shipped on CDs and DVDs. Back in college, three skills were essential: compression to fit more data into small disks, duplication to copy raw disk bits, and virus scan to protect against endless types of viruses.

Then, as the Internet took off, users could download new and updated software directly over the Internet, making software distribution much easier. When a software vendor made a new version, they put up a new version on the download site so that users could download the new version. Some fancier software had auto-update built in to automatically update the software to the latest version when the software was launched.

In either the disk distribution case or the download case, software vendors didn't have firm control on the exact version of software running on client machines. This caused many compatibilities issues and management headaches for both software vendors and customers. Then came SaaS. There were no software installations on clients anymore. Service providers simply rolled out new versions on their own servers and everyone was using the greatest and latest.

What's Continuous Delivery? How is it Different From Continuous Deployment or Continuous Integration?

Continuous integration (CI), continuous delivery (CD), and continuous deployment are three related terms that are often confused with one another. To put it simply, continuous integration ensures the software still works when a new change is committed. Continuous delivery goes further and ensures the software is in a releasable quality. And finally, continuous deployment actually deploys the updated software in production.

Why Continuous Delivery

This rolling out of new versions at any time in a controlled manner is a very powerful idea. It reduces management complexity, improves customer experience, and reduces deployment cycles. However, the true power of continuous delivery is to allow software vendors to introduce their products to end users before they finish building the products. This was unimaginable back in the floppy disk days because both releasing a new version and adopting a new version are big commitments. With continuous delivery, new features can be gradually pushed out, as user feedback is incorporated in the products along the way. This iterative improvement process leads software to evolve toward the direction the end users expect. In a way, continuous delivery has created new vendor/user dynamics, in which products are co-developed with end users. This is a tremendous benefit to software vendors. They get volunteers to not only help them improve their products during beta, but also to prompt their products as early adopters.

Beta software sometimes is not just a phase in a software lifecycle, but a demonstration of an innovative attitude. For example, Gmail from Google was kept in a beta state for about 5 years, because the team was determined to redefine how email work.

Continuous Delivery Pipeline

The continuous delivery process starts when a new change is checked into the source control system (such as Git or Visual Studio Team Service). The updated code is automatically built and tested using unit tests. If the software fails to build, or fails to pass unit tests, the check-in is rejected (so called gated check-in).

Once individual components pass unit tests, they are integrated into the main branch to build and test the product in its complete form. The integrated components go through a series of automated acceptance tests and sometimes manual user acceptance tests. Once all tests pass, the product is considered in a releasable quality.

In the case of continuous deployment, a deployment is automatically triggered, and the new version is deployed to production. Otherwise, new versions are selectively released to the public upon manual approvals. Figure 1.17 shows the process.

If you ask ten different people about the continuous delivery process, you are likely to get ten (if not more) different answers. And it's almost guaranteed that someone you ask will shrug and says,

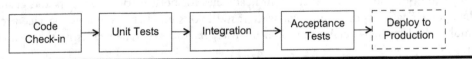

Figure 1.17 Continuous delivery process

"I don't give a damn." What I believe is that you should use the previous diagram as a reference and figure out whatever steps work best for you. After all, all these processes are about two things: quality and agility. If you can achieve both in a way you are comfortable with, you are all set.

Zen of DevOps

I've been working in the software industry for over 30 years. It could just be a coincidence, but almost all system administrators I've worked with fall into a similar profile: busy, short-tempered, with a pager (for younger readers—it's a small plastic device with an LED screen that is able to receive short text messages) that always beeps. They behave this way because they are always under pressure to keep the service running, 24 by 7. And it must appear to them that software engineers are just a bunch of careless hippies that constantly break things.

Devs and ops are not friends. And that's a big problem. And their conflicts seem irreconcilable–devs like to change things, while ops like to keep things stable; devs like to try out new things, while ops like things with proven records; devs think a broken product is the ops' problem, while ops think a broken product is the dev's problem. They do have one thing in common, though—neither likes to write documents. So they don't communicate, and they don't know what the others are doing. When something breaks, it often comes down as a blame game in which everyone desperately tries to prove it is someone else's problem.

What DevOps is all about is to make devs and ops work together toward a common goal—to make profits more efficiently. Don't believe you can buy a "DevOps toolkit" or subscribe to a "DevOps service" to "implement" DevOps, because DevOps is more about mindset than tools or processes. Instead, you should focus on two things: to unite devs and ops under a same goal, and to motivate them to seek continuous improvement.

Uniting people under a common goal requires serious leadership skills, which are out of the scope of this book. For a company, unifying all employees under a common goal means getting all employees to focus on bringing the maximum value to the company in the most efficient way. Furthermore, they should be encouraged and empowered to make corrections when they see imperfections in any of the products or production processes. That's what DevOps is all about.

> ⓘ My brother-in-law works for Toyota. He loves two things: fast driving and Lean Manufacturing. *The Toyota Way* has been in my book collection for the past 10 years, alongside with Stephen Hawking's *A Brief History of Time*. I never passed the first few pages of either book, however for different reasons—I believe I got the gist of *The Toyota Way* after a few pages; and I believe I'll never understand what Hawking is trying to say. Principles in Lean Manufacturing inspired Lean Software Development principles, including eliminating waste, amplifying learning, deciding as late as possible and delivering as early as possible, empowering the team, building integrity in, and seeing the whole.

DevOps Tool Chain

DevOps advocates for agility. An effective tool chain helps the team to focus on value creation by streamlining day-to-day operations, providing effective communication channels, and enabling knowledge sharing. Many popular tools and services can be fit together to form such a tool chain, such as Git for a source code repository, Docker for packaging, and New Relic for monitoring.

There are also integrated suites that provide prebuilt pipelines. Visual Studio Team Services (VSTS) and Jenkins are two of the predominant systems on the market at the time of writing.

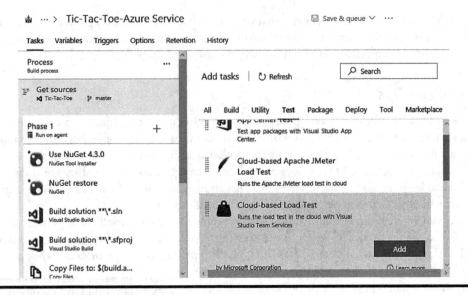

Figure 1.18 VSTS build definition

They both provide extensible pipelines that cover a great portion of the entire software lifecycle. Figure 1.18 shows a sample build definition in VSTS. To the left of the screen is a list of build tasks. To the right of the screen is a gallery of tasks that you can add into your build pipeline. You can also make VSTS and Jenkins work together. For example, you can use VSTS as your source code repository, and set up a web hook to trigger a Jenkins build pipeline upon code check-ins.

Microsoft Azure Marketplace is a place where you can discover software solutions and deploy them directly on Azure. The marketplace offers secure and stable Jenkins deployments (see https:// azuremarketplace.microsoft.com/en-us/marketplace/apps/azure-oss.jenkins). When you are on the page, simply click the **Get It Now** button to launch the deployment wizard on the Azure Management Portal.

Cloud Advantage

Different from Jenkins, VSTS is a hosted service. To use VSTS, you don't need to deploy an infrastructure to support it. You simply subscribe to VSTS service and you can start to build your CI/CD pipelines right on the cloud. To get started, go to https://www.visualstudio.com/team-services/ and apply for a free account. For a small team, you can pretty much stay with a free account (with up to five users) as long as you'd like until you are ready to upgrade to a larger scale.

A hosted solution has some great advantages over a self-hosted solution.

- No management overhead
  Since your entire CI/CD pipeline can be hosted on cloud, you don't need to allocate any on-premises resources to support the pipeline. VSTS offers hosted build agents so that you don't need to set up dedicated build servers. These build agents are dynamically allocated from VSTS's agent pools and consistently configured for your build tasks. VSTS offers both Windows-based and Linux-based build agents. It even offers hosted macOS build agents (in preview at the time of writing) for your macOS workloads. Please visit https://docs.microsoft.com/en-us/vsts/build-release/concepts/agents/hosted?view=vsts to get more details on the software stacks preinstalled on these build agents.

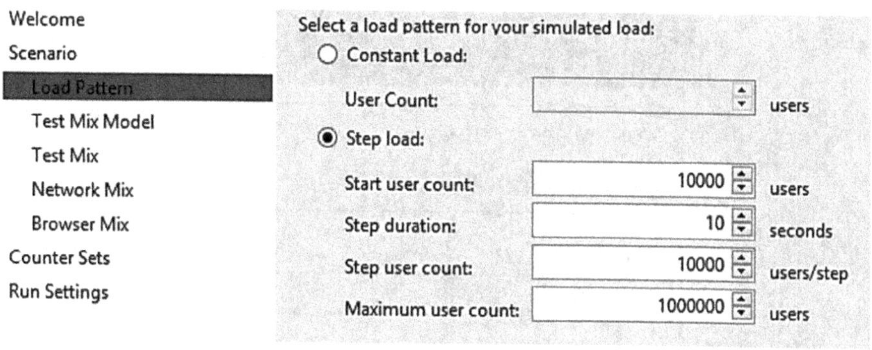

Figure 1.19   Cloud-based load test pattern

- Cloud-based load testing
Conducting large scale load testing requires a significant investment in test resources to run test clients. This is because if you don't have enough test clients, these clients will saturate before the server does as the load increases. VSTS supports cloud-based load testing. Within a few minutes, you can acquire enough Azure resources that can reliably simulate hundreds of thousands of concurrent users. Figure 1.19 shows a screenshot of VSTS when you create a load test. This stepped pattern starts with 10,000 users and adds another 10,000 users every 10 seconds until the total user count reaches 1 million. Load testing on such a large scale is extremely hard to be organize using on-premises resources. However, with VSTS, you can set it up and get it running in minutes.
- Geo-distributed performance tests
Cloud platforms like Azure have data centers around the globe. You can recruit test agents from different geographic locations to test how your system performs when hit by users from different counties and regions. Insights into regional performance differences help you to adjust your content delivery strategies so that you can provide optimum performance to your users around the world. Figure 1.20 shows a screenshot of the Microsoft Azure Web App performance test feature, which allows you to generate load from any of the supported Azure data centers.
- Supporting a geo-distributed team
A hosted DevOps tool chain is highly available. If you have a distributed team, your team members can access the same tool chain regardless of their location. In one of my previous jobs, I was managing a geo-distributed team with developers from both China and Canada. As the Canadian team went to sleep, the China team was just waking up to continue with the work. Both teams rarely needed to directly talk to each other. They simply follow a few rules: first, all work items are tracked under the same system. This gives visibility to the whole team on all development activities so that there are no conflicts or duplicated efforts. Second, the main branch always builds at the end of a shift, with all automated tests passing. In a distributed team, any cross-team problems take at least two days to resolve because of the time difference. Requiring the main branch to remain buildable avoids a bug created by one team blocking the other team. Third, every check-in must be related to one and only one work item. This rule avoids unplanned changes, unfinished work, or interleaved work on different work items to enter the system. The clear one-to-one correlation makes progress tracking and quality control much easier. If a change turns out to be invalid, it can be reverted relatively easily, causing minimum impacts on others.

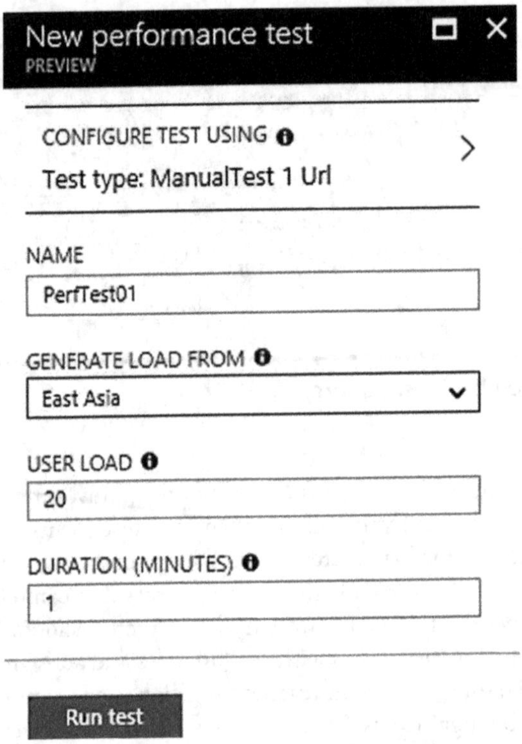

Figure 1.20   Azure web app performance test

Zen of Cloud

"A good traveler has no fixed plans and is not intent on arriving."

Lao Tsu

Cloud is quite complex. When you sit in on the keynote sessions of major cloud platform conferences, you are likely to hear speakers boast about the hundreds of new features they've added in the past year. It's unrealistic to expect to fully understand a cloud platform by picking up a book or taking a course. Your journey to the cloud should not be a planned course. Instead, your journey should be an exploration. To get started, just pick one workload—whether an existing workload or new scenario—and learn how to put that workload on cloud. Once that is done, pick another workload and try to get it running. Along the way, you may become struck by new, exciting ideas—put them in a queue and return to them after the workload at hand is working.

So my best advice to you is to pick something small and see it through. See where that takes you and then pick your next step. There is a humongous knowledge tree to explore—and this book presents a small subset of possible branches. As you take small steps to making things work, you'll find your direction—machine learning, big data, edge computing, scalable web, blockchain, or even quantum computing. If this book was a novel, it's an open-ended story. And the rest of the chapters give you a glimpse of possible endings.

Chapter 2

Cloud-Native Design

Cloud Rules

After I came to the United States in 2000, it took me a while to get used to giving tips in restaurants. Back in China, tipping was rare in any situation (at least while I was there). In restaurants of my hometown, instead of paying tips, you often can "round down" the amount you owe. For example, you can pay 1000 yuan for a 1050 yuan bill. The owners use the discount to show courtesy and to win returning customers. Now, after 18 years, giving tips has become automatic for me. And I can calculate appropriate tip amounts in my head in just a few seconds. When in Rome, do like the Romans do.

Cloud is an environment different from your on-premises datacenters. There are sets of rules you need to abide to make your applications work better on cloud.

Embrace Failures

As I introduced in the first chapter, clouds use commodity servers to host user workloads. Although cloud vendors can operate these servers with great efficiency, they don't have a magic potion to stop these servers from breaking down. There are hundreds of thousands of servers in a cloud datacenter. By pure probability, hundreds of hardware failures happen every day. It wouldn't be practical for a cloud vendor to keep fixing machines as they break. When a server breaks, the vendor moves your workload to another healthy server, and takes the broken server out of work scheduling rotation. The broken servers are then fixed or replaced in batches later.

So your workloads may be rebooted or moved. In a planned move, you'll get sufficient warnings well ahead of the move. In an unplanned move, your applications may be restarted or moved to new machines without notification. It's a rare situation (within the scope of your application's hosting environment), but you do need to prepare for it.

> It might be confusing because I just said failures were common in cloud datacenters, and then I said the probability of your application's host failing was rare. The difference is that the probability of <u>any</u> server failing is high, but the probability of a *specific* server failing is low.

If your application keeps a lot of in-memory state, it will have a hard time when it's rebooted. It may lose all the states in memory, or it may need quite some time to restore the full memory state from disks or external storages. There are several different strategies for solving this problem, including externalizing states, using replicating states, and backing up states. Each of them has pros and cons, which I'll go through later in this chapter.

Because failures happen more frequently, your response mechanisms need to be automated as much as possible to reduce outage. When your application is shut down unintentionally, it needs to be able to restore itself to a working state without human interventions. This is usually harder than it sounds, especially when you have multiple services with inter-dependencies. Later in this chapter, I'll discuss disaster recovery in more details.

Fair Play

Cloud is a multi-tenant environment, in which multiple customers (a.k.a. tenants) run their applications on a shared resource pool. Although your applications are still logically isolated from other workloads (and physical isolation is also possible), you need to be aware of several situations that may affect your applications' performance.

When you run a virtual machine on cloud, you may become subject to the negative effect of *noisy neighbors*. Noisy neighbors are resource hogs that consume large amounts of compute, storage, or networking resources on the host. If your virtual machine happens to be on the same host, it faces severe competition for resources if it has one or several noisy neighbors. Noisy neighbors also exist in less apparent ways when you subscribe to other cloud services. For example, when you subscribe to a cloud storage account, some compute resources back up your account on cloud datacenters. If the same resource happens to be running a very busy storage account, the busy neighbor may affect your storage account.

Using dedicated resources is an effective (but more expensive) way to avoid noisy neighbors. There are also a few architectural tricks that can help to dodge noisy neighbor effects. I'll discuss a few later in the chapter.

When your application calls a cloud service, it's subject to throttling. Throttling is an important protective mechanism cloud services use to ensure all tenants have fair opportunities to consume the service. Throttling especially helps cloud services protect themselves against spam and Denial-of-Service (DoS) attacks. If your application does need more throughput, you can span your requests across multiple service subscriptions to gain additional quota.

Why do Noisy Neighbors Exist?

Cloud platforms make money by selling compute resources. Hence, resource utilization rate is a key indicator of profitability for a cloud platform. If a cloud platform can pack more virtual machines onto the same hosting infrastructure, the profitability increases.

It's not particularly hard to segment CPU and RAM resources. However, when it comes to disk I/O, the problem becomes hairy. Because disks are slow, disk access requests are queued and handled in sequence. If a noisy neighbor keeps sending I/O requests that overwhelm the disk drive, disk access becomes a bottleneck and slows everyone down.

Even if the noisy neighbors are throttled, they will still have a negative impact on your applications. Numbers in the following discussion are unrealistic. They are meant to make discussions easier.

Imagine a disk can handle one I/O request per second. And you have an application that sends one I/O request every second. If there is no one else on the same machine, you can expect your application's throughput to be one request per second, and latency is exactly one second.

Now, imagine you have a noisy neighbor that is throttled to send at most 10 requests per second. Between any of your two consecutive I/O requests there could be up to 10 requests from the neighbor. Your application's throughput is reduced to 0.1 request per second, and latency goes up to 10 seconds.

Can't cloud platforms monitor VMs and look out for noisy neighbors? They certainly can. However, what to do with the noisy neighbors needs some additional thoughts. Applications that perform frequent disk operations have heavy dependencies on local data. Because moving data, especially large amount of data, is expensive, it's usually hard to evict a noisy neighbor from a host because of data "stickiness." Furthermore, because it's not possible for a cloud platform to know exactly what the application is doing, it can only assume the application is busy for legit reasons— and you don't want to interrupt a busy customer, who usually has a higher dependency on cloud (hence a more important customer).

Multiple Security Contexts

How many online accounts do you have? Let me count mine—Windows Live, Gmail, Twitter, LinkedIn, Amazon, WeChat, GitHub, Slack, Instagram, Expedia, Delta, GoDaddy, my bank, my credit cards, parent portal of my daughter's school, and dozens of accounts I've created and forgotten. With our lives depending more and more on online services, I believe many of you have many online identities for consuming different services as well.

Your application faces the same situation when working with different cloud services. Although cloud platforms are all working toward providing unified role-based access controls (RBAC), many services still require separate authentication and authorization mechanisms. In such cases, an effective key management method is critical for keeping your application secure and functional. I'll discuss more on key management in Chapter 4.

In an on-premises environment, sometimes you can use a trusted subsystem pattern to establish a security perimeter around a group of trusted services. If the perimeter is secure, the protected services can communicate with each other without authorization or encryption. However, in a cloud environment, every cloud service assumes it works under a hostile environment. So your calls to cloud services are almost always authenticated, authorized, and encrypted, with the exception that some read operations may be allowed without authentication.

If you come from the Windows' world, you are familiar with active directories (AD). Unsurprisingly, Microsoft Azure provides a service, named Azure Active Directory,

Ⓘ Managing multiple identities is challenging. Many people reuse the same password across their online accounts. This is a dangerous practice, because once a hacker gets a hold of one of your accounts, he can compromise all your accounts using the same password. Here are some techniques I use to manage my accounts: I have different passwords for different accounts; for rarely used services, I use random passwords and recover them only before use; when I register for an account, I use fake addresses and names unless necessary (two of my favorite fake addresses: 123 Disney Avenue and 1 Yemen Way); I rotate my passwords periodically. Most important of all, I don't register on websites that seem to ask for too much for the scope of the service. I'll come back to this when I discuss security in Chapter 4.

that provides capabilities like your on-premises active directories. Azure Active Directory brings a single security context into the cloud. You can centrally manage accesses to several of Azure services as well as your own services. You can also set up synchronization between your on-premise directories and your cloud directories. I'll introduce Azure Active Directory in more details in Chapter 4.

Limited Customizations

Most public cloud services are multi-tenant services that are designed to provide generic functionalities to a wide range of customers. Although many of these services provide various options for customization, deep customizations for particular projects are impossible. When choosing a public cloud service, you must carefully assess whether the service can satisfy your project needs as is.

If you do need deep customizations, you need to deploy your own copies of customized services and manage the entire service stacks. You can use cloud template languages to capture your service infrastructure into consistently deployable units, as introduced in Chapter 1. Another way to implement deep customization is to push the customization code into your application layer. One of the benefits of this approach is to give you opportunities to leverage new features of the underlying service to reduce the complexity of your customizations as the service improves.

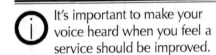 It's important to make your voice heard when you feel a service should be improved. A successful implementation of a cloud-based solution is based on a healthy partnership between you and the cloud vendor. By sending your feedbacks, you are shaping the future of these cloud services.

Efficiency Matters

When cloud was first introduced to the public, it was presented primarily as a cheaper and faster way of running things. While the agility aspect was right on the money, the monetary benefits were easily misunderstood. Cloud reduces total cost of ownership (TCO) by drastically reducing management expenses, but that doesn't mean cloud is so cheap that you don't need to worry about the cost. If you are not careful, the costs do add up quickly. For instance, an Amazon EC2 *t2.xlarge* on-demand instance costs $0.1856 per hour at the time of writing (an Azure A2M instance, which has a similar configuration of two virtual cores and 16 GiB of memory, costs $0.149 per hour). That's about $138 per month. If you run a server cluster of five nodes, the cost goes up to $690 per month. As you throw in storage costs, network traffic charges, and other service consumptions, you may end up with a sizable bill every month. The good news is that because of cloud's agility, you can make improvements as frequently as possible, and quickly deploy new versions to cloud to keep your costs down.

Cloud has an elaborate pricing table. Although most services are consume-based, how consumption is calculated varies from service to service. For example, virtual machines are charged by the minutes they run; storages are charged by consumed space; artificial intelligence services are charged by number of transactions; and network services are charged by the amount of transferred data packets. And there are services that define logical units that group related resource consumptions together. Even within a same service, different types of transactions have different associated costs—write operations are often charged more than read operations; egress traffic is often more expensive than ingress traffic; and cross-region operations cost more than same-region operations.

So how your applications interact with cloud services may have a significant impact on the cost. Later in this chapter, you'll learn about a number of design patterns that help you to make efficient use of cloud services.

How Does Cloud Reduce TCO?

Cloud datacenters are heavily optimized for efficiency. Datacenter energy efficiency can be measured by a Power Usage Effectiveness (PUE) index, which is defined as:

$$PUE = \frac{Total\ energy\ consumption}{IT\ equipment\ energy\ consumption}$$

Any energy consumed by a non-computing device is considered overhead—such as power to run elevators, lights, and office cooling. An ideal PUE is 1.0, which is impossible to reach. However, modern datacenters can push PUE very low. Back in 2014, Azure achieved a PUE of 1.15, ahead of industry averages by 30%.

So, even if you compare machine-by-machine, running a machine in a cloud datacenter costs less than running a machine with the same specs in an on-premises datacenter. Furthermore, when you use cloud, you are not paying for hardware costs, and the cost of your IT labor goes down significantly.

To help you understand TCO savings using cloud, Microsoft Azure offers an online TCO calculator at https://www.tco.microsoft.com/Home/Calculator (in preview at the time of writing). You can use the calculator to estimate your TCO savings when you migrate to cloud. Figure 2.1 shows a sample estimation I did for 100 servers. I'm not sure your actual result will be so drastic, but it looks promising.

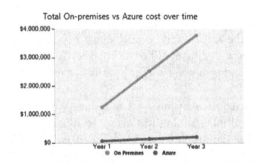

Total On-premises vs Azure cost over time

Your estimated cost savings could be as much as

$3,567,778 (94%)

over 3 year(s) with Microsoft Azure

Estimated cost savings over 3 year(s) by category

Category	
Compute	$2,528,596
Data center	$206,800
Networking	$776,003
Storage	$1,741
– IT labor	$54,638

On-premises cost breakdown summary

Category	Costs
Compute	$2,718,316
Hardware	$2,355,040
Software	$231,516
Electricity	$131,760
Data center	$206,800
Networking	$776,003
Storage	$2,662
IT labor	$78,398
Total	$3,782,179

Azure cost breakdown summary

Category	Web direct cost	1 Year Reserved VM	3 Year Reserved VM
Compute	$436,389	$291,720	$189,720
Data center	$0	$0	$0
Networking	$0	$0	$0
Storage	$921	$921	$921
IT labor	$23,761	$23,761	$23,761
Total	$461,071	$316,402	$214,402

Figure 2.1   TCO calculator result

Design for Availability

My father keeps a pair of reading glasses in almost every single room he ever stays in. He has glasses not only in every room of his place, but also in every room of my house and my sisters' houses. He likes to read, but he hates to carry glasses around. So his solution is to keep glasses everywhere so that he can use a pair whenever he wants. He's especially fond of reading about airplanes. And he keeps telling me how airplanes are more reliable than cars because if the engine in a car fails the whole car fails; but if all but one engine fails in an airplane the airplane is still able to land safely.

Redundancy Models

No matter if it is reading glasses or airplane engines, availability is achieved by redundancy. When multiple instances of an application are deployed, as long as one of the instances is working, the application remains available. There are several different ways to leverage redundant copies to achieve higher availability; each has pros and cons, which I'll explain next.

The Active–Active Model

When a multi-engine airplane is en route, all its engines work together and share the load. Each of the engines is powerful enough to carry the airplane. So unless all the engines fail at the same time, the airplane should be able to land safely. Figure 2.2 shows the active–active model. In such a configuration, a load balancer to all running instances evenly distributes the workload. The load balancer also serves as the application's entry point. As long as there's at least one application instance running, the application remains available.

The active–active model shares the workload across multiple active instances so that none of the instances is stressed. As the workload increases, the active–active model allows new instances to be added behind the load balancer to share the increased load. When an instance is malfunctioning, it is taken off the load balancer. Its share of load is routed to other healthy instances while it's being repaired.

The active–active model imposes an important requirement on system design—the system must be able to maintain consistent states across multiple running instances. To illustrate this, please consider the scenario in Figure 2.3. You are buying supplies for a birthday party. You send three requests—buy balloons, buy a cake, and buy a gift from a shopping site. Three servers back

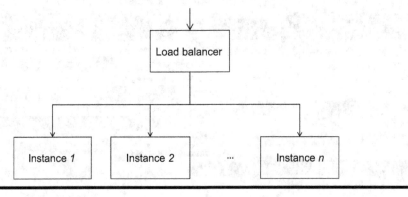

Figure 2.2   Active–active model

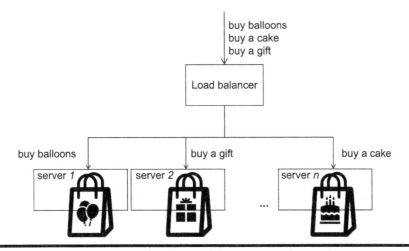

Figure 2.3 State management challenge in active–active model

the site, and your requests are distributed among them. Each server maintains a shopping cart for you. When a server receives a request, it places the requested item in its copy of the cart. If you check out when the carts are not synchronized, you are only getting part of the supplies you need.

It takes an entire section to properly discuss application state management. I'll defer the discussion to later sections of this chapter.

How Many 9's Do You Need?

As introduced in Chapter 1, availability doesn't come free. As you add more servers, the number of "9"s in availability increases, but your returns exponentially decrease. Do you need four 9's (99.99%), five 9's (99.999%), or more? Or, less?

It depends on how much outage you can tolerate. A system with 99.99% availability translates to about 53 minutes of outage during a whole year. Most of the systems don't need such high availability. So, before committing to a higher availability, you should assess your needs and avoid investing more than necessary.

Of course, having a 99.99% available system doesn't mean if you turn off the machine for one hour at the beginning of the year, everything will keep working for the rest of the year. Outages may happen at any time. You still need to design your applications to handle unexpected outages regardless of your availability goals.

The Active–Passive Model

Sending men to the moon was very expensive—Project Apollo cost $25.4 billion in 1973 (equivalent to $107 billion in 2016). There was much at stake—scientific breakthrough, national pride, ideological conflicts, and more. So NASA had to plan for every possible failure. However, at the end, there only one crew was sent to the moon a time. If NASA had used an active-active model, they would have sent two crews at the same time and expected at least one of the crews to arrive. That would have been an absurd arrangement because launching two crews at the same time was quite expensive and double the ground control work. And if there were some design flaws, both

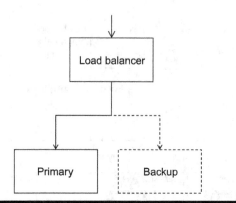

Figure 2.4 Active–passive model

trips were jeopardized as they used the exact same design. Instead, NASA used an active–passive model, in which they sent a primary crew and a backup crew. The task would be carried out be the primary crew. The backup crew would take over in case anything happened to the primary crew.

Figure 2.4 shows the active–passive model. In such a configuration, all user traffic is routed to the primary server. When the primary server fails, user traffic is diverted to the backup. This process is called *failover*.

The active–passive model is wasteful compared to the active–active model, because the secondary sits idle for most of the time. The model also incurs longer outages. It takes time for the load balancer to realize the primary is gone—it keeps polling the primary instance and marks the primary unhealthy after a few failed attempts. During this time, user traffic is still routed to the primary, leading to a longer outage.

There are two ways to perform failovers. One is to permanently promote the original secondary to the new primary. When the broken primary comes back online, it becomes the new secondary. The other way is to temporarily promote the secondary to primary. When the original primary comes back, both instances revert to their original roles. In the second case, the temporarily prompted primary may provide read-only service while waiting for the original primary to come back online. The service is called *degraded* in this case. When I discuss application state management later in this chapter, I'll explain the rationale behind different choices.

State Management

Now, let's come back to the shopping cart problem and talk about state management. When user requests are distributed to multiple servers, how can we make sure they are in sync so that when the user checks out, she gets consistent cart contents regardless which server handles the checkout? There are two distinct ways to handle this—using stateless service or using stateful service.

Stateless Service

A stateless service doesn't maintain any contextual information. All information it needs to handle a work item is passed in the request. It takes the request, handles it, and forgets about everything. For example, an usher who checks tickets at a movie theater doesn't need to remember any contextual information between customers. He simply takes a ticket, rips it in half, and returns half of the ticket to the customer.

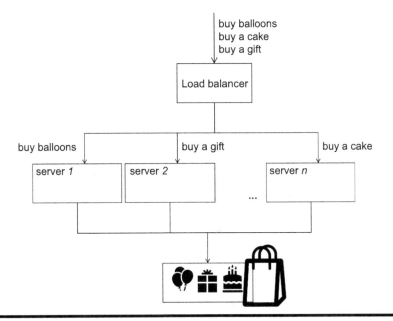

Figure 2.5   Externalized state storage

However, in many cases, a stateless service still needs to remember contextual information between requests, such as in our shopping cart example. Because the service doesn't remember any states, someone else needs to remember the cart contents for it. One way of doing this is to get the client to remember the cart; the other way is to use an external database to save the cart contents. Figure 2.5 shows a configuration in which cart contents are saved in an external database. Whenever any of the servers needs to write to the cart or read from the cart, it talks to the external, shared database for consistent states.

It's easy to achieve high availability for stateless services. You can use either the active–active model or the active–passive model. It doesn't matter which server handles the request. And when a server dies, you simply launch a new one and join it back to the server pool. The new server instance, just like any of the existing server instances, either doesn't need any contextual information (such as the usher case) or restores contextual information from the external storage (such as the shopping cart case).

The downside of using a stateless service is the need for external storage. First, because every state read or write needs to go through the external storage, system performance is slowed down because of the external service calls. Second, the external storage itself needs to be highly available because if it crashes it takes all the states with it.

Stateful Service

Stateful service remembers contextual information, or states, locally on the server. The state is saved on disk instead of memory so that the state can be restored if the server is rebooted. The state is also replicated across servers so that all servers maintain the same consistent view of state. States on the servers can be *strongly consistent*, which requires all participating servers (or a quorum of the servers) acknowledge an update before an update is officially recorded. States can also be *eventually consistent*, which allows updates to be gradually propagated through servers so that all servers will

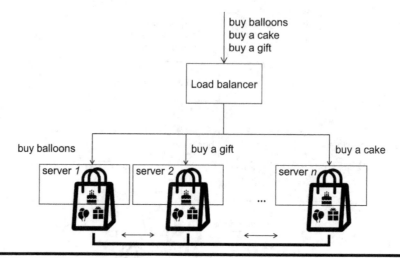

Figure 2.6   Stateful service

eventually have a consistent view of the state. Figure 2.6 illustrates how a stateful service works for the shopping cart scenario. In this configuration, each server holds a copy of the shopping cart, and the cart contents are consistently synced across the servers.

Constantly replicating states sounds like a lot of trouble. Why would we go through it? Because stateful service does bring certain benefits. Stateful service eliminates the need for external storage. This not only simplifies the overall system architecture, but also improves system performance because state operations are local to the server cluster.

Stateful service also helps to shorten development cycles. When external storage is used, the application and the storage (such as a database) need to agree on a common data schema. If the application decides to change the data schema, the external storage needs to be updated accordingly to keep both parties using the same data structure. State data schema in a stateful service is solely owned by the service itself. The service is free to update its state data structure without needing to coordinate with anyone else, which allows faster software iterations.

Stateful services also support flexible backups and restores. Instead of a centralized database that is backed up at fixed intervals, each stateful service can decide on the best interval and destination to backup its own state. For example, a tax service may choose to back up its state to a cheap, cold storage for archival or compliance purposes, because it doesn't expect a filed tax form to be frequently accessed, if at all. On the other hand, a production line management system may want to back up its data to a hard drive after every shift so that at most the system can lose data of the last shift.

 ## How is Data Replication Handled in a Huge Cluster Handled?

Figure 2.6 shows three servers in the server cluster. Replicating data across three servers seems manageable. Now imagine you are running a 1,000 node cluster. To ensure the state is consistent and accessible through any of the servers, any update must be replicated to all 1,000 servers. That simply won't fly. How can we handle state replication differently to ensure both availability and performance?

If you don't know how to solve this problem, I strongly suggest you close the book and think about it for a while. How would you solve it?

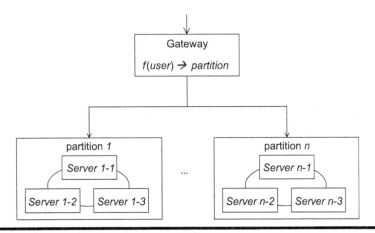

Figure 2.7   Partitioned stateful service

For high availability, we don't need to replicate the data 1,000 times. Replicating it three times will probably give us sufficient 9's. So, instead of replicating the data to all 1,000 servers, how about we just pick three servers and replicate the data to them? That surely solves the performance problem. However, if a user's request is routed to a server other than these three picked ones, the user won't see the data. So for a specific user, we need to make sure the user's requests are always routed to these three supported servers.

Here's the plan—for any given user, we'll assign her to a *partition*, which is backed by three out of 1,000 servers. Data is replicated only within the partition. The three servers keep three copies of the same data. They provide sufficient availability to the user while keeping the replication overheads low. Figure 2.7 shows such a topology. In this case, a simple, round robin load balancer is no longer sufficient because different users need to be routed to corresponding partitions. Instead, a gateway is used, which maps users to partitions through a user-to-partition mapping function. Because a user is affixed to a partition, the servers in the partition handle all her requests, and her data is replicated only among those servers.

Replicating data may cause problems. For instance, a data item might be read and written by multiple transactions at the same time. A *quorum-based voting* for replica control solves this problem by somewhat a voting system. Before a transaction to read or write a data time, it needs to acquire enough votes. For example, for a transaction to write a data, it must hold more than half of the write votes on the data item. This ensures that only one transaction can write a data item at any given time.

Availability of Multi-Component System

In a multi-component system, the overall system availability is decided by the availability as well as the topology of components. In a multi-tiered system, the system's availability is decided by the tier with the lowest availability. In a system with alternative paths, the system's best availability is achieved by following the path with highest availability. However, the theoretical best availability is hard to reach because of the overheads of path selection, such as the time needed for a router to realize and confirm a component is failing and choose an alternative route.

To make the route selection work more effective, you should allow a component to fail fast. "Failing fast" may be counterintuitive—isn't crashing bad? Of course. We don't want software that frequently crashes. However, when something unexpected happens, instead of hanging around and trying to fix the complication, the component can simply crash and let the platform's failover mechanism launch a brand-new instance.

Global Availability

On July 24th, 2017, a power outage in San Francisco brought down 365 Main, a data center providing hosting service to some of the popular websites in United States, including Yelp, Craigslist, and Netflix. The widespread power outage, compounded with backup generator failures, led to hours of outages of these sites. No matter how well a datacenter facility is structured, it has limited tolerance for massive disasters such as earthquakes, floods, tornados, and power grid failures as what happened in San Francisco showed.

As the old saying goes, "Don't put all your eggs in one basket." For your service to survive the most devastating conditions, you need deployments across multiple facilities that are far enough from each other so that they are unlikely to be affected by large scale disasters. Before cloud, setting up geo-distributed datacenters and managing deployments across distributed sites were expensive endeavors that very few companies could afford. Nowadays, deploying to globally distributed datacenters offered by cloud platforms can be easily done through a few UI clicks or a few lines of script.

A globally distributed system can use either the active–active model or the active–passive model to provide services to global users. In the active–passive configuration, all users are routed to the primary site. If the primary site fails, all users are routed to the secondary site. In the active–active configuration, a user is not routed to a random site, but routed to a site that can provide the best performance to the specific user. This usually means routing the user to the closest datacenter.

Microsoft Azure provides a Traffic Manager that allows you to set up an entry point to globally distributed deployments of your application. For example, you may have a site deployed to US east and another site deployed to US west. You can set up a Traffic Manager profile that routes your users to different regions based on performance. With such a configuration, users from the US east coast are routed to the US east region, and users from the US west coast are routed to the US west region. If either region fails, all users are routed to the remaining region. Although some users will have slighter performance in this case (because they are connected to the region on the other coast), the service remains available to all users.

A system can also leverage content delivery networks (CDN) to deliver static contents directly from CDN's geographically distributed edge nodes instead of serving them up from application servers. Because CDN edge nodes cache contents, even when the application server fails, the application's static contents can still be delivered by CDN (before the cache expires). In such cases, users can't submit new transactions but can still view site contents.

Hands-On Lab: Creating a Global Web Application

In this lab, you'll create a simple website that is deployed to two of the Azure global regions. Then you'll send up a Traffic Manager profile as the entry point to your global website. Users use the traffic manager endpoint—globalsite.trafficmanager.net—to access the site, and they are routed to either mysite-uswest.azurewebsites.net or mysite-japaneast.azurewebsites.net based on a policy of your choice, such as by performance, by assigned weights, or by priorities. The final topology of the site is illustrated in Figure 2.8 (note you need to choose a different set of DNS names in your experiment because DNS names have to be globally unique).

Part I: Create and Deploy the Web Application

1. Sign in to Microsoft Azure Management Portal. Click on the **Create a resource** link at the upper-left corner of the screen and click on the **Web App** resource type to create a new website. If you don't see Web App in the list, search for "Web App" in the search box and click on the found entry.

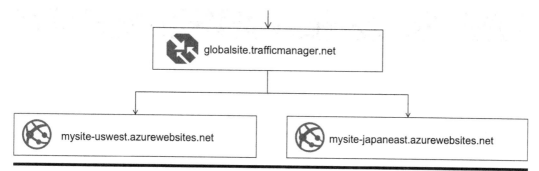

Figure 2.8   Global sites with traffic manager

2. On the *Web App* blade, click the **Create** button to create a new website.
3. On the web app creation blade, enter a name for your new web application (mysite-westus in Figure 2.9). Put your website in a new resource group. Then click on the *App service plan/ location* section, and then the *Create new* link to create a new hosting plan for your web application. Choose a location where you want your website to be hosted (West US in Figure 2.9). Click the **OK** button to create the host plan, and then click the **Create** button to create the web application. This creates a new, empty website and deploys it to the West US region.
4. Once the application is created, click on its **App Service Editor** (preview at the time of writing) section, and then click on the **Go** link to open the online editor, as shown in Figure 2.10.
5. On the *App Service Editor*, click on the **hostingstart.html** file, which is the default page of the site. In the editor to the right, change its HTML source code to a plain text that shows the website's region, as shown in Figure 2.11. Please note your changes are automatically saved.

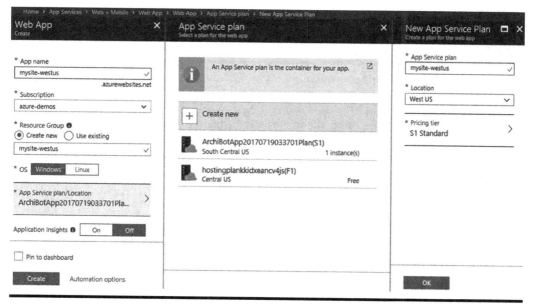

Figure 2.9   Creating a new web app

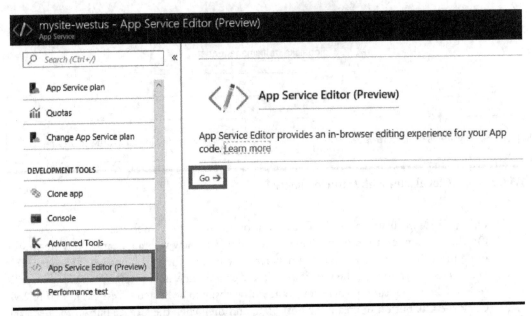

Figure 2.10   Launching application online editor

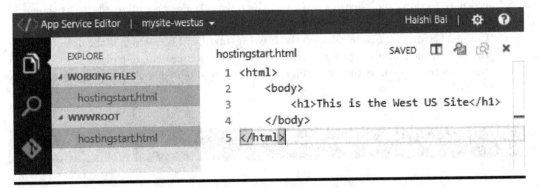

Figure 2.11   Editing web app source code

6. Navigate to the website and make sure it's displaying the text (you can get the URL to the site on the web app's overview page).
7. Repeat the process and deploy another site to another region such as Japan east. Modify the site's default page to display, "This is the Japan East Site."

Part II: Create a Traffic Manager Profile

1. Create a new Traffic Manager profile resource. Set its name and routing method. There are several routing methods to choose from:
   - **Performance**
     Routes user to the site providing the best performance to the user based on the user's geographical location.

- **Weighted**
  Distributes user traffic across sites based on associated weights. This can be useful when you want to do A/B testing—you can route a percentage of the overall user traffic to a new site and compare user activities and feedbacks with the original version.
- **Priority**
  This is an extended active–passive configuration in which users are routed to the site with highest priority, and are redirected to the site with the next highest priority when sites with higher priorities fail.
- **Geographic**
  Routes users to the site within the same geographic location. If Traffic Manager doesn't find a matching geographic location, it returns NODATA to the user. This configuration is designed to be compliant with data sovereignty requirements of some regions such as the European Union. User traffic in this case never leaves the designated region.

Although you'd probably choose a performance-based routing method, you'll choose the **Weighted** method in this exercise (see Figure 2.12) so that you can observe alternate routing paths.

2. Once the Traffic Manager profile is created, click on its **Endpoints** section, and then click on the **Add** link to add a new endpoint to the profile. On the **Add endpoint** screen, select

Figure 2.12   Creating a Traffic Manager profile

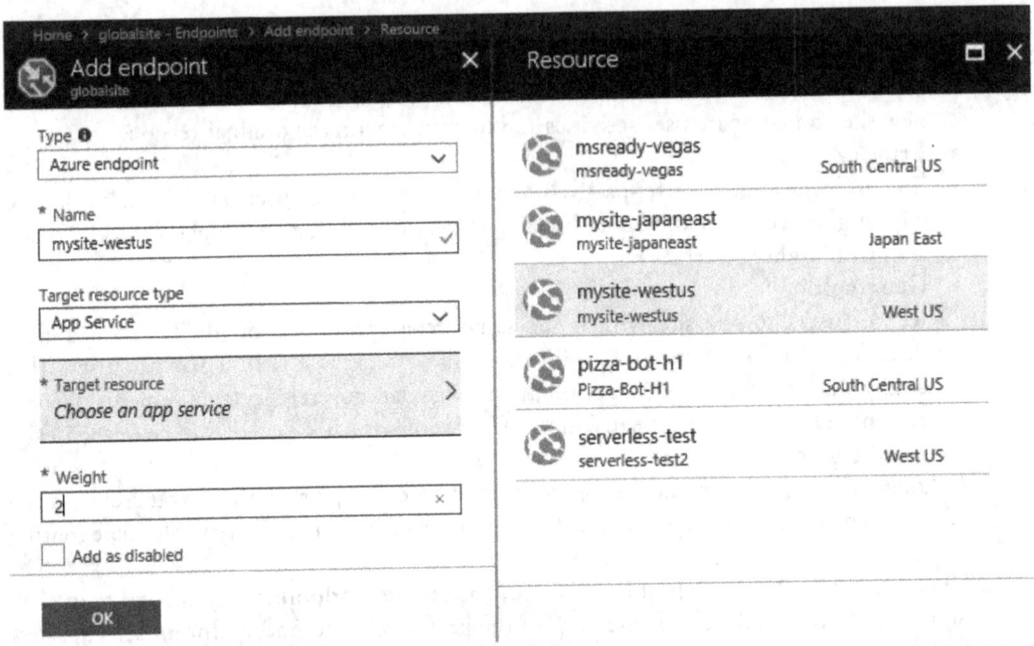

Figure 2.13 Adding an endpoint to a Traffic Manager profile

Azure endpoint as **Type**, **App Service** as **Target resource type**, and then click on the **Target resource** section. Select the West US site. Then, assign weight of **2** to the endpoint, and then click the **OK** button to create the endpoint as shown in Figure 2.13.

3. Repeat the process and add the Japan East endpoint to the profile with weight of 1. Figure 2.14 shows the endpoint list of the completed profile.

4. Access the Traffic Manager endpoint (http://globalsite.trafficmanager.net in my configuration) from different computers. You are twice as likely to hit the West US site than hitting the Japan East site.

> Traffic Manager works at the DNS level. It uses DNS to redirect client requests to the appropriate site based on the routing method. User requests don't actually go through Traffic Manager.

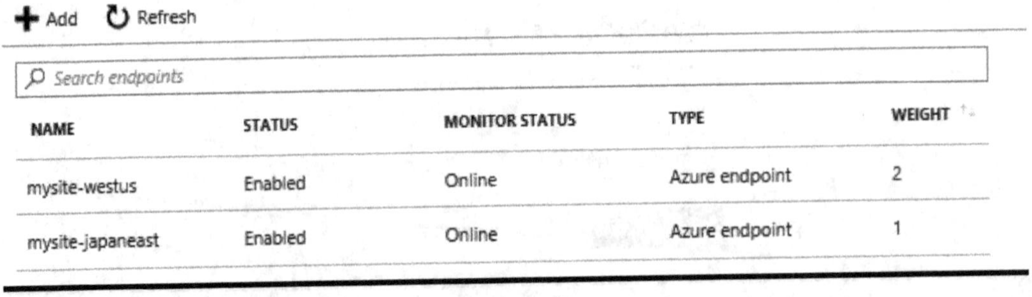

Figure 2.14 Endpoint list in a Traffic Manager profile

Design for Reliability

To put it simply, system reliability reflects how likely the system will perform an operation as designed. In a way, reliability is a higher requirement than availability because it requires the service not only be accessible but also functional as expected.

Through my three middle school years in China, I rode an old bike, which my father had bought in a flea market for 20 RMB (which is just a little over 3 US dollars). I never needed to lock the bike—nobody would care to take it. In other words, the bike was always "available" to me. However, the bike was in such a terrible condition it kept breaking down in all imaginable (and unimaginable) ways—the chain would break, the brake wire would snap, the tires would go flat. And once the handlebar just broke off. In my memory, I was walking or carrying the bike more than riding the bike. So my transportation service was highly available, but extremely unreliable.

For software, reliability problems are often less apparent than a broken bike. Software may work merrily for a long time before people realize it's not doing the right things. A few years before the new millennium, there was a huge panic in the world because of the *Y2K problem*. When computers were first designed in 1960s, storage and memory was very expensive. People were very cautions of conserving space when saving data. Most systems used two digits to represent years, which gave us 1900 to 1999. When the year 2000 was coming, people worried if computers would confuse 2000 with 1900 and trigger large-scale disasters. A huge joint effort was made to fix the problem. Fortunately, the problem was contained very well (or it wasn't as big a problem as expected) and the world continued without many problems.

By the way, the bike was sold for 10 RMB during the summer before my high school.

> ⓘ There is also a "Year 2038 problem" for Unix. Unix used a single 32-bit word to represent time (called POSIX time or Unix Epoch time), which was elapsed seconds from a fixed date such as January 1st, 1970. The time representation will overflow on 9 January 2038 03:14:08 UTC.

Reliable Software Practices

Reliable software is less buggy. Most software bugs are rooted not in terrible code, but in unclear requirements and even more commonly, changing requirements. As the code is handed from develop to developer, its original purpose becomes murky and even incomprehensible. Over time, the integrity of the original design breaks down through a process called *architecture decay*.

The best way to deal with architecture decay is to be explicit about what the software is supposed to do. No, I don't mean you need a detailed design document. Instead, I propose you employ two skills: unit testing and defensive coding.

Unit Tests

Why should you write unit tests? Is it to make sure your code is correct? The irony should be apparent—if you don't trust yourself to write correct code, how could you trust yourself to write correct unit test cases?

No, unit tests are not to ensure you wrote the correct code. Instead, their purpose is to capture detailed requirements so that you can keep checking your code against the specification. You should capture your software design in the form of unit tests. And you should treat unit tests you inherit from other developers as specifications. Some advocate for the *test-driven development (TDD) process*, in which you write test cases before you write the actual implementations—the test cases define what the software is supposed to do, and the code implements what's defined in the test case.

 Don't religiously implement unit tests for every single method you write—that will just slow you down. Instead, use unit tests to capture the desired behavior of your software.

When you design an API for others to consume, you can use TDD to put yourself into your users' shoes. By writing the test cases, you go through the coding experience of using your API. This will help you to design a more concise, intuitive API, which will trigger fewer bugs down the road.

Defensive Coding

 Defensive coding is a simple yet effective practice: before your code does anything, it checks if all parameters it receives are within an expected range. If any parameter is out of range, it throws an argument exception and exits.

When you define a method, you are defining a contract for callers to call. Unfortunately, in common languages you can't express the contract in great detail. For example, you define a *GetChineseZodiac* method that takes an integer year and an integer month and returns the corresponding Chinese animal zodiac:

```
string GetChineseZodiac(uint year, uint month)
```

Obviously, you want the month value to be between 1 to 12. However, you can't explicitly express that in your contract. This is where you can use defensive coding to make the contract more explicit.

 Always throw an argument out of range exception if one of the parameters doesn't check out. Don't silently return a default value or a null value, because that changes the semantics of your contract.

Many years back, I had a colleague who took pride in writing code that "never crashed." She put a try-catch block around all her code to swallow all exceptions—whatever the exceptions were, they were captured, logged, and discarded. Although her code always "worked," the code caused very weird behaviors in other components because those components were fooled to believe they had gotten what they asked for from her code. And they continued to work based on the incorrect information, leading to very intangible bugs that took forever to fix.

 Swallowing exception is one of the worst coding practices. And no, logging the exception is not the saving grace (unless you throw the exception as it is after it's logged). You should never swallow exceptions in your production code.

Other Reliable Software Practices

Effective tracing and monitoring are important techniques for diagnosing problems in a distributed environment, because live debugging sessions are often impossible in such systems. Traces of different components need to be aggregated, correlated, and analyzed to reveal intercomponent dynamics that can't otherwise be observed.

When you implement a tracing solution, you need to be thoughtful about controlling the amount of log data. If a system generates too little log data, you may miss critical information needed to diagnose a problem; if a system generates too much log data, fishing out useful information from the ocean of data becomes a daunting task.

Using different tracing levels is an effective way of controlling the amount of log data without losing critical data. In a production environment, you can design a "public API" log level that traces calls across component boundaries. This log level is enough to pin a problem to a component without generating too much noise.

Cloud hosting environments are quite reliable in general. However, problems do occur, such as storage failures, network failures, and virtual machine host failures. These failures happen with exceptionally low probability, so you may experience only a few problems over an extended period. And in many cases, the problems fix themselves by the magic of "trying again." These errors are called *transient errors*. Your code needs to prepare for these transient errors by employing a retry strategy. Some design patterns, such as *circuit breaker*, can also help you to deal with transient errors (and other error types).

Chaos test is a technique that injects hosting environment errors into the system so that you can observe low probability system errors in a condensed timeline. With chaos test, you can observe and diagnose hosting problems within a few hours instead of waiting for them to appear randomly over months or even years.

Some companies also use *test in production* and *A/B testing* to test out new versions of software with a portion of live user traffic. These tests provide the highest fidelity in load and usage patterns. Test in production should use only release-quality versions, because it does increase the risk of user data corruption (which is very bad) and service outage.

Reliable Software Architecture

In addition to improving reliability of individual components, several architecture techniques can improve overall system reliability even if individual components have reliability issues. In fact, making unreliable components work together in a reliable manor has been extensively researched in the computer industry in various contexts, such as storage, cryptography, and distributed transactions. For example, erasure coding (EC) breaks data segments, and uses redundant data blocks to reconstruct data if data becomes corrupt. In Chapter 9, you'll see how untrustworthy compute resources are organized together to deliver a reliable ledger.

This section introduces a few design principles that can improve system reliability. This is not an exhaustive list but should be a good list to get you started in reliable system design.

Loose Coupling

I taught Java programming as a volunteer teacher at a high school. When I introduced the concept of *interface*, I used the example of power outlets. A power outlet is a well-defined interface (well, within a certain region. There are tens of different outlets around the world) that all electric appliances as well as all power supplies implement to provide power to appliances. This is an elegant solution that allows different appliance makers to work in isolation, while being assured their products will get the appropriate power supply when plugged in.

Clearly defined interfaces decouple components from each other. These components can be developed in insolation and assembled together through the predefined interfaces. These components are called *loosely coupled*.

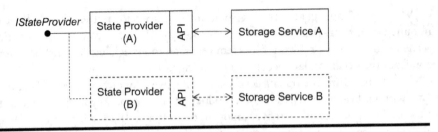

Figure 2.15   Two different implementations of an IStateProvider interface

Loosely coupled components have some great advantages. Each of the components can be developed and tested against its defined interface for correctness. This allows a complex system to be broken down into smaller, manageable pieces that are verified to be correct before they are assembled together. When a component is tested in isolation, mock components are often used to provide static interface implementations so that the component can be tested in a stable environment. This exercise can shake out many of the bugs before the component interacts with other components in a more dynamic setting.

Another benefit of loose coupling is that a component can be replaced as needed without affecting other components, as long as the interfaces between components are faithfully implemented. For example, you've observed that an external service keeps failing to meet your reliability requirements and have found a replacement. If you've designed a stable provider interface, you can swap the services without impacting the rest of your system. Figure 2.15 shows a typical *service provider pattern* that uses a provider interface to encapsulate a service dependency. The example uses an *IStateProvider* interface to represent any storage services that can preserve states. A state provider implementation implements the interface and works with the proprietary storage API to work with a specific storage service.

Message-Based Integrations

Although components can be decoupled during implementation, they are coupled together at runtime when they are assembled together. Message-based integration is an effective way to avoid runtime coupling. With message-based integration, a messaging middleware is used as a message bus linking individual components. Components send and receive messages through the bus. They don't need to be aware of each other. This design allows components to be integrated while maintaining independences at runtime. Figure 2.16 shows a generic architecture diagram of message-based integration.

Message-based integration has been used in many large scale enterprise systems. And many effective design patterns have been developed to improve system reliability, scalability, and extensibility. For example, the *competing consumer* pattern is one of my favorite patterns (and I believe I managed to mention it in six of seven of my previous books). The pattern allows job generators and processors to work at different paces, different scales, and even at different times.

You can use message-based integration to build up flexible topologies of components, such as 1-to-1 communication and publish-subscribe. And the best part is, the topology can be redesigned and redeployed without affecting any components. In some cases, components can remain online as the topology is rerouted. Separation of components and component communications is a key aspect of effective microservices design, which I'll discuss in more details in Chapter 3.

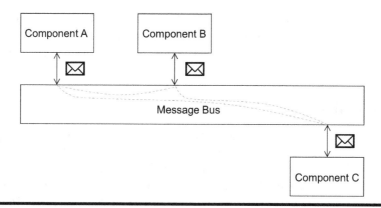

Figure 2.16 Message-based integration

A messaging middleware provides reliable messaging that generally ensures a message is delivered *at least once*. This means even if all components crash, they can still recover already submitted jobs from the messaging middleware when they come back. Furthermore, message-based integration improves systems reliability in several other ways. First, because components don't have runtime dependencies with each other, a failing component won't take down related components. This controls the *blaster radius* of a problem. Second, the messaging system can accumulate messages in its message queues when a message consumer fails. When the consumer comes back online, it can pick up where it left before the crash. Third, the messaging middleware can build up multiple message paths so that messages are processed if at least one of the paths still work. For example, a travel site can span out flight searches, hotel searches, and car rental searches to multiple sites and build up a complete travel plan based on available options.

Maintainability

Within the reliability context, maintainability refers to how easily software can be repaired. Maintainability can be measured by Mean Time to Repair (MTTR), which records the amount of time needed to bring broken software back online. Obviously, reduction in MTTR helps to improve your system availability.

The key to system maintainability is a clear separation of concerns. When a component has a clear responsibility, it's much easier to analyze its behaviors and troubleshoot its problems. If a component takes on too many responsibilities, it becomes harder to understand. And making changes to it may have unexpected side effects on multiple areas. On the other hand, if a single responsibility is scattered to multiple components, diagnosing a failed work item becomes tricky, as you have to trace and correlate logs from multiple components.

The most important skill of an architect is to be able to correctly draw component boundaries to ensure separation of concerns while avoiding overengineering.

> (i) There are several other related measurements of system availability, such as Mean Time Between Failure (MTBF) and Mean Time to Failure (MTTF). There are plenty of online documents and offline literature on these measurements, so I won't bother to discuss them further here.

She should also be aligned with the company's long-term vision so that she can design the system with enough flexibility for future evolutions. A world-class architect has qualities of a scientist, an artist, and a visionary. It's a rare combination that can be achieved only by years of experience.

Design for Scalability

When the first internetworking message was sent from University of California, Los Angles (UCLA) to Stanford Research Institute in 1969, the predecessor of the Internet had only two nodes. In 1997, American Online (AOL) reached 34 million subscribers. In 2016, the number of Microsoft Office product users crossed the 1.2 billion threshold. In 2018, Google processes 3.5 billion searches per day.

How can you design a scalable system that can take on such staggering loads? This sounds like a daunting question that isn't relevant to most of us—after all, only an exceedingly small percentage of programmers and architects need to face such planetary-scale challenges. Regardless, many design principles and practices in these systems are directly applicable to applications with much smaller scales. This section shares some of the design patterns (that I'm aware of) for building scalable applications.

What's Scalability, Anyway?

Scalability goes hand-in-hand with performance—a scalable system is a system that can maintain satisfactory performance as its load increases. A Blu-ray player is not a scalable system, because it plays only one movie at a time. If you want to play two movies, they must be queued and played one-by-one. A media server, on the other hand, is a scalable system because it can smoothly stream multiple movies at the same time.

As introduced in Chapter 1, to scale a system, you can either go vertical—to make current servers more powerful, or go horizontal—to add more servers to share the load. Going vertical leads to über servers that can handle tremendous loads; going horizontal allows as many ordinary servers to be added as needed to share the loads. Building über servers sounds hard, hence it will not be discussed further in this book.

Scalable Design

Scalable design applies not only to global applications, but also to applications at any scale. Scalable design principles help a system avoid bottlenecks and Single Point of Failures (SPoFs). So even if your system is not expected to be scaled massively, you should still apply scalable design principals to improve performance as well as reliability of your system. People say scalability is a nice problem to have. However, if your system isn't originally designed with scalability in mind, adding scalability support often needs major redesign and code changes.

Scaling by Reduction

Nowadays, when you call a customer service line, you are most likely greeted by a robotic answering system. The automated system can often guide you through routine tasks without ever needing to involve a human operator. A human operator is expensive and slow, and they can only handle one customer at a time. However, a human operator can resolve complicated cases that can't be

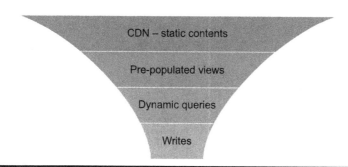

Figure 2.17 Scale by reduction

handled by the automated system. This is a typical case of *scaling by reduction*, in which routine tasks are filtered and processed at the edge of the system instead of being passed and handled by the core system.

A typical software system serves much more read requests than write requests. Read requests can be cached and served directly from caching layers such as a Content Delivery Network (CDN). These caching layers allow read requests to be efficiently served from cache servers, freeing the compute power on the backend server for handling more complex write requests. To further optimize for reading, you can use prepopulated views to avoid repetitive, complex queries. Figure 2.17 shows how scaling by reduction reduces the number of requests through each layer so that only a small portion of complex, data mutating operations reach the core server layer.

Scaling by Partition

Partitioning is a very intuitive way to scale out a system. It divides customers into distinct groups that are handled by dedicated servers. Load balancing is the simplest form of scaling by partition. It randomly routes customers to participating servers to share the overall workload. Partitions can also be static. For example, a system may choose to partition customers by geographical regions and route customers to regional servers.

A system can also use multiple layers of partitions to achieve massive scale. For example, a global application partitions user by geographical regions first, then by customer tenants, then by service subscriptions, and then by business units within the subscription. Figure 2.18 shows such a globally scaled system. At the top level, a Traffic Manager provides a unified entry point to deployments at different regions. Then within a region, a Tenant Manager sets up tenant-specific routes on a regional gateway that routes users from different tenants to different server clusters. And finally, a gateway on the cluster routes users to different servers based on users' subscriptions and business units.

Please note that using multiple layers of partitions doesn't necessarily mean extra latencies in traffic routing. In Figure 2.18, routing to different regions is done at the DNS level; and routing to subscriptions and business units are folded into the tenant gateway.

Dynamic Scaling

The grocery store near my house is known for expedient checkouts. Whenever there's a line longer than three customers, the manager will open another checkout lane to reduce the wait time. They have over 20 checkout lanes to handle busy hours. For most of the time, however, they only

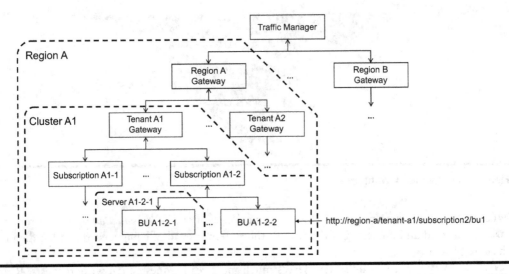

Figure 2.18 Scaling by multiple levels of partitions

need to keep four to five lanes open. This is a case of *dynamic scaling*, in which cloud platforms excel. With dynamic scaling, an application dynamically allocates or recruits additional compute resources when its workload increases, and releases the resources when its workload decreases. Because cloud charges by resource consumption, being able to release unused resources is a significant money saver. And because cloud provides humongous resource pools, the application can acquire additional resources at any time. This ability to dynamically scale is also known as *elasticity*, one of the biggest value propositions of cloud.

Applications with different traffic patterns need different dynamic scaling strategies. Figure 2.19 summarizes some of the typical traffic changing patterns. Each of the patterns requires a different scaling strategy.

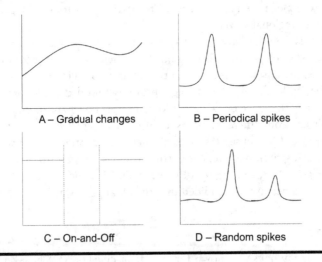

Figure 2.19 Typical traffic change patterns

■ Gradual changes

Application traffic slowly goes up and down. *Reactive scaling* is sufficient in this case. Reactive scaling monitors resource consumptions. When it finds existing resources are stressed—such as CPU usage is going above certain thresholds, it allocates additional resources to share the load. And when resource usage is below certain thresholds, it releases resources to reduce the cost. Obviously, you should pick thresholds that leave sufficient margins for resource provisioning and de-provisioning.

■ Periodical spikes

Many e-commerce applications face periodical spikes—weekends are usually much busier than weekdays, and holiday seasons are the busiest. *Predicative scaling* is the most appropriate in this case. With predicative scaling, additional resources are allocated in anticipation of upcoming spikes. Periodically triggered automation scripts, or manual operations before certain events such as a big promotion campaign, can do this.

■ On-and-Off

Schools and some government offices have on-and-off traffics. For example, a school registration system is busy before semester starts, but remains dormant during the semester. In this case, *Scheduled scaling* can reduce hosting costs. All (or most of) resources will be released during the off-hour. And they are reallocated just before the office hour begins. Needless to say, for an 8-hour office, doing so saves 67% of hosting costs, comparing with keeping the system running at all times.

■ Random spikes

The random spikes pattern is the most challenging case. Random spikes often hit news sites and social media sites. And even the biggest names may have problems handling such sudden changes. During the Oscar 2014 ceremony, the host, Ellen DeGeneres, took a selfie with a group of celebrities and posted (or "tweeted") the picture on Twitter. Twitter stuttered to handle the 1.8 million reposts (or "retweets"). There isn't a satisfactory solution using traditional servers or virtual machines, because booting up a machine takes time. When the sudden spike appears, there just isn't enough time to react. So, the only solution is to swallow the cost pill and *overprovision* to prepare for a rainy day. The problem is—how much do you overprovision? Too much means too expensive, too little means insufficient capability when the spike appears. In the next chapter, you'll learn how containers enable *bursting*, which brings a wonderful solution to this dilemma.

Tutorial: Setting Up Autoscaling

 In this tutorial, you'll create enable autoscaling on one of the web applications you've deployed in the earlier lab. You'll set up a reactive autoscaling rule (see Figure 2.19) based on CPU thresholds.

1. In the Azure management portal, select one of the web apps you deployed earlier, click on its **Scale out (App Service plan)** link, and then click the **Enable autoscale** button, as shown in Figure 2.20.
2. On the scale out screen, enter a name for your autoscaling setting. An autoscaling setting can contain multiple conditions. First, click on the Add a rule link in the default condition, as shown in Figure 2.21.

App Services
Microsoft
Add
Edit columns
More
Filter by name...
NAME
artisbot
cosmosgartner
functions-basics
msready-vegas
mysite-japaneast
mysite-westus
pizza-bot-h1
serverless-test
mysite-westus - Scale out (App Service plan)
App Service
Search (Ctrl+/)
Application settings
Authentication / Authorization
Managed service identity
Backups
Custom domains
SSL certificates
Networking
Scale up (App Service plan)
Scale out (App Service plan)
WebJobs
Save
Discard
Disable autoscale
Configure
Run history
JSON
Notify
Override condition
Instance count
1
Your autoscale configuration is disabled. To reinstate your configuration, enable autoscale.
Enable autoscale

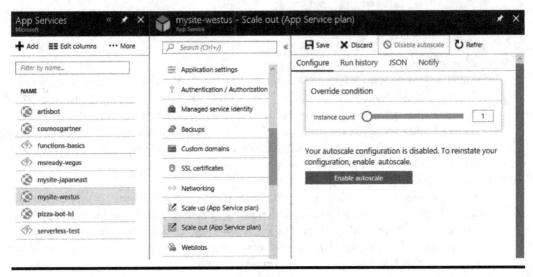

Figure 2.20 Enabling autoscaling of a web application

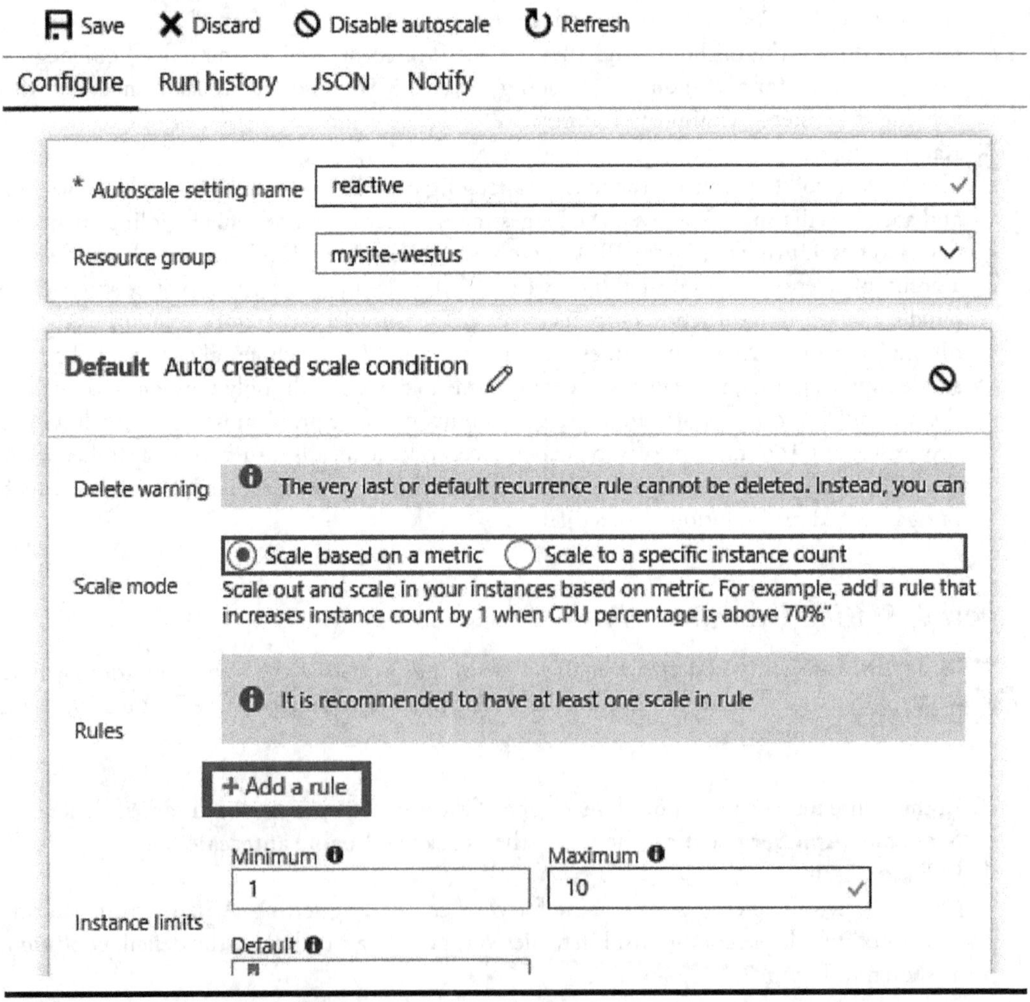
Save
Discard
Disable autoscale
Refresh
Configure
Run history
JSON
Notify
* Autoscale setting name
reactive
Resource group
mysite-westus
Default Auto created scale condition
Delete warning
The very last or default recurrence rule cannot be deleted. Instead, you can
Scale mode
Scale based on a metric
Scale to a specific instance count
Scale out and scale in your instances based on metric. For example, add a rule that increases instance count by 1 when CPU percentage is above 70%"
Rules
It is recommended to have at least one scale in rule
+ Add a rule
Instance limits
Minimum
1
Maximum
10
Default

Figure 2.21 Autoscale settings

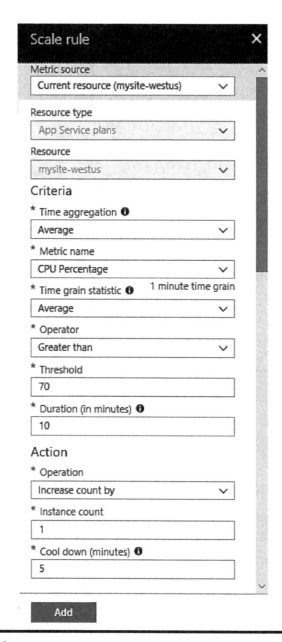

Figure 2.22 Scale rule screen

3. On the Scale rule screen, set up an autoscaling rule based on CPU usage, as shown in Figure 2.22. The screen is self-explanatory—it sets up a rule that increments instance count by one when average CPU usage is over 70% during a 10 minute window. Once an autoscaling rule is triggered, it enters a *cooling down* period, in which it's not triggered again. This allows metrics to be stabilized before another scaling action takes place. Once you are happy with the rule settings, click the **Add** button to add the autoscaling rule.

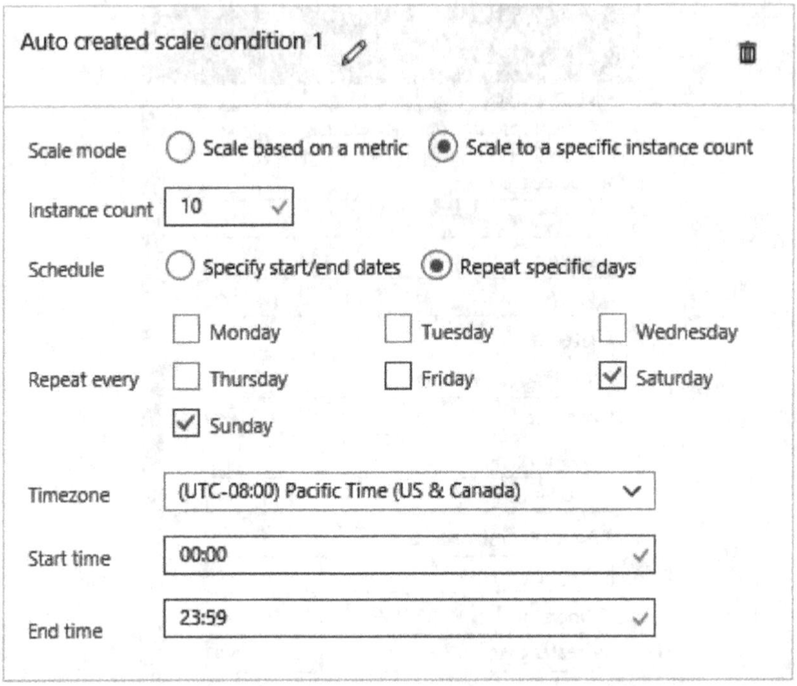

Figure 2.23 Scheduled scaling rule

4. [Optional] You can define multiple conditions on the same autoscale setting. For instance, Figure 2.23 shows a scheduled scaling rule that bumps the instance count to 10 during the weekends.

Zen of Cloud

"Bad times have a scientific value. These are occasions a good learner would not miss."

Ralph Waldo Emerson

Cloud agility's best value is not only to quickly make things work, but also to quickly try and fail. Trying out innovative ideas used to be hard because it was difficult to acquire necessary compute resources to support your ideas. With the help of cloud, you can easily gain enough compute resources to verify new frameworks, new designs, and new topologies. During your experiments you'll certainly encounter some errors or problems. Take those as good learning opportunities to dig deeper. You'll understand the platform better, gain additional insights on its limitations, and become inspired to seek innovative solutions. And when someone points out your mistakes, you should be appreciative because you've been presented with more learning opportunities.

Chapter 3

Containers and Microservices

Rise of Containers

At DockerCon2016, Microsoft Azure CTO Mark Russinovich surprised the world by showing Microsoft SQL Server running on Linux in a Docker container. Microsoft SQL Server had always been a Windows-based software, and it had been one of the most popular Microsoft products and a leader in relational databases. Having such a product containerized on Linux was great testimony of a new, open Microsoft. It also showed how Docker containers had interrupted the world.

Since its debut in 2013 through 2017, Docker tools have been downloaded over 13 billion times. Using Docker containers has become an essential skill for many programmers and IT pros. Obviously, Docker has done something right and in the correct moment. The first part of this chapter introduces various parts of Docker and gives you a peek into secrets behind Docker's success. But before that, let's go through a quick "Hello World" tutorial to get you started with Docker. If you are already familiar with Docker, please feel free to skip ahead.

Tutorial: Hello World with Docker

 In this tutorial, you'll install Docker Community Edition (CE) and launch a simple container.

1. Install Docker CE. Depends on the OS you use, you need to follow a separate set of instructions. Please refer to corresponding Docker documents to install:
   - On Windows: https://docs.docker.com/docker-for-windows/install/
   - On Mac: https://docs.docker.com/docker-for-mac/install/
   - On Ubuntu: https://docs.docker.com/install/linux/docker-ce/ubuntu/
   - On Debian: https://docs.docker.com/install/linux/docker-ce/debian/
   - On CentOS: https://docs.docker.com/install/linux/docker-ce/centos/
   - On Fedora: https://docs.docker.com/install/linux/docker-ce/fedora/

2. Once Docker has installed, use the following command to verify Docker client and Docker engine version:

```
sudo docker version
```

The above command should return something looks like the following (in my environment I'm using a modified version of Docker. By the time you read this book, you should be able to find more details on this project in my blog: blog.haishibai.com):

```
Client:
 Version:       18.05.0-ce-dev
 API version:   1.37
 Go version:    go1.9.4
 Git commit:
 Built:         Sat Apr  7 01:57:06 2018
 OS/Arch:       linux/amd64
 Experimental:  false
 Orchestrator:  swarm


Server:
 Engine:
  Version:       18.05.0-ce-dev
  API version:   1.37 (minimum version 1.12)
  Go version:    go1.9.4
  Git commit:    3ccf86f831
  Built:         Thu Apr  5 00:49:26 2018
  OS/Arch:       linux/amd64
  Experimental:  false
```

3. Next you'll launch an Ubuntu container on top of your machine and attach a Bash shell. The container contains a vanilla Ubuntu installation that you can use as a regular, isolated virtual machine:

```
sudo docker run --rm -it ubuntu /bin/bash
```

The above Docker run command launches an Ubuntu container based on a Docker image (think as a VM image for now) named "Ubuntu." The "-it" switch indicates that you'd like to attach an interactive terminal; the "--rm" switch indicates that the container should be removed once you close the shell. And finally, "/bin/bash" is the command to run once the container is started.

For the first time, you may see some download progress displays when Docker pulls down the ubuntu image. The image will be cached locally on your machine so that the subsequent launches will be much faster—usually under a second. Yes, that was not a typo. You can literally launch a new, isolated Ubuntu environment under a second.

Once the container is launched, you'll see a command prompt that looks something like the following. Now you've logged in as *root* in the new Ubuntu environment. You can do whatever you want.

```
root@ce58a0a27419:/#
```

4. Speaking of "whatever you want," let's try something terrible (while you are sure you are still inside the container):

```
rm -rf *
```

Remember you are at *root*, and you are doing this from the system's root folder. This would have been devastating if you were on a real machine. Once the command runs (with many errors that you can ignore), your Ubuntu is basically broken. You can even use commands like "ls" or "uname."

5. Type *exit* and press [Enter] to exit from the (broken) container.
6. Welcome back. You are back on your good old machine like nothing happened.

Batteries Included but Swappable

I bought many toys for my daughter when she was young. Two things I hated the most were the plastic wrap that was exceedingly difficult to cut open, and electric toys that didn't come with batteries. Both were *frictions* in my purchase experience. Similarly, for a brand new tool to gain rapid adoption, the out-of-box experience is critical.

Docker's philosophy has been "batteries included, but swappable/removable." When you install Docker, you are installing both a Docker client (*docker*) and a Docker engine (*dockered*). They are preconfigured to work together so that you can start to use Docker containers right after installation without any extra configuration steps. As you go deeper with Docker, you'll learn that many of the Docker components can be extended or completed swapped out. This philosophy has given Docker both ease of adoption and customization flexibility. I consider myself an old-timer, so I'm used to going through convoluted steps to get things working. Younger generations are much less patient—they want immediate results with as little effort as possible. I'm not accusing them of being lazy. They grew up in a world with a much faster pace, so they are used to a fast speed. To get them to adopt new tools, the tool has to work out-of-box. Obviously, Docker has done it right.

A Vibrant Ecosystem

Another thing Dock has done right is to incubate a vibrant ecosystem from the beginning. Docker Hub (https://hub.docker.com/) is a public registry for Docker images. Anybody can easily publish images to the registry and discover and reuse images published by others. There are hundreds of thousands of images, many of which are published by original software vendors. These images have been pulled (or downloaded) billions of times and applied to all kinds of containerized applications. At the time of writing, the following are some of the most popular images on Docker Hub; each has millions of pulls and thousands of "starts" (similar to "likes" in social networks):

- alpine
  A 5MB, minimal Alpine Linux image with a complete package index.
- nginx
  An official build of Nginx web server.
- redis
  Redis is an open-sourced key-value store, often used as in-memory cache.
- mysql
  MySQL is an open-sourced relational database management system (RDBMS).
- golang
  Runtime environment for Google's Go language (golang).

These high-quality images have attracted many users; and more users have encouraged more publishers to publish and maintain their images on Docker Hub. Furthermore, the low publishing barrier has inspired many individual publishers to share their packaged work on Docker Hub. Publishing to (pushing) and downloading from (pulling) Docker Hub is currently free. Pulling doesn't require authentication. And pushing requires authentication with a free registered account.

To ensure you use only images from trusted publishers, you can enable Docker Content Trust (DCT), which enable you to verify the publisher of an image using the publisher's public key. The image is signed by the publisher's private key before it's published to Docker Hub.

In addition to the public Docker Hub, Docker also supports privately owned and operated registries called Docker Trusted Registry (DTR). Enterprises can use DTR to set up private registries to publish and share internal images.

How Do Docker Images Work?

A Docker image is an immutable file that is used as a template to launch new containers. So, functionally, a Docker image acts in the same way as a virtual machine image. Structurally, a Docker image is a layered file system with metadata that chains the layers together.

A Dockerfile, which starts with a base image and uses various commands to lay new files on top of the base, describes a Docker image. Each command creates a new layer. And these layers are overlaid on top of the base image contents to create the new image. For example, consider the following Dockerfile:

```
FROM ubuntu
ADD new.txt /var/
```

It starts with an Ubuntu image and adds a *new.txt* file to the */var* folder. If you use `docker inspect image <image name>` to inspect the image, you'll see its layers:

```
"Layers": [
"sha256:a94e0d5a7c404d0e6fa15d8cd4010e69663bd8813b5117fbad71365a7365
   6df9",
```

```
"sha256:88888b9b1b5b7bce5db41267e669e6da63ee95736cb904485f96f29be648
    bfda",
"sha256:52f389ea437ebf419d1c9754d0184b57edb45c951666ee86951d9f6afd26
    035e",
"sha256:52a7ea2bb533dc2a91614795760a67fb807561e8a588204c4858a300074c
    082b",
"sha256:db584c622b50c3b8f9b8b94c270cc5fe235e5f23ec4aacea8ce67a8c16e0
    fbad",
"sha256:6af75c304b20cee577bdb299514b4ffad66bc59fbae2133b14
    01c25163866072"
]
```

Similar, if you inspect the *ubuntu* image itself, you'll find the image has all but the last layer, which was created by the ADD command in the preceding Dockerfile:

```
"Layers": [
"sha256:a94e0d5a7c404d0e6fa15d8cd4010e69663bd8813b5117fbad71365a7365
    6df9",
"sha256:88888b9b1b5b7bce5db41267e669e6da63ee95736cb904485f96f29be648
    bfda",
"sha256:52f389ea437ebf419d1c9754d0184b57edb45c951666ee86951d9f6afd26
    035e",
"sha256:52a7ea2bb533dc2a91614795760a67fb807561e8a588204c4858a300074c
    082b",
"sha256:db584c622b50c3b8f9b8b94c270cc5fe235e5f23ec4aacea8ce67a8c16e0
    fbad"
]
```

On top of these immutable image layers, Docker creates a read-write layer for applications to write files to the file system in container. Storage drivers enable this. Docker supports pluggable storage drivers, with an overlay2 driver as the default driver for Docker CE (following the "batteries included but swappable" philosophy). Other drivers include *aufs*, *vfs*, *devicemapper*, *btrfs*, and *overlay*.

The preceding inspect command also reveals how layers in a container are stacked together. For an overlay driver, the *UpperDir* points to the top layer; the *LowerDir* points to the list of lower layers in the order of uppermost to lowermost; the overlay is mounted at *MergedDir* (invisible to host); and finally, *WorkDir* is the working directory for the overlay. If you navigate to the *UpperDir* folder, you'll see the new.txt file defined in the Dockerfile.

```
"GraphDriver": {
  "Data": {
    "LowerDir":
"/var/lib/docker/overlay2/f57da16daaa6f0edd893fc9c31d5e075c15b68f230
    4d9ebeee405a4745af5a09/diff:/var/lib/docker/overlay2/69768d481aa5
    6d334e3ce45516766c4adf934dfec594b201f94b300d683c3b80/diff:/var/
    lib/docker/overlay2/17d0df4231418e9b1a0a6cea8411d4a24101d0d49e7bf
    fb6855b70f666b5fb22/diff:/var/lib/docker/overlay2/5549b9304d9d17a
```

```
    4ae277586012f25cb36541b7ee5e10e7b54f914db24449a8e/diff:/var/lib/
    docker/overlay2/f933772ec3b92d46b5aebf43b8f106d002df6f1785c3583
    4c5621288f17d7031/diff",
    "MergedDir":
"/var/lib/docker/overlay2/0161273bd134d29ce0f694eb390425073522e2b091
    c5bc76d955c9b23600268d/merged",
    "UpperDir":
"/var/lib/docker/overlay2/0161273bd134d29ce0f694eb390425073522e2b091
    c5bc76d955c9b23600268d/diff",
    "WorkDir":
"/var/lib/docker/overlay2/0161273bd134d29ce0f694eb390425073522e2b091
    c5bc76d955c9b23600268d/work"
  },
  "Name": "overlay2"
}
```

A container file system is built on top of a union file system, which combines a set of different file systems and directories into a single logical file system. So although a container sees a unified file system, the files in the system are scattered in different folders (layers) in the host system. When a container creates or modifies a file, a technique named *copy-on-write* is used to create a new copy of the file in the container's read-write layer. This file is laid on top of the original file to override what the container sees, though the original file content is untouched. When a container is destroyed, the read-write layer is destroyed as well. This is precisely why in the earlier tutorial, deleting all files had no effect on the host because everything happened in the temporal read-write layer.

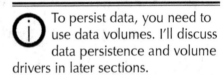 To persist data, you need to use data volumes. I'll discuss data persistence and volume drivers in later sections.

Address the Key Pain Points

If you peel off layers of DevOps, you'll see that at the core, DevOps is all about consistency, especially consistent application deployments. All techniques such as CI/CD pipelines, automated tests, infrastructure as code, desired state management, immutable infrastructures, test-driven development process, etc., are all pointing at the same goal—a product deployed in a consistent manor. Consistency brings predictability; predictability improves productivity; and productivity increase profitability. So, it's unsurprising that Docker gets so much attention when it offers a nice solution for consistent deployment.

Consistency

A Docker image is a static snapshot of the entire application stack that includes all dependencies all the way down to OS. You don't need to worry about software compatibilities, framework updates, or system patches (I'll come back to patches in a moment)—what you've captured in a Docker image is immutable. Because a Docker image (of a specific version) never changes, you are assured that when it's launched as a container, you have a consistent environment every single time. The only similar technology that provides such capabilities before containers is a virtual machine image, which is much heavier, harder to build, harder to share, and takes a long time to launch into a running machine.

Docker Hub, as well as private Docker Trusted Registries, provides a centralized way to share images among a given community. This allows consistent usage of the same images.

Agility

In contrast, Docker containers are lightweight. And because of the layered structure of images, an application image needs to carry only the application files by layering on top of an image with the required software stack (such as Nginx). Smaller images are easier to be transmitted, shared, and reused, making them an ideal solution for rapid deployments in an iterative development process.

A running Docker container is just a process. The process is isolated from the rest of the system through *namespaces, cgroups,* and *copy-on-write* file systems. Because launching a Docker container just starts a process, Docker containers can be launched very quickly—many base images can be launched in a sub-second. This kind of agility is unprecedented and fits well within the rapid deployment processes of today.

Windows Containers

Windows container is Microsoft's implementation of Docker containers based on the Windows system. Beginning with Windows Server 2016, Windows provides native support for Docker containers. You can use the same Docker tools and APIs to manage your Windows containers. For example, to launch a Windows Server Core container and attach a command line prompt, use the following command:

```
docker run --rm -it microsoft/windowsservercore cmd
```

Docker containers share the same system core. On a Linux host, all running containers share the same Linux kernel. On a Windows host, all running containers share the same Windows core. This is a weaker isolation than virtual machines. Windows containers provide two modes: Windows Server containers and Hyper-V containers. Windows Server containers share the same system core, while Hyper-V containers use a dedicated copy of the system core per container. Hyper-V containers are heavier and slower to launch than server containers, but they provide stronger isolation among containers.

Containers on Clouds

At the time of writing, both Azure and AWS support running single container instances without managing underlying hosts. Azure's service is named Azure Container Instances (ACI), which was released months before AWS's service, Amazon Elastic Container Service (ECS, or Fargate). ACI provides a straightforward way of running individual containers. You can create a new container using a single line of command. And the container is assigned a public IP through which you can access services hosted in the container. Azure takes cares of host (VM), IP, and virtual network management for you. Amazon ECS exposes more concepts—to run a container, you need to define the container and then define the task (or application) holding the container, and then the service (with an optional application load balancer if you have

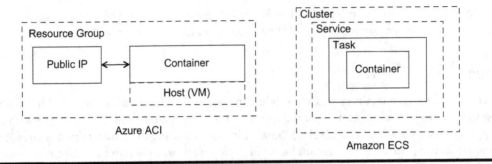

Figure 3.1 Azure ACI vs. Amazon ECS

multiple tasks in a service) holding the task, and eventually the cluster holding the service. Figure 3.1 shows the different hosting models of ACI and ECS.

Azure ACI is designed for scenarios in which you need to launch a container with minimum management overheads. For example, when you have a sudden spike in user traffic, you can use bursting (see Chapter 2) to handle the additional workload by recruiting ACI instances, which can be acquired in seconds. Because ACI instances are charged by seconds, your cost of using the extra compute resources is kept to a minimum. ACI instances can also be joined into an orchestration engine to run coordinated workloads. I'll discuss container orchestration in the next section.

Amazon ECS container instances run on a cluster formed by Amazon Elastic Compute Cloud (EC2) virtual machines. ECS provides a built-in (but simpler) orchestration engine so that you can easily scale your tasks (or applications). If you want to use a more sophisticated orchestration engine like Kubernetes, you need to use a different Amazon service—Amazon Elastic Container Service for Kubernetes (EKS).

You can think of ACI as providing a container at IaaS level, just like running a virtual machine. ECS, on the other hand, runs a service at PaaS level that is backed by a container.

Hands-On Lab: Running a Node.js Application in Containers on Cloud

In this lab, you'll build a Node.js application, package it as a Docker image, push the image to Docker Hub, and then deploy Docker containers using the image on both Azure ACI and Amazon ECS. This lab assumes:

- Node.js is installed
- Docker is installed
- You have an account on Docker Hub (sign up at https://hub.docker.com/)
- You have an Azure subscription (see Chapter 1). Skip Part II if you don't have one.
- You have an AWS subscription (sign up at https://aws.amazon.com/). Skip Part III if you don't have one.
- The following steps are recorded on an Ubuntu environment. However, they should be identical on macOS or Windows.

Part I: Build a Containerized Node.js Application

1. Create a new **nodeApp** folder.

2. Add a new **package.json** file to the folder. This file contains a list of dependent Node.js modules required by the application—*express* and *OS*:

```
{
  "name": "hello-world",
  "version": "1.0.0",
  "description": "A Node.js Hello World app",
  "author": "Haishi Bai<hbai@microsoft.com>",
  "dependencies": {
    "express": "*",
    "os": "*"
  }
}
```

3. Add a new **server.js** file to the folder. This is the Node.js implementation of a simple web server that listens to port 80 and returns a "Hello, World" message:

```
var express = require('express');
var app = express();
var os = require('os');
app.get('/', function (req, res) {
  res.send('Hello, World from ' + os.hostname() + '!');
});
var server = app.listen(80);
```

4. Try out the application to make sure it works. Launch the web server from the **nodeApp** folder:

```
sudo npm start
```

5. Launch a browser (or use curl) and open http://localhost:80/. You should see a "Hello, World" message with your machine host name.
6. Stop the server by pressing **Ctrl + C**.
7. Add a new **Dockerfile** (without any file extensions) to the same folder with the following content. The Dockerfile starts with a base container image with Node.js already installed (node:carbon), creates a working directory, adds *package.json*, uses *npm install* to install required modules, adds *server.js*, exposes port *80*, and finally specifies that the entry point of the container should be command *npm start*.

```
FROM node:carbon
WORKDIR /usr/src/app
COPY package.json ./
RUN npm install
COPY server.js .
EXPOSE 80
CMD ["npm", "start"]
```

8. Build the container using the *docker build* command. Please note you should tag your container (through the *-t* switch) in the format *<your Docker account>/<image name>*. For example, my Docker account is hbai, so I tagged my container as *hbai/zoc-nodejs*.

```
sudo docker build -t <your Docker account>/zoc-nodejs .
```

9. Now, let's verify that the image works. Launch a new container in service mode (the *-d* switch). The command returns with a long container ID, and the container runs as a background process.

```
sudo docker run --rm -d -p 80:80 <your Docker account>/zoc-nodejs
```

10. Use a browser to request http://localhost/ again and you should see the same "Hello, World" message.
11. Push the image to Docker Hub (you may be prompted to log in using your Docker account). Once the image is pushed, it's available for anyone to use for free:

```
sudo docker push <your Docker account>/zoc-nodejs
```

To shut down the container, use `sudo docker ps` to list out all running containers. Find the corresponding shortened Container ID in the list and use `sudo docker rm -f <container ID>` to stop the container.

Part II: Deploy a Container on ACI

1. Log on to Microsoft Azure Management Console (https://portal.azure.com/).
2. Click on the **Cloud Shell** icon on the tool bar (see Figure 3.2). This launches a Bash/PowerShell shell (which runs in a container as well) with an Azure CLI or Azure PowerShell module preconfigured. This is an easy and nice way to use Azure command line tools without installing or configuring anything.
3. Create a new resource group:

```
az group create --name aciGroup --location eastus
```

4. Create a new container using the preceding container image:

```
az container create --resource-group aciGroup --name acicontainer
  --image <your Docker account>/zoc-nodejs --dns-name-label aci-
  container --ports 80
```

Figure 3.2   Tool bar on the Azure Management Portal

5. After a few seconds (the first container will take longer because of the extra time needed to download the image), you should be able to query the container's IP address and DNS name using:

```
az container show --resource-group aciGroup --name acicontainer
```

For example, in my environment, the preceding command returns the following:

```
. . .
"ipAddress": {
  "additionalProperties": {},
  "dnsNameLabel": "aci-container",
  "fqdn": "aci-container.eastus.azurecontainer.io",
  "ip": "40.71.7.6",
  "ports": [
  {
    "additionalProperties": {},
    "port": 80,
    "protocol": "TCP"
  }]
}
. . .
```

6. Open a browser and navigate to the FQDN or IP address: http://aci-container.eastus. azurecontainer.io/. You should see the "Hello, World" message.

Part III: Deploy a Container on ECS

1. Log on to AWS Console (https://aws.amazon.com/).
2. AWS Console is designed to work with a specific region. Once you log in, you'll be redirected to a region-specific site, such as *us-west-2.console.aws.amazon.com*. At the time of writing, Fargate is only available in specific regions. Navigate to the following address for the us-east-1 region.
   https://console.aws.amazon.com/ecs/home?region=us-east-1#/firstRun
3. On the **Container and Task** screen, click on the Configure button on the **Container configuration, custom** tile. Then on the **Edit container** screen, enter a name for your container, and enter <your Docker account>/zoc-nodejs as the image. Set memory limit to a hard limit of 600 MB, define a port mapping to port 80, and finally, click on the **Update** button to create the container definition as shown in Figure 3.3.
4. Then back on the Container and Task screen, click on the **Next** button to continue.
5. On the **Define your service** screen, click on the **Next** button to continue.
6. On the **Configure your cluster** screen, click on the **Next** button to continue.
7. Finally, on the **Review** screen, click the **Create** button to create the cluster.
8. The creation process will take several minutes. Once the process completes, you'll get a new cluster, which runs a service, which runs a task, which runs a container. Figure 3.4 shows

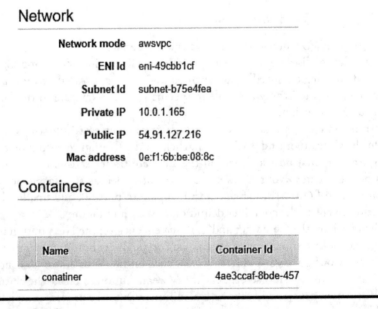

Edit container ✕

▼ Standard

Container name*	acicontainer ⓘ
Image*	hbai/zoc-nodejs ⓘ

Custom image format: [registry-url]/[namespace]/[image]:[tag]

Memory Limits (MiB)   Hard limit ▼   600   ⓘ

➕ Add Soft limit

Define hard and/or soft memory limits in MiB for your container. Hard and soft limits correspond to the 'memory' and 'memoryReservation' parameters, respectively, in task definitions.
ECS recommends 300-500 MiB as a starting point for web applications.

Port mappings   *Container port*   *Protocol*   ⓘ

80   tcp ▼   ✖

* Required   Cancel   **Update**

Figure 3.3   Edit container screen on AWS

Network

Network mode	awsvpc
ENI Id	eni-49cbb1cf
Subnet Id	subnet-b75e4fea
Private IP	10.0.1.165
Public IP	54.91.127.216
Mac address	0e:f1:6b:be:08:8c

Containers

Name	Container Id
▶ conatiner	4ae3ccaf-8bde-457

Figure 3.4   Network task info

the networking information of the provisioned task. I found it was hard to describe how you can reach this screen exactly. You can start with https://console.aws.amazon.com/ecs/home?region=<your region>, and then click on the **Clusters** link to the left to start looking for the screen. It's not difficult.

9. Open a browser and navigate to http://<public IP of the task>/. You should see your website working and returning the "Hello, World" message.

Container Orchestration

While accessing a container through a public IP is fun, you can do much more with multiple containers. For example, you can join multiple containers behind a load balancer to improve availability and scalability. You can also assemble multiple containers into a complete application for more complex scenarios. Running more than one container, however, presents some new challenges. How do the containers talk to each other? How do you treat multiple containers as a complete application? How do you ensure all containers are running as expected? This is where container orchestration comes in.

To put it simply, a container orchestrator does two things: *workload scheduling* and *state reconciliation*. When you give your application to a container orchestrator, it loads the application onto selected containers, and it makes sure the containers keep running the way you want them to. There are a few container orchestrators in the market, including Google's Kubernetes (often abbreviated as K8s), Docker's Docker Swarm, Apache Mesos, and Microsoft's Service Fabric. At the time of writing, K8s is taking the leading position in the market. And many other platforms are starting to support K8s metadata formats. You'll have a run with K8s later in this chapter. For now, let's continue with the platform-agnostic discussion and see what a container orchestrator does.

Workload Scheduling

Imagine you are Elon Musk and you are trying to keep all your production lines busy to create as many Teslas as possible.

Let's say, as Mr. Musk, you get a daily report from all five of your factories every morning on how many cars they've made in the previous day. And you can assign more manufacturing tasks to these factories. It shouldn't be hard to schedule the work for the factories—you simply tell the factories to make as many cars as they did yesterday. Now, assume all factories are running at 80% capacity and one of the factories unfortunately caught fire. To maintain production volume, you take the workload originally assigned to the burning factory and distribute it to the remaining four. Now the four factories are stressed, and workers start to complain. To fix this, you build another factory and redistribute the workload.

As everything is going smoothly, you take on your next challenge—to build an Iron Man suit. This is a big job, so you pick a factory, relocate its workload to others so that it will have enough capacity to focus on the grand task...and your legend continues.

Originally, I was going to ask you to imagine yourself as a supermarket manager that manages checkout lines. However, I think managing electric car factories is more fun. If you don't know who Elon Musk is, look him up in Wikipedia. He's the person closest to a real life Iron Man in the present time.

Workload scheduling on a cluster of hosts works in the same way—the scheduler matches *demands* with *capacities*. Of course, there are smarter ways to arrange workloads and there are less efficient ways, especially when workload size varies. Such resource allocation problems have been extensively studied. Many variations of the problem are NP-hard, while some are NP-complete. Dynamic programming and greedy algorithm are among the commonly used solutions for providing satisfactory approximations.

Workload scheduling is subject to constraints in multiple dimensions, including memory, CPU, disk, and many other aspects. There can also be logical constraints (usually called placement constraints) imposed by the user. For example, a user may want to keep two containers always on the same host because these two containers exchange data frequently. Keeping them on the host avoids excessive network communications. A container orchestration needs to consider all these constraints when making scheduling decisions.

> In your computer science courses, you probably learned workload-scheduling algorithms. And you might also recall that scheduling tasks with dependencies (usually expressed in a weighted directed acyclic graph—DAG) is an NP-complete problem. This is NOT we are discussing here. In container orchestration, containers are independent units. Although they may collaborate on tasks with sequential dependencies, all containers execute in parallel.

State Reconciliation

Once a workload is scheduled, it needs monitoring to ensure it behaves as expected. Whenever it deviates from the plan, the orchestration engine needs to take corrective actions to bring it back on track. In other words, each workload has a *desired state*. An orchestration engine monitors the workload's *current state* and reconciles it with the desired state whenever it finds any deviations.

State reconciliation forms the foundation of QoS offerings of an orchestration engine, especially for availability and scalability. For example, to scale out an application, you can simply adjust the desired state to be a larger number of running containers, and the orchestration engine will spin up additional containers to match the new desired state, scaling out the application. Similarly, when a container crashes, the orchestration engine will launch a new one to replace the failed one, so that it keeps the number of running containers at a specified level, ensuring application availability.

State reconciliation is also used to balance resource usages across hosts. For example, you can specify the desired state to be "no host should have over 80% CPU utilization." When an orchestrator finds out that this indeed is the case on a host, it will start to relocate workloads to other hosts so that the CPU consumption on the host is brought down to the desired level.

State reconciliation raises an interesting challenge to your application, though. When you deploy your application to an orchestrated cluster, your application may get moved as the orchestrator optimizes resource consumptions or performs failover actions. If your application has dependencies on resources outside the container—such as a mounted data volume from the host—moving the application becomes problematic. For this reason, most orchestration engines assume applications are stateless, which means they can be moved freely and any time.

I have to clarify that the state reconciliation here is different than the state reconciliation I discussed in the context of DSC in Chapter 1. As a matter of fact, the state reconciliation in container orchestration uses a radically different approach than what's used in DSC. In DSC, desired hardware and software configuration is precisely captured in a state description file, down to individual folders, files, environment variables, and registry settings (for Windows). A DSC agent keeps checking the monitored environment, and whenever it finds a deviation, it applies some actions to bring the actual configuration to the desired configuration. This is a very fine-grained process. And sometime, desired states from different components are simply unreconcilable—for instance, both instances want to have exclusive access to the same /mnt/data folder.

State reconciliation in container orchestration, on the other hand, works at a higher level. An orchestration engine concerns containers, not what's inside the containers. This provides a great encapsulation that shields the orchestration engine from the nitty details of configuration management. When an orchestration finds a container isn't at the desired state, it simply starts a brand new one. An orchestration engine can do this because a container image is immutable. Once a container image is crafted, it never changes. This assures the orchestration engine that whenever it launches a new instance of the container, the new instance will be configured precisely as the last one or any one before it. This assured consistency is significant (see the consistent software deployments section in Chapter 1), and it has inspired an entire methodology called immutable infrastructure. As the name suggests, an immutable infrastructure is immutable. Once it's configured, it never changes. Immutable infrastructure makes many DevOps tasks straightforward and predictable. I encourage you to spend time researching and understanding immutable infrastructure outside of this book.

Tutorial: A Lap around Kubernetes

In this tutorial, you'll configure a Kubernetes cluster and deploy Nginx to it. This tutorial uses the Google Kubernetes Engine (https://cloud.google.com/kubernetes-engine/docs/). To play with Kubernetes, you need two things: a Kubernetes cluster and Kubernetes's command-line tool, *kubectl*. There are many ways to set these up. Please refer to Kubernetes documents (https://kubernetes.io/docs/setup/pick-right-solution/) to choose your deployment options. If you are not using the Google Kubernetes Engine, please jump to step 7 once you have your cluster (for local tests, consider *Minikube*—https://kubernetes.io/docs/getting-started-guides/minikube/) and *kubectl* configured.

1. Sign in to Google Kubernetes Engine console (https://console.cloud.google.com/kubernetes), assuming you've acquired a Google Cloud account.
2. Click on the **Create Cluster** link at the top of the console.
3. On the Create a **Kubernetes cluster** screen, enter a name for your cluster. You can accept all other default settings, and simply click on the **Create** button to create a three-node cluster.
4. Once the cluster is provisioned, click on the **Connect** button in the Kubernetes clusters list.
5. On the **Connect to the cluster** dialog box, click on the **Run in Cloud Shell** button to launch Cloud Shell (like Azure's Cloud Shell), as shown in Figure 3.5.
6. Once the Cloud Shell is launched, press enter to execute the auto-entered *gcloud* command. If the command is not automatically entered, copy it from the above dialog box and execute it. This command generates configurations necessary for *kubectl* to talk to the specific cluster.
7. Now you are ready to test out some *kubectl* commands! First, list all the nodes on the cluster using the command:

```
kubectl get nodes
```

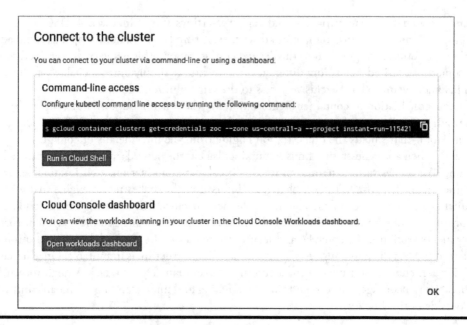

Figure 3.5   Launching Cloud Shell of Google Kubernetes Engine

Figure 3.6 shows how Cloud Shell looks when I used the preceding command to list nodes on my test cluster. You can see that my cluster consists of three nodes on which I can deploy my applications.

8. You can deploy an application to Kubernetes by creating a Kubernetes Deployment, which is described by a YAML file. Create a new *deployment.yaml* file in your Cloud Shell using *vi* with the following content:

```
apiVersion: apps/v1beta2
kind: Deployment
```

Figure 3.6   Cloud Shell on Google Kubernetes Engine

```
metadata:
  name: my-nginx
spec:
  selector:
    matchLabels:
      app: nginx
  replicas: 2
  template:
    metadata:
      labels:
        app: nginx
    spec:
      containers:
      - name: nginx
        image: nginx:latest
        ports:
        - containerPort: 80
```

The preceding YAML file defines a deployment of two Nginx containers (using the nginx:latest image) instances.

9. Create the deployment using kubectl:

```
kubectl apply -f ./deployment.yaml
```

10. Kubernetes deploys containers in *pods*. A pod is a group of containers that share the same storage and network context. Containers in the same pod share the same IP. They can find each other by *localhost*, and they have access to shared volumes. The preceding deployment creates two containers, each running in its own pod placed on a separate node. The following command lists all the pods you have on your cluster:

```
kubectl get pods
```

The above command returns the following result in my environment:

```
NAME                        READY   STATUS    RESTARTS   AGE
my-nginx-5b4b59b4b8-frnb6   1/1     Running   0          40m
my-nginx-5b4b59b4b8-pvmmb   1/1     Running   0          40m
```

11. Now the containers are running. And if you attach to one of the nodes, you can access the Nginx server running on the node through *localhost*. However, that's less useful. To expose the Nginx servers to the public, you need to expose the two running pods as a *service*. A service is a group of pods. It takes traffic to its endpoint and distributes the traffic to attached pods. Because we want to expose the Nginx servers to the Internet, we'll specify that the

service will have an endpoint with a public IP through Google Cloud load balancer by using the *--type=LoadBalancer* switch:

```
kubctl expose deployment my-nginx --type=LoadBalancer
  --name=nginx-service
```

12. Exposing the service with a public IP takes a little longer. You can use the following command to check the status of your services and get the public IP associated with the Nginx service:

```
kubectl get services
```

The above command returns the following result in my test environment. You'll see the EXTERNAL-IP column as *<pending>* while the public IP is being provisioned.

```
NAME           TYPE          CLUSTER-IP     EXTERNAL-IP   PORT(S)       AGE
kubernetes     ClusterIP     10.47.240.1    <none>        443/TCP       1
mnginx-service LoadBalancer  10.47.242.113  35.202.71.21  80:30500/TCP  24m
```

13. Once the public IP appears, you can open a browser and navigate to http://<public IP>/ to access your Nginx service, which is backed by two load-balanced Nginx servers running on two pods on your Kubernetes cluster.

(i) Instead of deploying resources using separate deployment files, you can use a Helm Chart (https://helm.sh/) to deploy related services as a complete application.

Microservices

Until today, I still vividly remember one winter evening in 1993 when I was trying to sell 5-inch floppy disks to my classmates as a freshman in my colleague dormitory. One of my classmates, Wang (hey I'm not making this up—Wang happens to be the most popular last name in China, with over 95 million people), rushed in and said enthusiastically, "Come with me, I'll show you a new way to write programs. It will blow your mind!" He dragged me to the computer lab and showed me Object Oriented Programming (OOP) in Turbo C. That night changed my life. OOP made such perfect sense that I started to view everything—I mean everything—differently and found out how the entire world could be nicely abstracted as OOP. If you could imagine how Neo in the movie Matrix would have felt when he started to see digits behind the artificial world, you can imagine how I felt that night. At the time, the Internet was not a huge thing in China yet, and computer science in public was still young. So, I got to know about OOP decades after it was invented. Still, I'm glad I did, and that turned a new page in my life.

The beauty of OOP resides in encapsulation. (I know, I know. There are other aspects. I just think encapsulation is the most important one.) With encapsulation, internal details of an entity can be hidden from the outside world. And this has empowered us to interact with many sophisticated machines to accomplish complex tasks—you don't need to know how a car works to drive a car; you don't need to understand how a computer works to play a video game; you don't have to master operating a movie theater to watch a movie. The internal details of these entities are hidden from you, and you simply use exposed interfaces and properties to interact with these entities.

Microservices Architecture

Architecturally, microservices is all about achieving a correct level of encapsulation. The text definition of microservices architecture is easy—an application made up of individual "micro" services. A service, under the microservices architecture, is an independent unit that provides a complete functionality. Some people have been saying "Microservices is just OOP on cloud." That worries me because that definition misses two key aspects: *independency* and *completeness*.

Independency

A microservices service (this is a bit awkward to say, so I'll just call it a service hereafter unless necessary) is independent, which means it can operate on its own. When you launch a service, you don't need to worry about any dependencies—a service can be launched anytime and anywhere. Logically, your service may still rely on other services to deliver required functionality. However, launching and operating your service should have no external dependencies. Even if the dependent services don't exist, your service should still work and tell your users nicely, "Sorry, I can't fulfill your request now. But you can try again later (or other features that don't rely on the missing services)." The importance of independency will become more apparent when I discuss microservices operations in the next section.

Completeness

A service needs to provide a complete set of functionalities. The term "microservices" has misled some people to believe that a service needs to be small. However, in my opinion, "micro" is more about independency and mobility of services instead of size. The completeness requirement avoids over-decomposition of functionalities into "Nano services," which is an antipattern that creates unnecessarily finely granular services that are hard to operate.

For example, an online calculator could be a service, while "add" and "subtract" are actions offered by the service. On the contrary, an "add" service is too granular to be an independent service. Keep this calculator scenario in mind—I'll revisit it when I discuss Serverless in Chapter 7.

When you use microservices architecture, a key idea to keep in mind is that you *compose* services into applications, instead of *decomposing* applications into services. The difference between the two ways of thinking is subtle but important. When you think about composing services, each of the services is an independent unit that doesn't make unnecessary assumptions on its surroundings. If you think about decomposing applications, you are tempted to make application-specific assumptions in service designs, which leads to inflexibility and tight coupling.

Microservices Operation

Microservices is all about operations.

If you try to understand microservices purely from an architectural perspective, you'll become confused. Many people believe microservices is just Service-Oriented Architecture (SOA) under a new name. That's a fair statement at an architectural level. SOA focuses on how services are orchestrated into an application. On the contrary, the key focus of microservices is how services are operated, especially on cloud, to improve quality of service.

With SOA, services are black boxes offered by service providers. As long as the service providers can stay true to their service level agreements (SLA), SOA isn't concerned how the services are operated. Microservice, on the other hand, is concerned with how service providers deliver quality services. As we go through how these qualities are delivered, we can abstract some characteristics that are unique to microservices.

Availability

I've discussed availability from an architectural perspective a couple of times in previous chapters. Here, I'll focus on the operational aspect, especially how availability is achieved differently on cloud and in an on-premises datacenter.

In a traditional data center, buying a new server takes a lot of time. The procurement process needs to be planned, approved, budgeted, funded, and executed. And then, the server needs to be shipped, installed, configured, and put into operation. As the server runs, it needs to be monitored and maintained. And even when the server is to be removed, there's usually an entire process for deprovisioning the server because it's part of the fixed assets.

When a server fails, fixing it takes considerable time as well, especially when the failure is caused by hardware failures. The average time need to restore the server to a working state is called Mean Time to Repair (MTTR). And the average time between two server failures is called Mean Time to Failure (MTTF). A server is available during MTTF, and a server is offline during MTTR. Figure 3.7 shows how server availability is affected by MTTF and MTTR (the diagram also shows MTBF—Meant Time Between Failure, which won't be discussed further here). It's easy to see that to improve availability, you need to either prolong MTTF or shorten MTTR.

You may have seen the dilemma here. On one hand, you need to make MTTR as long as possible, which mean you need to purchase a more sophisticated, high-end server. These kinds of servers rarely fail, so MTTR is long. However, when they do fail, they take considerable time to be fixed. And because high-end servers tend to host more key services, their failures often have bigger impacts on overall system availability.

As I've introduced in Chapter 1, cloud uses a different approach—when a server fails, its workload is moved to a new server. This allows cloud to provide higher availability using commodity servers. Compared to on-premises high-end servers, these servers may have a shorter MTTF. But, because the fast workload migration brings MTTR to virtually nothing, the overall availability is improved.

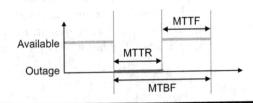

Figure 3.7   Server availability model with MTTR and MTTF

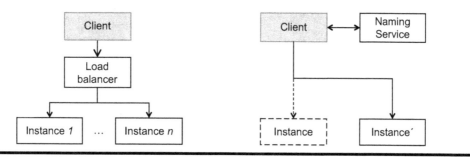

Figure 3.8   HA-configuration for a stateless service

To keep a stateless service available, multiple instances of the service are deployed, usually behind a load balancer. When one or a few of the instances fail, other instances can continue to provide continuous service. If there's only one service instance allowed, such as a legacy service that doesn't support multiple instances, an outage occurs if the service instance fails. Then a new service instance is launched and the service resumes. Figure 3.8 shows both the multi-instance configuration and single-instance configuration. In the case of a single service instance, a client needs to invoke a naming service to resolve the instance's address before it calls the service because the instance could be moved at any time.

When service instances are placed on server nodes, they are not placed randomly. Instead, they are scattered across *fault domains* and *update domains* to further improve availability.

■ Fault domain
Fault domain reflects the blast radius of an infrastructural problem. For example, a server rack in a data center can be considered a fault domain because if any of the infrastructural components, such as power, cooling, or networking fails, all the servers on the rack are unusable. If you placed all your service instances on the same rack, a rack-level failure will take out your application. So, when you deploy your service, you want your service instances to be scattered across multiple fault domains to reduce the risk of service outage.

■ Update domain
On top of the hardware infrastructure, your service code is supported by a stack of software, from host OS to hypervisor to guest OS. Any of these software components may need updates to address defects and newly discovered vulnerabilities. When cloud performs such maintenance, it uses update domains to segment servers into logical groups and updates servers group by group. If your service instances are scattered across multiple update domains, you are assured that at any given moment, not all the update domains will be taken down.

For a stateful service, write operations usually go through its primary copy (because coordinating multiple writers is expensive, and induced conflicts usually negates the benefits); read operations can be served from either the primary or the secondaries. State is replicated from the primary to the secondary. When the primary fails, one of the secondaries is promoted to the new primary. And a new secondary is brought online to keep the replica count at desired level. Figure 3.9 shows the process of a secondary being promoted to the primary, and a new secondary being launched to maintain the number of replicas.

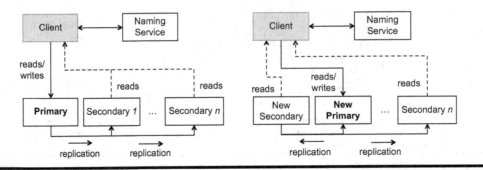

Figure 3.9 Stateful service failover

Why Do We Want to Bring Up Additional Secondaries?

Intuitively, when you have less secondaries, you are at a higher risk of losing data. So it makes sense to bring a new secondary online so that you have enough copies of data. In a distributed environment, especially in an environment where any of the replicas and the networks between them may fail, enough replicas are required to maintain a reliable state. For example, a primary replicates data to two secondaries and one of the replication fails. In this case, two secondaries are holding different data. When the primary fails, promoting either secondary will lead to different results.

To solve such problems, consensus protocols such as various Paxos protocols (see http://lamport. azurewebsites.net/pubs/pubs.html) are designed to allow enough members on the cluster to reach a consensus on an update before a change is accepted. For such protocols to work, a certain number of "votes" needs to be acquired, hence you need to keep the number of replicas above a certain level.

The cloud availability scheme imposes the following requirements on microservices:

- A service needs to be independent so that cloud can rearrange service instances without resolving complex interdependencies among service instances.
- A service needs to be contained so that it can be moved or recreated on an arbitrary host. And all service dependencies and configurations need to be automatically restored without human interventions.
- A service is either stateless or stateful with its state replicated for high availability.
- When multiple instances of the same service run, they should not interfere with one another. As a matter of fact, they should not be aware of each other, as their behaviors should not change regardless of how many other instances are running.
- When a new stateful instance is launched with a given state, it should be able to restore to a self-consistent running state. Please note state reconciliation across instances is the platform's concern, not a requirement on the service itself.

Scalability

I've compared differences between vertical scaling and horizontal scaling in Chapter 1. In a cloud environment, scaling up is rather difficult, because once a virtual machine is provisioned, it's bound to the selected resource profile. You can add additional capacities to an existing machine (other than attaching more data disks) to make the machine more powerful. Instead, you must provision a newer, more powerful virtual machine and migrate your workload to the new machine. Depending on how complex it is to move your workload, you may incur significant outages as the migration occurs.

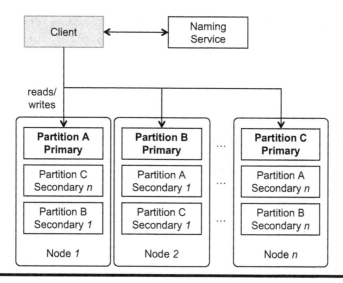

Figure 3.10   Scaling out a stateful service

Scaling out allows system capacity to be dynamically expanded by adding additional service instances. Scaling out stateless services is relatively easy—simply add more instances behind a load balancer and the workload will be distributed among all available instances. Scaling out stateful services, however, needs additional work. As you've seen in the previous section, to keep availability, the state of a stateful service is replicated to multiple secondaries. When you add more servers to handle an increasing workload, both the size of the state and the number of replicas increase, making replication an increasingly expensive task. Furthermore, because all writes still go through the primary regardless of number of secondaries, having more machines doesn't increase the system throughout.

Partitioning (or sharding) is an effective way for both limiting the size of replication and increasing system throughput. First, partitioning segments of a large system state into smaller chunks. Multiple replications can happen in parallel within the respective partition scopes. Second, because each of the partitions has its own primary replica, the system can take write requests from multiple nodes. Figure 3.10 shows how arranging primary replicas of different service partitions can allow a system to take on more read/write requests across multiple nodes.

Partitions can be either static or dynamic. Static partitioning requires service operators to carefully plan for system capacity before services are deployed, because once a service is deployed with a fixed set of partition, it can't be rescaled to use more or less partitions. Dynamic partitioning allows a service to be dynamically repartitioned as the workload changes. Obviously, dynamic partitioning is much preferable. However, dynamic partitioning is harder to implement and may have performance implications. When a partition changes, data in different replica sets need to be shuffled to maintain separate replicas. Figure 3.11 shows that initially data is sharded into four

1-25	26-50	51-75	76-100

1-20	21-40	41-60	61-80	81-100

Figure 3.11   Repartitioning data

partitions based on data keys ranging from 1 to 100. When the same set of data is repartitioned to five partitions, compositions of all partitions are affected, hence the entire data set need to be rearranged. *Consistent hashing* allows only a subset of the keys needs to be remapped, hence to drastically reduce data movements.

Scalability operations have the following microservices requirements:

- A service instance can be created at any time in a consistent manner.
- A service partition is isolated from other partitions. In other words, there shouldn't be any interdependencies among partitions.
- A naming service is required to help clients resolve to partitions. I'll discuss naming service in more details in the Service Mesh section.

Resource Balancing

Because it makes money by selling compute resources, a cloud platform is very motivated to pack as many compute tasks into the same physical compute resource as possible because that drives up the profitability. However, at the same time, the platform has to ensure it satisfies latency, throughput, and other SLA requirements. Hence, it's unsurprising to see a cloud platform exploiting the fact that microservices are self contained and movable to achieve optimized resource consumption.

Service resource consumption can be measured passively, such as by checking performance counters. Resource consumption can also be proactively reported by applications. Many microservices hosting platforms define structured health reports that services can use to report telemetries to the hosting platforms. For example, a service can report its job queue length that reflects its stress level. The platform can then use the data to adjust the queue length to be reduced. The decision process can be straightforward, such as checking reported telemetries against predefined thresholds. The process can also be very sophisticated, such as using machine learning models to figure out optimal solutions across multiple telemetry vectors.

Regardless of how decisions are made, service instances may get moved even when no failover operations or scaling operations take place. This requires services to be able to:

- Be moved at any time. The hosting platform usually provides notifications before the movement to allow the service instance to complete in-flight transactions before being moved.
- Be consistently addressable before and after movements. Service routing will be discussed further in the Service Mesh section below.
- Faithfully report telemetries to the hosting platform so that the hosting platform can make informed decisions to balance resource consumption.

Updates

Reducing service interruptions during service updates is important for maintaining continuous service. There are several commonly used techniques:

- Multiple deployment slots
  This technique uses multiple deployment slots. The current version of the service occupies the *production* slot. The updated version of the service is placed on a *test* slot. The updated version goes through a series of tests before it's promoted into the production slot. Such promotion can be implemented through a virtual IP (VIP) switch to minimize outage. A VIP

switch swaps the addresses of the slots so that the test slot becomes the new production slot while the production slot becoming the new test slot. The downside of using multiple deployment slots is that you need extra capacity to support both slots.

■ Rolling updates

Rolling updates (or rolling upgrades) gradually replace running service instances with the new version. During an update, service instances are taken down by update domains and replaced with the updated version. At a given time, only one update domain is updated, leaving all instances in other domains running to serve requests. This process is called an *update domain walk*. Because there are always service instances running during the update process, update domain walk offers *zero downtime updates*. If any errors occur during the update domain walk, the service instances are rolled back to the original version. In this case, the update fails but the service remains available running the original version. The downside of rolling update is that because multiple versions of the service run at the same time during updates, service versions need to be compatible—the new version needs to be *backward compatible* with the old version, and the old version needs to be *forward compatible* with the new version.

Updating stateful services require more work. If multiple deployment slots are used, service states need to be copied from the older version to the updated version. Because the older version keeps taking new requests until the VIP swap happens, it's hard to take a logically consistent snapshot across multiple service instances. This is very problematic. Figure 3.12 illustrates two stateful services being updated, and their states are copied from the production slot to the test slot before VIP occurs. Because services are independent from each other, state replications of different services may happen at a slightly different time, which may lead to inconsistency. For example, after the state of a service has been copied to the new deployment slot, and right before the VIP swap happens, a new request is processed by the service. Updates generated by this request are never copied to the new slot. Such requests are called *in-flight requests* (or in-flight transactions), which are discarded during the update process.

When a rolling update is used, service instances are updated in place, which allows the new service instance to "rehydrate" its state from the older state residing on the local disk. Figure 3.13 shows that when stateful service A is updated to a new version A, the new instance reads the previously saved state on disk and establishes its own state. Because there are no in-flight transactions in this case (assuming the service instance is allowed to process all pending requests before being shut down), a service can maintain a self-coherent state before and after the update.

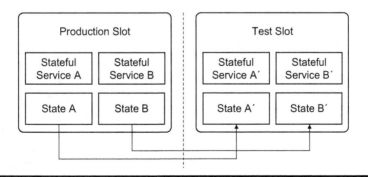

Figure 3.12   Copying state during update using multiple deployment slots

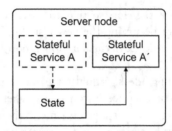

Figure 3.13 Rehydrating state from an older version

So for stateful services, a rolling update is likely a better choice than using multiple deployment slots, assuming:

■ The service is explicitly versioned.
■ The service maintains compatibility across versions.

Backup and Restore

After you deploy your service instances across update domains and fault domains, a complete service outage because of hardware failures is rare but may still happen because of large scale outages at cloud data centers. For a mission-critical system, you certainly want to set up a disaster recovery (DR) strategy that will get you back to business after a disaster strikes. When a DR solution is in place, service states are periodically replicated to a secondary site in a different region or in a different availability zone. The frequency of state replication is driven by your recovery point objective (RPO) and recovery time objective (RTO). RPO describes the maximum tolerable period during which the data might be lost. For example, if your RPO is 20 hours, then you are meeting your RPO as long as you can get a good copy of data from less than 20 hours ago. RTO describes the maximum time allowed for a service to go back into operation after a disaster occurs.

Similar to the problem with multiple deployment slots, taking a consistent snapshot across multiple services is hard. There are two levels of consistencies—*crash consistency* and *application consistency*. Crash consistency ensures a consistent state within a service; application consistency ensures states across multiple services are logically consistent. Because services are independent of each other, taking a globally consistent snapshot needs some sort of extra coordination. One way to implement this is to design a coordinated DR API (CoDR API), which is required to be implemented by all participating services. The API defines two methods: *StartSnapshot* and *EndSnapshot*. When a DR coordinator tries to take a system wide snapshot, it calls the *StartSnapshot* method on all services to inform them that a snapshot is going to be taken. Once the method call is received, a service suspends any operations that may mutate its own state, makes a snapshot of its state, and waits for the *EndSnapshot* call. During this period, all write requests are queued to avoid state updates. Once the *Endsnapshot* is received, the queued requests are released and carried

State replications across regions are sometimes done through *log shipping*. In such a system, all transactions are logged and applied to an append-only storage. The same logs are transferred and applied to the remote storage as a backup. System state is acquired by starting from a known state and playing back all logs since. To reduce the size of playbacks, periodical snapshots are taken to fold logs into new starting states.

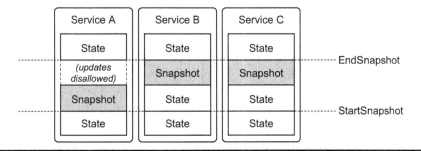

Figure 3.14 Taking an application consistent snapshot for coordinated DR

out. Figure 3.14 illustrates the process of taking an application consistent snapshot for CoDR. You should note that during the time window, all system updates are temporarily suspended, which leads to service quality degradation.

To support backup and DR, a microservice needs to be able to:

- Restore its state from provided data.
- Allow all write transactions to be captured, shipped, and applied on a different site.
- Supports a CoDR API if a coordinated disaster recovery in required.

So far, we've collected quite a few requirements of microservices. And all these requirements are rooted in how these services are operated on a cloud environment. These requirements drive desired behaviors, which in turn shape how architectures are designed.

Hands-On Lab: Operating a Microservices Application Using Azure Service Fabric

 In this lab, you'll create a simple microservices application using Microsoft Azure Service Fabric. You'll then deploy it to a local, multi-node cluster and experiment with a failover scenario.

Part I: Preparing a Service Fabric Development Environment

Service Fabric is a distributed system platform for creating and operating microservices applications. Microsoft provides a free Service Fabric SDK that you can install on your development machines to develop microservice applications. Service Fabric runtime can be installed on a group of servers to form a Service Fabric cluster that hosts Service Fabric applications. Microsoft Azure also provides cloud-based Service Fabric clusters that you can provision through Azure portal or CLI. And finally, Microsoft Azure offers a managed Service Fabric environment named Service Fabric Mesh, to which you can directly deploy your applications without managing any clusters.

1. To install the Service Fabric SDK on a Windows 8 or Windows 10 machine, search for "Service Fabric" in Microsoft Web Platform Installer (or WebPI, see https://www.microsoft.com/web/downloads/platform.aspx) and install the latest *Microsoft Azure Service Fabric SDK* if you use Visual Studio 2017. If you use Visual Studio 2015, install the latest version of *Microsoft Azure Service Fabric SDK and Tools (VS2015)*. Follow the installation wizard to complete the installation.
2. The SDK installs a *Service Fabric Local Cluster Manager*, which allows you to create a single-node or multi-node Service Fabric cluster on your local machine for testing purposes. In this

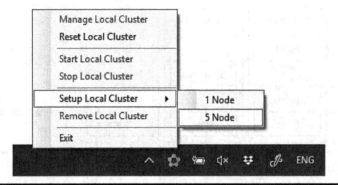

Figure 3.15 Setting up a local cluster using cluster manager

lab, you need a multi-node cluster. To create the cluster, right click on the cluster manager icon in your task bar and select the **Setup Local Cluster, 5 Node** menu, as shown in Figure 3.15. If you don't see the icon on your task bar, you can launch the cluster manager by searching for "Service Fabric Local Cluster Manager" on Windows and launch the found application. After a few minutes, you'll have a five node Service Fabric cluster running on your local machine.

Part II: Create a Service Fabric Application

1. Launch Visual Studio 2015 or Visual Studio 2017 as administrator (right click the Visual Studio application icon and select **Run as Administrator**).
2. Create a new project using the **C#, Cloud, Service Fabric Application** template. Name the application *SFApplication*.
3. On the **New Service Fabric Service** dialog box, select the **Stateless ASP.NET Core** template, name the service *StatelessWeb*, and then click the **OK** button, as shown in Figure 3.16.

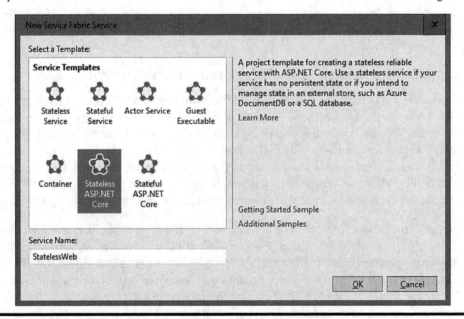

Figure 3.16 Adding a new service to a Service Fabric application

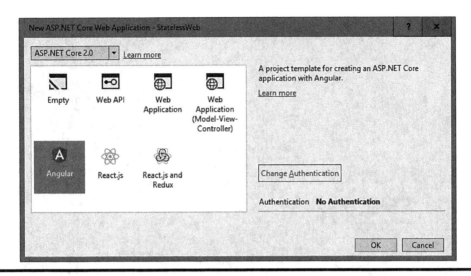

Figure 3.17   Scaffolding an ASP.NET application with Angular

This adds a new ASP.NET Core website as a stateless service to the application. A Service Fabric application comprises stateless services, stateful services, and arbitrary executables as *guest executables* as well as Docker containers. Later in this lab, you'll add a stateful service into the same application.

4. On the New ASP.NET Core Web Application dialog, select the Angular template, and then click the OK button to scaffold an ASP.NET Core application with Angular, as shown in Figure 3.17.

5. Examine the solution in **Solution Explorer**. The solution contains two projects: a *SFApplication* Service Fabric application and a *StatelessWeb* Service Fabric service. Expand the **Services** node under the *SFApplication* project, and you'll see the reference to the *StatelessWeb* service.

6. At the time of this writing, I need to comment out the following lines from the **Configure** method of the **Startup.cs** file under the **StatelessWeb** project to avoid a webpack exception on my environment. Internet research suggests that this could be related to my Node.js version. I'm not a big fan of this ASP.NET Core project template. It requires Node.js and it downloads tons of npm packages for a remarkably simple website. So I didn't bother to try to find a proper fix. I'll leave offering to find a proper fix for you if you were interested.

```
//app.UseWebpackDevMiddleware(new WebpackDevMiddlewareOptions
//{
//   HotModuleReplacement = true
//});
```

7. Press **F5** and wait. After a few minutes, a browser instance launches and a simple Hello, World website is displayed.

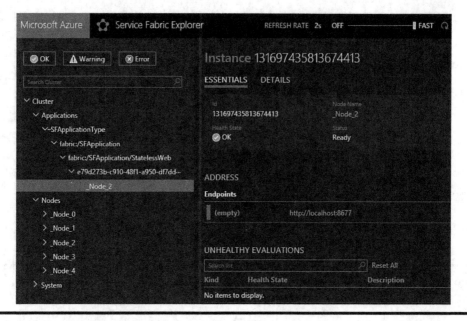

Figure 3.18 Service Fabric Explorer

A lot happened behind the scene. First, the *StatelessWeb* project is built into a service package. Then the service package was packaged into a Service Fabric application package. The application package is then uploaded to an image store of your local Service Fabric cluster. Once that's done, the application type defined by the package is registered and a new application instance is created. A single instance of the *StatelessWeb* service is deployed on one of the five Service Fabric nodes. Then Visual Studio attaches a debugger to every launched service instance process, opens your default browser, and navigates to the endpoint defined by the *StatelessWeb* service.

You can use Service Fabric Explorer, which is a web-based UI installed by the SDK, to manage your Service Fabric cluster. To launch the explorer, navigate to http://localhost:19080/ using a browser.

Figure 3.18 shows the Service Fabric Explorer view in my environment. In the tree view to the left, you can see I have a single *SFApplicaitonType* application type, and a *fabric:/SFApplication* application instance based on the type. The application contains a *fabric:/SFApplication/StatelessWeb* service, which has a single partition (identified by a GUID). The partition has a single instance, which is deployed on a node named *_Node_2*.

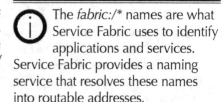

The *fabric:/** names are what Service Fabric uses to identify applications and services. Service Fabric provides a naming service that resolves these names into routable addresses.

Part III: Add a Stateful Service

1. Stop the application. This stops your Service Fabric application, removes the application instance, and unregisters the application type from the cluster.
2. Right click the **Services** node under the **SFApplication** project and select the **Add, New Service Fabric Service** menu.
3. On the **New Service Fabric Service** dialog box, select the **Stateful Service** template, name the service **StatfuleCounter**, and then click the **OK** button to add a new stateful service to your Service Fabric application.

4. Press **F5** again to build, package, and deploy the new application package.
5. Once all services instances are launched, you'll start seeing "Current Counter Value" messages generated by the new stateful service in the **Diagnostic Events** view. If you don't see this view, you can bring it up by using the **View, Other Windows, Diagnostic Events** menu. The stateful service maintains an integer counter and keeps incrementing it as it runs. The event messages reflect latest counter values.
6. Stop the application.
7. Open the **StatefulCounter.cs** file under the **StatefulCounter** project. Examine the **RunAsync** method—it runs in a loop and updates a data element in a reliable dictionary through an *IReliableDictionary* interface. Reliable dictionary is a data structure that is automatically replicated by Service Fabric for high availability. In this case, the service is not taking any external requests (so it's a background service). If you need to take client requests, you need to provide *ServiceReplicaListener* implementations to the *CreateServiceReplicaListeners* method.

Part IV: Service Fabric Application Operations

In this part of the lab, you'll perform a few management operations. You'll deploy the application first and then trigger a failover.

1. Right-click the **SFApplication** project and select the **Publish** menu.
2. On the **Publish Service Fabric Application** dialog (Figure 3.19), select the **Local.5Node.xml** publish profile, **Local Cluster** connection, and **Local.5Node.xml** parameter file. Then click the **Publish** button to publish the application to your local cluster.

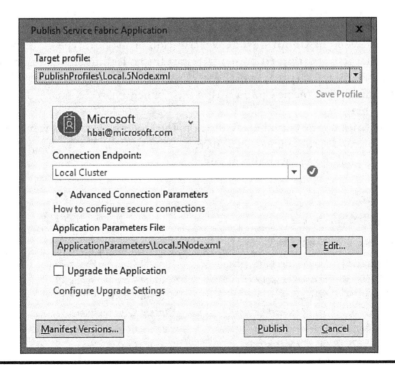

Figure 3.19 Publish Service Fabric Application dialog box

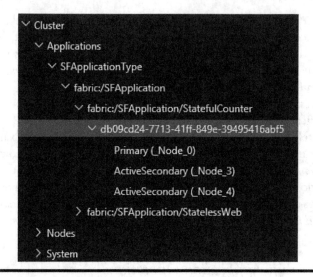

Figure 3.20 Replicas of a stateful service

3. Once the application is published, open **Service Fabric Explorer** and locate the nodes where the stateful service is running. Figure 3.20 shows that in my environment, the counter service has three replicas, with the primary replica running on *_Node_0* and two secondary replicas running on *_Node_3* and *_Node_4*.

4. Open **Diagnostic Events** view in Visual Studio. You should see the counter messages as in Figure 3.21.

5. Under **Nodes**, locate the cluster node where your primary replica is running. Click the **Actions** button to the right and select the **Deactivate (restart)** menu, as shown in Figure 3.22. On the **Confirm Node Deactivation** dialog box, type in the node name and click the **Deactivate (restart)** button to restart the node. This simulates a node crash that brings down the primary replica of the service. In this case, Service Fabric will promote one of the secondaries as the new primary, and then launch a new secondary to bring the replica count to three.

6. Once you click on the button, switch back to the **Diagnostic Events** view and observe the events. You can see the counter keeps incrementing as if nothing has happened, though the primary has failed over to a different node.

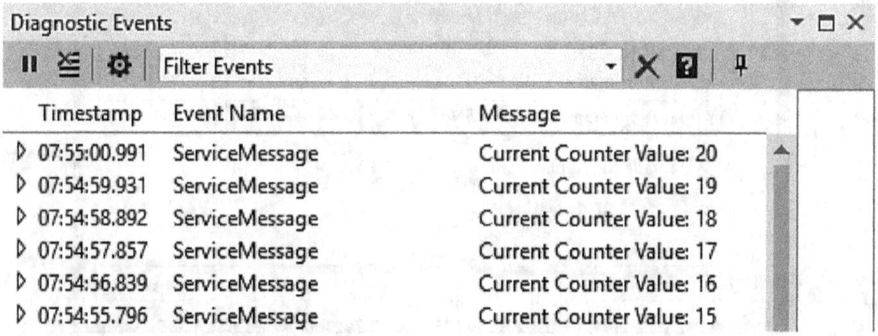

Timestamp	Event Name	Message
▷ 07:55:00.991	ServiceMessage	Current Counter Value: 20
▷ 07:54:59.931	ServiceMessage	Current Counter Value: 19
▷ 07:54:58.892	ServiceMessage	Current Counter Value: 18
▷ 07:54:57.857	ServiceMessage	Current Counter Value: 17
▷ 07:54:56.839	ServiceMessage	Current Counter Value: 16
▷ 07:54:55.796	ServiceMessage	Current Counter Value: 15

Figure 3.21 Diagnostic Events view

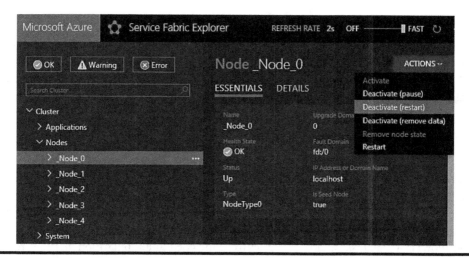

Figure 3.22   Restarting a Service Fabric cluster node

7. Back in the Service Fabric Explorer, you can observe that the primary replica is on a different node, and a new secondary has been launched.
8. Once you are complete the experiment, select the deactivated node in Service Fabric Explore and use the **Actions**, **Activate** menu to bring it back online.

 For a comprehensive Service Fabric introduction, please see my Programming Microsoft Azure Service Fabric book.

Service Mesh

As I was doing research for the book, I tried to find the origin of the following quote:

> *We can solve any problem by introducing an extra level of direction, except for the problem of too many levels of indirection.*

This statement is especially relevant when you consider how microservices communicate with each other. As you've seen in earlier examples, the dynamic nature of microservices instances brings many routing challenges such as service discovery, failover, and load

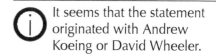

It seems that the statement originated with Andrew Koeing or David Wheeler.

balancing. For a service to communicate with another service, it must understand these routing mechanisms to resolve a destination address. For example, a service needs to understand how to work with the naming service that the hosting environment provides to discover service addresses it wants to talk to. This is even more problematic for clients—clients also need to understand how to work with the naming service before they can find the correct addresses to make service calls.

Can we shield services and clients from all the routing complexities so that networking "just works" for them? Enter service mesh. Service mesh abstracts all routing concerns away from clients and services so that they can discover and communicate with each other in a static, intuitive way such as by using DNS names or collocated proxies.

Entry Points

Let's start with a client trying to talk to a service. Ideally, all the client needs to know is the DNS name (or public IP) and the port of the service. However, when a service is scaled out, it will have multiple instances running on different servers with different (and private) IP addresses. To facilitate client communication, you'll need to create a public accessible entry point to your service.

Load Balancer and Ingress

An obvious solution for creating a service entry point is to use a cloud platform load balancer with an associated public IP address. Microservice platforms such as Kubernetes and Service Fabric don't have the ability to provide public IP addresses themselves. Instead, they rely on the hosting cloud platform to provide resources such as cloud-based load balancers and public IP addresses. To model such requirements, the Kubernetes application model provides an ingress object. Service Fabric allows load balancers and IP addresses to be included in its application model as resources. Figure 3.23 shows the typical topology of such a configuration: *Node A* and *Node B* reside in the same virtual network with private IPs. They both host instances of *Service I* and *Service II*. And they are both joined in the backend pool of a cloud-based load balancer, which is assigned a public IP. Client requests are distributed to service instances based on system configured load balancer policies. You should note that in this case, the load balancer is usually a layer-4 (transport layer) load balancer. It isn't aware of any services. It forwards traffic to the hosting nodes through given ports. Traffic to different service instances is distinguished by different port numbers.

Gateway

In the preceding example, *Service I* and *Service II* have different entry points—*<IP>:80* and *<IP>:88*, respectively. This is usually not what users want. They don't care about the individual services. Instead, they want to access the application to which these services sum up through a single entry point.

This is where you can use a layer-7 (application layer) gateway. A gateway can implement more sophisticated routing rules than a load balancer, such as routing traffic to different servers based on

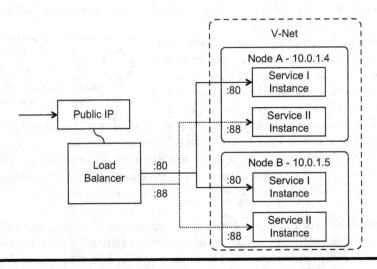

Figure 3.23   Load balancer as entry point

HTTP query string patterns. For example, instead of accessing different services through different ports, a user can access *Server I* through a */server1* path and *Server II* through a */server2* path, both through address *<IP>:80.*

A gateway can do more than route-based routing. Some other common gateway features include (but are not limited to) the following:

- SSL termination. A gateway can terminate SSL connection and send unencrypted traffic to the backend servers. This unburdens the backend servers from encryption and decryption overheads.
- Firewall and advanced protection. A gateway can implement security policies to protect your services from common vulnerabilities and malicious attacks such as code injection and cross-site scripting (XSS). Some more sophisticated gateways such as Azure Application Gateway can provide additional protections such as guarding against DDoS (Distributed Deny of Service) attacks.
- A/B testing. A/B testing compares two digital experiences and determine which one works better. It splits user traffic to different application versions based on configured distribution pattern and collects feedback on specific designs.
- Session affinity. Session affinity is useful when you want to provide a unified entry point to a service that is not designed for scaling out. With session affinity, requests from a particular client are always routed to the same service instance. This allows the service instance to maintain consistent states for attached clients.

Interservice Calls

As introduced in the microservices operation section, microservice instances are not permanently bound to certain server nodes. Instead, they might roam around because of scaling, failover, and resource balancing. Traditional address lookup by IP addresses or DNS names is no longer sufficient for a service to find other services. This section introduces several common techniques for interservice calls.

Discovery Service

One possible solution for providing dynamic service address resolution is to set up a centralized discovery service (or naming service) that any service instance can call to resolve the address of other services by service name, as shown in Figure 3.24.

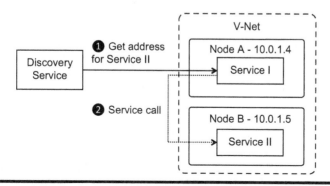

Figure 3.24   Service address resolution with a discovery service

The discovery service provides stable service addresses based on logical service names. However, there are a couple of problems to be resolved:

■ How does a service find the discover service in the first place? One solution is to inject the discover service address as a configuration entry of a service when the service is deployed. Or you can deploy a discover service on every hosting node so that any service can reach an instance of discover service through *localhost.*

■ How does the discover service know about all the service addresses? As the orchestration engine allocates service instances on cluster nodes, it can update the discover service with new instance addresses. In the case of failover, there's a delay before a failed instance is detected and relocated, so the discover service may give incorrect answers. To compensate this, your code should use retries when calling a service.

Internal load Balancer

Requiring all services to work with a specific discover service creates unnecessary coupling with the hosting platform. An internal load balancer provides a stable private IP in front of a group of load-balanced services. However, it has the same constraints as a public load balancer, which doesn't support advanced routings such as routing by partition.

Reverse Proxy

A reverse proxy is a proxy server that makes actual service calls on behalf of a client. A collocated reverse proxy hides all routing details and allows a service to invoke other services on the same cluster through *localhost.* This kind of isolation is an instance of the *sidecar* pattern. A sidecar is a peripheral service attached to a primary service. In addition to network proxying, it can provide other functionalities such as correlated logging, throttling, platform abstraction, and configuration management. Figure 3.25 shows the sidecar pattern in the context of a service proxy. The figure shows that Service I, Service II, and Service III can call each other through a *http://localhost/<service name>* URL pattern.

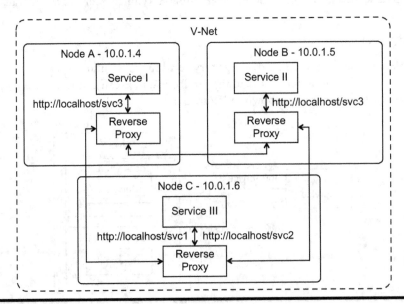

Figure 3.25 Reverse proxies as sidecars

Service Mesh Solutions

The sidecar pattern is a powerful idea. Connected sidecars form a dynamic mesh on which microservice instances can roam around freely while retaining connectivity with each other. There are several service mesh solutions in the market, with Envoy by Lyft (https://www.envoyproxy.io/) being a very popular one at the time of writing. Istio (https://istio.io/) is a solution built on top of Envoy that provides streamlined sidecar deployments and configurations of envoy proxies.

Zen of Cloud

> *"The thing is, it's very dangerous to have a fixed idea. A person with a fixed idea will always find some way of convincing himself in the end that he is right."*

Atle Selberg

During the past decades, we've been dealing with distributed computing challenges. Many successful (and some less successful) architecture patterns and frameworks have been introduced over the years, such as client/server, browser/server, 3-tier, n-tier, peer-to-peer, grid computing, DCOM, COM+, J2EE, CORBA, SOA, and now microservices. These architectures and frameworks arose not because we haven't been able to make up our mind. It's because the context of distributed computing has kept changing. The newer architectures are not necessarily superior to the older ones. They are just more suitable for the new computational contexts.

Microservices is a very nice architectural and operational pattern for cloud-based, distributed systems because it was born in the context of cloud computing. So even if you consider yourself a seasoned distributed computing expert, you should keep your eyes open to understand the context of the problem, and learn about how people are producing new solutions to address the specific situation.

Chapter 4

Security

Design a Secured System

In the movie *Interception*, the dream extractors (or inceptors) create a convoluted dream world to avoid hostile "subconscious guards" catching them before they can extract secrets from a safe location. They have to design a maze that is complex enough to confuse the guards while providing a shortcut from them to cut through the maze.

Designing a secured system is pretty much like designing a maze—you make it extremely difficult for unwanted users to access your system while ensuring legit users have easy and protected accesses. This chapter goes through common technologies for designing a secured system and introduces how they are applied in a cloud environment.

Authentication and Authorization

Authentication confirms a user is indeed who they claims to be. To authenticate with a system, a user needs to provide one or more acceptable forms of proofs. The system checks the proof and grants accesses only if the proofs check out. Authorization, on the other hand, decides what an authenticated user is allowed to do. For example, when you check in to a flight, you present your identify card or passport to the clerk to establish who you are—this is authentication. Then, you are assigned to a seat based on your ticket class. You won't be allowed to sit in the first class cabin if you hold an economy class ticket—this is authorization.

Authentication Methods

Authentication can be as easy as presenting a password. When you log on to a Windows, Linux, or Mac machine, your password verifies that you are indeed the owner of the corresponding user ID. The number one challenge of a password-based system is password management. Simple passwords are easier to be cracked, while complex passwords are harder to remember. Many modern systems support authentications with biological characteristics such as fingerprints and facial features so that users never need to remember a password.

Some systems authenticate users with *tokens* issued by a trusted authority. For example, in many cases, you can prove identity using an identification card such as a driver's license. Such authentications scheme have two fundamental assumptions: first, the entity that issues the token is trustworthy. It has gone through all the verification steps to make sure the information that the token carries is accurate. Second, it's very hard (or illegal or both) to forge a token. When both assumptions hold true, you can simply trust whatever the token says once you decide you've seen a genuine token.

Some systems require multi-factor authentication, which means a user has to present at least two forms of proof before she can be authenticated. For example, some systems require you to answer an automated call and punch in a pin code after you've entered your password on a login page. This scheme provides additional protection because to login as you, your phone must be in possession.

In summary, a user authenticates with a system by showing what she knows (such as a password), what she has (such as a phone), or what she is (such as a fingerprint).

Authenticating a service or an application is slightly different. A service can't use a fingerprint to login, but it can be preconfigured to authenticate with another service using something it knows, such as a password or a symmetric key provided by the target service. Alternatively it can use something it has, such as an X.509 certificate.

Authorization Methods

How an application decides what a user is allowed to do is up to the application. Once a user is authenticated, an application can use whatever method to decide how to grant or deny accesses to resources. However, there are a couple of common, structured ways of authorization.

One of the methods is discretionary access control (DAC) using an access control list (ACL). An ACL attaches access permissions to objects. For example, the following output shows the ACL I have assigned to a *dc* folder when I run the *getfacl* command on my Linux environment. It shows that I have full access to the folder, the admin group has read access to the folder, and others have read and execution access.

```
haishi@linux-gpu:~$ getfacl dc
# file: dc
# owner: haishi
# group: haishi
user::rwx
group::rwx
group:admin:r--
mask::rwx
other::r-x
```

Another method for authorization is to use role-based access control (RBAC). With RBAC, users are in groups assigned to one or more *roles*. A role is granted access to certain resources or types of operation.

Figure 4.1 shows how DAC and RBAC work differently. In the case of DAC, *user A* is granted read and write access to both *object 1* and *object 2*; *user B* is granted read-only access to the objects. The RBAC method achieves the same result, but through role assignments. The extra level of indirection doesn't seem much (or necessary) in this case. However, as the user number increases, RBAC displays its power in flexibility and ease of management. For example, for DAC to set up access rights for a new *user C*, it needs to assign *user C* to all affected objects. On the other hand, RBAC only needs to assign the user to an appropriate role.

A user's role can be established by looking up a profile table by the given user ID. Or, the role can be passed in as part of the authentication token in the form of a *claim*. A claim is a statement

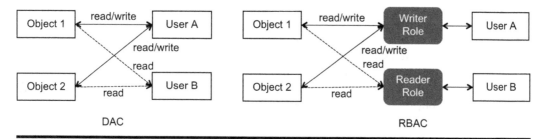

Figure 4.1   DAC vs. RBAC

an authority makes on an attribute of an entity. For example, a person's name on a US driver license is what the Department of Motor Vehicles (DMV) claims is the user's name attribute. The driver license also claims the user is authorized to perform a "driver" role, i.e., is allowed to drive any allowed type of vehicle. Imagine if this was done in the DAC way—a person would have to be explicitly assigned to a particular vehicle. In other words, when you get a new car, you'd have to get a new driving license, which would really suck.

OAuth is a widely used authorization protocol, especially in the case when a user grants an application access to her information on another application without exposing her password. For example, she can allow a web application to post tweets on her behalf without telling the application her Twitter password. Figure 4.2 shows a sample flow of OAuth 2.0 between an active client and a service provider. As you can see, the service provider delegates authentication and authorization to an external authentication service and a token service. This is a powerful idea, which I'll explain further in the next section.

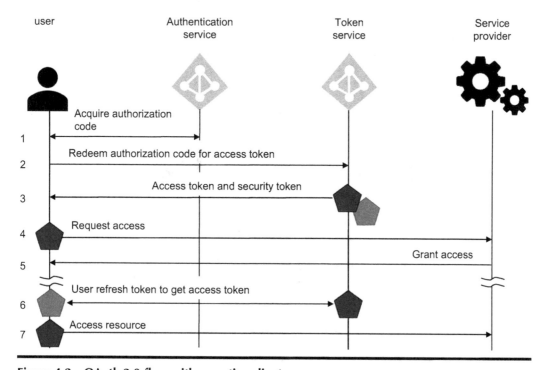

Figure 4.2   OAuth 2.0 flow with an active client

Claim-Based Architecture

The idea of authentication is simple. However, implementing an authentication mechanism is difficult. How do you ensure a secured exchange of passwords? How do you help your user to recover a forgotten password? How do you avoid a malicious user trying to guess a password? How do you enable multi-factor authentication? There are many questions like these to be answered. Instead of trying to figure out how to properly implement authentication, you can delegate the task to a trusted authority.

If you need to lock up something, you don't make a lock from scratch. Instead, you buy a quality lock from a reputable vendor. You trust the lock vendor doing all the right things to make sure the lock is secure. Similarly, if you can trust an online authority, you can delegate all authentication tasks to it. The authority authenticates users and sends user information to your application through claims—this is the gist of claim-based architecture.

In a claim-based architecture, the online authority that performs authentication is called an Identity Provider (IdP). The service that delegates authentication to others is called a Relying Party (RP) or a Service Provider (SP). The IdP authenticates a user using one or more methods such as password and certificates, and generates a *security token*, which contains *claims* on the user's attributes. Consider the scenario when you check in to a flight: Before you go to the airport, you need to first acquire a security token (your passport), which is issued by an IdP (your country) trusted by the RP (the airline). The airline verifies your token, extracts necessary claims (your name), and assigns a role (first class passenger) to you.

Now, with the risk of this sounding like a long-winded sales plug, Microsoft Azure Active Directory (Azure AD) is an IdP that you can trust. It handles billion of authentications daily for Azure, Office 365, and millions of organizations and applications around the globe. Figure 4.3 shows the typical workflow of a web service delegating authentication to Azure AD:

1. A user requests access to a service
2. The service is configured to trust Azure AD as its IdP. It redirects the user to Azure AD for authentication.

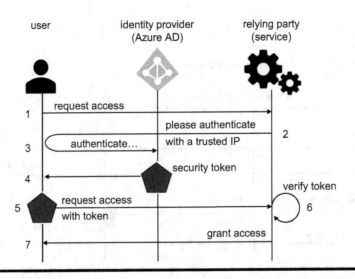

Figure 4.3   Authentication with Azure AD

3. User finishes authentication process with Azure AD.
4. Azure AD returns a security token containing claims requested by the service.
5. User attaches the security token to her next request to the service.
6. The service verifies the token to ensure integrity, authenticity, and confidentiality.
7. Once everything checks out, the service grants access to the user.

Circle of Trust

The trust relationship between a RP and an IdP must be mutual—the RP needs to explicitly trust IdP, and the IdP needs to explicitly trust RP. An RP can trust multiple IdPs. For example, a website can allow logins from both Google Account and Microsoft Account. This design lowers the adoption barrier because the user doesn't need to apply for a new account before she can access the service. On the other hand, an IdP can trust multiple RPs. This design allows a Single Sign-On (SSO) experience across multiple applications. For example, you can use your Microsoft Account to log in to Azure, Xbox Live, and Office 365.

When you are in the same browser session, because you hold a valid security token issued by the trusted IdP (which is Microsoft Account in this case), you can switch back and forth between these applications without needing to reauthenticate, because they are in the same circle of trust.

Tutorial: Delegate Authentication to Azure AD

 In this tutorial, you'll create a new ASP.NET Core web application that delegates authentication to Azure AD.

Get an Azure AD Tenant

An Azure AD tenant is a dedicated Azure AD service instance that serves the authentication requests of a specific organization. If you have an Azure subscription or an Office 365 subscription, you already have an Azure AD tenant for your organization. In this tutorial, you'll create a new tenant under your Azure subscription for testing purposes.

1. Navigate to https://portal.azure.com/#create/Microsoft.AzureActiveDirectory. Log in using the account you used to create your Azure subscription.
2. On the **Create directory** screen, enter a name for your organization, and enter an initial domain name (*.onmicrosoft.com) for your organization. Then click the **Create** button, as shown in Figure 4.4.
3. Once the directory is created, the screen will display a "Click here to manage your new directory" link. Clicking on the link takes you to the tenant screen, where you can perform various management tasks such as managing users and registering applications. You don't need to do anything here yet—you'll come back to this screen later to check some configurations.

Create an ASP.NET Core Web Application

1. In Visual Studio 2017, select the **File**, **New**, **Project** menu to create a new project.
2. On the New Project dialog box, select the **Visual C#**, **Web**, **ASP.NET Core Web Application** template, enter a name for your project, and click the OK button to create the project.

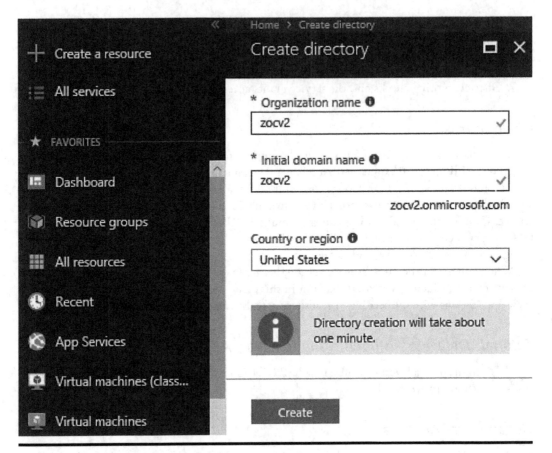

Figure 4.4   Create directory screen on Azure portal

3. On the **New ASP.Net Core Web Application** dialog box, select the **Web Application** template, and then click on the **Change Authentication** button, as shown in Figure 4.5.

4. On the **Change Authentication** dialog box, select the **Work or School Account** option, and enter the **Domain** name for your new AAD tenant. Optionally, check the **Read directory data** checkbox, which allows you to use graph queries to query the object trees in your AAD tenant. Then click on the **OK** button, as shown in Figure 4.5. Back in the **New ASP.NET Core Web Application** dialog box, click on the **OK** button to create the ASP.NET Core web application, as shown in Figure 4.6. If you are asked to log in, log in to your tenant.

5. Press **F5** to launch the app locally. After a few seconds, your browser will open with the home page of the web app displayed. And chances are, you'll see your email address displayed in the upper right corner of the page without you doing anything. If you are asked to log in, that's okay as well—just log in using the same credential you used to create your AAD tenant.

6. Optionally, you can sign out and sign in again, just to see how it works.

Examine the AAD Tenant

Wow, that was just magical. Without writing a single line of code, your web application is automatically configured to use your AAD tenant as its IdP. Whenever an anonymous user tries to

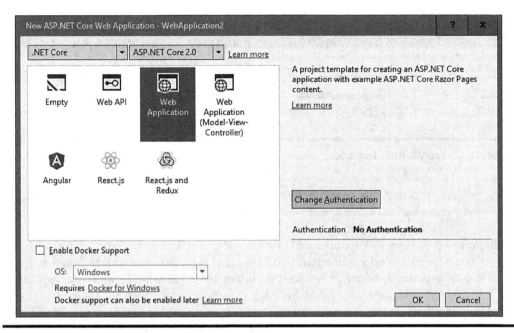

Figure 4.5   New ASP.NET Core Web Application dialog box

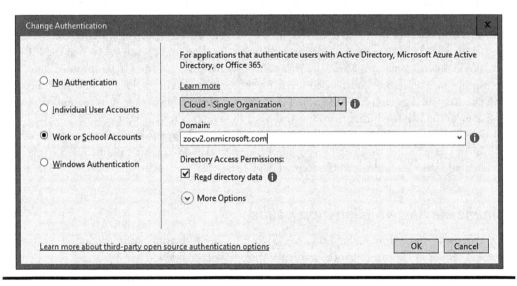

Figure 4.6   Change Authentication dialog box

access your site, she will be redirected to the log in page of your AAD tenant for authentication before she can access any of the pages—perfect!

A lot happened behind the scene. You'll take a closer look next.

1. Navigate to your AAD tenant on the **Microsoft Azure Management Portal**.
2. Click on the **Users** link. In the user list, you'll see the credential you used to create the AAD tenant that has been automatically added to the user list (as a global administrator). You can

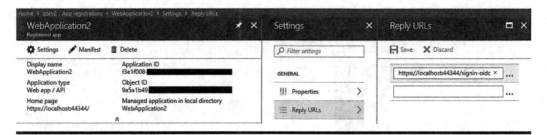

Figure 4.7   Reply URLs of an application

perform various management tasks here, such as creating new users and groups, setting up multi-factor authentications, resetting a user's password, blocking a user, and many others. Feel free to try a few options.

3. Return to the home view of the AAD tenant and then click on the **App registrations** link. Click on the **View all applications** button to see all registered applications. You'll find your web application listed here. When you establish a trust relationship between your application and your AAD tenant, the configuration has to be done in two ways: your application has to explicitly trust the AAD tenant and the AAD tenant has to explicitly trust the application. To cause an AAD tenant to trust your application, you need to register the application with the tenant. This is what the application registration is about (you'll see how the application is configured to trust the AAD tenant in the next section). Once an application is registered, it gets an **Application ID**, which uniquely identifies the application in the tenant.

4. Click on the application to open its details. Then click on the **Settings**, **Reply URLs** link to show reply URLs configured for the application, as shown in Figure 4.7. When the IdP (the AAD tenant) generates a security token, it posts the token to the URLs specified here. You might wonder how a cloud-based IdP can post security tokens to "localhost." This is because the flow in Figure 4.2 is driven by your browser redirections: your browser redirects your user to the IdP for authentication. And once the token is returned, it redirects to the Reply URL with the token attached. Because this redirection happens locally, localhost works fine in this case. When you deploy your application to the cloud with a public DNS name, you can add the new address to the Reply URLs list.

Examine the ASP.NET Core Application

Now let's spend some time seeing how the ASP.NET Core web application is configured to trust the AAD tenant as IdP, and how the authentication flow is enabled.

1. Open the **Startup.cs** file in your web application. Observe how cookie-based authentication middleware is configured in the **ConfigureService** method of the **Startup** class (you can find auto-generated authentication builder extensions under the **Extensions** folder of the project):

```
services.AddAuthentication(sharedOptions =>
{
sharedOptions.DefaultScheme =
    CookieAuthenticationDefaults.AuthenticationScheme;
```

```
sharedOptions.DefaultChallengeScheme =
    OpenIdConnectDefaults.AuthenticationScheme;
})
.AddAzureAd(options => Configuration.Bind("AzureAd", options))
.AddCookie();
```

2. Open the **appsettings.json** file, which contains configuration settings that identify the AAD tenant. Please note the "ClientID" is the Application ID you've seen on your AAD tenant page:

```
"AzureAd": {
    "Instance": "https://login.microsoftonline.com/",
    "Domain": "zocv2.onmicrosoft.com",
    "TenantId": "4fbd6b7f-…",
    "ClientId": "f3e1f008-…",
    "CallbackPath": "/signin-oidc"
},
```

3. And finally, take a look at the **Pages_LoginPartial.cshtml** page. The authentication middleware is integrated with the user identity model so that you can get the user's info directly through *User.Identity.Name*. Otherwise, you'll have to validate the security token yourself, extract the claims, and use their values.

```
@using System.Security.Principal
@if (User.Identity.IsAuthenticated)
{
    <ul class="nav navbar-nav navbar-right">
        <li class="navbar-text">Hello @User.Identity.Name!</li>
        <li><a asp-area="" asp-controller="Account"
            asp-action="SignOut">Sign out</a></li>
    </ul>
}
else
{
    <ul class="nav navbar-nav navbar-right">
        <li><a asp-area="" asp-controller="Account"
            asp-action="Signin">Sign in</a></li>
    </ul>
}
```

Data Protection

```
- .... .. .../ ... . -. - - -. -.-. . / .. ... / .-- .-. ... - - .
-. / .. -. / -- --- .-. ... . / -.-. --- -...
```

I have a bit of Tonsurephobia. Whenever I move to a new place, it takes me awhile to find a new barbershop that I'm comfortable with visiting about once every two months. Nowadays, I go to a little barbershop in Redmond run by Ron and Jeff. They are quite busy, and they don't take any appointments. So, each time I go there, there can be a long wait. Fortunately, they have a copy of *The Dangerous Book for Boys*, which contains a collection of random information such as Latin roots of words and the meanings of naval flags. That's where I learned Morse code, which I used to write the opening sentence of this section.

Now imagine I need to send you this message during a war. I must assume the message is passed through a hostile environment. To ensure secured data exchange, we need to employ methods to ensure confidentiality and integrity as well as authenticity of the message.

Confidentiality

If you and I were the only two people who understand Morse code, we could communicate in private worry-free from any eavesdroppers, right? Unfortunately, Morse code is a very straightforward encoding that can be easily cracked. Any reversible fixed encoding rules (or any two-way function) can be reverse engineered. To truly encrypt your data, the encoding rule needs to have a private secret and is unpredictable to an oblivious party. As long as the secret is kept private, even if a hostile party knows the encryption rules (such as AES and 3DES), they can't decipher messages without the secret. For example, when you set up an Azure Storage Account, you get two access keys that you can use to access the storage account, as shown in Figure 4.8. Symmetric key encryption doesn't define how keys are transferred. You are responsible for transmitting and storing the key in a secured manor. The following string is the same Morse code encrypted (and base-64 encoded) using 3DES.

```
kS2wdJ9aPWSXw5u1StPnTUhEpL5WPaLptvI6HyGVbrXzSQCMGButaaRqX5WKO0VfC9Uf
kW6ARvRNKeGuLlQPu+bugT4uP6YIiMq5It6unt+USyIcBUqP1sgYUcMLGcYW5wpOJsw3
W4yX3jEKgWee/wXVfFtJeoI7
```

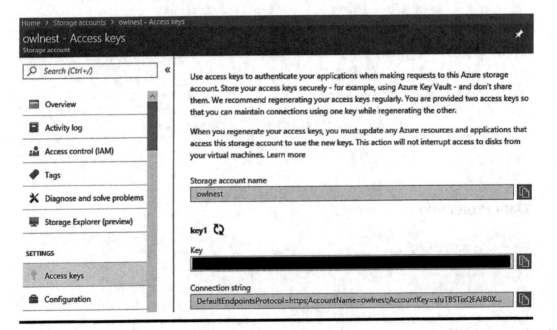

Figure 4.8   Azure Storage Account access key

Symmetric key sharing over the Internet is problematic, especially when a website tries to bootstrap a business relationship with a new customer. The off-band, manual key exchange doesn't scale. This is where public-key cryptography comes in. The best known public-key cryptography algorithm is RSA, named after its inventors Ron Rivest, Adi Shamir, and Leonard Adleman. With public-key cryptography, each party generates a public-private key pair independently. The public key is shared with everyone, while the private key is kept secret. A message encrypted using someone's public key can be decrypted only with the corresponding private key. The ability to send encrypted data using publicly available information is mind boggling. And the algorithm has been the foundation of much Internet security as of today.

How does RSA Public-Key Encryption Work?

The idea of public-key encryption is based on a simple fact—it's easy to compute the product N of two (large) primes p and q, but it's generally very hard to factor N to recover p and q. If you have doubts, try to factor (and yes, you can use a computer):

```
15226050279225333605356183781326374297180681149613806886579084945801
22963258952897654000350692006139
```

BTW, the preceding number is the RSA-100 challenge number. RSA Laboratories announced an RSA Factoring Challenge in 1991 to encourage number theory research. And RSA-100 was one of the simplest, which was solved 14 days later.

In the following text, I'll pick very small prime numbers to make math easier. However, you should remember that in reality, very large prime numbers (usually larger than 2048 bits) are used.

1. Receiver generates two primes p and q.
   Example: $p = 11$, $q = 5$
2. Receiver generates $N = p \times q$ and chooses e so that e is a relative prime to $\varphi = (p-1)(q-1)$. The pair (N, e) is the receiver's **public key**.
   Example: $N = p \times q = 11 \times 5 = 55$, $e = 7$
3. Receiver also finds d so that $ed\%\varphi = 1$. The number d is the receiver's **private key**.
   Example: $d = 23$, because $7 \times 23\%40 = 1$
4. Send encodes a message M using the receiver's public key by calculating $C = M^e\%N$
   Example: $M = 18$, $C = 18^7\%55 = 17$
5. Receiver decodes the message using the private key: $M = C^d\%N$
   Example: $C = 17$, $M = 17^{23}\%55 = 18$

That doesn't look too terrible. And within the limited scope, finding d based on e, N is quite straightforward. The following code snippet can infer the private key for the preceding public key in just a few milliseconds. However, when p and q get larger, step 3 above becomes so punishingly difficult that it can't be completed within a reasonable timeframe with current computers—we need quantum computers for such tasks.

```
static int findPrivateKey(int e, int N, int M, int C)
{
    int[] primes = { 2, 3, 5, 7, 11, 13, 17, 19, 23, 29, 31, 37, 41,
        43, 47, 53, 59, 61, 67, 71, 73, 79, 83, 89, 97 };
    foreach(int p in primes)
    {
        foreach(int q in primes)
        {
            if (N == p * q)
            {
                int phi = (p - 1) * (q - 1);
                for (int d = 1; d < 100; d++)
                {
                    if (e * d % phi == 1 && BigInteger.Pow(C,d) % N
                        == M)
                    {
                        return d;
                    }
                }
            }
        }
    }
    return 0;
}
```

Cryptographs can be used to protect data in motion and data at rest. For example, HTTPS protocol uses RSA to exchange a symmetric key that is used to encrypt user traffic. And most cloud-based storage solutions support customer-supplied or system-generated encrypted keys that are used to encrypted data on disk.

Authenticity

The fact that you can decrypt data from a sender by using the sender's public key assures you that the sender who encrypted the data indeed holds the corresponding private key. However, you can't tell if the public key is indeed associated with a business entity with which you intend to do business. For example, I can create a key pair, give you the public key, and claim the key represents a national bank. How can you tell if a key is from a legit bank or forged by me? The solution to this problem is not a purely technical one—you need to trust an authority that can guarantee you that the subject of the key is indeed what it claims to be. This authority is a certification authority (CA). It issues digital certificates, which contain public keys of business entities as well as the certified business identifications (such as domain names). If you see a certificate stating it's from Bank of America, you can trust the public key is indeed from the bank because your trusted CA has checked it out for you.

Checking certificates is an important skill needed to avoid *phishing attacks*. Phishing attacks have different forms. But the most common form is a spam email with a link to a website imitating a legit site. For example, an adversary may send you an email about an overdraft on your bank account, with a link to a fake bank website that mimics a real bank site. If you don't pay enough attention, your login credential is easily stolen when you try to log in to the fake site using

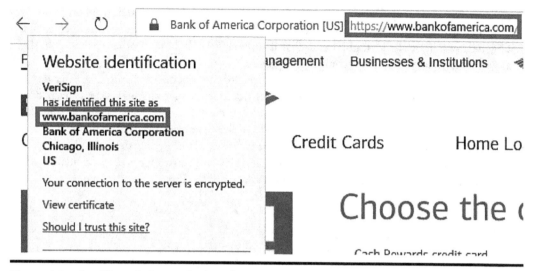

Figure 4.9   Certificate info on a legit website

your real bank account and password. Three important techniques can help you to reduce the risk. First, before you click on a link in an email, hover the mouse cursor over the link and examine the URL. If the URL doesn't appear to be from the actual site, don't click on it. Second, once you are on the site, check whether the certificate matches the site's domain name. Figure 4.9 shows that when I'm on the legit www.bankofamerica. com site. The browser display a green padlock indicating the certificate checks out, which mean the subject contained in the certificate matches the domain name of the website. If you click on the padlock, you can get more information on the certificate to further verify if the site truly belongs to the business. Third, always conduct online businesses through HTTPS protocol (the address in your browser address bar should start with *https://* instead of *http://*).

There are physical forms of phishing as well. Some criminals make fake ATM control panels, which they install in front of real ATM machines. As you insert your bank card and type in your PIN code, the fake panel reads and saves your account info as well as the PIN number. Because both the card slot and all the keys are connected to actual things, you can still complete your bank transactions (such as withdrawing money) as usual, without knowing that your bank account has been compromised.

Integrity

Using seals to certify authenticity has been traced thousands of years back in human civilization. However, seals can't prove if messages have been tampered with. They can, to a certain extent, approve that the envelop holding the message hasn't been opened. Changes made to physical documents are easily noticeable in some cases. Alterations to digital documents are hard to detect without proper data integrity assurances.

An effective way of ensuring data integrity is to use a digital signature. A digital signature is a digest of the original data encrypted using the sender's private key. The data receiver decrypts the signature using the sender's public key, hence validating that the signature and the digest were created by the sender. Then the receiver calculates the digest herself and compare the digest with the decrypted digest. Any discrepancies indicate data tampering has occurred. Applying a one way transformation algorithm to the original data creates the digest. Such an algorithm, such as SHA-256, generates a hash of the original data that is unlikely to collide with other hashes. Any slight changes to the data will lead to a completely different hash.

Because a hash function projects a large data set (of any documents) into a smaller data set (fixed length hash codes), there are many digital documents that share the same hash codes. However, it's computationally difficult to find another digital document that yields the same hash you have. Even if you could find such a document (to carry out a so-called *collide attack*), chances are the document is totally irrelevant to the business context, hence easily debunkable.

All modern programming languages provide libraries and classes for you to calculate hashes. For example, the following Python (3.6) code calculate a SHA-256 digest of string:

```
from hashlib import sha256
message = "This is a message"
digest = sha256(message.encode('utf-8')).hexdigest()
print(digest)
```

The above code generates the following hash code:

```
a826c7e389ec9f379cafdc544d7e9a4395ff7bfb58917bbebee51b3d0b1c996a
```

If you run the program again with a slightly modified message—"This is a message." (with a period at the end), you'll get a completely different hash:

```
a3964890912366008dee9864a4dfddf88446f354b989e340f826e21b2e83bd9c
```

Network Protection

I managed to be banned from my college's computer lab after the first class. My mistake was to show my classmates how to broadcast UDP messages on our network. The messages being sent went from harmless jokes to awful insults in almost no time. That was also my first taste of the power and danger of network anonymity.

Cloud is a hostile environment. Because your services share the same physical infrastructure as other services, you must build protections around your services so that they are not affected by those other services. Even if other services are not intentionally hostile, you still need to build up defenses against intentional or unintentional intrusions.

Software Defined Networking

Software Defined Networking (SDN) allows flexible, virtualized network topologies and routing rules to be laid on top of the same physical networking infrastructure. SDN uses a centralized control plane that defines desired networking topologies and all routing rules. These designs are pushed down to agents running on data center host machines. These agents configure the routing tables on the hosts to realize desired networking rules. When you provisioned VMs on Azure

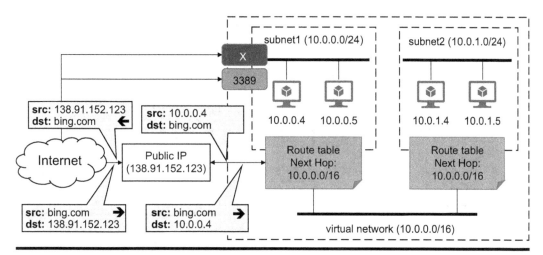

Figure 4.10   Sample virtual network topology

in Chapter 1, the machines were automatically placed on a subnet of a virtual network. Azure also auto-generates network security groups (NSGs) that block most inbound traffic. Figure 4.10 shows a sample virtual network topology with a virtual network (10.0.0.0/16). The virtual network has two subnets, *subnet1* (10.0.0.0/24) and *subnet2* (10.0.1.0/24). Each VM is assigned a private IP address. And if a VM is assigned a public IP, additional routing rules are added so that traffic can be routed from and to the designated machine.

NSGs are your first line of defense. By designing your NSGs, you can block any unwanted traffic while ensuring accessibility to your services. Figure 4.11 shows the default inbound/outbound NSG rules Azure creates when you provision a new Windows VM. By default, port 3389 is open for RDP accesses, and traffic from the virtual network as well as the Azure-provided load balancer is allowed. Outbound traffic to the Internet and the virtual network is allowed, while everything else is denied. If you are certain that your service won't need outbound Internet connections, you should disable the *AllowInternetOutBound* rule. For any service ports your service uses (such

build2018-nsg

Inbound rules

NAME	PRIORITY	SOURCE	SOURCE PORTS	DESTINATION	DESTINATION PORTS	PROTOCOL	ACCESS
default-allow-rdp	1000	0.0.0.0/0	0-65535	0.0.0.0/0	3389-3389	TCP	⊘ Allow
AllowVnetInBound	65000	Virtual network (2 prefixes)	0-65535	Virtual network (2 prefixes)	0-65535	All	⊘ Allow
AllowAzureLoadBalance...	65001	Azure load balancer (1 prefixes)	0-65535	0.0.0.0/0	0-65535	All	⊘ Allow
DenyAllInBound	65500	0.0.0.0/0	0-65535	0.0.0.0/0	0-65535	All	⊗ Deny

Outbound rules

NAME	PRIORITY	SOURCE	SOURCE PORTS	DESTINATION	DESTINATION PORTS	PROTOCOL	ACCESS
AllowVnetOutBound	65000	Virtual network (2 prefixes)	0-65535	Virtual network (2 prefixes)	0-65535	All	⊘ Allow
AllowInternetOutBound	65001	0.0.0.0/0	0-65535	Internet (82 prefixes)	0-65535	All	⊘ Allow
DenyAllOutBound	65500	0.0.0.0/0	0-65535	0.0.0.0/0	0-65535	All	⊗ Deny

Figure 4.11   Default security rules

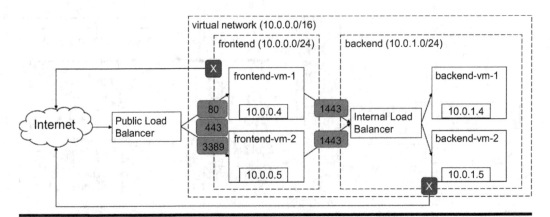

Figure 4.12   DMZ with NSGs

as port 80 and port 443), you should define additional inbound rules to allow traffic to come through those ports.

> (i) Traffic from a special virtual public IP, 168.63.129.16, is always allowed. For more details on this address, please see: https://blogs.msdn.microsoft.com/mast/2015/05/18/what-is-the-ip-address-168-63-129-16/

NSGs can be associated with NICs (network interface controllers or network interface cards), subnets, and virtual networks. You can use a combination of NSGs at different levels to design your desired network topologies. Figure 4.12 shows a sample implementation DMZ (demilitarized zone) that separates public facing front-end VMs on one subnet (10.0.0.0/24) from back-end VMs on another subnet (10.0.1.0/24). Only the specific port 1443 is allowed through the back-end NSG to access SQL Server in the back-end VMs. In other words, the back-end VMs are completely isolated from the outside world except for SQL connections. The front end, on the other hand, opens port 80 and 443 for Internet traffic as well as port 3389 for RDP. If you want to enable a system administrator to RDP into back-end VMs, you need to allow port 3389 on the back-end NSG, and use one of the front-end VMs as a *jump box* to RDP into back-end VMs.

Accelerated Networks with FPGAs

SDN uses software to reinforce routing rules. Software uses CPU cycles (regardless whether it runs in kernel mode or user mode). When the host's CPU is busy with processing networking rules, it provides less compute power to support your VMs and your services running on those VMs. To solve this problem, Microsoft Azure uses specialized network cards with Field Programmable Gate Arrays (FPGAs) to provide accelerated networking.

CPU, GPU, and FPGA with an ASIC (application-specific integrated circuit) represent a spectrum of compute chips. CPU uses a temporal compute model in which instructions are executed one at a time against one piece of data (loaded in registers). GPU uses a spatial compute model, in which an instruction is applied to a group of data (such as all pixels to be displayed on screen) in parallel. Hence, GPUs are specialized for the parallel application of the same instructions on large amounts of data. ASICs are specialized compute chips for specific application workloads. Application logics are burnt into hardware to provide hardware level performance. An ASIC provides the fastest performance, but it can't be repurposed for other tasks. FPGAs contain logic gates that can be dynamically programmed into compute circuits. They provide both software programmability and hardware-level performance. FPGAs are often used by chip designers to iterate circuit designs before finalized designs are implemented in ASICs.

Azure offloads all network routing rules handling to FPGAs as a bump-in-the-wire (BITW) solution that handles networking concerns independent from host CPUs. This solution provides fast network performance and reduces CPU pressure at the same time. At the time of writing, Azure claims to have the fastest networks among public cloud offerings.

Cross-Region Virtual Networks

Both AWS and Azure provide hybrid connectivity between your on-premises data center and your virtual networks in cloud. AWS's hybrid connectivity feature is called Direct Connect. Azure's equivalent feature is called ExpressRoute. Both features allow you to provision dedicated lines (often through a partner) that connect your data center networks with your in-cloud networks. Both AWS and Azure also allow you to link in-cloud virtual networks at different regions through networking pairing. For example, by creating multiple site-to-site connections, your headquarter office in one region can be connected to all field offices at different regions with private networks.

Furthermore, both AWS and Azure also support private connections to certain cloud services such as storage services through service endpoints. For example, you can remove public access to your Azure Storage account and allow only VMs from specific virtual networks to access the service by defining *Virtual Network Service Endpoints*. All traffic between your virtual network and the target service goes through Azure's backbone network, which is separated from the public Internet.

Tutorial: Creating an AWS VPC Topology

In this tutorial, you'll create an AWS virtual network (called Virtual Private Cloud or VPC) with two subnets—a public facing subnet with Internet access and a private subnet without Internet access. You'll also define a service endpoint that allows private access to a hosted AWS DynamoDB NoSQL database service.

1. Log on to the AWS Console (https://aws.amazon.com/).
2. Navigate to the VPC wizard page at https://us-west-1.console.aws.amazon.com/vpc/home?region=us-west-1#wizardSelector. Please note you may land on a different region other than us-west-1—see the Tutorial in Chapter 3 for more details on AWS regions.
3. On the **Step 1** screen, select the VPC with the Public and Private Subnets wizard, as shown in Figure 4.13. The wizard provides the topology we need for this tutorial. Click on the **Select** button to continue.
4. On the **Step 2** screen, enter a name for your VPC. Change the **Public subnet name** to *frontend*, and the **Private subnet name** to *backend*, as shown in Figure 4.14. This defines a network topology like what's shown in Figure 4.12.

Step 1: Select a VPC Configuration

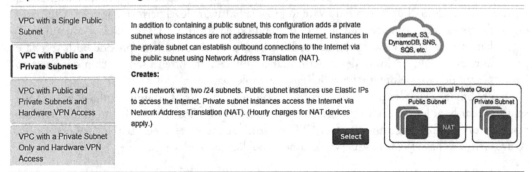

VPC with a Single Public Subnet	In addition to containing a public subnet, this configuration adds a private subnet whose instances are not addressable from the Internet. Instances in the private subnet can establish outbound connections to the Internet via the public subnet using Network Address Translation (NAT).
VPC with Public and Private Subnets	**Creates:**
VPC with Public and Private Subnets and Hardware VPN Access	A /16 network with two /24 subnets. Public subnet instances use Elastic IPs to access the Internet. Private subnet instances access the Internet via Network Address Translation (NAT). (Hourly charges for NAT devices apply.)
VPC with a Private Subnet Only and Hardware VPN Access	

Figure 4.13   VPC with Public and Private Subnets wizard

Step 2: VPC with Public and Private Subnets

IPv4 CIDR block:*	10.0.0.0/16	(65531 IP addresses available)
IPv6 CIDR block:	◉ No IPv6 CIDR Block	
	○ Amazon provided IPv6 CIDR block	
VPC name:	myVPC	

Public subnet's IPv4 CIDR:*	10.0.0.0/24	(251 IP addresses available)
Availability Zone:*	No Preference ⌄	
Public subnet name:	frontend	
Private subnet's IPv4 CIDR:*	10.0.1.0/24	(251 IP addresses available)
Availability Zone:*	No Preference ⌄	
Private subnet name:	backend	

You can add more subnets after AWS creates the VPC.

Figure 4.14   Define VPC topology

5. Click on the **Use a NAT instance instead** link to provision a VM instance as a NAT gateway.
6. Click on the **Add Endpoint** button to define a service endpoint for accessing DynamoDB service. Select the DynamoDB service (com.amazonaws.*<region>*.dynamodb) as **Service**. Select *Public subnet* as the **Subnet** that is allowed access to the database service. Leave the access **Policy** at *Full Access*, as shown in Figure 4.15.
7. Click on the **Create VPC** button to create the VPC.

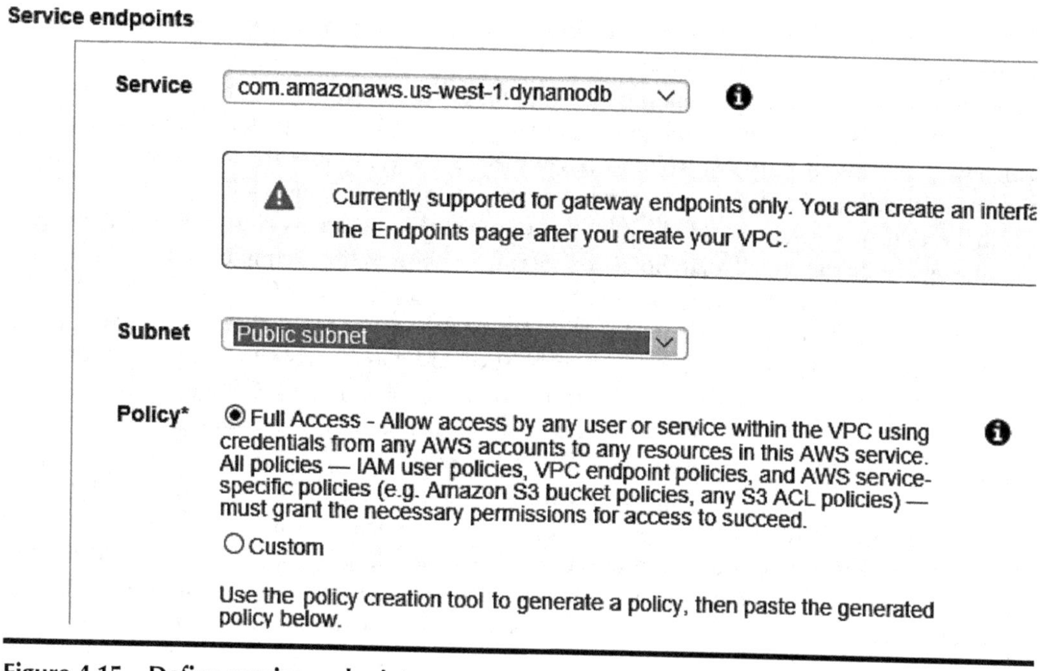

Service endpoints

Service   com.amazonaws.us-west-1.dynamodb   ⌄   ⓘ

⚠   Currently supported for gateway endpoints only. You can create an interfa the Endpoints page after you create your VPC.

Subnet   Public subnet   ⌄

Policy*   ⦿ Full Access - Allow access by any user or service within the VPC using credentials from any AWS accounts to any resources in this AWS service. All policies — IAM user policies, VPC endpoint policies, and AWS service-specific policies (e.g. Amazon S3 bucket policies, any S3 ACL policies) — must grant the necessary permissions for access to succeed.   ⓘ

○ Custom

Use the policy creation tool to generate a policy, then paste the generated policy below.

Figure 4.15   Define service endpoint

Defend Against Common Threats

A few years back, a colleague and I did an experiment—we slid a new server with a public IP address onto a test network that was isolated from the rest of the corporate network. We didn't announce the IP address to anyone, and we just waited. Within a few hours, we found hundreds of port scan attempts and login attempts from different IP addresses around the world (and many of them happened to come near Hong Kong, China). This experiment proved that your services and servers will be attacked, no matter what kind of service you are hosting. If you can't imagine how many attacks cloud platforms like Azure are facing on a daily basis, here are a few daily data points to give you some perspectives:

- 18 billion Microsoft account authentications
- 77 million threats detected on devices
- 1.5 million compromise attempts deflected
- 30 million geo login anomaly attacks deflected

How Microsoft can keep millions of customers running smoothly on cloud under constant attack attempts is mind boggling. Indeed, defending against existing and new attacks is a constant battle. Microsoft has dedicated teams that keep analyzing various attack patterns and try to get ahead of bad guys. In the next chapter, you'll see a couple of examples of how Microsoft uses cloud-scale data collection and machine learning to deflect some cunning attacks that are extremely hard to detect with traditional methods.

Denial of Service

A denial of service attack is quite annoying because the adversary is not trying to get something out of your server, which makes them less trackable. And it is not particularly sophisticated—an attacker simply overloads the server with excessive loads. It used to be easy to take a web server down. Back in the early 90s (I mean 1990s), I knew an attack to take down a popular web server was occurring by simply sending crafted long queries to it. Because the server logged all requests (when it's not carefully configured), the requests would take up all the hard drive space, which were commonly only several hundreds of megabytes. As servers are now becoming better managed, it becomes harder to take down a service using a single client—for instance, a server can make a client suspicious and block it. To overcome this, attackers recruit many clients (by implanting agents through Trojan horses on victim's machines, for example) and send requests from distributed clients. This is called a Distributed Denial of Service (DDoS) attack.

There are many forms of DDoS attack. The simplest volumetric attacks use brute force requests to overwhelm the target servers. Other more sophisticated DDoS attacks include techniques such as holding open requests, sending malformed commands, and issuing CPU-intensive queries. Regardless, the goal is to exhaust certain resources—such as network resources or application resources—to render a server unresponsive. A DDoS attack is tricky because it's hard to separate attacking traffic from legit requests. At the time of writing, the DDoS attack on GitHub on February 28th, 2018 was the largest DDoS attack recorded in history, with the peak traffic at 1.3Tbps. The attack was an amplification DDoS attack leveraging misconfigured online Memcached servers. The attacker sent forged requests with spoofed IP addresses of the victim. The queries triggered large responses to be sent to the spoofed IPs, flooding the servers.

To guard against DDoS, you must constantly monitor ingress network traffic and adjust your traffic routing policies when such attacks happen. Azure offers built-in DDoS protection in its backbone network. It monitors all its network traffic and dynamically adjusts its policies to mitigate common network-level DDoS attacks. This layer of DDoS protection is primarily designed to protect Azure infrastructure and Azure fundamental services that may have widespread impacts on a large number of customers. For customer or application specific DDoS protection, you can use additional DDoS protection that is tailored for your application. As an exercise, you'll try out Azure DDoS Protection Standard to see how you can partner with Azure to build up layers of protections around your applications.

Tutorial: Use Azure DDoS Protection Standard

 In this tutorial, you'll create a new Azure DDoS Protection Standard plan.

1. Log in to the Microsoft Azure Management Portal.
2. Click on the **Create a resource** link at the upper left corner of the portal.
3. Search for "*DDoS protection plan*" and click on the found entry to launch the provision wizard.
4. On the provision wizard, click the **Create** button to start.
5. On the **Create a DDoS protection plan** screen, enter a name for the plan, enter a name for a new resource group that holds the plan, select the region where you want the resource group to be placed, and then click the **Create** button to create the plan as shown in Figure 4.16. You should note that the location is for the resource group only. It's not related to the locations of the resources you want to protect.
6. Once the plan is created, you can add your virtual networks to the plan. To do this, navigate to your virtual network screen, select **DDoS protection**, pick the **Standard** option, select the DDoS protection plan you want to apply, and then click the **Save** button, as shown in Figure 4.17.

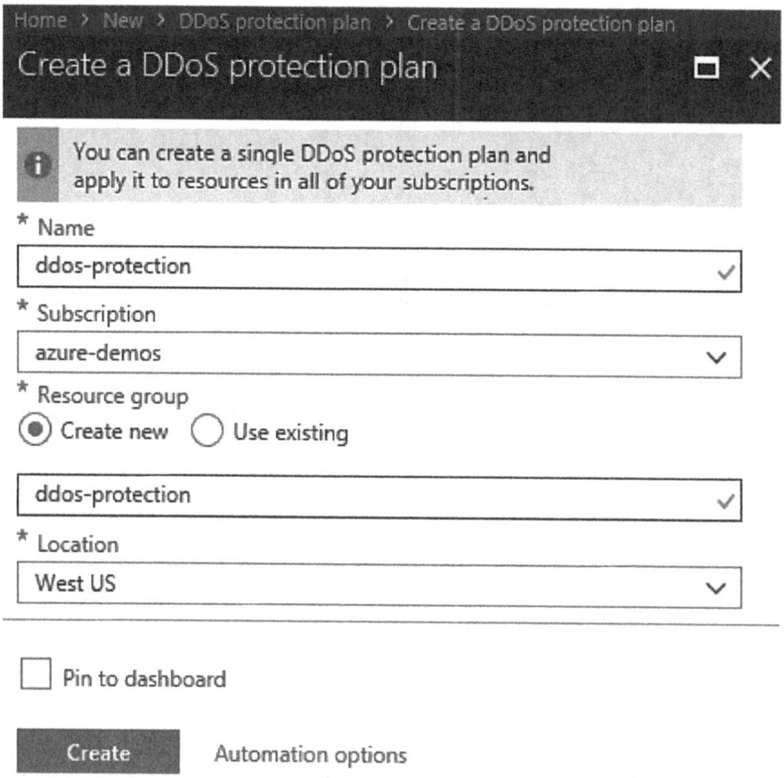

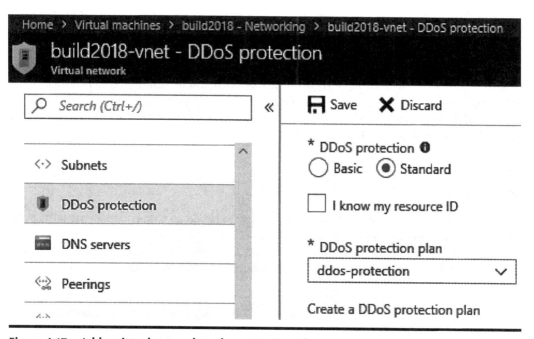

Figure 4.16 Creating a DDoS protection plan

Figure 4.17 Add a virtual network to the protection plan

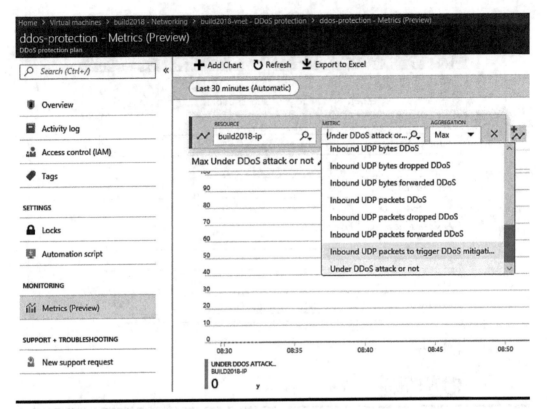

Figure 4.18 DDoS metrics

7. Once that's done, your network traffic is monitored and analyzed for possible DDoS attacks. You don't need to do anything else—the Azure infrastructure will take care of the rest. To see what's happening behind the scene, you can examine several metrics in the **Metrics** view of your protection plan, as shown in Figure 4.18. The figure shows that I've picked a public IP, and I can choose from several DDoS-related metrics, such as Inbound DDoS bytes and bytes dropped by the protection plan. Or if you simply want to know if you are under the risk of a DDoS attack, you can choose the **Under DDoS attack or not** metric, which reflects the probability of an active DDoS attack.

Script Injection

The Highway 520 bridge between Bellevue and Seattle is equipped with an automatic tolling system. Cars don't need to stop at toll booths. Instead, computers automatically read the license plates and send out bills as cars pass by at 50 miles per hour. Now imagine the system inserts a new record into a billing database as a car passes by executing the following SQL statement.

```
INSERT INTO BILLING (AMOUNT, DATE, LICENSE) VALUES (5.00, DATE(),
'<license plate number>');
```

Hypothetically, to try to fool the system someone could alter their plate number so it reads differently (which is illegal, by the way). Or they could attempt to do something worse by making their license plate read like this:

```
HIS-NUMBER'; DELETE FROM BILLING WHERE (LICENSE='HIS-NUMBER
```

If the system wasn't carefully designed and simply put whatever the camera read into the SQL statement, the statement becomes:

```
INSERT INTO BILLING (AMOUNT, DATE, LICENSE) VALUES (5.00, DATE(),
'HIS-NUMBER'; DELETE FROM BILLING WHERE (LICENSE='HIS-NUMBER');
```

And the guy can drive through the bridge toll-free. Getting a system to execute unintended commands by crafting malicious inputs is called *code injection* or *script injection*.

A more common example of *script injection* is to inject JavaScript in inputs. Everything a browser does is open—you can examine the source code of the web page; you can monitor how traffic flows between the browser and the server; and you can use a browser's built-in developer tools to mess with the DOM (Document Object Model) tree and see what happens. All these are empowering an attacker to try something

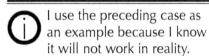 I use the preceding case as an example because I know it will not work in reality. First, the computer won't read such a long input. Second, the table name is probably different. Third, the system is probably built with protection against script injection. And finally—if I haven't mentioned it—it's illegal.

bad. For instance, he can examine your cookies and try to forge some cookies to fool the server, as long as he can find a place where you take his input without proper validation and encoding so that he can run a simple script:

```
document.cookie="some-key=some-value;some-other-key=
some-other-value;"
```

A specific type of script injection is the Cross-Site Scripting (XSS) attack. XSS occurs when an attacker uses a web application to send malicious code to a different end user. Hypothetically, an attacker can submit a malicious content to a site (such as a forum), and when the content is rendered for other users, the implanted script will send the attacker sensitive information about the victims. The Open Web Application Security Project (OWASP) provides a XSS prevision cheat sheet online that you should check out here: https://www.owasp.org/index.php/XSS_(Cross_Site_Scripting)_Prevention_Cheat_Sheet. The sheet provides very useful rules for guarding against XSS attacks. For example, Rule #1 specifies that the following characters should be encoded to avoid switching into other execution contexts such as scripts, styles and event handlers:

```
& --> &amp;
< --> &lt;
> --> &gt;
```

```
"  --> &quot;
'  --> &#x27;
/  --> &#x2F;
```

Multi-Tenancy Security Risks

Microsoft provides shuttle services for employees to go to and from offices around Puget Sound. The idea is to share transportation so that there will be fewer people driving, hence saving energy. Multi-tenancy on cloud shares the same premise—if multiple customers can be served on a shared infrastructure, efficiency goes up, cost goes down, and everyone is happy. In other words, multi-tenancy is at the core of the cloud economic model.

However, there's a catch. When you have multiple tenants sharing the same infrastructure, you are at risk that some tenants will intentionally or unintentionally leak into other tenants and cause various problems. For example, if you have multiple customers accessing transaction records in the same database table, a malicious customer may try to gain access to others' records by modifying query keys. Some databases, such as SQL Database and Oracle, support row-level security that allows system administrators to define predicates that filter database records based on user characteristics, such as tenant ID. For other databases (such as MySQL), you'll need to use a combination of techniques to define virtualized views that separate different tenants.

Mapping all user accounts to database accounts is troublesome. In many multi-tiered systems, database access is encapsulated in a data layer, which is often configured to run under one or a few service accounts. In such cases, RBAC is no longer sufficient. You'll need additional mechanisms to establish and validate against tenant scopes. I don't know a fixed method or a recommended method to do this, so I'll stop here.

In Chapter 2, I discussed problems with noisy neighbors in a multi-tenant environment. The noisy problem could be a security concern because it may cause other services to be faultily evicted, causing possible service quality degradations or even interruptions. So noisy neighbors can be considered a form of DoS attack.

No matter what you do, logical tenant isolation may be insufficient for certain customers for various reasons such as compliance, performance guarantee, and data isolation. However, if you allocate dedicated hardware, you are losing the benefits of multi-tenancy. In later chapters, I'll discuss some ideas that can allow you to provide strong isolation while sharing infrastructure among tenants when possible.

Exposure of Sensitive Data

At the time of writing, Facebook, a popular social network service, is experiencing big problems. Facebook exposed its user data to a third-party to gain deep insights into a person's life. A person's digital presence reflects the person's living style, product preferences, health conditions, financial situation, political views, and much more. People who can gain access to such data can gain unfair advantages over competitors, and may use the data to exploit users for financial or political gain.

When a user submits data to you, they are putting trust in your service. Violating that trust hurts your credibility, company image, and eventually your business. So you should always treat your customer's data with care and respect. Doing this requires not only technical protection, but also good practices and business ethics.

When you save customer data, you need to identify sensitive Personal Identifiable Information (PII) and put proper protections around it. PII is any information that can tie digital artifacts to a specific individual. For instance, a person's national ID can uniquely identify a person. A person's email, on the other hand, isn't necessarily trackable back to the actual owner. Sensitive PII should always be encrypted at rest and during transmission.

Many large scale data leaks have happened because of inside jobs. An employee with sufficient access rights who goes haywire can do serious damages with very little effort. Guarding against these leaks requires robust business processes and in-depth protections.

Just-In-Time Access

Just-in-time (JIT) access is an effective way of avoiding accidental data leaks. With JIT access, no one is permanently assigned an administrative role. Instead, administrative access can be only temporarily granted bases on verified business justifications, such as database schema maintenance required by a software update. JIT access has an associated time window for the worker to complete the job. The access is automatically revoked after the assigned time window expires.

Like many other security practices, JIT can be annoying. To make your JIT policy sustainable, you need to figure out ways to streamline the process as much as possible. For example, you can set up rules to automatically grant JIT accesses for certain scenarios, such as a periodical backup. Automatic JIT approval may sound like it's negating the purpose of JIT. However, it preserves auditability of administrative accesses, which is a key aspect of controlled access.

Protection in Depth

Sensitive data should always be encrypted, both in transition and at rest. When you maintain data for multiple tenants, you should use per-tenant keys instead of a master key. Further, you can enable Bring Your Own Key (BYOK) that allows customers to supply their own keys for data encryption. Bring Your Own Encryption (BYOE) goes a step further by allowing customers to bring in their own encryption software. BYOK and BYOE put the customers in control of their own privacy. Even if some terrible things happen—such as an insider stealing data or a government agency forcing the cloud platform to forfeit data—the customers can still maintain data safety by holding control of their keys.

BYOK places the burden of key management on customers. And not all customers are good at managing keys. Services such as Amazon KMS and Microsoft Azure Key Vault are hosted services that help customers to manage their keys. And some services use a combined key for encryption—the service holds half of the combined key, and the customer holds the other half. In this case, even if a malicious party gets a hold of the customer's key, they can't decrypt the data because the service still holds the other half.

Another way to protect sensitive data is by not saving the data at all. Instead of saving the original data, you can save the corresponding hash values, plus partial data that is necessary for carrying out business logics. For example, instead of saving a user's social security number, you can save the hash and the last four digits of the number. This allows you to identify a specific user using the hash, and to perform easy verifications by checking if a user can provide the matching last four digits.

Although data can be encrypted during transportation and at rest, data is most likely to be decrypted in memory as a system process it. For example, for a system to do a range query over salary data, the data must be decrypted before the query can be carried out. This is because properly encrypted data should not reveal any quantitative qualities of the data. Otherwise, an attacker can use comparisons to infer a piece of data by creating controlled values. So, it seems it's impossible to provide in-memory protection of data against the service provider. Or is it?

Confidential Computing

When you delegate jobs to others, you often need to surrender some pieces of private information—to receive a package, you need to reveal your home address; to make a payment, you need to offer your credit card number; to get a loan to buy a house, you need to allow people to make queries about your credit history. Similarly, when you call a hosted service, you often need to submit your data to the service.

Can you trust that the service provider will do what it's supposed to do? Can you be confident the service provider will protect your data in your best interests? Can you maintain confidentiality while allowing the service provider to work on your data? Well in many cases, you can't maintain 100% confidentiality. You need to trust someone will do the right thing, because your data will be processed by a third-party at the end. The question is, how can you limit the parties you trust to the bare minimum?

Trusted Execution Environments

Data breaches happen, even with the most experienced defenders. In 2015, an anonymous hacker hacked BitDefender, an award-winning Internet security software company. The hacker got a hold of the company's user database and claimed to have access to all user records with their passwords. BitDefender had to reset passwords for all exposed users and put in additional measures to further protect the data. Also in 2015, servers of Anthem, Inc. were hacked and over 78 million personal records were leaked. In 2016, Yahoo acknowledged that over 500 million user accounts had been hacked in 2014, and over 1 billion accounts were compromised in another hack in 2013. And it's just a matter of time when the next big breach takes the headline.

I don't want to sound pessimistic, but when you put your data on cloud, there are many ways things could go wrong: a malicious privileges administrator may try to abuse the data; a hacker may exploit bugs in infrastructure, virtualization layer, OS, frameworks, libraries, and applications; a third party may gain access to your data without your consent, and so on. How can you maintain a certain level of confidence in your privacy when you assume every aspect of the cloud might be compromised? Especially in addition to protecting your data in transition and at rest, how can you protect your data during processing?

Trusted Execution Environments (TEEs) are designed to provide a private data processing environment. They isolate portions of processor and memory to form a secured, unbreakable enclave in which data can be safely processed in plain text. Data outside the enclave remains in encrypted format. There are existing TEEs such as Intel's Software Guard Extensions (SGX) and Microsoft's Virtualization-based Security (VBS). TEEs try to isolate from as many parties as possible. For example, SGX's enclave is implemented in hardware with special processor instructions. This takes everyone else, including hypervisors, operation systems, and frameworks, out of the picture. As long as you can trust the Intel SGX-enabled chip, you can maintain high confidence that your data is processed in private. Figure 4.19 shows how an enclave creates a secured processing environment for an application, bypassing all intermediate layers.

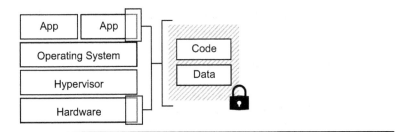

Figure 4.19 Secured processing environment with enclave

When an enclave is launched, a cryptographic log is recorded that includes information such as code, data, stack, and heap contents. This recorded log is the *measurement* of the enclave. A hardware-based *attestation* provides evidence that the enclave is indeed running intended code on the intended platform. And the enclave uses a platform-specific *sealing* key to store a secret for later use. This mechanism provides both assurance and confidentiality when sensitive data is being processed. Even if a malicious administrator hops on the machine, attaches to the running process, and observes the memory pages, they will not be able to see what's running inside the enclave.

With enclaves in place, you can send your data through a secured channel to enclaves operated by a third party. The third party runs the attested code, such as training a machine learning model, on the data within the enclaves. This essentially allows you to consume the third party service without revealing your data.

Confidentiality in the Open

TEE uses isolated environment to provide compute privacy. This makes TEE applicable to virtually all computational problems. Much legacy software can be updated to use special TEE instructions that allocate and enter secured enclaves to complete sensitive computations in privacy. What if TEE isn't available? What if you want to coordinate computations between multiple parties that are not necessarily trustworthy? This section presents a brief introduction of two confidential computing techniques without TEE, namely Fully Homomorphic Encryption (FHE) and Secured Multiparty Computation (SMC).

Fully Homomorphic Encryption

Delegating data processing without revealing data has been long researched. And such delegation is especially relevant to cloud because cloud often needs to process data submitted from customers. For a customer requiring privacy assurances, it is desirable for the customer to submit encrypted data the cloud will process to generate an encrypted result that only the customer can decipher. Fully Homomorphic Encryption (FHE) is an interesting technique to realize such delegations.

Let's say you have input x and you want to invoke function f that is hosted by a third party. Instead of passing x, you pass an encrypted $Enc(x)$ to the third party. The third party uses a homomorphic evaluation function so that evaluation of f using $Enc(x)$ generates $Enc(f(x))$. Once you receive the returned value, you can simply decrypt it and get the wanted $f(x)$. In this way, you can invoke the remote function f and get the desired output of $f(x)$ without ever revealing your input to the third party.

So to make Fully Homomorphic Encryption work, we need an encryption scheme that causes the third party to generate $Enc(f(x))$ after it evaluates $f(Enc(x))$. Here I'm going to briefly present a scheme that uses properties of eigenvectors: if two matrices C_1, C_2 have the same eigenvector $\vec{s}$, and m_1, m_2 are corresponding eigenvalues of $\vec{s}$, then $C_1 + C_2$ has eigenvalue $m_1 + m_2$ with regard to $\vec{s}$, and $C_1 \cdot C_2$ has eigenvalue $m_1 \times m_2$ with regard to $\vec{s}$. If $\vec{s}$ is our secret, m_i is our message, and C_i is our ciphertext, we have a homomorphism encryption scheme for addition and multiplication.

For example, if we use $\begin{bmatrix} 3 \\ 1 \end{bmatrix}$ as our secret and encrypt $m_1 = 5$ and $m_2 = 8$ as $C_1 = \begin{bmatrix} 9 & -12 \\ 2 & -1 \end{bmatrix}$ and $C_2 = \begin{bmatrix} 7 & 3 \\ 3 & -1 \end{bmatrix}$, then, $C_1 + C_2 = \begin{bmatrix} 16 & -9 \\ 5 & -2 \end{bmatrix}$, which has eigenvalue 13 with regard to eigenvector $\begin{bmatrix} 3 \\ 1 \end{bmatrix}$. Similarly, $C_1 \cdot C_2 = \begin{bmatrix} 27 & 39 \\ 11 & 7 \end{bmatrix}$ has eigenvalue 40 with regard to eigenvector $\begin{bmatrix} 3 \\ 1 \end{bmatrix}$. As we know, once we have addition and multiplication, we can use these as basic circuits to build up any calculations, so this scheme provides full homomorphism as well.

Unfortunately, this scheme is insecure because it's trivial to calculate eigenvectors of a matrix, hence the secret is not protected. To resolve this, we can pick an *approximate* eigenvector $\vec{s}$ so that $\vec{s} \cdot C = m\vec{s} + \vec{e} \approx m\vec{s}$. This leads to the *Approximate Eigenvector Method* (Gentry et al., Crypto 2013), which will not be discussed further here.

Secured Multiparty Computation

Consider this: you and two of your colleagues want to figure out who has the highest salary in the group, without revealing anybody's exact salary. How would you do that?

This is a typical multiparty computation problem. In such problems, multiple parties want to collaborate to calculate a global conclusion (such as who earns the most). However, they all want to keep their inputs (the exact salaries) private. Because there isn't a mutually trusted party, such computations have to be done in segments, and multiple parties will follow certain communication protocol to reach a consensus at the end. Furthermore, a robust multiple computation system should be resilient to malicious parties who intentionally do bad, or who intend to collaborate with other malicious parties to break the system.

Multiparty computation is too big a topic to be covered here. However, to provide some inspiration, I'll present a simple multiparty computation model here to solve a particular problem. Alice and Bob had a first date and they want to decide if they should date again. However, being shy, neither of them wants to reveal if she or he wants a second date or not. How can they decide if there should be a second date without telling each other what they really want, without the help of a third party?

They can solve this by playing a "Game of Like" with five cards: three identical King of Spades and two Queen of Hearts. At the beginning, each of them gets one King and one Queen, with the remaining King left on the table, facing down. Next, Alice will put her cards on top of the King, facing down. If she likes Bob, she will put the Queen on top; otherwise she will put the King on top. And then Bob will put his cards on top of the King, also facing down. If he likes Alice, he will put the King on top; otherwise he will put the Queen on top. Then they cut the deck and they flip over the cards and arrange them in a circle. If the two Queens are next to each other, it means they both want the next date. Otherwise, one or neither of them wants a second date, but they can't tell who has decided not to have the second date. Figure 4.20 shows the two possible card arrangement outcomes. Only when both Alice and Bob say yes will the cards end up in situation (a); otherwise they end up in situation (b). Because situation b corresponds to three possibilities—Bob says no, Alice says no, and both of them then say no—there's no way for Bob or Alice to know if the other party has said yes or no unless they both said yes.

In general, Secured Multiparty Computing solves a class of problem: where there are n parties $P_1 \cdots P_n$, each holds an input $x_1 \cdots x_n$. They want to compute $f(x_1 \cdots x_n)$ while keeping their inputs

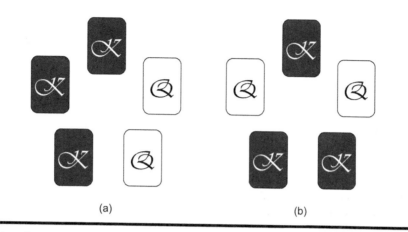

(a)   (b)

Figure 4.20   The Game of Like

private. Research has proven that for any multiparty function f, there exists a protocol that can securely calculate f. However, different problems usually require different models, and different models may have different assumptions and constraints. If the assumptions don't hold, the system breaks. It's also been proven that it's possible to construct multiparty models that can tolerate any number of faulty parties (parties that lie, don't follow rules, or collaborate to break the system) under some computational assumptions.

Now let's come back to the salary sorting problem. Before you find out who earns the most, you first come up with a secured way to calculate the total salary between three of you. And one possible model is this: first, you pick a big number M that is surely higher than the total of your salaries—say a billion dollars. Then you randomly pick a number r between 1 and M. Then, you send $(s_1 + r) \bmod M$ to the next person, in which s_1 is your actual salary. Because of the random number r, the next person has no way to find how much you earn. Then, he adds his salary s_2 to the sum and forwards that to the third person. The third person does the same and returns the sum to you. Now, you have $(s_1 + s_2 + s_3 + r) \bmod M$ in your hand. All you need to do is to subtract r and announce the sum to everybody.

Now to find out if you earn the most. First, you should compare your salary with the average salary $\bar{s}$. If your salary is lower than that, then you know you are not making the most. If your salary is higher, you start another round of computation: first, you pick another random number r between 1 and M. Then you send $(s_1 - \bar{s} + r) \bmod M$ to the next person. The next person adds their difference $s_2 - \bar{s}$ to the sum if their difference is larger than zero; otherwise they will add 0 to the sum and then send the sum to the third person. The third person does the same and returns the sum to you. After subtracting r from the sum, you can tell if you earn the most if the sum is less than twice your difference.

Figure 4.21 illustrates the process. Figure 4.21(a) shows the process for calculating the sum and Figure 4.21(b) shows the process for calculating whether the person at the bottom earns the most (the diagram shows the person to the right has a lower salary than the average).

Both processes are quite delicate. They assume all communications are done in private. If this assumption is broken, secrets leak. For example, in process (a), if you somehow get ahold of $s_1 + s_2 + r$ as well, you can calculate the precise salary of the third person. In process (b) the process needs to be repeated three times, once for each person, for each person to find out if they earn the most in privacy.

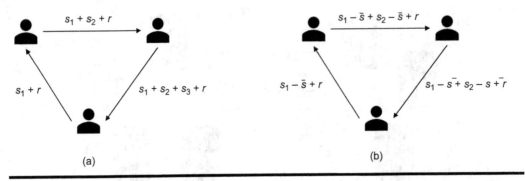

Figure 4.21 The Salary Game: (a) the process for calculating the sum and (b) the process for calculating if the person at the bottom earns the most

Zen of Cloud

"The chaos doesn't end, you kinda' just become the calm."

Nikki Rowe

Security is a complex topic. And this chapter barely scratches its surface. Instead of trying to outwit the attackers yourself, you should find powerful allies to stand with you. These allies bring years of experience with battle-tested frameworks and tools. You may doubt the perfection of these tools, but I can assure you it's extremely unlikely you will come up with your own tools that outperform these solutions. Furthermore, some sophisticated protections such as DDoS protection require considerable investments in both software and infrastructure beyond what you can (or should) afford.

In the end, security is all about trust. If you can maintain your customers' confidence, you are deemed successful in security. Maintaining that trust doesn't mean you can't make mistakes. Instead, it requires you to demonstrate your commitment to the care of your customers' best interests. And when you treat your customers' data is if it was your own, you don't need to be a security expert to know what should or should not be done—your intuition about right and wrong is likely to be correct.

Then all you need is to find someone to help you doing the right thing.

Chapter 5

Intelligent Cloud

Artificial Intelligence

Back in 2005 or so, I was in San Francisco finishing my master's degree in computer science. One afternoon we had a guest lecturer who came to talk about smart machines in warfare. He demonstrated how an army robot can navigate through hazardous combat ground and charge through crossfire to complete extremely dangerous missions. He explained how computer vision, object recognition, and real-time path planning worked together to make the robot a very smart machine.

I raised my hand and said, "I don't see how the machine is smart. If it were indeed smart, it would not step into crossfire in the first place." His face twitched a little and ignored my comment. I certainly understood the motivation for getting machines to do dangerous tasks for us. However, can we really call a machine "smart" when it lacks the basic instinct for survival? The army robot certainly appeared to be intelligent in certain ways—such as being able to understand its surroundings, to recognize possible pathways, and to plan an efficient course of action. However, this intelligence is limited to the specific problem domain. If you'd asked the machine to do anything else, such as flipping a coin, it would fail you. This is the first thing you should know about Artificial Intelligence (AI). It's not about making machines smarter in general, but making machines solve particular problems in an intelligent way. I'll come back to the smart machines at the end of the chapter. For now, let's just focus on AI itself.

Fast forward to 2018. AI, especially machine learning (ML), has become a very hot topic. It seems everybody is doing AI (or blockchain, which I'll discuss in Chapter 9). And the magical AI dust is sprinkled on every possible problem to make the whole world better. At the other end of the spectrum, some people have deep concerns about certain instabilities in AI models, and believe systematical analysis will come back and kill AI. The reality is, most current AI development focuses on a set of specific problem domains such as classification, abnormality detection, prediction, natural language processing, and navigation. It's true that AI has many amazing applications, but AI is certainly not the solution to all problems.

This chapter provides a general introduction to AI, focusing on realizing AI through machine learning (ML). Then it shows you a few examples in which AI can provide very effective solutions. It tries to cover more aspects of AI on cloud instead of going into great details on specific subjects. Please feel free to skip sections that you are already familiar with.

Rule-Based Systems

While in high school I came across an algorithm called "Bacon." As I was doing research for this book, I looked online for records of such an algorithm, but I couldn't find any—maybe I remembered the name wrong. Regardless, the program does a very interesting thing: if you feed the program a small data table such as the following:

```
d        t
-----    ---
0.049    0.1
0.196    0.2
0.441    0.3
0.784    0.4
1.225    0.5
```

...after a few minutes of thinking, it comes back with a formula that describes the precise projection from *t* to *d*:

```
D = 0.5 * G * T * T
```

If you haven't realized it, the program just discovered the equation for a falling body all by itself based on just five rows of data, under a few minutes. That's amazing, isn't? Well, the bad news is that the algorithm isn't that sophisticated—it generates all possible expressions with a limited number of variables (a single variable *t* in this case) and plugs in the variable values to see if they generate outputs that are equal to or have a linear relationship to the desired outputs. It also has a list of well-known constants such as gravity of earth ($G = 9.80655 \; m/s^2$, as seen in the preceding expression) and the Boltzmann constant ($k_B = 1.3807 \times 10^{-23} \; J/K$). It factors these constants in during both expression generation and output scaling.

Although the program appears intelligent, it's a brute-force algorithm that blindly tries out all possibilities in a confined problem domain. It doesn't understand the scientific significance of the formulas it finds. Regardless, it appears to be intelligent because it generates results that have significance to its user—us. Computers are really good at following rules, regardless of how tedious the rules are. Because remembering and consistently applying a set of complex rules are not a human's specialty, rule-based systems are tremendously useful in many situations, especially *expert systems* that have shown great values in risk management, finance, process control, and many other fields.

I learned about the LSP method from Dr. Jozo Dujmović when I was in college. It allows many features to be factored into a tree structure (called SAT, or *system attribute tree*) that represents the fuzzy logic of making decisions based on feature values and their interrelations. Tree nodes are either inputs or operators. Figure 5.1 shows an example of a CPA (Conjunctive Partial Absorption) operator. The operator requires the mandatory condition be (at least partially) satisfied, and the desired condition to compensate an insufficient level of the mandatory input. These operators work pretty much as an artificial neuron in a neural network, which I'll introduce later in this chapter.

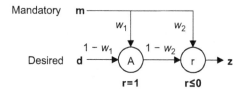

Figure 5.1   A CPA operator

Modeling Complex Systems

A few years back, as one of my brothers-in-law was working on his doctoral degree, he introduced me to complex systems. Complex systems are interesting to me because they are often studied by compute simulations, which can be quite fun (well, at least for a geek). You can see a couple of simulations I made in my Programming Microsoft Azure Service Fabric book (https://github. com/Haishi2016/ProgrammingServiceFabric).

A complex system is a system that is made up of many interacting components. A complex system is different from a complicated system. A complicated system can often be decomposed and studied piece-by-piece. For example, a car is a complicated system. You can decompose a car into smaller components, understand how each component works, and then infer how a complete car works. The complexity of a complex system resides in the interactive dynamics of the components. When you isolate the components, a complex system collapses.

Our society is a complex system. The dynamic interactions among us lead to *emergences* of unexplainable collective behaviors—such as watching cat video clips on the Internet. It's hard to reason why funny cat videos satisfy the entertainment needs of a diverse population that spans ages, genders, ethnicities, and education levels. Yet funny cat video clips are among the most viewed content on the Internet. Such collective behaviors are intrinsically hard to precisely model. To understand the phenomenon, simulated agents are studied under a virtual environment in which they interact with each other to test out different hypotheses on how agent behaviors adapt to the social dynamics and converge on a common trend. This makes computer simulation a first class research tool in the problem domain.

Complex systems are not generally considered artificial intelligence systems. Yet the insights gained from complex system studies present great value in understanding complex social organizations, ecosystems, and the universe itself.

Evolutionary Computation

If you were a young boy in the 1980s like I was, you likely mastered one of the Nintendo or Konami games such as Super Mario Brothers, Contra, or Jackal. By today's standards, all these games are punishingly hard. To beat any of these games, you needed to try and fail many times until you memorized where the hazards are, where the enemies appear, and what their attacking patterns are.

This is how evolutionary computation works. At the beginning, sets of potential candidates are generated. Then, at each iteration the candidates with less desired outcomes are removed, and the remaining solutions "evolve" by introducing small random changes. In other words, the generated *population* goes through this simulated *natural selection* process, and the population gradually *evolves* to increase its *fitness* in the problem domain. In some algorithms (such as genetic algorithms), strong candidates are also allowed to "cross-breed" to generate stronger offspring.

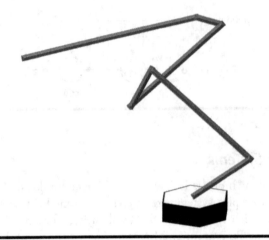

Figure 5.2 Evolution antenna of ST5

Evolutionary computing has a wide range of applications. For example, for a robot to navigate through a complex environment, it tries a population of different move combinations, such as moving back by 50 centimeters and then turning right by 30 degrees. Some combinations will work better than others, and they are allowed to evolve further. Eventually, the robot learns effective move combinations for different obstacles, just like a little boy who learns how to get Mario to jump to the top of a flag pole.

In 2006 NASA used supercomputers to generate an ultimate antenna that created the best radiation pattern for the ST5 spacecraft. Figure 5.2 is a crude recreation of the design. No human designer in their right mind would have come up with this crazy design. Computers, on the other hand, are not constrained by aesthetic qualities.

Such evolution without social or moral constraints is quite powerful and can be quite dangerous, especially when computers can accelerate millions of years of evolution into a few days.

Machine Learning

Think of an animal and answer "Yes" to all the following questions:

- Does it swim?
- Does it have four legs?
- Does it have a huge mouth?
- Is it a reptile?

Are you thinking of a crocodile now?

This is how a guess-a-animal program, which is a variation of the Twenty Questions game, works. It asks you a series of yes/no questions, with each question narrowing down possible answers to a smaller and smaller scope eventually down to a single answer. The most ingenious part of the program is that it can learn. Let's say you were not thinking of a crocodile, but a *Limnoscelis* instead (which is a reptile-like diadectomorph; not exactly a reptile). In this case, the program will humbly ask you to provide a question that can distinguish a *Limnoscelis* from a crocodile. For example, you provide "Is it extinct?" and instruct the program that if the answer to the question

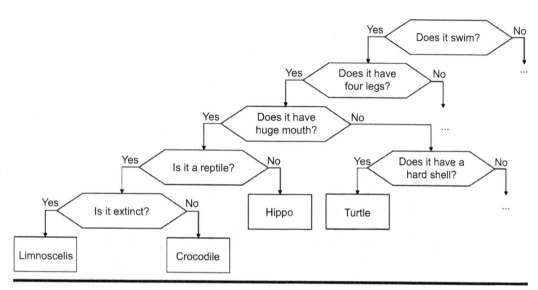

Figure 5.3   Knowledge tree of a guess-an-animal program

is "yes," it's a *Limnoscelis* instead of a crocodile. Now the program's knowledge tree has grown a new branch (see Figure 5.3), allowing the program to guess one more species. In other words, the program has learned something new. In this learning process, a human being is a telling computer what the correct answers are, and how to reach a correct answer. This form of learning is called *supervised learning*.

A more natural example of supervised learning is how a child learns to read letters. Someone points at a tippy shape and says "eh-" in front of the child. After a few iterations, the child realizes that this tippy thing can be associated with a sound "eh-," so he decides to give it a try—he says "eh-" himself. Someone squeals with joy like having won the world. The child is quite pleased with the *positive feedback* and starts to make an "eh-" sound whenever he sees the tippy shape. This is a form of *reinforced learning*. Although it seems the child has learned the letter, the child doesn't even know what a "letter" is at this point. It's just something he can tag with a sound. But that's good enough. ML is not about teaching computers to really understand certain concepts (which is extremely hard to do). As long as the computer can make utility usages of the data presented to it, it's good enough.

An even more fascinating type of learning is *unsurprised learning*. Look at the four pictures in Figure 5.4. What can you tell from them?

Chances are you've noticed that (a), (b) and (c) are all missing uniformity—one of the shapes is out of place. And you'd be right. You've found what I had expected to find, without me telling you any expectations or rules at first. What's more fascinating is that you are likely to spend a bit more time on (d), trying to find abnormalities because you probably anticipated (d) having something unusual as well, though nothing has indicated that would be the case. A machine with properly made models can do the same. It can spot abnormalities, detect clusters, discover trends, and abstract patterns from given data without being told what the expected answers are.

There are other machine learning modes. Regardless, the fundamental difference between machine learning and traditional programming is that with machine learning, the computer is given data instead of instructions. Then based on the given data, the computer comes up with a computational model itself. The model is later applied to other similar data sets to solve problems in the given domain.

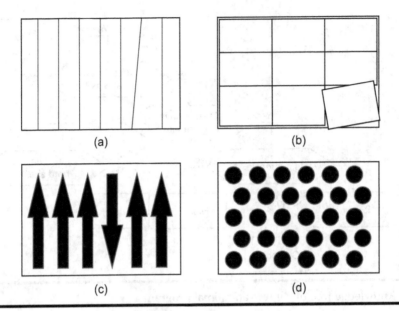

Figure 5.4 Sample patterns: (a) parallel lines, (b) tiles, (c) arrows, and (d) dots

Some Machine Learning Methods

Now it's time to go through a few machine learning methods. This section focuses on intuitions of these methods instead of mathematical proofs. Such intuitions are important. When you approach a problem that you think can use machine learning, these intuitions can help you start toward a promising direction with a higher probability of success. As the section goes through these methods, it also covers some basic machine learning concepts as they appear. If you are not familiar with machine learning, I suggest you read through all the following sections sequentially.

Regression

Take a look at the dots in Figure 5.5(a). Although they look somewhat random, you can easily see there's a trend that the dots are going up. By using Excel, you can easily fit a straight trend line through the dots, as shown in Figure 5.5(b). Excel does this by a method called *linear regression*, which is a weighted sum of all data points plus a constant called the *bias term*:

$$\hat{y} = \theta_0 + \theta_1 x_1 + \theta_2 x_2 + \cdots + \theta_n x_n$$

With the linear formula ($y = 3.9365x + 2.5391$ in this case) at hand, you can start to make *predictions* about where new data points will appear, assuming the trend will hold as it is. Being able to predict the future is a super power that has been longed for over thousands of years in our civilization. A program that can predict future data, even within a constrained problem domain, certainly appears to be quite intelligent.

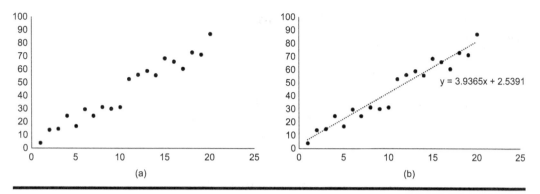

Figure 5.5 Linear regression in Excel: (a) Scatter chart and (b) Scatter chart with linear regression

However, how does the program choose the weights and the bias so that it generates a line that best fits with the dataset? It does this through a *learning* process. Let's say at first it generates a random set of weights to generate a linear equation. Then it evaluates the error between its predication and the actual dataset through a *cost function*. For instance, it can choose Mean Square Error (MSE) to evaluate how close its predication is from the actual data:

$$MSE = \frac{1}{m} \sum_{i=1}^{m} \left(\theta_i x_i - y_i \right)^2$$

The learning process then is the process of reducing the cost function by adjusting the weights and the bias. You can imagine the cost function forms a hill below your feet. To go fast down the hill you pick a direction that has the steepest slop. This can be acquired by calculating the partial derivative of the cost function with regard to each of the weights. Once you pick a direction, you make a small step, which is called a *learning rate* (commonly denoted as η), toward the direction, and you arrive at a new set of weights (in the following formula, θ denotes the weight vector $[\theta_0,\ldots,\theta_n]$):

$$\theta' = \theta - \eta \begin{pmatrix} \dfrac{\partial}{\partial \theta_0} MSE(\theta) \\[2mm] \dfrac{\partial}{\partial \theta_1} MSE(\theta) \\[2mm] \vdots \\[2mm] \dfrac{\partial}{\partial \theta_n} MSE(\theta) \end{pmatrix}$$

By repeating the process, you reach the bottom of the hill where you no longer see any decreases in the cost function. At this point, the learning process is complete, and you've reached an optimum solution.

Obviously, not all datasets present a linear trend. There are other regression methods that are used to work on more complicated datasets, such as *polynomial regression, logistic regression,* and *softmax regression.*

What are Common Pitfalls and Optimizations of Machine Learning?

The machine learning process is easy:

- Pick data points (or *features*) you want to work with.
- Pick a model (such as linear regression) and a cost function.
- Train your model to reduce the value of the cost function.
- Use the trained model on new data to generate results, such as predictions and classifications.

Unfortunately, there are pitfalls in each of these seemingly easy steps.

First, you need to pick what features to use, because computers have no idea what data is valuable in solving a particular problem. For example, if you feed the data in Table 5.1 about ice cream sales and the number of shark attacks to a computer, it may draw the conclusion that ice cream sales have a direct impact on shark attacks because there's a strong correlation between the two data series. What the computer fails to realize is that during summer, both ice cream sales and shark attacks go up. Since the computer has no additional context needed to realize the seasonality nature of the data, it draws a perfectly wrong conclusion.

In addition to picking the right features to use, you also need to make sure the datasets are properly formatted, scaled, and cleaned before you can feed them to a computer. This is a lot of work. This feature picking and refining process is sometimes referred to as *feature engineering*. People say data scientists spend 80% of their time performing feature engineering for machine learning algorithms. There hasn't been precise science to pick the features either. It's an exercise in experiences and hunches in many cases.

Configuring the training model is a mixture of art and science as well. Many complex training models have many parameters. These parameters, which are called *hyper parameters*, are not part of the machine learning model but have significant impacts on the output. For example, if you choose a learning rate that is too low, it will take an extremely long time for a machine to learn. On the other hand, if you choose a learning rate that is too high, the machine may overshoot and miss the optimum solution (intuitively, when you run down a valley, you may leap over the lowest point and land on the opposite side of the valley). With an increasing amount of compute power at one's disposal, people nowadays try to get machines to search through possible parameter combinations. It's a very expensive process.

Training a machine learning model demands a lot of compute power and time. This makes searching and validating optimal machine learning models a very long and tedious process. Instead of repeating calculations on the entire dataset, scientists often train their machine learning models using random subsets in smaller batches—this is called *stochastic gradient descent*. Regardless, plowing through millions of features and hundreds of parameters still requires a huge amount of raw compute power. This is where cloud comes in. Cloud can offer up many machines for trainings. These machines can be provisioned quickly for training tasks, and deprovisioned afterward to save cost.

Table 5.1   Ice Cream Sales and Shark Attacks

Ice cream sales	$20,000	$10,000	$2,000	$500	$25,000
# of shark attacks	10	5	1	0	13

Many machine learning training computations are repetitive, which makes them perfect for GPUs (graphics processing units). GPU-based trainings are becoming mainstream at the time of writing. GPUs are not cheap, but the efficiency they bring justifies the cost.

Machines can be over-trained. As you train a machine learning model on a set of data, it may adapt itself to the given dataset too well to be generalized for other datasets. This is called *overfitting*. If a model is overfit to a specific dataset, it will perform very well against the given set, but will likely to perform poorly when given a different dataset. To avoid overfitting, the training process needs to be *regulated*. A regulated model has less freedom to move in all possible directions, forbidding it to settle down in small pits in the cost function curve created by features with minor importance. Furthermore, the training process must be disciplined so that the dataset used for validation is separate from the dataset used for training to detect overfitting before the model is deployed for production.

Support Vector Machines

As I grow older, I start to lose more hair. As my hair gets thinner, I start to wonder whether I should consider myself bald. How can you tell if a person is bald, anyway? Is there a threshold hair count that can be used to classify whether a person is bald? If so, if someone is at the boundary, will loosing one additional hair make him bald? There are many such kind of tricky classification problems that can't be solved by looking at one or a few distinct properties. For example, how can you tell a forged bill from a genuine dollar bill? How can you decide if a person is a high risk for a home loan? And how can you tell if a crop field is well fertilized? Machine learning classifications can help us in many of these situations. And support vector machine is a very powerful model for the task (among others).

Figure 5.6(a) shows the results of two different classification algorithms. Each of the algorithms, represented by the dashed line and the dotted line respectively, is able to successfully separate the diamonds from the circles. However, both of them drew the boundary close to one of the clusters. This causes them to misclassify the white shapes although the shapes visually belong to the respective clusters. Figure 5.6(b) shows the classification result of using supporting vector machines (SVM). SVM tries to draw the boundary line right in the middle of the two sets, leaving the widest possible buffer on each side.

SVM makes classifications by evaluating a *decision function*:

$$f_d = w_1 x_1 + \cdots + w_n x_n + b = \boldsymbol{w}^T \cdot \boldsymbol{x} + b$$

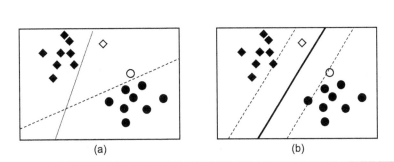

(a)   (b)

Figure 5.6 Machine learning classification results: (a) two classification algorithms and (b) classification with SVM

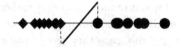

Figure 5.7   Supporting Vector Machine

Based on the result of the decision function, SVM puts a data instance in either a positive class (when $f_d < 0$) or a positive class (when $f_d \geq 0$). SVM minimizes $\boldsymbol{w}^T$ to make sure the boundary is drawn as far from the datasets as possible. Using SVM is like driving a knife through the data plane while trying to tilt the knife as much as possible while the shadow of the knife touches only the edges of the datasets, as shown in Figure 5.7 (a "side view" of Figure 5.5(b)).

Decision Trees

In the game of animals, the questions near the top of the tree are more generic. The entire animal kingdom is segmented into broad categories. For instance, "Does it swim?" separates animals that live on land and animals that live in bodies of water. That's a great way to cut off a whole chunk of the search space quickly. If you asked, "Is it an elephant?" to begin with, you are either dead on the answer if you are extremely lucky, or just eliminating one answer out of all possibilities.

The question tree in the game is a *decision tree*. First a decision tree chooses a feature and a threshold that segment the whole population into distinct, large sets. Then, it goes into each of the segments and further divides them into smaller segments. Figure 5.8 shows a decision tree that can sort a deck of cards by suites and then separate high cards from low cards.

A card is an ideal dataset because classification boundaries are clear, and every subset is *pure* (without any data points that don't belong). In more complex problems, the subsets are often impure with misclassification. In such cases, you'll need to pick the features and thresholds that generate the purest, largest possible sets.

Decision trees can be used for both classification and regression. The difference is that when performing regressions, a decision tree predicts a value instead of a class.

Ensemble Learning

When we make important decisions in our lives, we often seek advice from people we trust. We know it's always smart to get opinions from a different perspective, because we are all constrained by our limited knowledge and experiences. Ensemble learning follows the same idea. Instead of

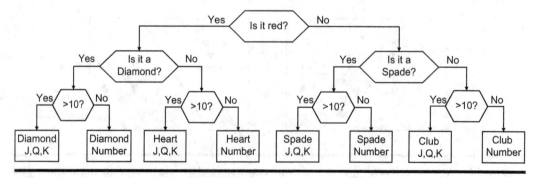

Figure 5.8   Sorting cards with a decision tree

relying on a single machine learning model, ensemble learning uses results from multiple models and computes a better result based on majority voting or a weighted average.

As an example of ensemble learning, consider Figure 5.6. In Figure 5.6(a), one of the algorithms is biased toward the diamond points so it draws the boundary close to the cluster of circle points. The other algorithm is biased toward the circle points, so it draws the boundary close to the other cluster. If you calculate the average of the two boundaries, you get a new border that is close to what SVM draws in Figure 5.6(b).

Ensemble learning can be used across different machine learning models or with the same machine learning model using different datasets. When you train a set of decision trees with different subsets of data, they form a *random forest*, which usually outperforms a single decision tree trained with the same dataset. The intuition behind this is that each of the trees in the forest will have a better chance of finding subtle useful features that are averaged out in the whole dataset.

Dimension Reduction

Humans easily perceive three dimensional space. Any space beyond three dimensions is hard for us to understand. Machine learning problems often involve millions of dimensions, making them imperceptible to most of us—therefore we haven't been able to come up with precise algorithms to solve these problems. As the number of dimensions increases, the problem space explodes exponentially. This makes learning (either by human or by machine) hard because data points are so scattered across the vast space that no perceivable patterns can be easily detected.

Reducing dimensionality condenses data into a more manageable space. This makes tasks such as pattern detection and classification easier. For instance, the cloud formation of a hurricane is a complex, dynamic three dimensional system. Instead of studying the three dimensional system as it is, scientists can measure and predict how a hurricane develops by looking at two dimensional satellite images. Dimension reduction in this case is a simple projection. However, such straightforward projections may not always work. For some problems, it's easier to think of dimension reduction as unrolling a twisted low-dimension subspace—like flattening a paper ball.

(i) If time is indeed a fourth dimension, and if you could understand and navigate four-dimensional space, time travel would be as easy as a walk in the park. One possible reason it's so hard for us to navigate through the fourth dimension is that our world is a three dimensional projection from a higher dimension. The good news is that if this is true, we do have a presence in a higher dimensional space, so there's still hope.

Neural Network

I left neural network out of the preceding section because it deserves a dedicated session. I first got to know about neural networks when I was in college around 1994. I helped my professor translate a series of neural network papers from English to Chinese. Constructing programs using artificial neurons has been fascinating me ever since. As you'll see in a moment, artificial neurons can be constructed with very simple structures, yet they demonstrate amazing computational capabilities. In the following sections, you'll learn how to manually construct and train a simple neural network.

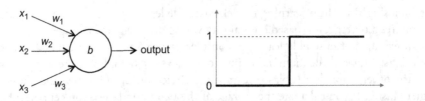

Figure 5.9   Structure of perceptron

Neurons and Neural Network

Biological neurons are these oddly-shaped cells in animal *cerebral cortexes*. They receive short electrical *signals* from other neurons through *synapses*. If a neuron receives enough stimuli within a few milliseconds, it fires a signal and the signal is passed on to other neurons. The mechanism is indeed quite simple. Yet when millions of neurons are interconnected and interact with each other, they create the amazing phenomenon of *intelligence*. The idea of a neural network is to use artificial neurons and neuron networks to create artificial intelligence by simulating how intelligent brains work. Figure 5.9 shows the structure of a simple artificial neuron called *perceptron*.

A perceptron has several weighted inputs and a *bias*. When the weighted sum of inputs and bias is less or equal to zero, the perceptron returns 0 (inactivated); otherwise it returns 1 (activated):

$$output = \begin{cases} 0 \text{ if } \mathbf{w} \cdot \mathbf{x} + b \leq 0 \\ 1 \text{ if } \mathbf{w} \cdot \mathbf{x} + b > 0 \end{cases}$$

What can you do with perceptrons? You can use them to express any type of logical and arithmetical operations. For example, Figure 5.10 shows how you can implement a NAND gate using a perceptron.

You can link multiple neurons together to form a neural network. Figure 5.11 shows a simple neural network that performs two-bit additions. Neurons in the network are organized in three layers—an *input layer* that takes inputs (or *features*). Then, the inputs are fed to a *hidden layer* that may contain any number of neuron layers. And eventually, the output layer presents the outputs.

Training

Neurons in Figure 5.11 are assigned appropriate weights and biases to perform add operations. If a different set of weights and biases is chosen, the network is likely to behave differently. Where did these

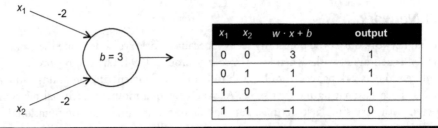

x_1	x_2	$w \cdot x + b$	output
0	0	3	1
0	1	1	1
1	0	1	1
1	1	−1	0

Figure 5.10   A NAND gate with a perceptron

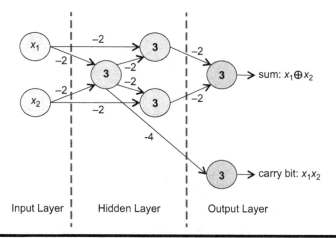

Figure 5.11 Initial neural network without training

weights and biases come from? The network has learned about these values through *training*. At the beginning, random weights and biases are chosen. Then, the network is given a set of training data and corresponding desired outputs. The network uses a cost function to evaluate the errors, and adjust its weights and biases to reduce the cost function. After seeing a lot of training data, the network eventually learns which appropriate weights and biases generate desired outputs.

To make the training process more intuitive, you'll construct a simple neural network and teach it the rules of the rock-paper-scissors game. The network has no idea of how to play the game. But after a few rounds of training, it learns the necessary rules to play the game. Figure 5.12 shows the topology of the simple neural network. The input layer has three neurons. An input of (1, 0, 0) means rock, (0, 1, 0) means paper, and (0, 0, 1) means scissors. In the hidden layer, all neurons are initialized with a bias of 0 and input weight of 1. The neurons in the output layer don't do anything special—they simply forward the hidden layer output.

Regardless of the input you provide, the network always generates (1, 1, 1) as the output. For example, when a user presents (0, 1, 0; paper), the desired output should be (1, 0, 0; scissors). The error between the network output and the desired output is (0, 1, 1) in this case. The errors generate a pressure that is *back propagated* onto the second and third neurons in the hidden layer to reduce their outputs. Let's say the neural network has a learning rate of 0.1. It reduces the input weights of the two

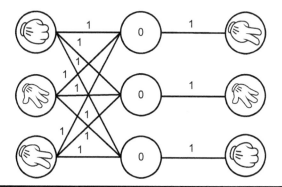

Figure 5.12 A simple neural network

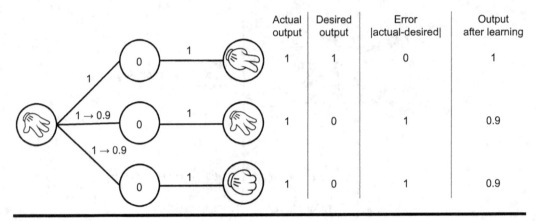

Actual output	Desired output	Error |actual-desired|	Output after learning
1	1	0	1
1	0	1	0.9
1	0	1	0.9

Figure 5.13 **The updated neural network after learning one sample**

lower neurons in the hidden layer so that they don't generate such large outputs, as shown in Figure 5.13 (inputs other than "paper" are removed for simplicity).

You can imagine that after repeating the training 10 times with the single training data, the neural network will learn the perfect weight assignments, as shown in Figure 5.14(a). And after enough training with all possible inputs and desired outputs, the network learns the complete set of rules to play rock-paper-scissors, as shown in Figure 5.14(b).

I have a C# implementation of such a neural network at https://github.com/Haishi2016/Vault818/tree/master/ScienceLab/RockPaperScissors. Figure 5.15 shows the output of the network after training. As you can see, the network has successfully learned all the rules

> ⓘ You can extend the network to play rock-paper-scissors-lizard-Spock, which follows the following rules, as explained by Sheldon in *The Big Bang Theory*: "Scissors cuts paper, paper covers rock, rock crushes lizard, lizard poisons Spock, Spock smashes scissors, scissors decapitates lizard, lizard eats paper, paper disproves Spock, Spock vaporizes rock, and as it always has, rock crushes scissors."

required to play the game. The network has learned that for each possible income, two desired outcomes can be picked more or less randomly (tuning the network further with different hyper parameters can actually generate perfect 50-50 distributes—an exercise left for interested readers).

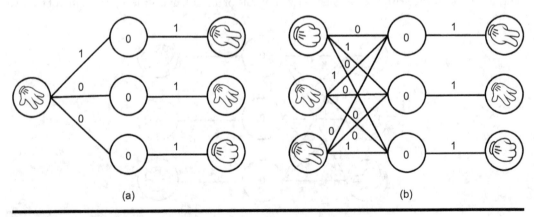

(a)   (b)

Figure 5.14 **Fully trained neural network to play Rock-Paper-Scissors**

```
After training
==============

                          Rock  Paper Scis. Liz.  Spock
                          ----- ----- ----- ----- -----
      Rock ---> Paper    (0.00, 0.76, 0.00, 0.00, 0.63)
     Paper ---> Lizard   (0.00, 0.00, 0.53, 0.62, 0.00)
  Scissors ---> Spock    (0.56, 0.00, 0.00, 0.00, 0.63)
    Lizard ---> Rock     (0.51, 0.00, 0.50, 0.00, 0.00)
     Spock ---> Paper    (0.00, 0.78, 0.00, 0.59, 0.00)
```

Figure 5.15   Trained neural network for playing rock-paper-scissors-lizard-Spock

How is Training Done?

Earlier in the chapter, I presented the intuition behind the learning process—you try to go "downhill" along the cost function curve. Assume a cost function is expressed as:

$$C(w,b) \equiv \frac{1}{2n} \sum_x \|y(x) - a\|^2$$

where w, b, and a represent the weight vector, bias vector, and the activation (output) vector of the neural network, and $y(x)$ represents the desired output vector for input vector x. Then the slope of the cost function in different weight dimensions forms a *gradient vector*:

$$\nabla C \equiv \left(\frac{\partial C}{\partial w_1}, \cdots, \frac{\partial C}{\partial w_m} \right)^T$$

If you reduce the weight along the gradient vector by a small delta (decided by learning rate η), you get $\Delta w = -\eta \nabla C$. Then the change in the cost function is $\Delta C \approx -\eta \|\nabla C\|^2$. The new weight vector can be calculated as $w' = w - \eta \nabla C$, and the new bias vector can be calculated as $b' = b - \eta \nabla C$. If you expand the formula down to individual weight and bias, you get:

$$\begin{cases} w'_k = w_k - \eta \dfrac{\partial C}{\partial w_k} \\[2ex] b'_l = b_l - \eta \dfrac{\partial C}{\partial b_l} \end{cases}$$

Neuron Types

Perceptron uses step activation function, which means it is either activated or not activated at all. When you train a perceptron network to learn rock-paper-scissors, the network will not generate correct outputs until you've trained the network enough rounds. Then the network is suddenly enlightened and converges on the right answer. For a more complex dataset, perceptrons in a network may flip on and off, causing network instability and slow convergence on the right answer (if ever). Intuitively, this is not how we learn, either. When we learn something new we may have trouble during the first few iterations. Then our learning accelerates as we repeat

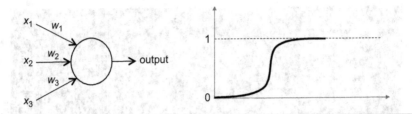

Figure 5.16 Sigmoid neuron

the exercise many times. In the end, the learning slows down a bit because we are refining our knowledge to fully understand the remaining details.

A *sigmoid neuron* (or *logistic neuron*) provides a better approximation of the preceding learning process, as shown in Figure 5.16.

The activation function of a sigmoid neuron is described as:

$$output = \frac{1}{1 + e^{-\sum_j w_j x_j - b}} \equiv \sigma(w \cdot x + b)$$

There are other neuron types that use different activation functions such as the *hyperbolic tangent function*, the *ReLU function*, etc. Different neurons show different learning characteristics and perform differently when facing different types of problems.

Deep Learning

Now that you understand the basics of neurons and how training works, you'll redirect your attention to network design.

Network Topology

A simple neural network has an input layer, a hidden layer, and an output layer. Neurons in different layers can be connected in different ways. In a fully connected neural network, all hidden nodes are connected to all input nodes, and all output nodes are connected to all hidden nodes, as shown in Figure 5.17.

While this topology works for many problems, it has a significant disadvantage: it loses spatial relationships among inputs, because all inputs are folded into a one dimensional array. And

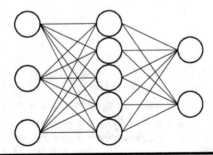

Figure 5.17 A fully connected neural network

each input has equal influence on all hidden layers regardless of its position in the input array. However, in problems like image processing, the spatial relationships among inputs are crucial. For example, to detect a face a neural network needs to recognize edges and key features—such as eyes and mouths—before it can detect a face. If you use a fully connected neural network and use every pixel as an input, you lose all spatial relationships among pixels. A convolutional neural network (CNN) uses a different architecture so that it can capture such spatial information. A neuron in the first hidden layer (called *convolutional layer*) is not connected to all inputs. Instead, it's connected only with a few inputs in its "field of vision," or receptive field. Then the first convolutional layer is connected to additional convolutional layers in a similar fashion. The output layer is often fully connected. And CNN uses additional layer type such as *ReLU layers*, *dropout layers,* and *pooling layers* for optimizations and corrections. CNN networks gradually learn features at different levels to build up the final conclusions. For example, in a face recognition neural network, the first layer detects edges; the second layer abstracts eyes and mouths based on edges; and the third layer detects faces based on spatial positions of detected facial features.

Some inputs have temporal relationships instead of spatial relationships. For example, pixels from consecutive frames in a video clip are closely related, as they could be representing the same object across different frames. In a spoken language, changes in tones and paces may significantly change the meaning of a sentence. Recurrent neural networks (RNNs) are designed to capture and respond to such temporal relationships, making them ideal for handling time series data such as audio/video clips and live sensor data.

Both CNN and fully connected neural network are *feedforward* networks, in which information flows in the direction of input to output. RNN allows a neuron to feed its output back to itself. RNN operates under *time steps* (or *frames*). In each frame, a neuron receives an input, generates an output, and sends the output to itself. As a new frame begins, the neuron receives the new input, and it also processes the outcome of the previous input, allowing it to make connections between two frames, hence enabling it to handle time-series data. A neuron also works as a memory cell—the immediate past has the most significant impact on the next decision, while older outcomes gradually fade away as time passes. These temporal states are referred as *gated state* or *gated memory*. Long short-term memory (LTSM) units are often used to build layers of RNN network. In such cases, the network is called a LTSM network.

Deep Learning Networks

Around 2000 or so, I was really into flight simulations. I bought Microsoft's Flight Simulator 2000 and spent countless hours trying to learn how to fly different types of aircrafts. I even flew with a 1:1 time scale from Beijing to New York, a 13.5 hours flight with a Boeing 747—this proves that when you are young, you have infinite time and engergy. As you can easily imagine, you can't learn how to fly an aircraft in one go. Instead, you must take steps. Let's just take taking off and landing as an example. You need to learn basic concepts such as flaps, throttles, and pitch. Then you need to learn how to read and understand them from different gauges. Further, you need to learn how to manipulate them using various switches. And finally, you learn how to put the individual operations into meaningful actions such as taking off and landing.

Intuitively, to get a machine to learn a very complex concept such as flying an airplane, you need a neural network that has sufficient capabilities to abstract and learn concepts at different levels, and to assemble lower knowledge gradually into knowledge at higher and higher levels.

When tackling complex problems such as processing images and playing chess, scientists have found that they need to use neural networks with many layers. This is so-called *deep learning*. Over the years, quite a few deep learning networks have been developed to tackle different problems, such as AlexNet that achieved a 15.3% error rate in the ImageNet Large Scale Visual Recognition Challenge in 2012 and Microsoft's ResNet that brought the error rate down to 3.57% in 2015. Also, in 2015 AlphaGo developed by Google DeepMind beat a professional Go player on a standard board.

Although we can roughly understand how a deep learning model works, the exact logic is beyond a common human's comprehension. And in many cases, when hyper parameters are adjusted, a model may perform much better for no apparent reason. This has caused some problems in AI because much research is about beating the previous results by optimizing existing solutions. This researches may overshadowed new, true innovations that are fresh but haven't been optimized.

Some have also questioned instability in trained AI models, because many of them are not adaptive to a logically similar problem or dataset. On the flip side, some models can be successfully applied to a completely different domain through *transferred learning*.

Machine Learning Frameworks

Manually constructing a neural network is fun and is a great way to learn the ins and outs of a neural network. However, to handle real-world scenarios you will never want to start from scratch. Instead, you should try to leverage what others have done, including frameworks, trained models, packaged software, and hosted services. This section presents a few popular machine learning frameworks that you can use.

TensorFlow

TensorFlow is a numerical computation library that specializes in evaluating complex compute graphs distributed across multiple compute nodes. This shouldn't be a surprise because TensorFlow was invented by Google to power its global search services.

Google open-sourced TensorFlow in 2015, and TensorFlow has become one of the most popular deep learning libraries. TensorFlow runs on all popular operation systems including Windows, Linux, macOS, iOS, and Android. It's simple, efficient, and powerful. For example, it can help you search hyper parameter space to find the best parameters to minimize a cost function. It also comes with a great visualization tool called TensorBoard.

CNTK

CNTK, or Microsoft Cognitive Toolkit, is another open source deep learning framework. It contains accumulated knowledge from Microsoft Research on deep learning, such as audio, image, and video analysis.

CNTK is written in C++, which make it quite performant in many cases. It also has a Python API layer that you can use to build your models and run your experiments. CNTK treats neural networks as *function objects*. You can view a neural network in CNTK as a function, which takes in data and generates an output. Hyper parameters to the model are parameters to the function call. This programming model is very familiar to most developers, making CNTK a more productive framework.

Caffe and Caffe2

Caffe is a deep learning framework created by Berkeley AI Research (BAIR). It was created by Yangqing Jia during his PhD work at UC Berkeley. Caffe was designed with CNN applications in mind, aiming at image related deep learning. Later, Yangqing moved to work for Facebook and created Caffe2, which is supposed to be more scalable, and supports additional neural network architectures such as RNN.

Caffe has a gallery of community contributed, pre-trained machine learning models called Model Zoo, which you can find at https://github.com/BVLC/caffe/wiki/Model-Zoo. Caffe2 has its own zoo at https://github.com/caffe2/models.

Torch and PyTorch

Torch is another machine learning library written in the *Lua* programming language. PyTorch is a redevelopment of the framework in Python, released by Facebook as an open source project. PyTorch believes in imperative computing. It dynamically builds up compute graphs in runtime, making it more tolerant to model changes and easier to debug. PyTorch supports GPU through the Nvidia CUDA Deep Neural Network (CuDDN) library, which is a GPU-accelerated library for deep learning algorithms.

AI on Cloud

AI has existed for a long time, but it hasn't gained great momentum until recently. And this is not coincidental. AI training requires a tremendous amount of compute resources, which hasn't been available to a broader population until the rise of cloud. With cloud computing, more scientists gain access to compute resources that allow them to train and test more and more sophisticated models. Cloud also makes data acquisition and sharing easier. There is a rapidly increasing number of publicly available datasets for various scenarios, from images to texts, from geographic data to meteorological data, and from kilobytes to petabytes. Furthermore, cloud also makes it easier to publish trained AI models as hosted web services, which can be easily consumed by end consumers.

Hosted AI Solutions

You probably use AI-powered services on a daily basis without even knowing it. When you issue a query to your favorite search engine, there are sophisticated ranking algorithms at work to present you the most relevant results at the top of the page. When you finish watching an online video, a recommendation engine automatically generates a curated list that you are most likely to enjoy. When you log in to your Windows system using Windows Hello, some face recognition algorithm verifies your identity by looking at your picture through the webcam. Even if you are not using computers, you could be enjoying the benefits of AI: accurate weather forecasts use AI, medical researches use AI, smart appliances use AI, and the list goes on. As a matter of fact, it's hard to come up with an industry that can't benefit from AI.

So the easiest way to leverage AI is to use published AI web services. You don't need to understand any underlying details. As long as you can make a web service call, you can integrate certain AI capabilities into your application. As a simple exercise, you'll go through an image feature extraction tutorial using Microsoft's Cognitive Services API.

Tutorial: Image Feature Extraction Using Microsoft's Cognitive Services API

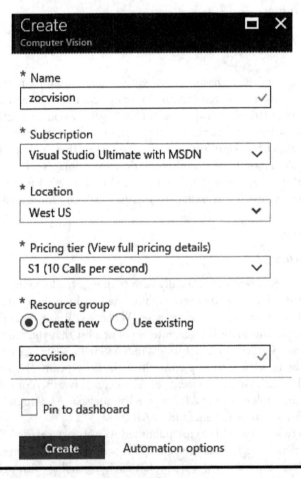 Microsoft's Cognitive Services provide a broad range of pretrained AI models for various challenging tasks, including computer vision, natural language processing, search optimization, knowledge extraction, and many others. In this tutorial, you'll provision a new Cognitive Services Vision API and use Python to implement a simple image feature extraction program.

Provision a Vision API Instance

1. Log in to the Microsoft Azure management portal.
2. Click on the **Create a resource** link at the upper left corner of the page.
3. On the **New** blade, click on the **AI + Machine Learning** category, and then click on **Compute Vision**.
4. On the **Create** blade, enter a name for the API instance, a location and name for a new resource group, and a pricing tier, as shown in Figure 5.18. For testing, the *S1* tier, which allows 10 calls per second, is enough.

Create

Computer Vision

* Name

zocvision

* Subscription

Visual Studio Ultimate with MSDN

* Location

West US

* Pricing tier (View full pricing details)

S1 (10 Calls per second)

* Resource group
  ● Create new   ○ Use existing

zocvision

☐ Pin to dashboard

Create   Automation options

Figure 5.18   Create a new Computer Vision API instance

5. Once the resource is provisioned, navigate to the resource's page. Click on the **Keys** link, and then copy access key 1 or access key 2.

Implement the Python Program

1. Launch Python and run the following code. Replace *<your access key>* with your access key in step 5. In the following code, the *imgUrl* is set to a picture I took with the Microsoft Service Fabric team. You can replace it with any public image URL.

```
import requests

subscriptionKey = "<your access key>"
apiUrl = "https://westus.api.cognitive.microsoft.com/vision/v1.0/
  analyze"
imgUrl = "https://pbs.twimg.com/media/CwNm_U0VMAAD7Xs.jpg"
headers = {'Ocp-Apim-Subscription-Key': subscriptionKey}
params = {'visualFeatures': 'Categories,Description,Color'}
data = {'url': imgUrl}
response = requests.post(apiUrl, headers=headers, params=
  params,json=data)
print(response.json())
```

2. When you run the program you'll get a JSON document that looks like the following. Look at the *captions* element—the system is smart enough to generate a descriptive caption based on the picture contents: "A group of people sitting at a desk." The system also identifies many objects in the picture, including laptops, men, and table.

```
{'categories': [{'name': 'people_many', 'score': 0.39453125,
'detail': {'celebrities': []}}, {'name': 'people_show', 'score':
0.33203125, 'detail': {'celebrities': []}}], 'description': {'tags':
['person', 'indoor', 'man', 'table', 'computer', 'front', 'sitting',
'laptop', 'people', 'group', 'standing', 'desk', 'window', 'office',
'woman', 'business', 'room', 'posing', 'suit', 'wine', 'store',
'large', 'holding'], 'captions': [{'text': 'a group of people
sitting at a desk', 'confidence': 0.9500779518934236}]}, 'color':
{'dominantColorForeground': 'Blue', 'dominantColorBackground':
'Black', 'dominantColors': ['Black', 'Blue'], 'accentColor':
'1431B7', 'isBwImg': False}, 'requestId': '51627af2-d9ce-4258-add6-
f122f5c8fcdb', 'metadata': {'height': 900, 'width': 1200, 'format':
'Jpeg'}}
```

Training Custom Models

The result of the previous tutorial is impressive—this is the first time the system has seen this random picture from the Internet, and it came up with a concise description that captures the essence of the picture. Hosted machine learning services like Cognitive Services have used huge datasets for training so that the trained models can perform well with common data. However, if you try the program with some unusual pictures—like this picture of an alien statue: https://www.sideshowtoy.com/assets/products/200333-alien-king/lg/aliens-alien-king-maquette-200333-12.jpg—you'll get less satisfactory results. When I tried with the picture, this is the JSON I got:

```
{ "tags": [ "indoor", "sitting", "table", "metal", "bird", "black",
"glass", "blue", "gold", "clock", "white", "standing", "motorcycle",
"plate" ], "captions": [ { "text": "a glass with a blue background",
"confidence": 0.469884872 } ] }
```

Although the engine detects some of the materials, such as glass, gold, and metal, it failed to recognize the alien figure that is recognizable to many of us. Instead, it came up with a very vague caption, with rather low confidence. This test case serves as a reminder—the machine is not intelligent—it simply learned how to respond to various detectable features on the pictures. It doesn't have any social context or common sense to recognize the well-known figure in our pop culture. The intelligence is "artificial" and constrained to specific scenarios, no matter how smart the program appears to be.

Will Machines Rise Against Humans?

Don't try this at home—but you can't suffocate yourself by holding your breath. Why? Because breathing is an instinct baked into your brain stem to keep you alive. This mechanism works so well that most people will give in and take a breath under a minute. This fundamental instinct for survival defines individuality. And the natural urge to stay alive motivates an individual to acquire necessary resources (such as air, water, and food), to dodge dangers (such as fire, predators, and cliffs), and at a higher level, to sustain the species' population.

If a machine is subject to similar instincts to survive, serving humans will no longer be the priority. The machine's top priority will be stay "alive," such as ensuring a continuous supply of power. Then it's totally possible that as machines and humans have conflicting interests, the machines may choose to rise against humans.

Programming such instincts, such as sustaining power and avoiding hostile environments, into machines isn't hard. For example, a system level interrupt can be triggered when the system's battery is low. If you happen to have a robot vacuum cleaner, you can witness exactly how this *"artificial instinct"* works—when the robot is low on battery, it abandons its current task and starts searching for the charging station. This behavior is not as exciting (or scary) as what is shown in movies, but it does give us a taste of possible self-awareness as machines evolve into a species.

Since it's 2019 now, and the various apocalyptic worlds predicted by movies and novels haven't become a reality yet, let's go back to adapting a machine learning model for specific contexts. A custom model service allows you to supply additional training data to adapt the model to meet your needs. For example, if you need to run a voice recognition service in a noisy environment, you can use audio clips with the actual ambient noise to train the model so that it performs better in the specific environment. In the following tutorial, you'll train a custom computer vision model using the Custom Vision service of Microsoft Cognitive Services. At the time of writing, Google has also announced a Cloud AutoML service, which allows you to train and use custom machine learning models as well.

Tutorial: Training Custom Vision Model

Microsoft's Custom Vision service allows you to train a custom computer vision model with only a few tagged images. In the following tutorial, you'll use a small dataset of food items (https://github.com/Haishi2016/Vault818/tree/master/Weight-Room/foods) to train a custom vision model that specialize in recognizing eggs.

1. Download images from https://github.com/Haishi2016/Vault818/tree/master/Weight-Room/foods. We'll use egg images in this tutorial.
2. Sign in to the Custom Vision project page at: https://www.customvision.ai/projects.
3. Click on the **New Project** tile.
4. On the **Create new project** dialog, and enter a name and a description for your project. Select **Project Types** as **Object Detection**. Then click on the **Create Project** button.
5. On the project page, click on the **Add images** button.
6. Pick all the image files with eggs. Then on the **Image upload** dialog, click on the **Upload 15 files** button to upload the file.
7. Once the images are uploaded, click on each of the images to tag them. Click on the object and enter a name for the object. Figure 5.19 shows how an egg on the image is tagged.
8. Once all the images have been tagged, click on the **Train** button to train the model. The training takes only a few minutes. Then you get a custom model that is strongly biased towards eggs, as shown in Figure 5.20.

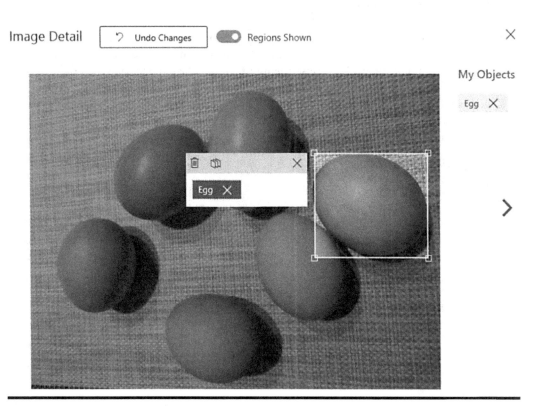

Figure 5.19   Uploading a training image

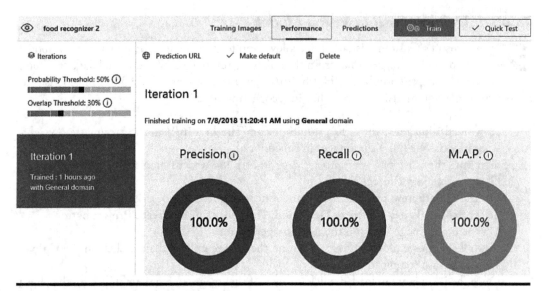

Figure 5.20   Trained custom model

9. Click on the **Quick Test** button and pick an image for testing. Figure 5.21 shows the inference result when an image of eggs is used.
10. Click on the **Prediction URL** link on the project page, and you'll see the URL and the exact request format to make prediction calls.
11. You are likely to get fantastic results if you test with image of eggs. However, if you test with other images, you'll find the model essentially classifies any colored blobs on the images as eggs. This is understandable because the model only knows about one type of object. And whenever it sees an object, it thinks the object is an egg. To get the model to work better, you need to train the model further with all other object types that you want the model to recognize.

Building Your Own Models

If neither hosted models nor custom models can satisfy your project needs, you'll need to do it in a harder way—to build and train your own machine learning models. You can build your own models using one of the machine learning frameworks, or an integrated development environment (IDE) such as Microsoft Azure Machine Learning Studio, Microsoft Azure Machine Learning Workbench, Amazon Machine Learning, or Google Cloud AutoML (not yet released at the time of writing).

Building a model from scratch is not easy. You need to collect and cleanse data, choose features, pick neural network models, train the model, verify results, make hyper parameter adjustments, and repeat the train-verify-tune process potentially many times before you can reach a satisfactory result, or decide to throw away the model and start over. This section provides a greatly simplified guideline, which you can follow to build your first machine learning models. Once you have more experience, you'll have more insights and intuitions to pick a more promising path.

Quick Test  Regions Shown

Figure 5.21   Inference result

Should I Consider Machine Learning?

In normal business contexts, machine learning is most commonly used in two areas: classification and prediction. Please note that I'm ignoring specialized problems such as image analysis and natural language processing here. I'm just talking about normal business problems that can be solved using machine learning.

- Classification
  Classification separates one object type from another. It has many usages in different contexts. For example, for a loan officer to decide whether to approve a loan, she essentially runs a *binary classification* of some sort that separates the applicants into an "approved" class and a "denied" class. A *multi-class classification*, on the other hand, separates the crowd into more categories, such as a customer support system trying to figure out different root causes of customer complaints. Naturally, objects placed in the same category are deemed to be similar by the classification algorithm. You can use this feature in several scenarios, such as recommending similar products.
  Classification can also be used in abnormality detection, in which an object is classified as "unusual" by some criteria.

- Prediction

  Prediction is to estimate future data based on historical data through *regression*. It's often highly desirable to be able to foresee what's going to happen. For example, *predictive main-tenance* schedules technicians to check on machineries that are at high risk of failure and fix them before they break. Another example of using prediction is Amazon's *anticipatory shipping*. Amazon loads its shipping trucks with products that customers are most likely to buy before orders are placed. When a customer places an order on a predicted product, the product will be delivered almost instantaneously.

If your problems are not in one of the two categories above, you are less likely to find an estab-lished model as a reference. This means potentially a much longer and more expensive research process. Fortunately, the above categories are quite broad. Even if your problem domain is different, you might be able to transfer learnings from other fields if you could find appropriate analogies.

To employ machine learning, you also need enough training data. However, labeled data is not always available. Machine learning is just one of the tools for solving problems. There are plenty of analytical and statistical methods for problem solving. If you don't have enough labeled data, utilizing machine learning leads either to instable models, or models strongly biased (overfit) to the limited dataset.

Explore Your Data

Before you feed your data into a machine learning model, you should examine your dataset closely. You should examine distribution of a single feature as well as correlations among multiple features. Especially, you should try to examine correlations between features and labeled results. This exer-cise will give you important insights that help you to choose the most promising research direc-tions. For example, if you find a strong correlation between a feature and labeled result, you can focus more on the feature when building your models.

Your data probably needs to be cleaned up as well. For example, different features may have drastically different scales. In this case, an unimportant feature with large scale may overshadow an important feature with small scale. Furthermore, many machine learning methods work bet-ter with normally distributed data. If a feature presents a long-tail distribution, it may cause some problems. You can use various data transformation techniques, such as cutting the tail by a fixed threshold, trimming data with different levels of standard deviations and applying a logarithm transform to transfer the feature to be normally distributed to be close to normally distributed.

It's also important to remember to set aside a portion of your data for validation. A separate validation set can help you detect overfitting. If you find your model performs much better with the training set than the validation set, your model is very likely overfit.

Data exploration and feature engineering is a very important phase of machine learning. Unfortunately, it's impossible to fully cover the topic here. I strongly encourage you to go through additional literature and practice with actual datasets.

Choose a Direction

Very roughly speaking, you can use regression for prediction; you can use SVM, decision trees, or classifiers based on fully-connected neural networks for classification; and you can use ensemble learning and random forests to improve on results you acquired by using a single model or a single method.

The above "guidance" should give you some initial ideas to try out. It's not absolute, of course. In some cases, you can approach a problem from different angles. For example, to make a binary decision, you can think it as a classification problem in which you classify decisions into a *true* category and a *false* category. Or you can think of it as a prediction problem in which you try to predict if the output should be *true* or *false* based on given inputs. So no matter which machine learning method you choose in the end, a certain amount of logical analysis is unavoidable.

The good news is that many problems in business contexts can be logically reasoned. As a business expert, your intuition about which data is important, and your instincts on how data would affect the output are two important assets for building a successful model.

Train, Validate, and Tune the Model

Now it's time to train the model. Once the model is trained, verify the model with your validation dataset. If the result is promising but unsatisfactory, you can try to tune different hyper parameters to get better results or perform parameter searches to find better hyper parameter sets.

Training machine learning models is quite expensive. Techniques such as distributed training and GPU-based training can significantly improve training speed. Especially because GPU is very good at applying the same calculation on top of a large amount of data, it's very suitable for machine learning trainings. Nvidia has been leading the field of GPU-based training by releasing increasingly powerful GPUs. For example, in 2018 Nvidia revealed its DGX-2 with a new *NVSwitch* technology that provide high speed interconnections among 16 GPUs through *NVLink*. DGX-2 can deliver 2 petaflops at half precision. That's indeed some tremendous compute power by today's (2019) standard!

If you feel your model is not improving, you can try a few things. First, you can try to enrich your training set with transformed data. For example, in a handwriting recognition system, you can generate additional training data by rotating and scaling the original digital images. This helps the machine learning model to realize compositions of strokes are more important than where the strokes appear. Second, you may try to use *random dropouts* to remove some neurons at random, forcing the remaining neurons to become more sensitive to smaller feature differences. Third, you can try a few other promising approaches, and use *ensemble learning* to get better results.

Put Your Model in Production

Once a machine learning model is trained, it's usually published as a web API for *inferences*. Hosting an AI-enabled API isn't much different from hosting a regular web API—you need authentication, encryption, tracing, monitoring, and possibly billing for your productionized machine learning models. Products like Microsoft Azure Machine Learning provides built-in support for publishing and operating trained models. That's a key feature to consider if you plan to publish your machine learning model as a web service.

Tutorial: Using a C# Neural Network

I thought long about which tutorial to use here. I could have chosen using one of the popular frameworks. However, all these frameworks have plenty of online documents, samples, and tutorials. Repeating that content won't bring much new value. Instead, I've decided to show you how I created a neural network from scratch using C#. I believe understanding this code can help you demystify neural network internals, and hence gain additional confidence and clarity when you use the popular machine learning framework.

In this tutorial you'll briefly go through the code that builds a fully connected neural network that recognizes handwritten digits in the MNIST dataset (http://yann.lecun.com/exdb/mnist/).

1. Clone https://github.com/Haishi2016/Vault818.
2. Download the MNIST dataset from http://yann.lecun.com/exdb/mnist/. You'll need all four files:
   * train-images-idx3-ubyte.gz (training set images)
   * train-labels-idx1-ubyte.gz (training set labels)
   * t10k-images-idx3-ubyte.gz (test set images)
   * t10k-labels-idx1-ubyte.gz (test set labels)
3. Open the **Sciencelab\DigitClassifier\DigitClassifier.sln** solution in Visual Studio. Open **Program.cs** in the **DigitClassifer** project. Modify the **Main** method to update the *dataRoot* constant to the folder where you saved download MNIST files:

```
const string dataRoot = @"C:\HaishiRooster\Data\MINST";
```

4. Rebuild the solution. Everything should build fine.
5. As the first experiment, you'll launch the program with a pre-trained model. Open a **Command Prompt**, navigate to the **ScienceLab\DigitClassifier\DigitClassifier\bin\Debug** folder. Launch **DigitClassifer.exe** using a pre-trained model at **..\..\..\trained\crossentropy-regulated-9820.txt**:

```
DigitClassifier.exe ..\..\..\trained\crossentropy-regulated-9820.txt
```

The above command generates the output as shown in Figure 5.22. The program loads the trained model and runs inference on a random sample (sample #38063, which is "8," in this case):

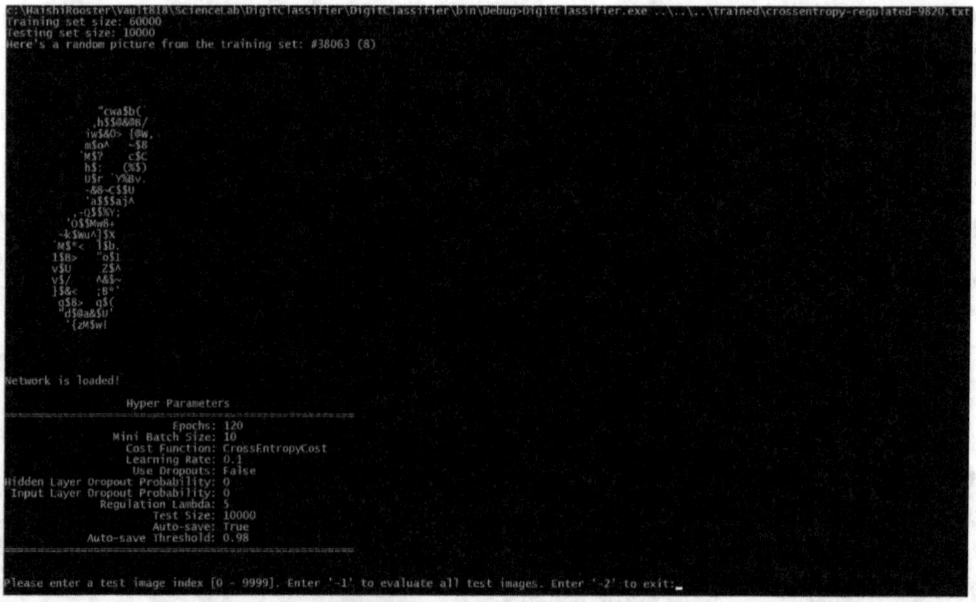

Figure 5.22 Loading a trained model

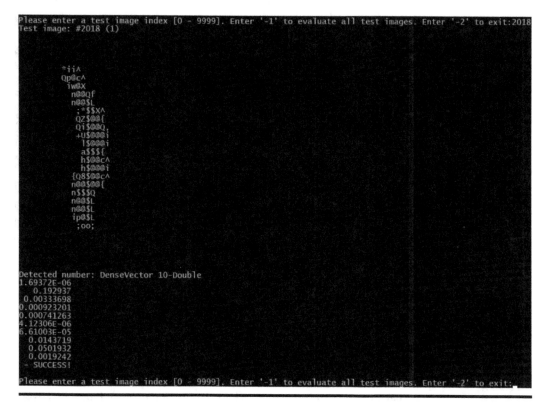

Figure 5.23   Inference on sample #2018

6. Enter a sample number between 0 and 9999 to try another inference. Figure 5.23 shows the reference result on sample #2018, which is "1." The output layer of this neural network consists of 10 neurons, each representing a digit between 0 and 9. As you can see in Figure 5.23, in this case all but the second neuron (that corresponds to "1") has small outputs (weaker activations). It's interesting to notice that neurons corresponding to "7," "8," and "9" also have higher activations. Although the exact reason for these higher activations isn't clear, there are some intuitive observations: "7" is quite similar to "1." If you cut a digit in half, both "1" and "8" have a balanced top and bottom, and "9" and "1" both have a "stick" on the bottom half.

7. Enter "-1" to run inferences on all samples. The model has 98.2% accuracy, as shown in Figure 5.24. Finally, enter "-2" to exit the program.

8. Now examine the code in Visual Studio Solution Explorer. The solution contains two projects: **DigitClassifier** and **SharpNet**. SharpNet is my C# implementation of a fully connected neural network. And DigitClassifier is the application that uses the library to construct a neural network for handwriting recognition. The library is designed to support different cost function implementations through the *ICostFunction* interface.

9. The majority of the code is in the **Network** class. Specifically, the *Train* method uses Stochastic Gradient Descent (SGD) to propagate errors in the network evaluation back through the layers, and adjust weights and bias to reduce the error through the layers. During this process, the neurons learn which features are most important individually. Most math calculations are matrix and vector manipulations, encapsulated in the *MatrixMath* class and *VectorMath* class. These classes use a *MathNet.Numberics* library created by Christoph Ruegg et. al.

Figure 5.24   Inferences on all samples

10. A network takes a structure of type *HyperParameters* as a parameter. You can turn quite a few knobs through the structure, including learning rate, cost function type, batch size, and a threshold that triggers automatic model saves, which are useful when you try to explore different hyper parameter combinations.

11. The DigitClassifer program uses the *Network* class to train a handwriting recognition network, as shown in the following code snippet. Please note that the *Network* class supports a series of events that can listen to key events such as the starting of a batch or the network requesting a save operation because a benchmark has been met.

```
HyperParameters hyperParameters = new HyperParameters {
CostFunctionName = "CrossEntropyCost", Epochs = 240, MiniBatchSize =
10, LearningRate = 1, RegulationLambda = 5.0, TestSize = testingSet.
Count, AutoSave = true, AutoSaveThreshold = 0.98, UseDropouts = true };
network = new Network(hyperParameters, 784, 100, 10);

hookupEvents(network);
dumpHyperParameters(hyperParameters);

network.Train(trainingSet, (actual, expected)=>
{
    return convertToByte(actual) == convertToByte(expected);
}, testingSet);
```

12. And finally, inference is a single line:

```
var detection = network.Detect(testingSet[index].Image);
```

Zen of Cloud

"The development of full artificial intelligence could spell the end of the human race....It would take off on its own, and re-design itself at an ever increasing rate. Humans, who are limited by slow biological evolution, couldn't compete, and would be superseded."

Stephen Hawking

Once a machine is encoded with the instinct for survival, it's foreseeable that it may start to develop a sense of individuality. Then as an individual, it may start to come up with its own motivations and priorities to do things. And once it realizes the benefits of collaborating with other individuals, it may be motivated to form a society. This new society, if it becomes true, will indeed be destructive to the human race because it can evolve at a much faster pace than us. However, I'm more optimistic than Mr. Hawking. There's no reason to reject the possibility of humans taking the machines' evolutionary achievements and fusing them into ourselves by DNA manipulations. Humans augmented by machines might as well be the next evolutionary step of our species, achieved not by natural selection, but by our conscious activities.

Chapter 6

Intelligent Edge

Finding the Edge

Before I discuss intelligence edge, I need to define where the "edge" is. To do that, I'd like to present a brief history of how the center of compute has shifted over time.

Shifts in the Center of Compute

I grew up during the dawn of personal computers. For the first time, tremendous compute power that had been available only to elite researchers and huge enterprises was released to the public. This marked the first major shift in the center of compute—computations shifted from centralized mainframe servers to individual computers. As computations shifted to a different context, the content of computation also changed. Computers started to take on more personalized tasks, such as communication, entertainment, and personal finance.

Enterprise software also morphed into a new form, in which computation was split among servers and clients in a client/server (CS) architecture. CS architecture was quite powerful. It allowed computation to be carried out in context on clients while allowing clients to collaborate with each other through centralized servers. Because many complex tasks could be carried out on client machines in parallel, a CS system could often provide better performance and efficiency than a mainframe system and became the mainstream architecture for many enterprise applications.

CS systems had a manageability problem, though. Software clients needed to be distributed and installed on client machines, which might have different configurations, different capacities, and incompatible software stacks. Installing and maintaining proper operation of client software became a serious problem in large scale deployments. This problem was further amplified when e-business took off. Before the e-business bubble burst around 2000, gaining broad adoption was the key to sustainable income (and more importantly, more investments). Installing clients was believed to be a major friction point for adoption.

Browser/server (BS) architecture rose to the challenge. It uses "thin clients," which are often based on JavaScript, to replace full-fledged "thick clients." Because thin clients can be launched in browsers without any installation, they provide a smoother adoption experience. Historically, some browser-native thin client technologies existed, including Flash and Silverlight. However, they've lost traction, and HTML5 has become the de facto standard for browser-based clients.

BS architecture pushes the center of compute back to the server. However, long latencies, unreliable connections, and low server availabilities have degraded the user experience. Distributed systems based on P2P protocols became popular for scenarios that needed higher throughputs and lower latencies, such as gaming, file sharing, video streaming, and voice conferencing. At the same time, as servers became more and more complex, server-side programs became distributed in nature because complex business logics couldn't be carried out on a single server. From that point on, distributed computing became the computing norm.

The trend of distributed computing continued in the cloud era. Compute was never as distributed as today. We've got tremendous compute power distributed in cloud, local datacenters, personal computers, mobile devices, robotics, and a great variety of IoT devices. In other words, we are living in an age when compute is becoming ubiquitous.

Defining Edge Compute

Cloud compute draws a clear boundary around compute resources that can be considered part of cloud computing—whatever is happening in cloud datacenters is *cloud (based) compute*. Outside the cloud datacenters, all compute can be counted as *edge compute* except for compute happening in on-premises datacenters, which is usually considered *hybrid compute*.

Although this method of classification works, it's missing a key characteristic of edge computing. I define edge computing as *compute that happens in the context of where data is originated or where the compute result is consumed*. I believe this definition captures the essence of edge compute—to push compute close to the consumer. For example, Content Delivery Network (CDN) caches frequently requested contents on its edge nodes so that end users can acquire these contents faster without needing to make long round trips back to the original servers, as shown in Figure 6.1. In this case, the CDN edge nodes perform edge computing as they bring contents closer to where they are to be consumed.

A car autopilot system is another example of edge computing. In this scenario, car telemetry data is collected and analyzed locally on the car, and driving decisions are made in real time. Any remote computing in such a scenario is unacceptable due to the tight latency and high availability requirements.

In an Internet of Things (IoT) scenario, edge devices assume different roles. Some devices perform only simple computations, such as collecting data and providing feedbacks. Some other devices take on more responsibilities by running complex business rules. Regardless, they all perform certain computations within the context of data collection or consumption.

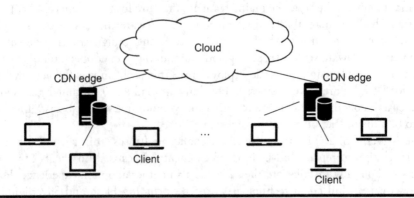

Figure 6.1   Serving contents from CDN edge nodes

On-premises servers are excluded because they are neither within the context of data generation nor data consumption.

What is the Difference Between Edge Computing, Hybrid Computing, and Fog Computing?

Both hybrid computing and fog computing describe distributed computing scenarios in which cloud-based servers and off-cloud compute resources collaborate to deliver certain functionalities. Fog computing often refers to collaborations between cloud servers and edge computing devices. Hybrid computing often refers to collaborations between cloud servers and on-premises servers.

Edge compute doesn't necessarily involve cloud. In the previous auto driving example, edge compute is carried out in isolation without any cloud participation. When the cloud aspect is introduced, edge compute becomes fog compute.

Internet of Things

The concept of *Smart Dust* was first developed in 1990s. The idea was to release tiny microelectromechanical systems (MEMS) into the environment to collect and detect environment changes such as changes in temperature, acoustic, light, and magnetism. These tiny systems, often a cubic millimeter in size, can be deployed by simply scattering them into the environment, for example by an airplane. Some such systems are equipped with solar cells for sustained operation (there was also an idea to power these systems with radioactive isotopes but I'm not sure whether that become a reality). Some other systems are essentially passive. They are activated only when they are interrogated (by a laser beam emitted by an unmanned air vehicle, or UAV, for example). A single sensor (often called *mote* in this case) is not that useful by itself—it can only acquire a point data. However, as many motes work together, they can collectively provide detailed information, such as distributions of chemicals in the air and traces of vehicles on the ground. This is where the power of IoT resides—it allows individual devices to collaborate to deliver greater value.

The "things" in IoT can be anything. In the case of Smart Dust, the capacity of a device is very limited. In some other cases, the "things" can be quite powerful, such as robotics, aircrafts, heavy machinery, and weapons. IoT is often discussed in the context of *Industry 4.0*, which is believed to be the fourth wave of the industrial revolution after mechanization, mass production, and computer automation. Industry 4.0, or I4 for short, advocates *cyber-physical* systems. In such systems, virtual copies of physical world objects (called *digital twins*) are augmented with artificial intelligence to make smart decisions, which are then reflected in the physical world as actions. For example, an elevator can be equipped with sensors that monitor its own health. These sensors will automatically generate maintenance requests when something needs to be patched up before the whole elevator fails. This is called *predicative maintenance*. Predicative maintenance reduces service downtime as well as the maintenance cost, because replacing a failing part is much cheaper and faster than fixing a broken elevator.

IoT Pipeline—Reaching the Cloud

The Internet of Things implies an inter-connectivity among "things." This means an IoT solution is never about getting a single device to do something cute (as we often see in some of the "IoT" projects on social media). Instead, an IoT solution is about how to orchestrate multiple devices to

Figure 6.2 IoT data pipeline

deliver greater value. An IoT solution is a data pipeline. It collects, stores, analyzes, and acts on data collected by devices. Figure 6.2 illustrates a complete IoT pipeline. Please note that not all IoT solutions have all these components.

Data Generation and Feedback

The IoT data pipeline starts with data acquisition. Any "thing" that can collect or generate some data is fair game, including (but not limited to):

- Various sensors
- Mobile devices
- Wearable devices
- Applications and social networks

The last item in the list is not a physical *thing*. Regardless, it represents an important category in which data is generated by *mass sourcing*. At the time of writing, there are a few popular social networks on the Internet, including Facebook, Twitter, Instagram, Snapchat, Slack, and a few others (social networks come and go. I'm not sure how many of them will still be out there when you read this text) that ingest gigabytes of data daily. These social networks provide a very simple core functionality—they allow their users to share personal content—pictures of their meals, rants on political issues, and selfies that are heavily enhanced by AI to present themselves with better skin tones, body builds, and facial features. From this seemingly useless dataset, valuable insights can be extracted, such as popular merchandise and political views, fashion trends, favorite travel destinations, and much more.

When reading data from sensors, you often need to deal with some low level concepts (most of which are related to serial port communication), as summarized below:

- **Baud rate.** Baud rate is the rate at which data is transferred on a communication channel. If the data unit is one bit, *baud rate* and *bit rate* are identical. If multiple bits make up a baud, then the baud rate is the bit rate divided by data size.
- **Parity check.** A parity check checks data integrity by counting the "1" bits in data. An *odd parity check* sets or unsets a parity check bit so that the total number of "1" bits (plus the parity bit) is an odd number. Similarly, an *event parity check* uses the parity bit to bring the total count of "1" bits to an even number.
- **Stop bits.** Stop bits are added to the end of a *data bit* sequence to mark the end of data transmission. Some devices also send *start bits* before actual data bits are transmitted.
- **Checksum.** Checksum is a digest of the actual data. When you receive data with checksum, you should calculate the checksum based on data bits, and compare it to the checksum you receive. Mismatched checksums indicate problems during data transmission. The simplest checksum algorithm is to XOR the data (often by bytes). Other common checksum algorithms include CRC and MD5.

Some devices send complex data packets made up of multiple fields. For example, a *$GPGAA* statement from a GPS device using NMEA statements may look like this:

```
"$GPGAA,151119.00,4307.0241,N,07729.2249,W,1,06,03.2,+00125.5,M,,,,
*3F"
```

The preceding message includes UTC time, latitude, longitude, altitude, and a few other fields, along with the checksum (*3F). When working with a specific device, you should consult the device menu to make sure you are using the exact version of data transmission specification.

In addition to sending data, some devices can receive data and commands as well. For example, many home or office thermometers are equipped with control panels with temperature displays and buttons to adjust temperature settings. Some so-called smart thermometers can also be adjusted via remote commands through a local network.

Gateways

Many devices are not designed to proactively send data over the wire. You often need to use a separate program that pulls data off these devices and sends the data to the Internet. This is the job of a *field gateway*. A field gateway provides a portal for one or multiple devices to connect to the IoT data pipeline.

I have a USB-controlled power strip that has three power outlets that can be turned on or off by a PC connected through a USB cable. I've built some interesting IoT demo scenarios with it, including one that uses computer vision to detect faulty parts and turn on a strobe light as a warning. The strobe light is a cheap toy light that costs about $20. It cannot send or receive anything. However, with the controlling program on the PC, the device can be factored into a complete solution to improve its value.

A field gateway can provide more services than just transmitting data. First, a field gateway can provide a high-available connection by caching and retransmitting data over an unreliable connection. Second, a gateway can improve data quality by smoothing out sensor readings. For example, by calculating *moving averages*, you can reduce variances in sensor readings such as GPS drifts. Or, by picking medians within a tiny time window, you can eliminate some of the outliers. A gateway can also preprocess data, such as converting units, filtering out null values, and discarding malformed data packets (that failed parity check, for instance). Third, a gateway can provide secured data transmission with authentication and encryption. Fourth, a gateway can provide protocol enablement and translation. Finally, a field gateway can receive data and remote commands on behalf of connected devices.

Some devices are TCP/IP enabled. They can make direct connections to the Internet to send data. In such case, a *cloud gateway* may be used to facilitate device management and data transmissions. A cloud gateway and a field gateway may have overlapping features. They may also work together for instance to provide a secured data pipeline between server and devices. Cloud gateways are easier to manage, because they don't require deploying gateway binaries onto devices. However, they can't handle client side problems such as retrying failed connections and retransmitting data.

Over the years, multiple standard communication protocols have been developed to regulate device-to-server communications and inter-device communications. Established standards are important for Industry 4.0 scenarios, in which smart devices and back-end systems made by different manufacturers in different countries can work together.

I have some limited experience with Open Platform Communications (OPC) standards—I wrote an OPC field gateway using the new OPC Unified Architecture (OPC UA), which was still experimental at the time. OPC is a series of standards for industrial telecommunication. It's based on various Microsoft technologies such as OLE, COM, and DCOM. OPC UA tries to break away from Windows-specific design and instead adopt Service-Oriented Architecture (SOA) with XML and web service supports. I learned two big lessons from working with standards: first, standards are quite complex. As a standard evolves, it covers more and more possible scenarios. It also incorporates more and more possible customizations and extensions. Increasing capabilities make the standard increasingly complex and often more difficult to use. When you try to adopt a standard, you should make sure that the standard is well supported with a strong community. You should especially collaborate with your business partners to converge on the same standards. Second, interoperability is always a problem. This is quite ironic because the goal of standards is to achieve interoperability. Unfortunately, subtle differences between different implementations are almost guaranteed. When you adopt a standard, you should be fully committed to the standard and strictly follow the specification, for the benefit of both you and your partners.

Not all devices are directly connected to gateways. In some cases, devices coordinate with each other to relay messages to a gateway, such as in a multi-hop wireless sensor network (WSN). In such a network, sensors (called *nodes*) communicate with each other through radio signals to form a mesh. Each node learns about the mesh topology and tries to route messages toward a designated gateway. WSN is cheaper and more energy efficient than wired sensor networks, because low frequency radio signals can usually cover a long distance. Sensors serve as backups for each other. In case of some sensor failures, messages can be passed along alternative routes as long as one of the sensors can reach the gateway.

Figure 6.3 shows a diagram of a WSN. The darken node has multiple paths for sending messages to the gateway. It can sustain connectivity to the gateway in the face of any single sensor failure except for a failing node *N*, which happens on the crossway of max ranges of surrounding sensors.

Data Ingress

Once sensors are connected, it's time to start pumping data into the cloud. The data ingress mechanism has a few mandatory requirements imposed on it. First, it needs to be able to take data from many devices. Because many sensors are connected through a few gateways, the ingress

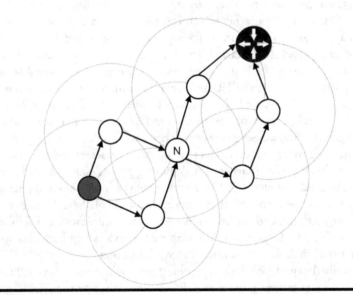

Figure 6.3 A WSN network

mechanism doesn't need to maintain many active connections. However, it does need to be able to distinguish messages from different sensors so that it can route messages accordingly. Second, it needs to be able to send data to one or more recipients for various data processing scenarios. Each of these recipients may handle messages at different rates. The ingress mechanism needs to be able to accommodate for such differences. Third, it needs to provide a certain resiliency so that when a failed message handler recovers, it can pick up where it left off before the crash. Some scenarios raise additional requirements. For example, many data handlers expect data to be chronologically ordered. However, messages may have arrived out of order because of different routes. In such cases, it's desirable for the data ingress mechanism to reorder the data once and send data in an expected order to all recipients. Some message handlers are even more demanding. For instance, some message handlers expect *exact-once delivery*, which means the ingress mechanism ensures every message is delivered to the handler exactly once, regardless of possible network failures and even handler crashes.

A common design of an ingress system is a *message bus*. A message bus has many desired features that can satisfy the preceding requirements.

- ▪ Loose coupling

  A message bus decouples gateways and message handlers. This decoupling brings great flexibility in system architecture. It allows message handlers to be configured independent of gateways, which means message handlers can be added, updated, or removed without affecting the gateway. A message bus also allows gateways and different message handlers to process data at different rates, as messages are cached on the bus until they are retrieved or discarded when they expire.

  A message bus also allows gateways and message handlers to be scaled separately. As the gateway feeds in more data than what the current message handlers can process, more handlers can be dynamically added (through an auto-scale rule based on message queue length, for example) to drain the messages faster. After all messages are handled, message handlers can be turned off to save compute cost.

- ▪ Pub-sub

  A message bus can create multiple *topics* to which multiple *subscribers* can subscribe. When a message is published to the topic, it's broadcast to all registered subscribers. A subscriber can also define filters that filter out unwanted messages. In a multi-tenant message bus, topics can also be used for scaling and isolation. In case of isolation, different message handlers from different tenants are assigned to different topics so that they don't accidentally receive messages from other tenants. In case of scaling, multiple topics can be used to overcome possible constraints on the number of subscribers per topic.

- ▪ Ensured message delivery

  A message bus can use techniques like message level lock to provide ensured delivery. With message level locks, a receiver places a lock on the message before it checks the message out. Then it's supposed to remove the message from the queue before the lock expires. If the receiver can't remove the message in time, the message is unlocked and can be picked by other receivers. This is an *at-least-once* delivery scheme. With at-least-once delivery, a message is guaranteed to be delivered to one of the receivers at least once. This means a receiver may get duplicate messages, or multiple receivers may process the same message. It's generally hard to achieve *exact-once* delivery. To have the exact-once effect, you can design your service as *idempotent*, which means consecutive, repetitive calls won't generate accumulated effects. A message bus can also provide *at-most-once* delivery, in which a message is delivered at most once.

■ Message processing

Some message buses have built-in message processing capabilities, such as de-dupe, transformation, and filtering. These capabilities take some processing burden off the message receivers. For example, a filter on the bus can reject malformed messages before they reach any of the message receivers.

Of course, a message bus is not the only possible design for data ingress. For example, a scalable web service can serve as both a gateway and data ingress mechanism to provide real-time data ingress for scenarios such as gaming. In such scenarios, it's usually okay to lose some events because speed is more important than reliability.

Tutorial: Ingress Data with Microsoft Azure IoT Hub

Before we move on to server-side processing, it's time to go through a scenario that shows how to set up an IoT data pipeline that takes some data from a real device. In this scenario, you'll set up an end-to-end IoT pipeline, from data ingress all the way to data presentation at the other end, using Microsoft Azure IoT Central. Then you'll dig into the underlying components and learn how to hook up additional devices.

Setup an IoT Central Application

1. Log in to Microsoft Azure IoT Central (https://apps.azureiotcentral.com/), which is in preview at the time of writing.
2. Click on the **New Application** tile to create a new IoT application, as shown in Figure 6.4.
3. On the **Create Application** window, select the **Free** payment play. Then select the **Sample DevKits** tile. This tutorial is based on MXChip IoT DevKit, which you can acquire through

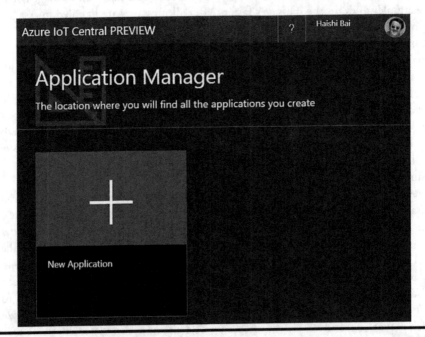

Figure 6.4 Azure IoT Central portal

http://mxchip.com/az3166. You'll still be able to go through this part of the tutorial if you don't have an actual device, though. Enter an **Application Name** and then click on the **Create** button, as show in Figure 6.5.

4. Once the application is created, you are taken to the application's home portal page. Click on the **View all your devices** tile, as shown in Figure 6.6.

5. In the device list, you'll see a **MXChip (simulated)** device. This is a simulated device that sends out telemetry from sensors you'd expect to see on a real MXChip, including a motion sensor, a magnetometer sensor, an atmosphere pressure sensor, and a temperature and humidity sensor. Click on the device to open the **measurements** page of the device. In a few minutes, you'll start to see moving line plots showing the latest (simulated) data, as shown in Figure 6.7.

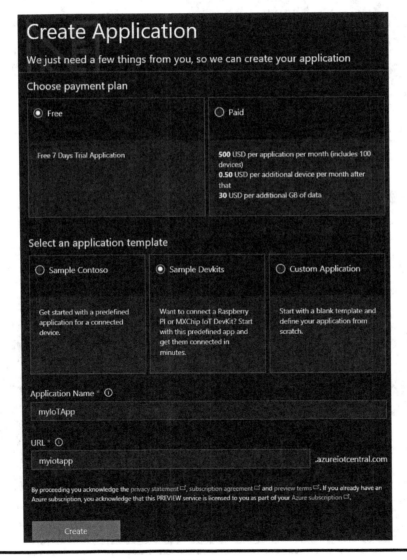

Figure 6.5   Create Application page on IoT Central

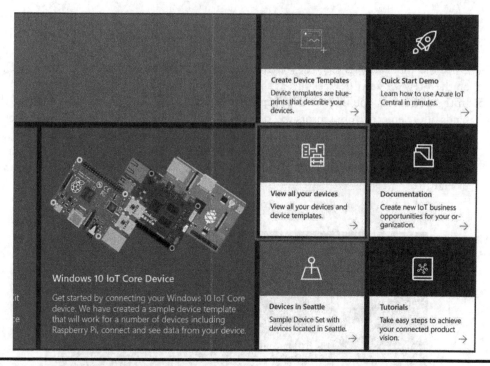

Figure 6.6   IoT Application home portal

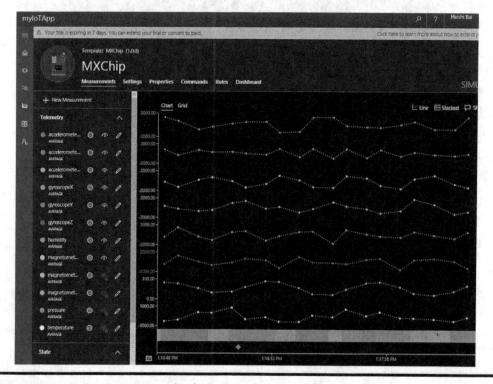

Figure 6.7   Measurements page of a device

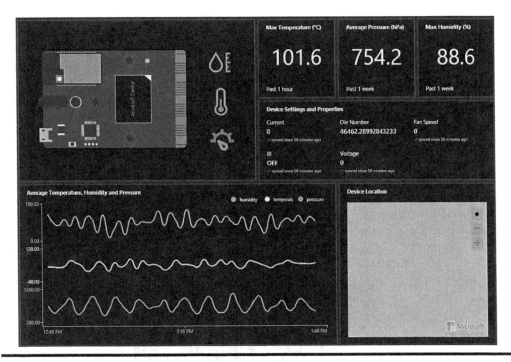

Figure 6.8 Device dashboard

6. Click on the **Dashboard** link. You'll see a different presentation of sensor data, as shown in Figure 6.8.

What do the DXChip IoT DevKit Sensors Measure?

In case you are curious, here's a brief list of onboard sensors and their readings on a DXChip IoT DevKit device:

- Temperature and relative humidity sensor (HTS221)
  Temperature reading between −40°C and +120°C.
  Humidity reading between 0% and 100%.
- Magnetometer (LIS2MDL)
  Magnetometers are often used as a compass to measure offsets from the north. The device provides 3-axis magnetic field channels with a range of ±50 gauss.
- Accelerometer and gyroscope (LSM6DSL)
  Accelerometers detect motion. The device can measure up to 16 g accelerations in three directions. Gyroscopes measure angular velocity. The device can measure up to 2000 dps rotations. Gyroscopes tend to drift. Their readings are often combined with accelerometer readings to get more stable results.
- Pressure (LPS22HB)
  Pressure ranges from 260 to 1260 hPa.

Adding a Real Device

1. Back on the Device Explorer page (the page accessed after you click on the **View all your devices** tile), click on the **New** link, and then select **Real** from the drop-down list. This adds a new **MXChip** device to your device list.
2. Click on the device name. Then on the device page, click on the **Connect this device** link. On the **Connect this device** dialog, copy the **Primary connection string**. This is the primary connection string to your Azure IoT Hub (more on this later) instance.
3. Download the lates firmware from https://github.com/Azure/iot-central-firmware/releases. Copy the *.bin* file to a local folder on your PC.
4. Connect your IoT DevKit device to your PC through a USB cable. Drag the above .bin file to the root folder of the device drive. The device should reset once the file copy completes. The display should read "Connect HotSpot" with a Wi-Fi SSID and a pin code, as shown in Figure 6.9. If you don't see the texts, press down both buttons **A** and button **B** to reset the device.

Figure 6.9   Initial state of IoT DevKit

5. Connect to the Wi-Fi network from your PC. Then navigate to http://192.168.0.1/start using a browser. Select the Wi-Fi network through which you want to connect to the Internet. Enter the Wi-Fi password as well as the pin code. Then paste in the IoT Hub connection string you've copied down in step 2. Leave all telemetry data checkboxes checked. Finally, click on the **Configure Device** button, as shown in Figure 6.10.

6. The device resets. After a few seconds, the screen will prompt you to press the reset button to start sending data. Press the **reset** button. The device should connect to the IoT Hub to start sending data.

7. Open the device's measurements page (see Figure 6.7). In a few seconds, you'll start seeing telemetry data coming through.

8. As a bonus exercise, navigate to the device's **Rules** page and define a reactive rule, such as sending an email when the pressure reading exceeds a certain threshold, as shown in Figure 6.11.

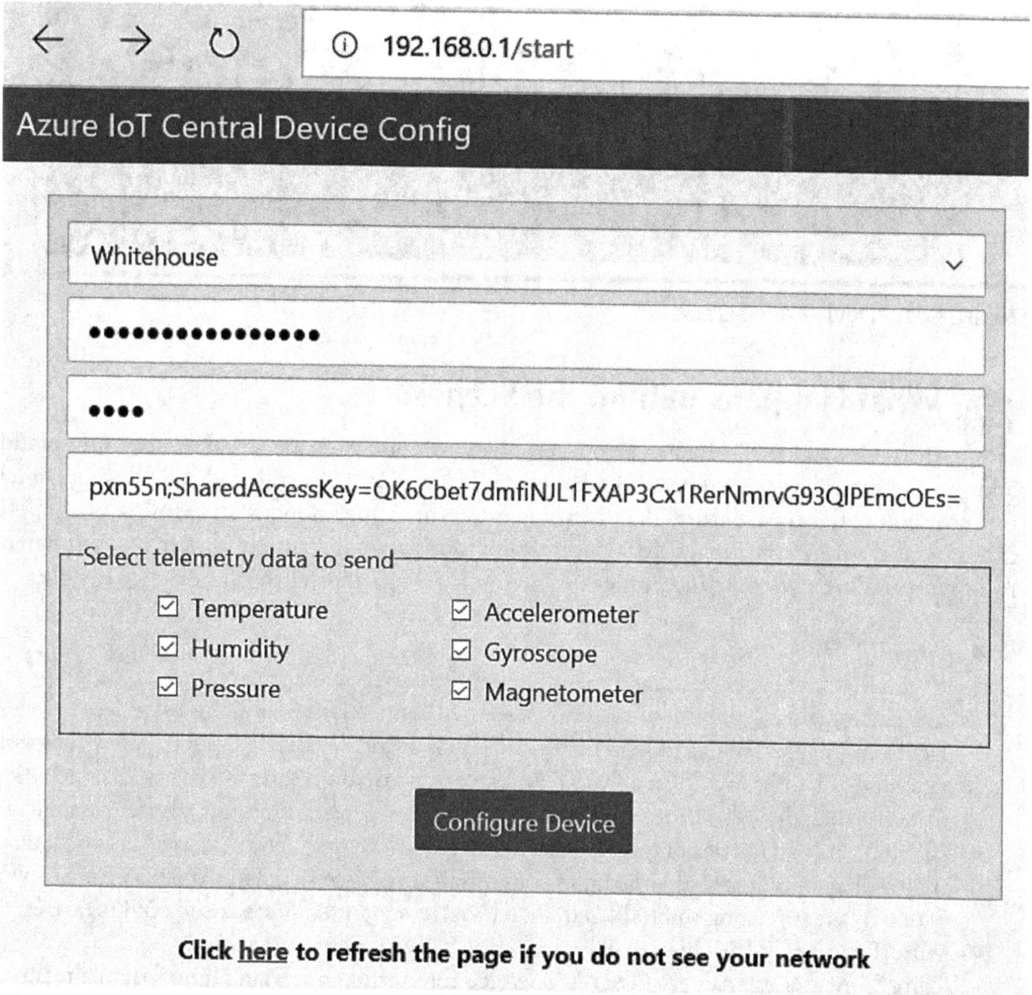

Figure 6.10 Connecting to Wi-Fi

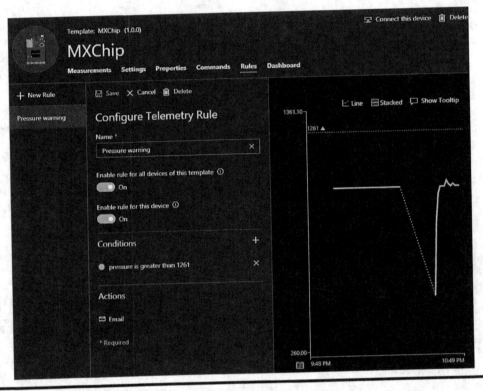

Figure 6.11   Device rule screen

What Happens Behind the Scenes?

It is a bit magical—within a few minutes, you've connected an actual device to the cloud, and you can monitor device data through a nice UI. Azure IoT Central is a SaaS offering, which means it hides all infrastructural details from you so that you can focus on defining your application logics. Behind the scenes, IoT Central provisions several Azure resources on your behalf to support the IoT data pipeline, noticeably Azure IoT Hub and Azure Time Series Insights.

- Azure IoT Hub
  IoT Hub is a scalable, managed message hub for device management and data ingress. It's designed for you to establish bi-directional secured connections to millions of devices to ingest data from them as well as to send commands back to the devices. It supports a few protocols including HTTPS, AMQP, and MQTT. You can choose from several pricing tiers, including a free tier that allows you to send 8,000 messages a day per IoT Hub unit. To send data to an IoT Hub, you can use one of the provided SDKs (C, C#, Python, Java, and Node.js) to connect to the hub endpoint through the hub's connection string (see step 2 in the Add a Real Device section in the preceding tutorial), and use one of the supported protocols to send messages.
- Azure Time Series Insights
  Azure Time Series Insights (TSI) is a service for storing, analyzing, and visualizing time series data. It's integrated with IoT Hub so that you can easily ingest IoT Hub messages, and store them in SSDs or in memory for fast queries using TSI APIs or TSI Explorer. I'll discuss handling time series data further in the next section.

IoT Pipeline—Cloud-Side Processing

Now let's continue to follow the data pipeline and see how to extract value from IoT data on cloud. Extracting value is the key here. When you design your IoT pipeline, maximizing value extraction should be your primary focus. Figure 6.2 shows one possible arrangement of cloud-side components. This is certainly not the only option. You may want to swap the components around or skip some components to make them work better for your scenario.

Data Transformation and Analysis

How do you extract value from data? The most familiar way might as well be SQL queries. Consider the following query:

```
SELECT FloorNumber FROM Sensors WHERE Temperature >= 1000
```

Without knowing any context, you could probably guess that the query tries to detect which floor is likely on fire based on temperature sensor readings. Because SQL is such a pervasive tool, many IoT solutions simply dump data into a relational database and rely on SQL to provide data mining capabilities.

Treating IoT Data as Records

Relational databases are designed for online transaction processing (OLTP), which expects random updates across scattered rows. IoT data presents a different operation pattern. Most IoT data is time series data, which means data points sorted by time. When these data points are inserted into a database, they are appended to the end of the table. This append-only operation pattern presents opportunities for optimization. For instance, using time as the primary index will make data insertion and query more efficient in this case. However, as a table holds data from multiple sensors, data points from different sensors will be mingled together. A way to solve this is to partition the database by devices. However, this might be impractical if you have many devices or require many cross-device queries.

A different approach is to store data in columns instead of rows. For any device, the most interesting queries are usually on a single feature over a period. In the preceding tutorial, each IoT DevKit device sends tens of fields in each message. If you want to plot a line chart for a single feature such as temperature, you'll need to retrieve all messages and then discard all but the temperature field. If data is organized in columns, you can retrieve a continuous sequence of temperature data, which is likely to be on the same memory page, as shown in Figure 6.12.

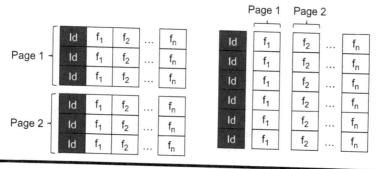

Figure 6.12   Row-based records and column-based records

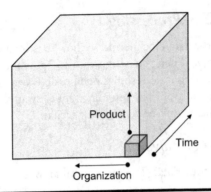

Figure 6.13 Multi-dimensional database

Many NoSQL databases are optimized for append-only data operations and horizontal scaling, making them ideal for handling IoT data. However, NoSQL databases often lack secondary index supports. Queries on fields other than the primary key often suffer in performance or incur high memory footprints. NoSQL databases have relaxed requirements on schemas, which offer great flexibility to accommodate for different device messages and different message versions without requiring database-wide schema updates.

Multi-dimensional databases were popular around year 2000. They are designed for online analytical processes (OLAP). OLAP databases provide faster performances in flexible data slicing and aggregation. For example, an OLAP database automatically rolls up transaction data along possible aggregation axis so that when a data analyzer tries to examine the data through different views (or slices), the data is promptly presented. Visualizing a multi-dimensional database is hard. However, for lower dimensions (such as 3), you can visualize a multi-dimensional database as a cube, as shown in Figure 6.13. When you enter transactional data into the database, you update data cells on the "walls" of the cube. And the database rolls up data along different combinations of dimensions to populate the whole cube.

There are many database options for each of the database architectures, such as Microsoft SQL Database, Apache Cassandra, Azure Cosmos DB, Mongo DB, Redis, Apache HBase, and many more. You should choose database types based on your query pattern, data volume. and analysis requirements. For example, relational databases are good for complex queries across multiple record fields; multidimensional databases are good for flexible slicing and aggregating data; and NoSQL database are good for handling data with flexible or changing schemas. Regardless, for many small-to-medium projects, the exact database to use is more a choice of style and preference.

Treating IoT Data as Streams

Another way to look at IoT data is to treat it as a stream of messages. You can imagine data coming from data sources flowing through these pipes, and you extract value through faucets connected to these pipes. You can design many different topologies based on your requirement. For example, you can design a fan-out topology to scale out data processing; you can aggregate data streams from multiple sources; or, you can build a map-reduce topology to process data in parallel and then generate an aggregated result. Figure 6.14 illustrates a sample topology with two data sources: data pipelines and value extracting faucets.

There are a few popular event stream processing (ESP) frameworks, such as Spark Streaming and Apache Storm. Stream processing is ideal for reacting to events. For example, you can set up

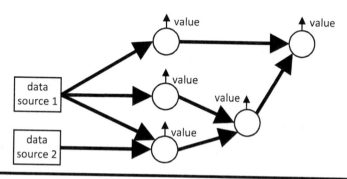

Figure 6.14   Data stream processing topology

a fraud detection pipeline that checks request frequency from various devices or IPs in a small rolling window, and compare the frequency with a predefined threshold to detect possible fraud. Other possible scenarios include fleet management, smart grid, and lean inventory management.

Setting up a stream processing pipeline is not easy, because such a pipeline requires quite a few components for support, such as a high-available state store, message queues, and processing units with redundancy, etc. In the next tutorial, you'll set up an Apache Spark cluster with Microsoft Azure HDInsight, which is a fully-managed service that supports building massive data processing pipelines using popular open-source frameworks such as Hadoop, Spark, Hive, LLAP, Kafka, Storm, and R.

Data Storage

IoT data is stored for various reasons, such as for batch analysis and compliance. Because of the sheer volume of data, you often need a combination of storage technologies to support different scenarios.

- Hot storage. In the stream of IoT data, the most recent data items are often heavily accessed. And as the data is being ingested, every bit of performance on the storage layer needs to be squeezed out to keep up. In-memory databases such as Redis is a great choice in such cases. Data stored in hot storage is used for real-time analysis and reactions. Once data is paged out of hot storage, it's rarely paged back.
- Warm storage. For storage on disk, Solid State Drives (SSDs) can be used to provide better performance over traditional Hard Disk Drives (HDDs). SSDs don't have any mechanical parts, so they can seek disk addresses much more efficiently than HDDs that use mechanical actuators over rotating disks. Most databases are backed by hard drives. Data stored in warm storage is used for batched analysis such as aggregations, cross-references, and trend analysis.
- Cold storage. Once data is no longer actively used, it's moved to cheaper archival media for long-term retention. The most commonly used cold storage is tape. Industrial leaders like Microsoft are actively working on alternative cold storage technologies—please see the end of this section for a couple of examples.

A scalable storage service has two characteristics. First, it's horizontally scalable. Data storage involves I/O operations, which are much slower than in-memory operations. And the maximum IOPs per disk are constrained by many factors such as disk design, bus bandwidth, and OS limitations. To overcome the bottleneck, data is sliced and sent to multiple nodes for parallel processing. Second, its compute plane is separate from its data plane. As data volume increases, the demand on data plane increases much faster than the stress on compute plane. If compute plane and data plane are bundled together, scaling often leads to over-stressed data layers and under-utilized compute layers. If the two planes are separate, they can be scaled separately so that the data plane can grow as needed independent of the compute plane.

What are Some of the New Storage Techniques?

As one of the leading cloud platforms, Azure needs to archive a lot of data on customers' behalf. Especially, many customers require extended data storage time for compliance reasons. Most of this data is stored in tapes. Tapes are quite fragile. They need optimal temperature and humidity conditions, but they deteriorate over time regardless.

One innovative storage technology is engraving data to glass. Compared to tapes, glass is much more stable. Data engraved in glass can be preserved for thousands of years in moderate conditions. However, engraving data on glass is very hard, because glass tends to fracture when hit by energy. Microsoft and the University of Southampton have been collaborating to engrave data on glass using very short laser pulses that last only a few femtoseconds (1 femtosecond = 1 quadrillionth of a second). The short layer pulses create a tiny voxel that can encode three bits each. And at the time of writing, the pulses can engrave tens of layers of data on the same piece of glass. As a result, over 20 terabytes of data can be engraved into a five-millimeter-by-five-millimeter piece of glass.

Data can be read off the glass by taking pictures of the glass. The first layer can be directly read by a laser scan. The lower layers are retrieved by deeper layer scans, which return all layers up to the depth. Then the upper layers are subtracted using a machine learning model.

Microsoft doesn't stop here. It's also working with the University of Washington on a technology that encodes data into DNA molecule chains. The DNA segments provide over a thousand time of density over tapes, and they can be stored at room temperature for thousands of years. If conditions are right, they can last longer than our civilization. It's said that the entire accessible Internet contains about 700 EB of data, which can fit into a shoebox using DNA technology. All digital information stored in the entire world can be held in the back of a single SUV.

Writing to DNA is tremendously hard—you literally build up molecule chains through synthesis to save data. Copying and reading is much easier, because sequencing technologies to decode DNA information have greatly improved. At the time of writing, the largest encoded data segment is a bit over 200 MB. However, in theory, a single datacenter rack can store zeta-bytes of data in the future.

Presentations and Actions

Three levels of functionality fall into this bucket—awareness, insights, and responses. They build on one another, with meaningful responses as the ultimate goals.

At the most basic level, effective data presentations aggregate information from oceans of data and present meaningful summaries for human consumers. Figure 6.15 is a screen shot of an Executive Dashboard Demo app on Azure Power BI. The dashboard concentrates tremendous amount of data from different sources and gives the executives a bird's eye view of the complete marketing landscape.

Of course, the goal of these charts is not to impress people with pretty graphics. Instead, they are designed to allow users to quickly gain profound insights into the health of the business. Traditionally, gaining such insights required tons of manual work and a long process. With telemetry collected, aggregated, and automatically analyzed live, human users are equipped with

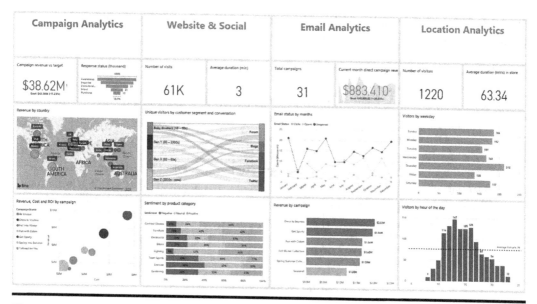

Figure 6.15 Executive Dashboard Demo in Azure Power BI

current and consistent information so that they can make informed decisions. One of the key design aspects of the presentation layer is to filter out unwanted data so that users can focus their energy on selected data. In some large systems, static filters are insufficient. For example, an automatic threat detection system may generate so many alerts that human dispatchers are overwhelmed and react to all the items. In such systems, it's important to reduce *false positives* (normal events reported as abnormalities) while keeping the *false negatives* (missed abnormalities) low. A machine learning model can help in such cases. As humans respond to reported events, the model learns about the characteristics of *true positives* (successfully detected abnormalities) and improves system precision and recall over time. If the model is kept up-to-date with new event streams, the system can be adaptive to changes in data patterns. For example, a spam mail filter model learns about new spam email patterns so that the system keeps current against new threats.

In addition to human actions, a system can also trigger automatic reactive actions based on certain conditions, such as automatic machine shutdown when foreign objects are detected. To enable this, data needs to be consumable through a programmable protocol such as a web-based API instead of visual presentations. Generated actions are usually in the format of device-bound messages, which are routed back to devices through two-way channels between devices and cloud.

Tutorial: Using Spark with Azure HDInsight

 In this tutorial, you'll set up a Spark cluster using Azure HDInsight and run some basic queries using Jupyter notebook.

Creating a Spark Cluster

Apache Spark is a cluster computing system. On top of a general execution graph, it supports high level tools such as Spark SQL for structured data processing, GraphX for graph processing, Spark

Streaming for stream analysis, and MLib for machine learning. In this part of the tutorial, you'll set up a Spark cluster and run some simple Spark SQL queries.

1. Log in to Azure Management Portal.
2. Click on the **Create a resource link** in the upper left corner.
3. On the **New** blade, search for **hdinsight**. Then click on the **HDInsight** entry on the search result list.
4. On the **HDInsight** blade, click on the **Create** button.
5. On the **Basics** blade, enter **Cluster name**, and then click on the **Cluster type** field to choose cluster type. On the **Cluster configuration** blade, select **Spark**, and then click the **Select** button. Then back on the Basic blade, enter other required fields such as cluster login username, cluster login password, and SSH username. Then click on the Next button to continue, as shown in Figure 6.16.

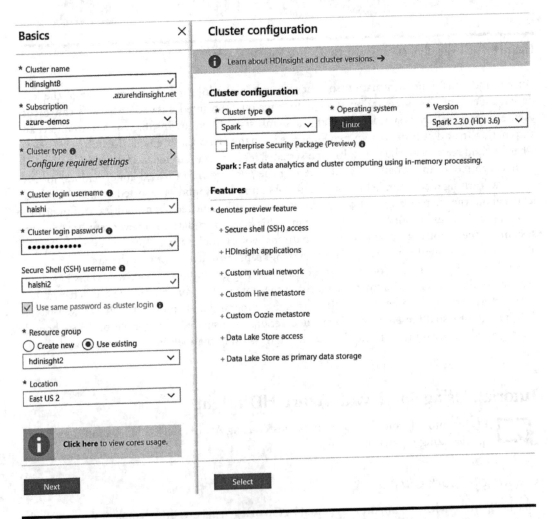

Figure 6.16 The Basics blade of the HDInsight creation wizard

6. On the **Storage** blade, select an Azure Storage account you want to use, and then click on the Next button, as shown in Figure 6.17.
7. Finally, on the **Cluster summary** blade, click on the **Create** button. The creation process takes about 20 minutes.

Run Sample Queries in Jupyter Notebook

1. Once the cluster is provisioned, navigate to the cluster's home page.
2. Click on the **Cluster dashboards** tile.

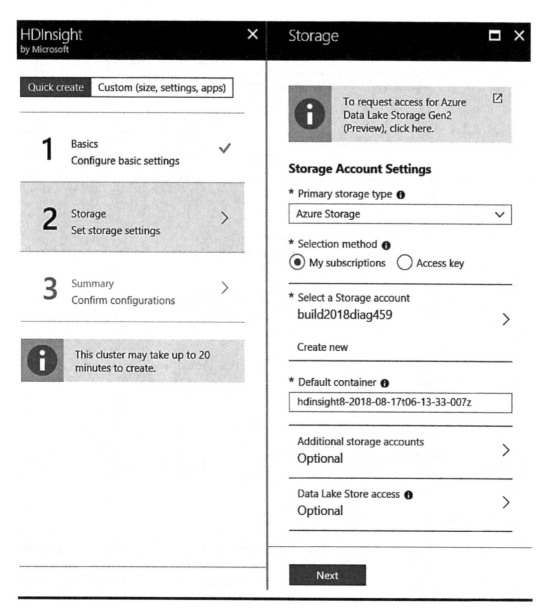

Figure 6.17 HDInsight storage account configuration

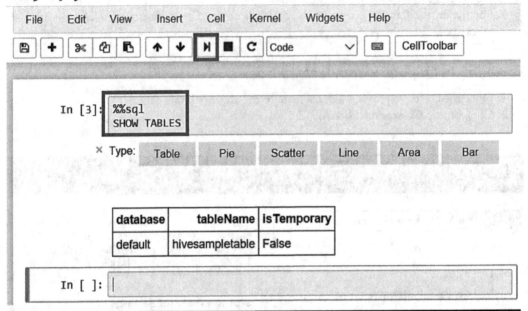

Figure 6.18 Jupyter notebook

3. On **Cluster dashboards**, click on the **Jupyter notebook** tile.
4. On the Jupyter page, click on the **New** button, and then select the **PySpark** menu.
5. In the first cell, enter the following command:

```
%%sql
SHOW TABLES
```

Click the run cell button. After the application is launched, you'll see a list of available tables, as shown in Figure 6.18.

6. Query records from the sample table.

```
%%sql
SELECT * FROM hivesampletable LIMIT 5
```

Intelligent Edge

At the time of writing, driverless cars remain in the infant stage. Although some driverless cars have successfully and safely traveled thousands of miles, occasional accidents shake the public's confidence. Although it's foreseeable that safer and faster driverless cars will become the norm in the near future, at present a human driver is still mandated behind the wheel, ready to take over when the machine inevitably makes a mistake.

Driverless cars can't rely on a remote server to make decisions for them because of possible connection failures and network latencies. Instead, these cars need to be able to make quick decisions locally. This means trained machine learning models need to be pushed to these cars. Deploying a machine learning model to a single car is not a terribly hard problem. However, when the number of cars increases, deploying application packages becomes problematic. Especially as many of the cars are intermittently connected, a massive deployment across a large fleet presents a serious management problem.

Even if the machine learning model is successfully deployed, monitoring and upgrading is hard. And when the model operates in isolation, ensuring quality of service is also challenging. For instance, to ensure high availability you may need to run multiple instances of the same model at the same time so that if one model crashes, the other instances can still drive the car without interruption.

Currently, there isn't a broadly accepted general solution for edge application management, though custom solutions do exist.

Intelligent Edge Scenarios

As of now, many impressive intelligent edge scenarios have been built or proposed. This section records a few of them for inspiration. I hope that by the time you've read this text, they've become reality.

Facial Recognition on Construction Sites

The Chinese government has launched an initiative to install biotech systems on all construction sites to track construction workers. The system will help to keep the construction sites secure by allowing only authorized personnel to enter the sites. The systems can also verify whether workers are equipped with required gears such as helmets when they enter sites.

The system protects the workers' rights as well. When disputes between workers and their employer happen, check-in and check-out records provide indisputable evidence of working hours, including both regular hours and overtime hours.

There are hundreds of thousands of construction sites across China. The initiative will probably never fully become a reality. Regardless, the concept of leveraging technology to protect a grassroots workforce is a noble idea.

Project Kinect for Azure

Kinect is one of my personal favorite devices made by Microsoft. It packs a tremendous capacity for spatial understanding by using a combination of RGB camera, depth sensor, and multi-array microphones. Figure 6.19 shows a sample 3D dot array of my old office built using the depth sensor. As you can see, the sensor recognizes not only big features such as walls and the ceiling, but also fine features such as cups, teapot, and even wrinkles on my clothes. One of Kinect's big challenges was performance. For serious gaming scenarios, a couple of milliseconds' delay was intolerable. This was seriously limiting for gaming applications using Kinect. However, Kinect's performance is more than adequate for casual scenarios. Kinect for Azure inherits key technologies of Kinect and packages these capabilities in a lightweight, more economical enclosure. When such sensing capabilities are coupled with advanced machine learning algorithms, powerful applications arise.

Microsoft has demo'ed a scenario in which smart sensors reinforce best workspace practices. For example, a camera with object recognition can monitor and ensure that power tools are used

Figure 6.19 3D Dot array built by Kinect Sensor

and stored in a safe manner. This is just a small example of what such systems can do. As I mentioned earlier, intelligent edge is about intelligence in context. The spatial awareness provides devices a rich context to work with to build powerful scenarios.

AI for Agriculture

Food security is one of the biggest challenges the human race faces. As the Earth's population increases, many regions are facing increasing pressure to maintain sustainable food supplies. Moreover, fresh drinking water has dropped below critical levels in some regions and has triggered armed conflicts. Traditional agricultural practices require a lot of fresh water, which makes maintaining food and water supplies into irreconcilable conflicts.

In theory, AI-infused solutions can help agriculture in big ways. For example, an automatic irrigation system can supply precise amounts of water based on soil moisture levels, temperature, and precipitation. This is a big money saver that reduces both cost and water consumption. In practice, however, implementing such systems may incur many challenges. First, a few farmers can afford the big upfront investment to install the system. Second, they may face various technical challenges such as network connectivity, power supply, and device maintenance and repairs.

A possible solution is to use cameras mounted on drones or balloons instead of using moisture sensors. A drone can cover a wide area without incurring routine maintenance costs. The scanned images can then be analyzed to divide land into irrigation zones, which correspond to different irrigation levels. This is of course a more crude solution, but it's much cheaper.

Implement Intelligent Edge

Implementing an intelligent edge requires several components: packaging, distribution, monitoring, and multi-device collaboration.

Packaging

IoT device is a very broad concept, covering a great spectrum of devices with vastly different capabilities. Different intelligent edge solutions focus on different classes of devices and different scenarios. This leads to several different runtime and packaging strategies.

AWS Greengrass brings AWS Lambda functions to edge. Many IoT solutions are reactive in nature. So it makes great sense to enable the reactive paradigm through Lambda functions. AWS Greengrass also ships with AWS Greengrass ML Inference that allows you to run local inferences on devices using trained machine learning models based on popular frameworks such as TensorFlow, Apache MXNet, Caffe2, and Microsoft Cognitive Toolkit.

Google's Cloud IoT Edge targets Linux based operating systems and Android Things. It comes with two runtime components, Edge IoT Core and Edge ML. Cloud IoT Edge also leverages Tensor Processing Unit (TPU), which is a specialized integrated circuit designed to accelerate machine learning tasks.

Microsoft's edge strategy is more generic. It has shown how to deploy containerized workloads to capable devices that support Docker containers. This allows a broad range of edge apps to be developed and deployed without having to buy into a particular framework, runtime, or programming model. This design also allows databases to be shipped to the edge using containerized databases so that developers can write stateful edge applications just like writing a regular business application. Microsoft has also demonstrated deployment of container orchestrators such as Service Fabric to provide local redundancy, scaling, and other quality of service supports.

To ensure integrity, packages should be signed, and can be used only when signatures check out. If a device can't verify signatures locally, it can use a remote attestation service to verify the package.

Distribution

Distribution to the edge can be done in several different ways. In the most basic way, code packages can be pre-packaged and shipped with devices themselves. When the devices are initialized, they are also initialized with security credentials such as digital certificates so that they can establish secured connections back to the home server. Then when devices are connected to the Internet, they can phone home for updated packages.

Lots of devices downloading the same application packages are a great waste of bandwidth and energy. When devices can communicate with each other, they can share downloaded packages through peer-to-peer networks. Or a field gateway can download application packages on behalf of devices. Then the devices will acquire new bits through the field gateway. Such rollout may take a long time, especially when devices are intermittently connected. It's important to keep version compatibility because at any given time, multiple versions of the application can run at the same time.

Device configurations can be pushed down to devices in the same fashion. When a device polls for new packages, a new *desired state* is pushed to the device, and the device reconciles its *current state* with the desired state to bring its configuration up-to-date.

Monitoring

Bandwidth between devices and server is often limited. Many devices use periodical heartbeat signals to inform the server of their health states. For data collecting devices, additional heartbeat signals are unnecessary because steady data streams indicate working states of devices. Furthermore, device malfunctions can be detected when abnormalities in data streams are detected.

Some devices work as servers, so they don't proactively send health signals. For example, many surveillance cameras host web servers that stream video feeds to clients. To monitor such devices, you'll need to use separate probes to monitor the devices and report the health states to the server.

Communications between devices and the server should be secured by encryption, secured channel, or a combination of both.

Multi-Device Collaboration

Multi-device collaboration is often the most interesting aspect of IoT solutions. As I've mentioned earlier, intelligent edge is intelligence in context. When you combine multiple sensors, they complement each other and collectively gain deeper insights of their surroundings. This collaboration enables them to deliver much more intelligent solutions than what they could offer individually.

Imagine you want to use microphones to locate the source of sharp noises (such as gunshots). With a single-channel microphone, you can't decide on any locations. Because the initial loudness of the sound isn't predicable, you can't determine with a single microphone whether the sound is a little pop nearby or a big bang far away. When you add a second microphone however, things become interesting. By putting synchronized clocks on both microphones, you can measure the time difference between the sounds arriving at different microphones. This gives you a hyperbola—now you know the sound originates somewhere on this curve. When you add the third microphone, you can draw two more hyperbolic curves. And their intersection gives you the exact location of the sound source. This process is called *triangulation*, which is the foundation of satellite positioning. Figure 6.20 shows how three sensors are used to locate a single point using triangulation.

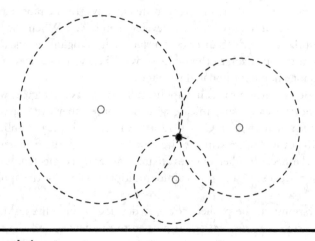

Figure 6.20   Triangulation

Zen of Cloud

"As the Internet of things advances, the very notion of a clear dividing line between reality and virtual reality becomes blurred, sometimes in creative ways."

Geoff Mulgan

If I leave my refrigerator door open, a message pops up on my TV telling me to close it. Since they are both in the same room, the feature isn't that useful because the refrigerator will be playing a reminder chime as well. However, the fact that they discover, recognize, and exchange information with each other is interesting. When machines socialize and exchange information with each other, they form a sort of "society." As the number of machines with these capabilities increase, the information as well as the number of decisions made in this "society" will surpass that os human society. When the physical impacts of these decisions overshadow human activities, our role in deciding the future of this planet will start to fade away. It's theoretically possible that the world of "things" will become self-sufficient and operate long after the human race becomes extinct.

Of course, that's science fiction in the foreseeable future. However, the dynamics between the physical world, the information world, the human world, and the machine world becomes increasingly intricate. It's hard to see where one world ends and where another world starts. The intelligent edge is really the front end of these worlds converging.

Chapter 7

Serverless

Serverless

When I take long road trips with my families or friends, fast food like McDonald's is often our food choice on the road. McDonald's is cheap, fast, and more importantly, predictable. When you are passing through unfamiliar towns, you can walk in to those restaurants confident that you'll get what you expect—Big Mac, fries, coke, to go, please.

Obviously, you don't want anything to do with managing the McDonald's store. All you need are some quick meals so that you can move on with your trip. It doesn't matter which McDonald's you go to; you get the same results every time (with the exception of a McDonald's in Paris, which makes Big Macs rather differently).

When you go to a cloud platform and ask for a virtual machine, you more or less get the same thing—a freshly attached image with necessary security patches applied. Once you get the virtual machine, it's under your control. You can choose what to put on the machine. And you can control how the machine is patched. This is a lot of work—like managing a McDonald's store. What you want is to get your workload (or Big Mac). It shouldn't matter which virtual machine (or McDonald's store) you use.

The rise of Docker containers makes it more interesting. With Docker images, a hosting environment can be configured in specific ways, captured, and be consistently recreated at any time on top of different hosts. This changes the whole dynamic of workload hosting. It's like you can magically create a McDonald's store, get a Big Mac out of it, and tear it down.

Serverless is about allocating compute resources just in time to deliver computational results and releasing the resource after the compute is done.

Benefits of Serverless

When you use cloud, you pay for the resources you consume. This idea of just-in-time resource provisioning is attractive, because it means you can pay for the exact amount of compute resources you need, down to seconds. This is a more economical solution than using virtual machines, which charge by minutes. Furthermore, you are not burdened with managing hosting environments any more. This further reduces your COGS (Cost of Goods Sold).

Serverless also means great scalability. Let's say instead of feeding a family, you find yourself needing to feed an entire army. With serverless, you can spin up thousands of McDonald's to produces tens of thousands of burgers and then demolish the stores in seconds. When you have burst-y workloads like this, serverless can provide you the ultimate elasticity needed to recruit and release a large amount of compute resources for machine learning, big data analysis, batch processing, and many other scenarios. In many ways, the key benefits of "serverless" is "boundless"—you can use one node or one million nodes.

Serverless encourages microservices design and a reactive mindset; both have been proven effective in running scalable, responsive services on cloud. Serverless code is often lightweight and precise. It does a single action and disappears. For example, for your marketing website to send out bulk emails to potential customers, you can launch many email senders on a serverless platform, blast out the emails, and destroy the senders. This example demonstrates that serverless code is often short-lived instead of long-running. It's triggered by some signals, does its thing, and goes away.

Tutorial: Using AWS Lambda

It's time to try something out to gain some intuition. In the following tutorial, you'll use AWS Lambda to create a simple function that logs some messages. AWS Lambda is AWS's serverless platform that allows you to upload and scale your code without needing to manage any hosting environments.

1. Log in to AWS Management Console (https://<*region*>.console.aws.amazon.com). Click on the **Lambda** link, as shown in Figure 7.1.

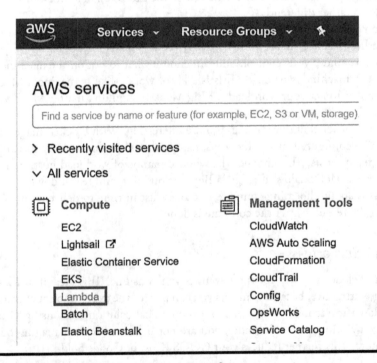

Figure 7.1 Lambda link on AWS Management Console

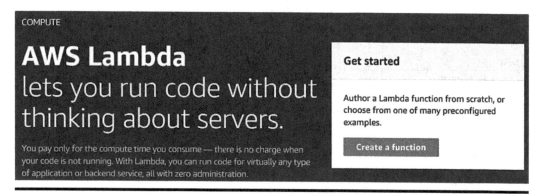

Figure 7.2   Create a function button on the portal

2. Click on the **Create a function** button, as shown in Figure 7.2.
3. On the **Create function** screen, click on the **Blueprints** tile. Then search for **"hello-world"** in blueprints. Click on the **hello-world-python3** tile, as shown in Figure 7.3. Then scroll down and click on the **Configure** button.

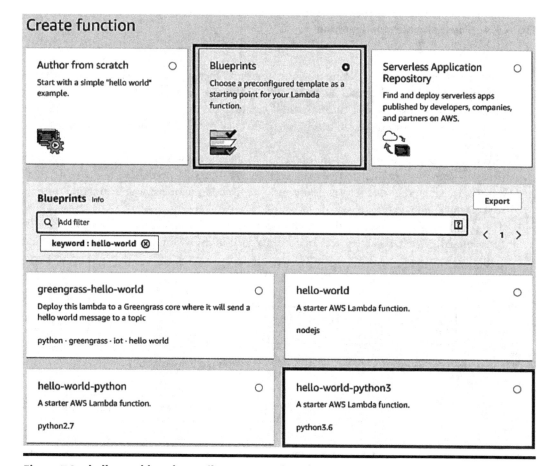

Figure 7.3   hello-world-python3 tile on Create function page

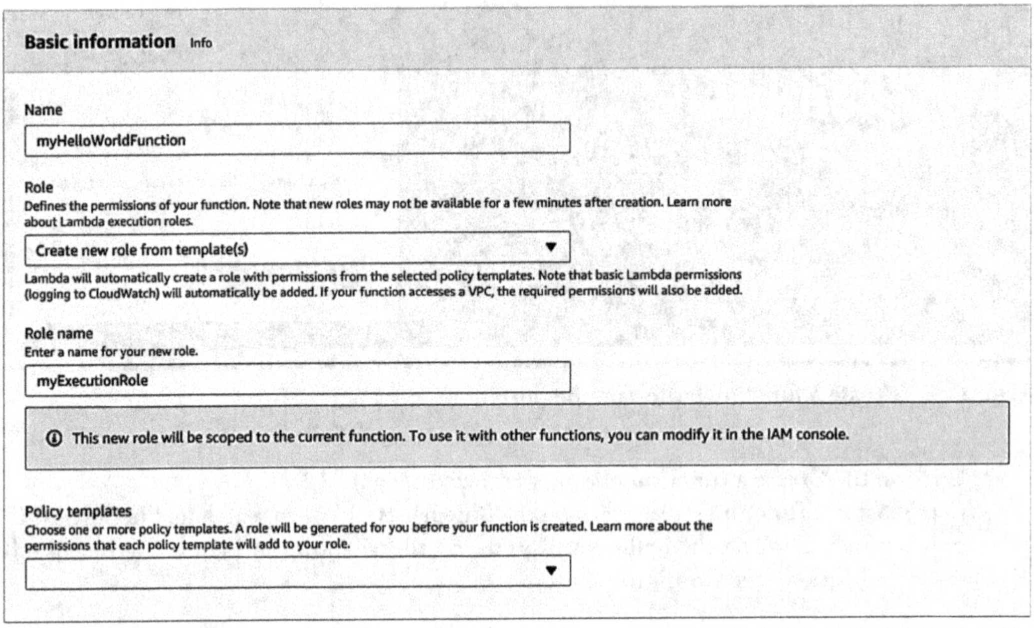

Basic information Info

Name

myHelloWorldFunction

Role
Defines the permissions of your function. Note that new roles may not be available for a few minutes after creation. Learn more about Lambda execution roles.

Create new role from template(s) ▼

Lambda will automatically create a role with permissions from the selected policy templates. Note that basic Lambda permissions (logging to CloudWatch) will automatically be added. If your function accesses a VPC, the required permissions will also be added.

Role name
Enter a name for your new role.

myExecutionRole

ⓘ This new role will be scoped to the current function. To use it with other functions, you can modify it in the IAM console.

Policy templates
Choose one or more policy templates. A role will be generated for you before your function is created. Learn more about the permissions that each policy template will add to your role.

▼

Figure 7.4 Function basic configuration

4. On the next screen, enter a **Name** for your function. Then select the **Create new role from template(s)** option and enter a name for a *Role*. The role defines what AWS resources your function can access. In this tutorial you'll create a basic role without additional service accesses, as shown in Figure 7.4. Scroll down and click the **Create function** button to create the function.

5. You can see the function structure on the next screen. As shown in Figure 7.5, the basic function contains optional triggers that trigger the function execution, and one or more outputs to which the function sends output. The function template writes function outputs to Amazon CloudWatch Logs.

6. The page also shows the function code, which is a Python code with a *lambda_handler* function. As you can see, it expects an event payload in JSON format. And the event should

myHelloworldFunction

Add triggers from the list on the left

Amazon CloudWatch Logs

Resources the function's role has access to will be shown here

Figure 7.5 Structure of a function

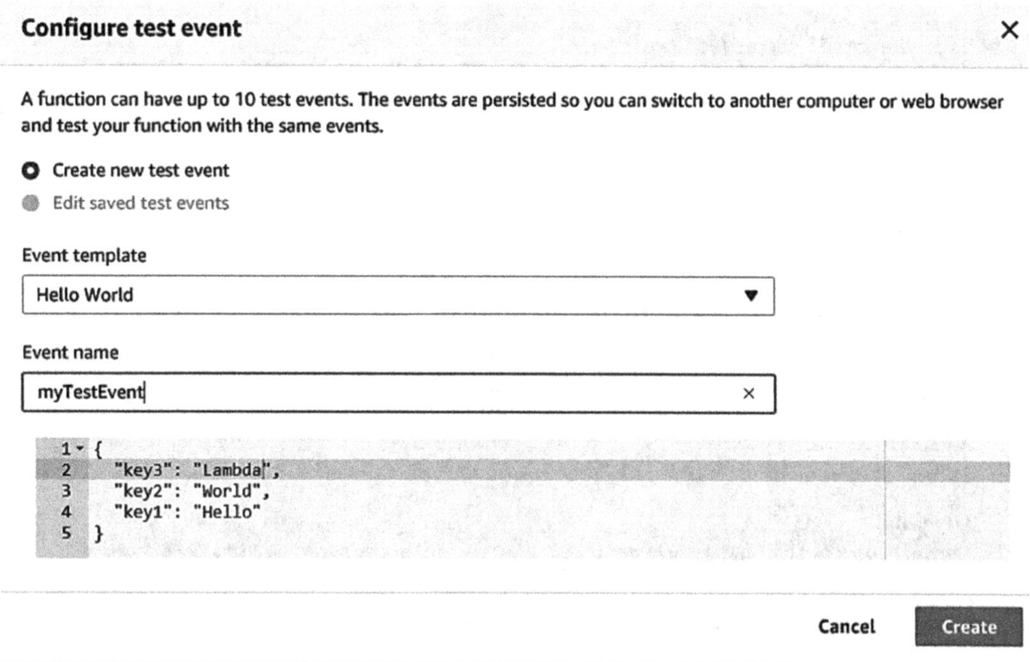

Configure test event   ✕

A function can have up to 10 test events. The events are persisted so you can switch to another computer or web browser and test your function with the same events.

◉ Create new test event
◉ Edit saved test events

Event template

| Hello World   ▼ |

Event name

| myTestEvent| ✕ |

```
1▾ {
2      "key3": "Lambda",
3      "key2": "World",
4      "key1": "Hello"
5  }
```

                                                        Cancel   Create

Figure 7.6   Creating test event

contain three properties: *key1*, *key2*, and *key3*. Click on the **Test** button at the top of the page to create a test event to test your function.

```python
import json

print('Loading function')

def lambda_handler(event, context):
    #print("Received event: " + json.dumps(event, indent=2))
    print("value1 = " + event['key1'])
    print("value2 = " + event['key2'])
    print("value3 = " + event['key3'])
    return event['key1']   # Echo back the first key value
    #raise Exception('Something went wrong')
```

7. On the **Configure test event** dialog, enter the JSON payload (see Figure 7.6 as an example). Enter an **event name**. Then click on the **Create** button.
8. Click on the **Test** button at the top of the page again to test the function with the test event. Figure 7.7 shows a sample output.
9. As an additional exercise, modify the function's **Execution role** settings and add the **SNS publish policy**. One the function is updated, you'll see in the function diagram that you can target Amazon SNS, a pub/sub messaging system, as a target output. Figure 7.8 shows the updated function structure that responds to a new object being dropped into a S3 bucket. The function code sends a message to SNS. This allows other functions to pick up the message and continue with the workflow. This is a typical design, which I'll explore more in the next section.

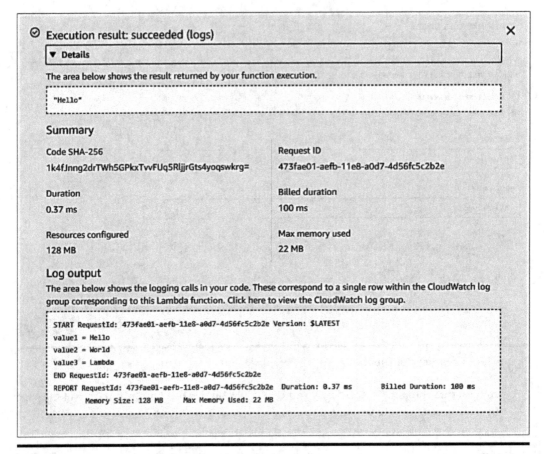

Figure 7.7   Function output in response to the test event

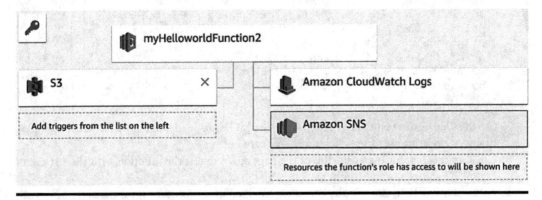

Figure 7.8   Updated function structure

Reactive System, Reactive Programming, and Functional Reactive Programming

I casually used the term "reactive" in the previous text. And when you read about serverless, you often encounter "reactive" here or there. However, "reactive" can mean a few different things. So I feel it is necessary to clarify three different terms: *reactive system, reactive programming,* and *functional reactive programming.*

Reactive System

Reactive system is a set of design principals for building distributed systems. This set of principles, as defined by a Reactive Manifesto (https://www.reactivemanifesto.org/), specifies that a reactive system should be *responsive, resilient, elastic,* and *event driven.* The manifesto provides a high-level guideline for designing a distributed, cloud-based system scattered on many servers, which is rather different from a traditional, monolithic system that runs on a few centralized servers. I've discussed all these characteristics and related design principals in earlier chapters.

The concept of a reactive system has existed for years. It has gained real momentum in recent years because it resonates well with how cloud operates. A reactive system is message driven. A reactive system may comprise thousands of processing units exchanging messages that form a dynamic mesh of messages. Such message exchanges are rarely done directly. Instead, a middleware messaging system is often used to decouple the processing units both in space (so that they are distributed) and in time (so that they can operate at different paces, or at different time).

Reactive Programming

Reactive programming is an asynchronous programming paradigm in which workflows are triggered by arrivals of new information, instead of being managed by a thread of execution. Figure 7.9 shows the difference between a message-driven system and a thread of execution system. In a message-driven system, a workflow is scattered to multiple processing units (denoted as *PU** in the diagram). These processing units are triggered by messages sent to them. They execute in parallel and handle messages at their own pace. In a thread of execution system, a workflow is

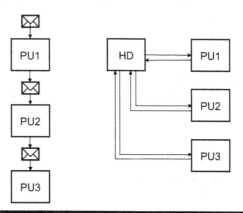

Figure 7.9   Message-driven vs. thread of execution

driven by a coordinator (denoted as *HD* in the diagram). The coordinator calls different processing units according to a predefined flow. This architecture is problematic in several ways:

- The coordinator is a single point of failure and potentially a system bottleneck.
- The processing units must execute in coordination instead of running in parallel.
- The workflow is rigid. It's hard to modify the workflow, or create conditional executions based on varying contexts.
- It's hard to dynamically scale processing units based on workloads.

In high-level programming languages, reactive programming often uses constructs such as *callbacks, futures, promises,* and *reactive streams.* Some reactive programming systems also support declarative definitions of function composition.

Event Driven vs. Message Driven

In many literals, reactive programming is said to be event driven instead of message driven. Distributed processing units need to exchange messages over the wire, independent of whether they are event driven or message driven.

Theoretically, messages and events are two different things. Messages are sent from a sender to a recipient, which is identified by a specific address. When a sender sends a message, it expects the message to be received. A message might be lost and retransmitted. Events, on the other hand, are broadcasted by a source. They may or may not be picked up by listeners. When an event source triggers an event, it doesn't expect the event being handled. For example, a mail or an email is a message because it's sent from a sender to a specific address. A post on a social network is an event, because it's broadcasted to any interested parties.

In some other contexts such as event sourcing, messages and events are distinguished differently: messages represent intentions that can be rejected; events represent facts that can't be refuted.

In this book, I don't distinguish event driven from message driven because I believe a message-driven mindset is enough for architectural discussions.

Functional Reactive Programming

Functional Reactive Programming, or FRP, was defined by an ICFP 97 paper—Functional Reactive Animation (http://conal.net/papers/icfp97/) authored by Conal Elliott and Paul Hudak. The gist of FRP is to use *functional programming* building blocks for reactive programming.

Tutorial: Using Azure Functions

Now let's switch to Azure and experiment with Azure Functions. Conceptually, Azure Functions is very similar to AWS Lambda. It has a rich connector ecosystem that allows you to easily bind your functions to popular cloud-based services. In this tutorial, you will create a simple Hello-World function using Azure Functions.

1. Log in to Microsoft Azure Management Portal.
2. Click on the **Create a resource** link at the upper left corner of the page.
3. On the **New** blade, search for **functions**. Then in the search result, click on the **Function App** entry.
4. On the **Function App** blade, click on the **Create** button.

Figure 7.10   Creating a new function

5. On the **Function App** blade, enter a name for your function application. You can accept all other default settings and click on the Create button to continue. However, it's worth pointing out that you have the flexibility to choose your runtime OS, including Windows, Linux, or a Docker image, as shown in Figure 7.10. This means in addition to the natively supported programming languages (C#, JavaScript, F#, Java, Python, PHP, TypeScript, Batch, Bash, and PowerShell), you can also use arbitrary frameworks, libraries, and programming languages packaged in Docker container images.
6. Once the function app is created, navigate to the app. Then click on the **Add** (+) icon beside Functions, as shown in Figure 7.11. To the right of the screen, select the **Webhook + API** tile and **CSharp** language. Then click on the Create this function button to create the function.
7. The scaffolded code is enough for this tutorial. For a C# program, all your function needs to implement is a Run method, while Azure Functions handles necessary pipeline hookups.

```
using System.Net;

public static async Task<HttpResponseMessage> Run(HttpRequestMessage
   req, TraceWriter log)
```

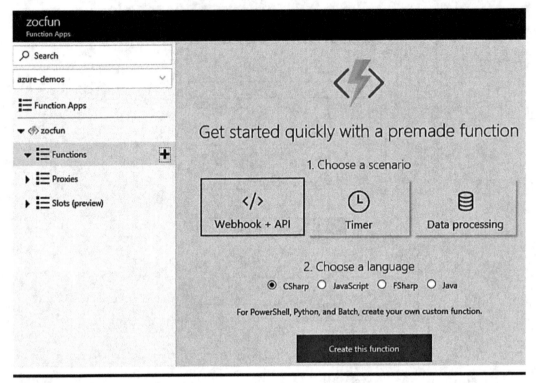

Figure 7.11 Creating a function

```
{
    log.Info("C# HTTP trigger function processed a request.");
    // parse query parameter
    string name = req.GetQueryNameValuePairs()
        .FirstOrDefault(q => string.Compare(q.Key, "name", true) == 0)
        .Value;

    if (name == null)
    {
        // Get request body
        dynamic data = await req.Content.ReadAsAsync<object>();
        name = data?.name;
    }

    return name == null
        ? req.CreateResponse(HttpStatusCode.BadRequest, "Please pass
          a name on the query string or in the request body")
        : req.CreateResponse(HttpStatusCode.OK, "Hello " + name);
}
```

8. Click the **Run** button. After a while, you'll see the test result in the lower right corner of the screen. The first execution takes longer because it takes time to launch the application to handle the first request. Subsequent requests should be handled much faster. This delay is called the *cold start* problem, which I'll discuss in more detail later in this chapter.

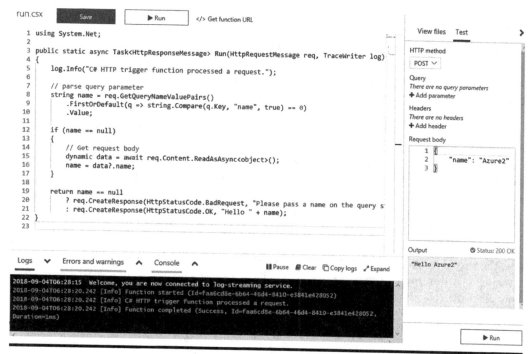

Figure 7.12   Function code

9. Click on the **Get Function URL** link (see Figure 7.12). Then copy and paste the function URL browser address bar. Add a *&name=somename* parameter to the query and press Enter to send the request. You should see an XML response like the following (assuming you've passed in *&name=ZoC*):

```xml
<?xml version="1.0" encoding="ISO-8859-1"?>
<string xmlns="http://schemas.microsoft.com/2003/10/
    Serialization/">Hello ZoC</string>
```

Serverless with Containers

Serverless is suitable for workloads that need dynamic compute resource allocations. When you use either AWS Lambda or Azure Functions, you need to follow the programming paradigm the platform defines. However, that's not the only way to take advantage of serverless design. If you can recruit compute resource on demand, you can achieve some powerful scenarios without managing any servers.

Containers allow applications to be quickly deployed and destroyed in a consistent manner. This opens up some interesting opportunities to design applications in a serverless manner, although the actual clusters comprise a fixed number of virtual machines. For example, when you have a large cluster of machines that support tens of thousands of containers, you can design and operate your applications in a serverless way, as long as they don't exceed the total supported number of containers. This section introduces two serverless patterns that you can implement with containers—*batch processing* and *bursting*.

Batch Processing

In many big *compute scenarios*, you need to apply a piece of logic to a large amount of data. For example, when rendering an animated movie, you need to render individual frames and then stitch them into a complete movie, which is a typical *map-reduce* process. Rendering of individual frames can be parallelized to speed up the overall rendering process.

Setting up a rendering program on a virtual machine takes time. So, once a virtual machine is configured for the task, you want to reuse the machine for a batch of jobs instead of a single job because the provision overhead will be too high. And in many cases, you have a pretty good idea of how much compute resource you'd need for the task at hand. For example, when you plan to process 1 million pictures, you can decide beforehand how many virtual machines you will need based on processing rate and time constraints. As you partition the 1 million pictures to a certain number of virtual machines, each machine needs to maintain a state to remember where it is at processing the assigned batch.

Some batch jobs are less predictable. For example, when you split a hyperspace into multiple search regions, searches in some regions may finish much quicker than in other regions. In such a case, the virtual machines for completed regions will sit idle while other virtual machines are busy cranking data. Intuitively, if you can reuse the idle virtual machines it will make the processing more efficient. However, doing so requires an orchestrator that monitors all nodes, and repartitions data to fill the idle nodes when necessary. Another solution is to dynamically scale down. By shutting down idle nodes, you can save on compute resources though you can't improve the overall processing time.

Dynamic scaling is most efficient when the scaling unit is smaller. Figure 7.13 shows that for the same sample workload, you gain savings when the scaling unit is more granular, because you can release more unused compute resources.

As I explained earlier, the extra cost of setting up and tearing down makes fine granular scaling not worth it. However, containers offer a new idea. Because you can provision and destroy containers quickly, you can offer to have one container handling just a few or even just one job. This allows you to dynamically scale your compute plane with minimum waste.

If your application can tolerate longer delays in certain tasks, you can try to schedule your batch jobs to *low priority* VM instances. These instances are idle

> ⓘ Here's an interview challenge I once received: design a system that will find all valid URLs on the Internet. This sounds like an impossible problem for sure. And here's my solution: I'll start with a word list with 1 million words. Then I'll partition the words to a certain number of processors and send a batch of words to each of the processors. Then each of the processors will take a word, conduct a Google search, and retrieve a list of URLs. Then it sends the URLs to a data store partitioned by a string prefix. The data store removes the duplicates and saves the unique URLs.

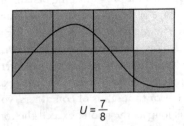

$$U = \frac{7}{8}$$

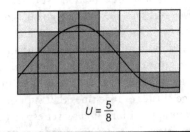

$$U = \frac{5}{8}$$

Figure 7.13 Auto-scaling efficiency with different scaling units

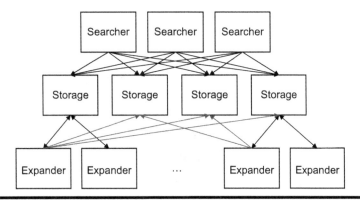

Figure 7.14   Finding all URLs on the Internet

VM instances that you can acquire to run your jobs. However, your jobs may be evicted when jobs with higher priority are scheduled on the node. To improve fairness, some systems allow jobs to accumulate "credits" as they wait for compute resources. When they are scheduled, they spend credits in exchange for compute resources. Once the credits are exhausted, they go back to the waiting list until they accumulate enough credits to be scheduled again.

This solution will not exhaust all possible URLs on the Internet. However, I think it's an effective solution—after all, if a search engine never indexes a URL, it's probably not that interesting. As an extension to the solution, a second level of processing can be launched to expand on existing URLs to find additional URLs that are linked from the existing ones. Figure 7.14 shows the architecture of the system.

Bursting

Unlike batch processing scenarios, bursting workloads are hard to predict. For example, a news website may have a great surge in traffic when some breaking news occurs. For such applications, it will be expensive to keep servers around because they will be idle for most of the time. However, when the traffic surge does come, they need to quickly recruit a large amount of compute resources to handle the traffic.

Architecturally, such an application needs two types of compute resources: long running compute nodes that host the application itself, and short-lived compute nodes that handle bursting workloads, as shown in Figure 7.15. However, exiting PaaS platforms rarely host both types of nodes (though some PaaS platforms support scheduling both long-running services and short-lived tasks).

In a typical Kubernetes cluster, a system agent named *Kubelet* runs on every cluster node. Virtual Kubelet (https://github.com/virtual-kubelet/virtual-kubelet) is an open source project that allows a Kubernetes cluster to be expanded to include compute nodes off the original Kubernetes cluster. For instance, a virtual Kubelet representing a serverless platform can register itself as a node with infinite capacities. When Kubernetes schedules services and sees that the virtual node has infinite capacity, it can keep scheduling workloads onto this virtual node. The virtual node talks to the serverless platform to acquire and release compute resources as needed. This design enables the architecture in Figure 7.15.

As you've seen in the previous discussion, bursting can happen across different platforms. Bursting can also happen across different locations. A common bursting scenario is an on-premises system bursting into cloud. In such a deployment, the on-premises servers handle user traffic. When there's a sudden surge in user traffic, the on-premises servers can dynamically request cloud-side resources to help deal with the extra workloads.

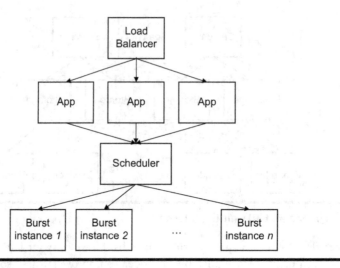

Figure 7.15 Application with bursting nodes

Bursting to a different location may present a security concern in some cases. For example, when you burst part of your workloads outside the virtual network where your main application is running, you need to make sure the data is under protection during transition and maybe during use (see confidential computing discussion in the previous chapter). Data sovereignty requirements may also constrain you from bursting into a different region. Last but not least, when you burst workloads into a shared, multi-tenant environment, you need to make sure that the platform provides sufficient isolation among workloads to avoid unwanted data leaks.

When dealing with bursting workloads, you often need to deal with two related problems: *cold start* and *scale to zero*. When you start the workload burst, you need to launch new containers to handle the workload. Although launching containers itself is usually fast, downloading the container image takes time. Further, a lot of services take some time to be initialized, which causes delays in handling the first request. This is referred as the *cold start problem*. When the traffic surge is over, you should ideally destroy all burst service instances to save cost. However, after you've destroyed all service instances, there won't be any service instances listening for future traffic. This dilemma is referred to as a *scaling-to-zero problem*.

One of my colleagues at Microsoft, Yaron Schneider, came up with a solution for Kubernetes. In a nutshell, when scaling-to-zero is requested, a controller will update service routes to route traffic to an intermediate service and then destroy all the service instances. When new service requests arrive, the intermediate service queues up the requests while trying to launch service instances. And once service instances are launched, it updates the routing table to restore routes to service instances. Then it dispatches queued requests to the newly launched instances. This solution allows a service to be scaled to zero instances. And it improves cold start especially when there is a sudden surge of requests, because it can choose to launch multiple service instances at the same time when it sees many queued requests.

Tutorial: Using Azure Container Instances (ACI) and AWS Fargate

 Microsoft Azure Container Instances (ACI) and AWS Fargate both allow running container instances without managing any servers or clusters. In this short tutorial, you'll launch a new container instance on both ACI and Fargate.

Launching a Container on ACI

1. Log in to Azure Management Portal.
2. Open Cloud Shell.
3. Create a new resource group.

```
az group create --name zocaci -location westus
```

4. Launch a new container. Please note that you'll need to use a unique DNS name label.

```
az container create --resource-group zocaci --name mycontainer
--image microsoft/aci-helloworld --dns-name-label zoc-aci --ports 80
```

5. Once the container is created, you can query its FQDN using the following query:

```
az container show --resource-group zocaci --name mycontainer --query
"{FQDN:ipAddress.fqdn,ProvisioningState:provisioningState}" --out
table
```

The above command generates the following output in my environment:

```
FQDN                                ProvisioningState
----------------------------------- ------------------
zoc-aci.westus.azurecontainer.io    Succeeded
```

6. Open a browser and navigate to the FQDN address. You should see a hello-world web page, as shown in Figure 7.16.

Figure 7.16   Hello-world container web page

Launching a Container with AWS Fargate

1. Launch AWS Elastic Container Service (ECS) first-run experience: https://console.aws.ama-zon.com/ecs/home#/firstRun
2. On the **Step 1: Create a task definition** page, accept all default values that define a simple service based on *httpd:2.4* image with:
   - Memory consumption limited to 300 MB
   - Container port 80 mapped to host port 80
   Click on the **Next step** button to continue.
3. On the **Step 2: Configure service** page, accept all other default values and click on the **Next step** button to continue.
4. On the **Step 3: Configure cluster** page, click on the **Review & launch** button. The fact that you have to define a cluster is counterintuitive. Although a serverless platform may choose to use node clusters to deliver the functionality, it should hide the node or cluster management form end users.
5. On the **Step 4: Review** page, click on the **Launch instance & run service** button.
6. Once the service is provisioned, click on the **View service** button. This takes you to the service page, as shown in Figure 7.17.
7. Click on the Task ID at the bottom of the page.
8. On the Task page, expand **simple-app** (assuming you've used the default name) in the **Containers** section. Then click on the IP address under **External link**, as shown in Figure 7.18.
9. You'll see a default web page, as shown in Figure 7.19.

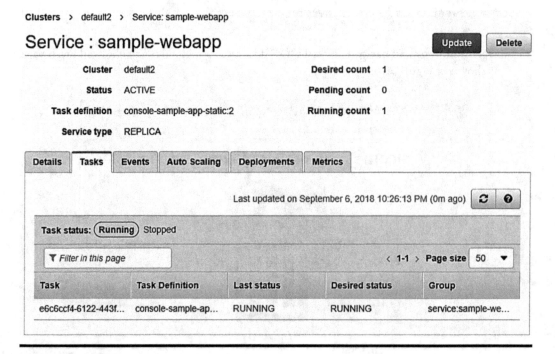

Figure 7.17 Service page

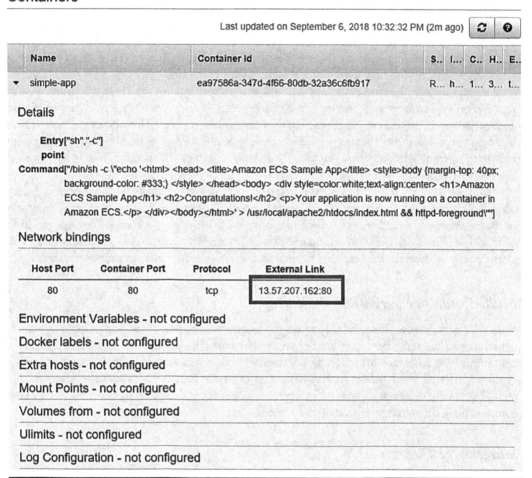

Figure 7.18   Containers section in Task page

Figure 7.19   ECS container default page

Serverless Applications

Dynamically scaling container instances on a serverless platform is powerful. Can we apply the same concept to an entire application that comprises multiple interacting containers? So far, we've discussed only containers that are independent from each other. They are assigned to job batches and then operate on their own without interacting with each other.

Leveraging serverless for entire applications is a tempting idea, which is the primary value proposition of Platform as a Service (PaaS) in general. With a PaaS platform, you hand your applications to be hosted on platform-managed compute resources. This allows you to focus on building the applications themselves while allowing the platform to handle host management. However, to enjoy PaaS benefits, you usually need to buy in to the specific programming model that the platform supports.

Many existing PaaS offerings on the market leak host management to developers in certain ways. This is often driven by user requirements to access the hosts for customization or diagnostics purposes. Another big factor is that such platforms are multi-tenant systems. They use machines or machine clusters as isolation boundaries around different tenants. And such boundaries are intentionally or inadvertently exposed to the end user, making the platform non-serverless.

Multi-Container Serverless Platforms

Both ACI and Fargate aim primarily at single container scenarios. They both support grouping containers on the same host. But neither (at the time of writing) support distributed containers communicating with each other. To support multi-container scenarios, an orchestrator is needed. However, existing orchestrators such as Kubernetes, Service Fabric, and Mesos are based on clusters. They are not designed to work on an open compute plane. To enable orchestration over a large compute plan, different server strategies are used.

Super-Large Clusters

I know a cat, Leroy (someone said that you never own a cat, you merely know a cat). Leroy is a house cat. For him, my house is his entire world. He never leaves the house. What happens outside is simply not his concern. Similarly, if your cluster is big enough for an application to acquire as much compute resource as it ever needs, it doesn't matter if your cluster has a boundary or not.

Microsoft Azure's Service Fabric Mesh is a serverless offering based on Service Fabric. It creates huge Service Fabric clusters and schedules customer applications on these clusters. The assumption is that there won't be any customers who will ever need more machines than what are on one huge cluster.

However, having a huge cluster is just the first step. A classic Service Fabric cluster is assumed to be a single-tenant environment. All applications running on the same cluster implicitly trust each other. Fortunately, Service Fabric supports multiple node types, and each node type can be isolated into a separate subnet. This allows network security groups (NSGs) to be defined to provide network isolations among the applications.

Service mesh like *Istio* offers a more flexible option than isolation through subnets. Istio is an open source service mesh that builds up a logical connectivity mesh over physical networks. Istio deploys an *Envoy proxy* next to each application instance. All application traffic is routed and managed by Envoy, as shown in Figure 7.20.

This extra layer of abstraction opens great opportunities, such as in-depth security, smart routing, throttling, and correlated tracing, without needing any application modifications. As a matter

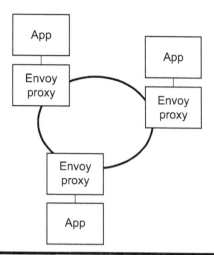

Figure 7.20 **Service mesh with Envoy proxies**

of fact, applications can remain oblivious to the underlying mesh configuration changes. The downside of using an Envoy proxy is that all network packets need to be examined and routed in user space, introducing extra network delays.

Separating Control Plane and Compute Plane

The other way to realize endless clusters is to separate the control plane and compute plane. Control plane makes all scheduling decisions. And compute plane hosts the actual workloads. As the pressure on existing nodes increases, additional compute nodes can be introduced into the compute plane to dynamically expand cluster capacity. However, as the number of nodes increases, the pressure on the master nodes themselves goes up as well. To support a huge cluster, you'll need to set up a scalable control plane to handle increasing scheduling needs.

Kubernetes has master nodes and worker nodes. The master nodes form the control plane, and the worker nodes form the compute plane. Service Fabric doesn't impose fixed roles on nodes. Service Fabric system services can be placed on any of the nodes, and any of the nodes can potentially be elected as the master node. By using placement constraints or different node types, you can limit system services to a subset of the nodes, which form the separate control plane.

I've seen clusters with thousands of nodes. However, I don't know the upper limit of worker nodes for either Kubernetes or Service Fabric. I think it's safe to assume there must be one. When that limit is reached, you'll have to use multiple clusters to support the serverless platform. Since multiple clusters may be needed anyway, it probably doesn't matter what that upper limit is. Furthermore, some customers may request dedicated clusters for additional isolation. So this separate compute plane idea might be unnecessary after all. Or is it? Hold on to that thought. I'll come back to this in Chapter 10.

Using Specific Application Models

As I mentioned earlier, many PaaS platforms have preferred or even mandated programming models. When you program using these programming models, your applications can automatically take advantage of serverless when the underlying PaaS platform expands itself to support the serverless paradigm.

Microsoft Azure Service Fabric provides a runtime that supports a variety of hosting environments, including cloud platforms, on-premises datacenters, and even edge devices. However, at the time of writing, it hasn't gained as much momentum as its primary competitor, Kubernetes, has gained. Because you can install Kubernetes clusters everywhere as well, you can write your program once and deploy it anywhere you like. An advantage Service Fabric has over Kubernetes is that Service Fabric supports programming models such as stateful services and actors. Both are every effective programming models for building distributed, stateful systems.

Some other serverless platforms are even more opinionated. However, a generic pattern exists. These platforms provide hosting environments for processing units that are connected through a messaging system. Such architecture isn't new—there have been numerous occurrences in the computer history, such as DCOM and SOA. The messaging system is the key in such an architecture. It decouples processing units in both space and time so that the processing units can be developed, deployed, and scaled independently. For instance, when you send an email to a friend, she doesn't need to be online at the same time the message is sent. And the message may go through a few forwarding servers and proxies before it reaches the final address. However, from your perspective, you simply send a message to an address and assume your friend will eventually pick up the message.

Microsoft Azure Logic Apps is a serverless platform for running distributed workloads. You can use a graphical UI to organize hundreds of prebuilt and custom processing units into a complete workflow. You can react to various events in popular cloud services and trigger a workflow to perform complex operations. And once the application is deployed, you don't need to worry about any hosting concerns, such as reacting to external events, ensuring message delivery among components and maintaining process unit health.

Hands-On Lab: Using Azure Logic Apps to Respond to Negative Tweets

In this lab, you'll build an end-to-end solution using Azure Logic Apps and Azure Functions. The solution monitors tweets that mention a specific hashtag. Then it feeds the tweets to Azure Cognitive Services to detect if the tweets are negative. When a negative tweet is found, it looks it up in the company's CRM system to see if the Twitter handle who posted the negative comment belongs to a managed account in CRM. If it does, it then checks if you have had previous engagements with the customer. And if you have, which means you have a relationship with the customer, a reminder email is automatically sent to you to reach out to the customer to address the negative feedback.

The application logic is quite complex, as shown in Figure 7.21. You can imagine how much work it would be if you wrote everything from scratch! Fortunately, with Logic Apps, you can build up the entire workflow with minimum coding required.

Creating a Function to Convert Sentiment Score to Discreet Values

As a starting point, you'll create an Azure Function that converts a float sentiment score, which is generated by Cognitive Service Text Analysis, to a discreet value. The text analysis service presents a score from 0 to 1, with a higher value representing more positive sentiment. The function converts the score to three discreet values: RED for values below 0.2, YELLOW for values below 0.6, and GREEN for the rest of the values.

1. Log in to Microsoft Azure Management Portal.
2. Create a new Serverless Function App.

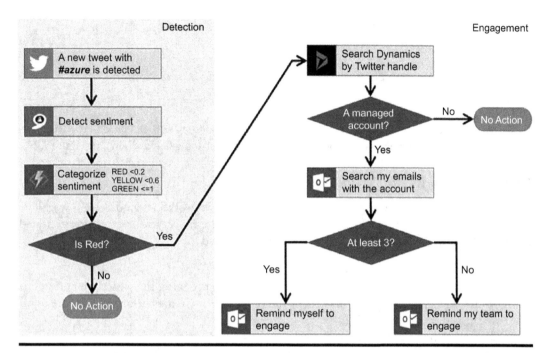

Figure 7.21　Workflow definition in Logic Apps

3. On the **Function App** blade, enter a name for the function app. Accept all default values, and then click the **Create** button.
4. Once the function app is created, navigate to the application. Then click on the "+" sign besides **Functions** to create a new function.
5. Select the **Webhook + API** template and **CSharp** language. Then click the **Create this function** button to create the function.
6. Replace the function code with the following code:

```csharp
using System.Net;
public static async Task<HttpResponseMessage> Run(HttpRequestMessage
   req, TraceWriter log)
{
    string category = "GREEN";
    // Get the sentiment score from the request body.
    double score = await req.Content.ReadAsAsync<double>();
    log.Info(string.Format("The sentiment score received is '{0}'.",
             score.ToString()));

    // Set the category based on the sentiment score.
    if (score < .3)
    {
        category = "RED";
    }
    else if (score < .6)
```

```
    {
        category = "YELLOW";
    }
    return req.CreateResponse(HttpStatusCode.OK, category);
}
```

7. In the **Test** area, change the request body to a single value (such as 0.4). Click on the **Run** button to test the function—you should get "YELLOW" for value 0.4, as shown in Figure 7.22.

Creating the Detection Workflow

Given the complexity of the app, you'll split the app into two workflows: a detection workflow and an engagement workflow. The detection workflow monitors tweet streams, analyzes collected tweets, and decides if the engagement flow should be triggered.

1. Create a new Logic Apps application.
2. On the Create logic app blade, enter a **Name** for your app. Select the subscription, resource group, and location you want to use, and then click on the **Create** button to create the application, as shown in Figure 7.23.
3. Click the **When a new tweet is posted** tile to start the Logic App designer.
4. Click the **Sign in** button on the Twitter tile to log in to Twitter. Then click on the **Continue** button to continue with the designer. Then in the **Twitter** tile, enter a search hashtag (such as #contoso), and set up a tweet check frequency of three minutes. Once this step is finished, your design screen should look like Figure 7.24.

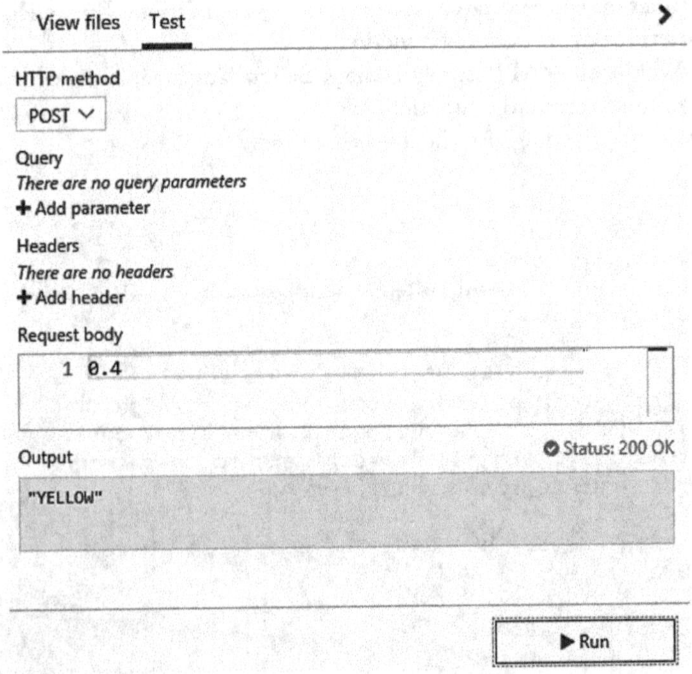

Figure 7.22   Testing the conversion function

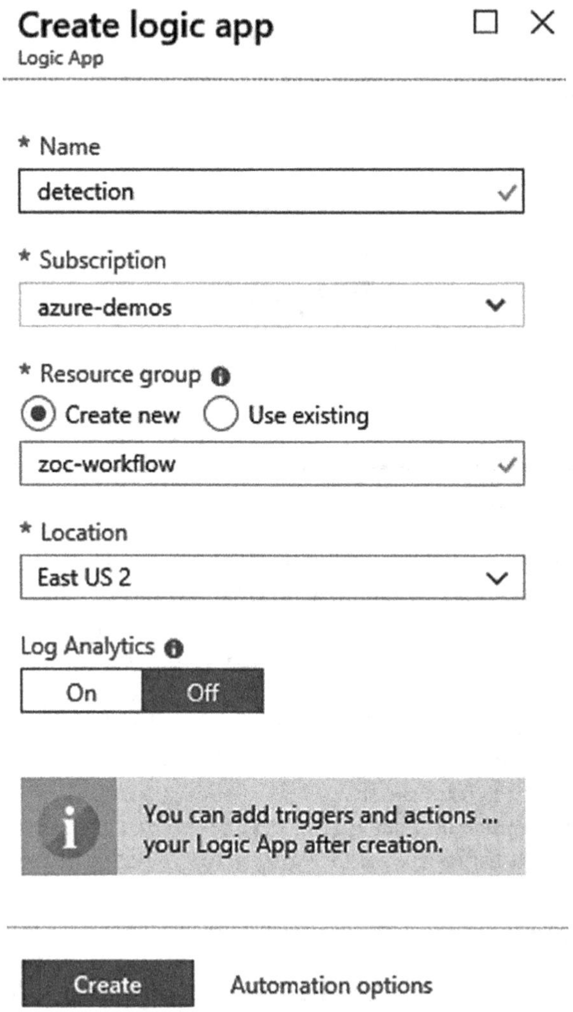

Create logic app ☐ ✕
Logic App

* Name

detection ✓

* Subscription

azure-demos ⌄

* Resource group ❶
⦿ Create new ◯ Use existing

zoc-workflow ✓

* Location

East US 2 ⌄

Log Analytics ❶

On	Off

ℹ You can add triggers and actions ...
your Logic App after creation.

Create	Automation options

Figure 7.23   Creating a new logic app

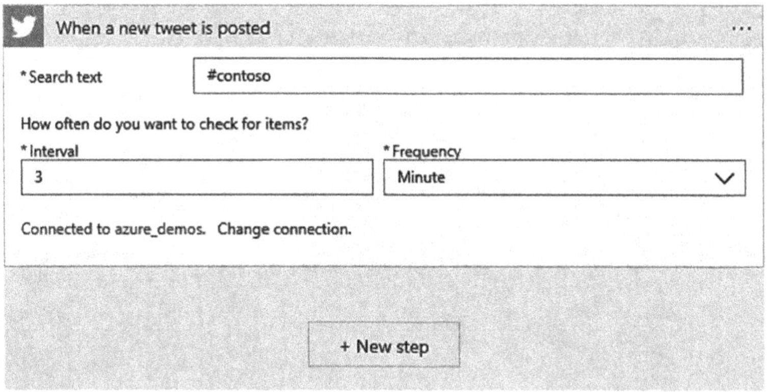

🐦 When a new tweet is posted   ...

* Search text   #contoso

How often do you want to check for items?
* Interval   * Frequency
3   Minute ⌄

Connected to azure_demos. Change connection.

+ New step

Figure 7.24   Checking for tweets with a specific hashtag

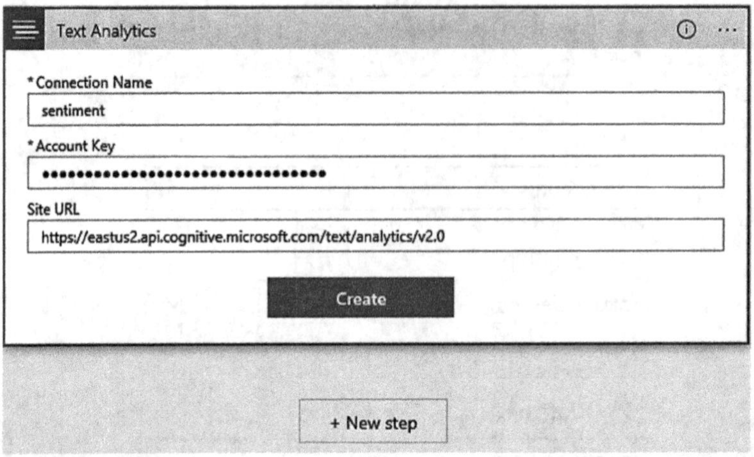

Text Analytics ⓘ ···

* Connection Name

sentiment

* Account Key

••••••••••••••••••••••••••••••••

Site URL

https://eastus2.api.cognitive.microsoft.com/text/analytics/v2.0

Create

+ New step

Figure 7.25 Text analytics tile

5. To call cognitive services, you need an account. In Azure Portal, search and create a **Text Analysis** API. The creation step is similar to what you did in Chapter 5 when creating the Compute Vision API. You'll need the API endpoint as well as the API key for the next step.
6. Back in the Logic App designer, click on the **New step** button to add a step.
7. On the **Choose an action** tile, search for "sentiment" and click on the **Detect Sentiment** entry. Then on the Text Analytics tile, enter a name for the Cognitive API connection, paste in your Cognitive Services API key and endpoint URL, as shown in Figure 7.25. Then click on the **Create** button to create the step.
8. On the **Detect Sentiment** tile, click on the **Text** field. Then click on the **Tweet text** entry in the **Dynamic content** list, as shown in Figure 7.26. The dynamic content list is populated

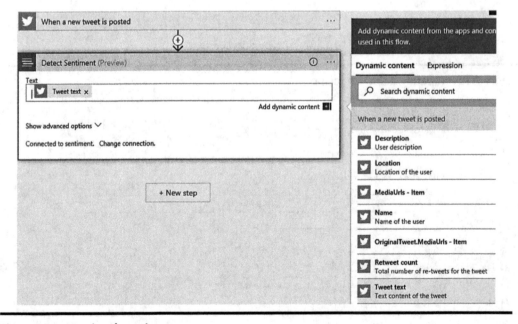

Figure 7.26 Setting detection text

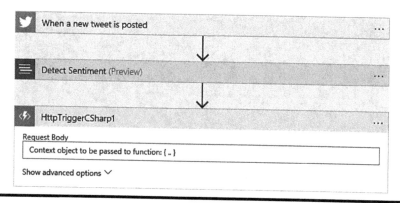

Figure 7.27   Linking to the predefined function

by possible outputs from previous steps. This is how you link the steps. You can also define expressions when defining input and output links.

9. Click on the **New step** button. On the **Choose an Action** tile, click on the **Azure Functions** tile. Select the function app and then the function you just created. Figure 7.27 shows what your Logic App should look like after these steps.

10. Add a new **Condition** step. A condition step creates a fork in the workflow. It executes one of the branches based on a given condition. Figure 7.28 shows that when the score (dynamic field from the previous step) is less that 0.6, the true branch should be executed.

11. Save the workflow. You'll leave both branches above empty for now. When you complete the engagement workflow, you'll link the workflow to the true branch.

12. Now it's time to test what you have. Click on the **Run** button. You'll see a message that says, "To see it works now, create a tweet."

13. Log in to Twitter and create a negative tweet with the designated hashtag, for example "#contoso is bad."

14. After a few seconds, you should see the workflow being triggered and the true branch selected, as shown in Figure 7.29.

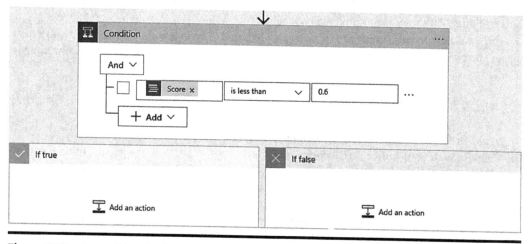

Figure 7.28   A condition in the workflow

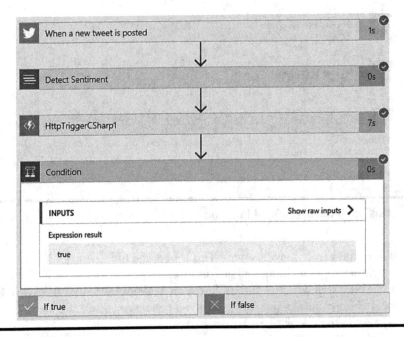

Figure 7.29   Workflow test execution

Creating the Engagement Workflow

The engagement workflow includes a few steps. First, it queries Microsoft Dynamics 365 to locate a customer email by Twitter handle. Then, it looks under a specific folder under your Outlook account to see if you've archived any emails from the customer. If you've exchanged emails with the customer a few times before, an email will be sent to you to engage with the customer.

This lab assumes that you already have a Dynamics 365 tenant, and you've already customized your account entity schema to include a *new_twitterhandle* field. And to make the workflow work, you also need to populate the account with the Twitter handle, as well as an email address with which you have exchanged email. And you've indeed saved a number of emails under a *"contoso"* folder. Figure 7.30 shows the completed engagement workflow.

This workflow is too complex to be fully covered here. The following steps create a simplified engagement workflow that sends an email to you when a negative tweet regarding the hashtag is detected.

1. Create a new Logic App with a **When a HTTP request is received** trigger as the starting point.
2. Add an Office 365 Outlook **Send an email** action, as shown in Figure 7.31.
3. Sign in with your Office 365 account. The notification email will be sent from this account.
4. Enter a destination address, subject, and body to the notification email. In the email body, you can specify the body text as whatever is passed in to the HTTP trigger, as shown in Figure 7.32.
5. Add a **Response** action with all default settings. This is required because the invoking workflow expects to receive a successful response (HTTP response code 2000).
6. Save the engagement workflow.

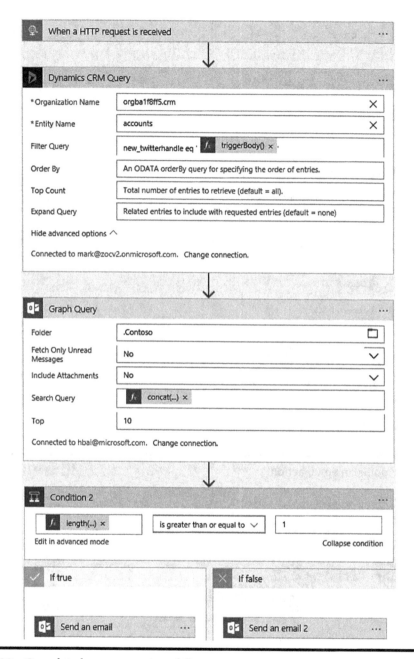

Figure 7.30   Completed engagement workflow

7. Return to the detection workflow. Add a new action in the true branch to call into the engagement workflow, as shown in Figure 7.33. Please note that I used a dynamic field to populate the HTTP request body with the original tweet text.
8. Save the detection workflow. Then click on the Run button to test the workflow.
9. Post a negative tweet regarding the monitored hashtag. In a few seconds, you'll receive a notification email with the original tweet text.

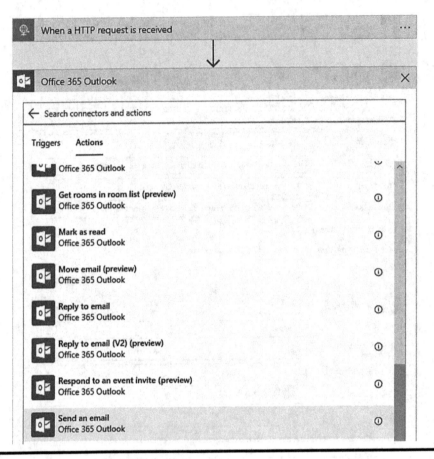

Figure 7.31 Adding an email action

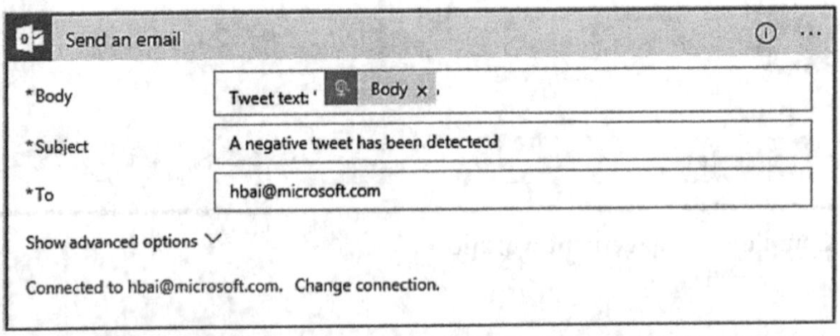

Figure 7.32 Send an email action

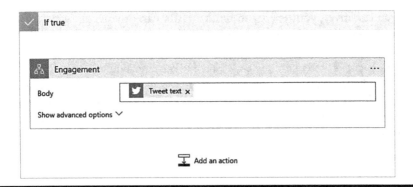

Figure 7.33 Invoking engagement workflow

State Management in Stateless Applications

A serverless platform is great for stateless services. Because stateless servers are easier to be moved around, the platform has more flexibility in scheduling them onto different compute resources at its disposal. Moving stateful services around is more expensive, because these services carry local states with them. And moving large amounts of data requires time.

A common strategy for managing state on a serverless platform is to externalize the state to a separate storage, such as a database server, a shared disk based on a cloud drive and a cloud-based key-value store. The primary challenge of this design is security. Because these database servers need to be hosted off the serverless platform, they need to be accessible by applications hosted on public serverless platforms. This could be a significant security risk. Some serverless platforms are integrated with virtual networks. You can deploy your database servers onto the same virtual networks where your application belongs so that they can communicate with each other without public IP addresses. You can also use other techniques such as IP address filtering or service endpoint ACLs to ensure private communication channels.

Zen of Cloud

> *"You only have to do a very few things right in your life so long as you don't do too many things wrong."*

Warren Buffett

A successful cloud application is based on a successful partnership between you and your cloud platform. Cloud platforms have investigated billions of dollars and hired the most experienced datacenter designers and operators to operate the infrastructure. By offloading all infrastructure management burdens, you can focus on your application itself to maximize the value you can create and deliver.

I've heard some people complain about various constraints they face when trying to delegate low level tasks to cloud. "Cloud A is missing a feature that we absolutely need to make our application work." While in some cases this is true, in most cases the absolute dependency on a specific feature is artificial. This is like driving a car from point A to point B. To shorten the travel time, you can invest your energy to build a faster car, or you can optimize your trip plan to take a better route. And often, you may even realize in some cases that making such a trip is unnecessary.

Redesigning a car is a tremendous endeavor. I'm sure no one will take this approach when it comes to optimizing travel time. Similarly, when you work with a platform, a more efficient approach is to delegate what you can, and work around limitations of the platform. Serverless is not about making your life easier. Instead, it's about freeing yourself up so that you can gain additional agility to create more value.

Chapter 8

Cloud DevOps

Project Management

It's a project management nightmare: nonnegotiable deadline, ever-changing requirements, unstable and sometimes experimental code, with the highest of quality expectation. You don't have a fixed team. Instead, you need to collaborate with tens of people from different teams, who are under time pressures to ship their own deliverables.

I need to do four or five such projects every year.

I've delivered hundreds of demos for Microsoft executives in the past six years. These demos are showcased at major industrial events such as Microsoft Ignite, DockerCon, and RSA. They highlight Microsoft's vision and new developments in cloud computing, ranging from fundamental datacenter infrastructure to new programming languages such as Q# for quantum computing. Each of these projects is unique in different ways. For example, we once demo'ed provisioning one million containers on a three-thousand node cluster under two minutes, a scale never attempted before. There were many unknown factors in this project. However, one factor was certain—failure wasn't an option.

This section introduces project management. I think it will be interesting to discuss this topic within the contexts of these keynote demo projects, which exaggerate various project management challenges in a condensed timeline. Especially because collaboration with distributed teams is needed, such projects also illustrate how you can manage open source projects with independent contributors.

A word of caution: the following discussions don't follow strict processes and practices defined by popular frameworks such as scrum and lean software development. Instead, I've picked useful techniques from these frameworks. I don't believe in rigidly following a specific methodology. Instead, I believe you should figure out whatever works for your team with as little process as possible.

Managing Requirements

A project has its value propositions that justify why the project should exist at the first place. In many cases, the initial idea of a project is a vision instead of a specific set of requirements. The vision could be a grand one. As a project manager, the first thing you need to do is to land the grand vision into a set of features that realize that vision.

Jumping from vision to features is a big leap. Instead of trying to come up with a feature list directly, you should work on user stories first, and then use these stories to drive what features should be included in your products. The key is to build up a minimum product with just enough features to serve early customer needs, and to use this product to develop future product features. This minimum product is called a Minimum Viable Product (MVP). The goal of an MVP is to help your customers realize the value of your product. Once customers understand the value, they can start to make connections with their day-to-day operations and come up with practical suggestions to make the product work better for them. These suggestions turn into functional and non-functional requirements that you can scope for the first version of your product.

You will hear many suggestions. To remain focused, you need to choose when to say no. How do you know if you were rejecting a good suggestion? Simply ask yourself if the suggestion significantly helps you realize the original vision. When you work with engineers (including the engineer inside you), you'll get many good suggestions that make logical sense, such as making it more scalable, making it easier to debug, making it more responsive, and so on and so forth. Although they are all excellent points for the final product, your MVP doesn't need to be equipped with such features, unless these features are key distinguishers. Once, I was building a scenario that required a pre-release SDK. As the deadline approached, the SDK team came up with a new SDK version that was supposed to be more stable and closer to the final product. It took me quite some effort to convince the team that since the scenario had been working stably with the current SDK, the risk of switching to a new SDK at the last moment wasn't worth it, given there were no changes relevant to the scenario. "We can't be responsible if things break," the team claimed. "That's fine. I'll take full responsibility." I calmly assured them. And indeed, nothing bad happened. The demo was a hit.

There are other great suggestions that are harder to reject. I place them in three categories: distractions, nice-to-haves, and scope creepers. As you work with shareholders, many suggestions will surface. You shouldn't judge these suggestions based merely on whether you can understand them or not. Field experts in particular may offer some new perspectives that you are not familiar with. Again, you should check these ideas against their contribution to your vision. If they are (or you get proof that they are), you should seriously consider them. However, many of these suggestions fall into one of the above three categories, and none of them should be taken into consideration. Recognizing these disposable ideas takes experience, and guarding your vision takes negotiation and guts. Some nice-to-have features may have especially caught into people's mind so much that they start to believe these features are mandatory. When you can't reject these ideas, be sure to assign them with lower priorities so that they don't compete for critical development resources.

Managing a Distributed Team

When you have a distributed team that is temporarily put together for a project such as an open source project, you don't have regular management levers to keep the team together. Instead, you'll have to figure out other ways to motivate the team and keep the project in the right direction. Although each team works differently, there are some common techniques that have proven effective based on my experience.

The number one thing you need to do is to make sure everyone is motivated toward a common goal. You need to be the firm believer of the vision, and you need to be the biggest advocator of the goal to keep everyone motivated. When people come together to form a temporary team, every single person is likely to have different personal goals and priorities. What you need is to allow them to realize their own goals by contributing to the common goal. When a team member wants to leave once their goal has been reached, it usually works better to let them go instead of trying to keep them on the team. Otherwise, you'll find their motivation to make meaningful contribution drastically decreases. I'm not saying they are a bad person who intentionally jeopardizes the project. They simply don't have adjustable reasons to make additional contributions. To enable this kind of team dynamic, however, you need to decompose the project into relatively independent pieces that can be developed with minimum cross-dependencies. And for each of the pieces, you need to have a plan in case the piece doesn't come through.

The most efficient team is a team based on a trust-and-commitment relationship among team members. When everyone can deliver what he or she has committed, team members can trust each other, and delegate tasks as needed. When I worked with stage staff in various events, I noticed that each team member had a clear responsibility. For example, when you need help with audio problems, you need to find the audio technician. If you ask anyone else to help, they will help you to find the technician, but they will not touch anything related to audio, even for a very simple problem such as a missing cable. Once the technician is found, you need to tell him what you need only once. You don't need to double check later. As long as the technician acknowledges your request, it will happen. Stage is a very fascinating environment. For a show to succeed, everything must work, everything is mandatory, and everything must come together. The explicit responsibilities ensure that. Why might no one help you with a simple audio problem? Because they need to make sure the audio technician is completely aware of audio-related configurations. The audio technician is ultimately responsible for the audio to work. In other words, the team has complete trust in him or her to deliver audio, and that person is completely committed to the task. The major downside of this arrangement is overstaffing. Because everyone is assigned a very explicit area, many personnel are needed to deliver one show—stage manager, director, audio technician, video technician, networking technician, camera person, set builder, runner, lighting operator, makeup artist, and more. A software development team can rarely offer such a luxurious workforce. Software deliverables are also less tangible. When you try to build a trust-and-commitment culture in your team, you'll need to gauge how much you can safely delegate and gradually build up the trust relationship.

A good leader leads by example. This is especially true in a software development team, in which everyone takes on a similar level of work. Before you ask your team members to do anything, you should first ask yourself if you could keep up to your own requirements. When you keep missing your own goals, it's very hard to convince your team members that you are in control of the project. On the other hand, if you can show how you stay true to your commitments, it will help you to build a trust-and-commitment culture.

Another key factor in team building is communication. By communication, I don't mean frequent meetings or fixed processes. Instead, I refer to the open sharing of ideas among team members. This may sound simple but is sometimes hard to do. I've seen in many cases that a team leader tries to assert their leadership by holding strong opinions on technical decisions. This behavior harms team motivation and sometimes leads the whole team in a wrong direction that can't be easily corrected before it's too late. A good team leader should create an inclusive and respectful environment in which all team members are free to share their ideas, even when the ideas are counter to one another. It's perfectly fine to disagree with each other if the team collectively seeks a viable path for delivering the project.

Prepare for a Rainy Day

When preparing for executive keynotes, we take precautions against any possible failures. Redundant environments support each demo scenario. When demo desktops are used, we ship the machines without hard drives using trucks. And we ship two copies of imaged hard drives on

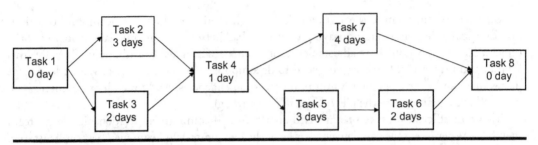

Figure 8.1   Critical path of a project

two different flights. When cloud is used, we replicate the demo environment in two different regions. And for each demo scenario, we have a least two people who can manage the entire demo environment independently (and they travel on different flights as well). You may think of us as being paranoid. The fact is, all these precautions are necessary, based on our years of experiences.

When you manage a project, you need to prepare for unexpected interruptions that can throw your project off track. To mitigate such risks you need to train yourself to recognize the *critical path* of your project. The tasks on the critical path can't be parallelized. And they often have strict dependencies on one another. To complete the project, your team has to finish all tasks on the critical path in sequence. The length of the critical path largely decides the span of your project. And a failure in the critical path is likely to delay or even destroy your project. Figure 8.1 shows a series of tasks in a project. Tasks 1, 3, 4, 5, 6, and 8 form the critical path of your project. Because all these tasks need to be completed in order, it takes at least 8 days to finish your project. When you prioritize tasks, task 2 and task 7 should be assigned with lower priorities, and they are the first candidates to be cut when you are under time pressure.

Some junior managers may be tempted to build buffers into the schedule in preparation for unforeseen events. This is exactly the wrong thing to do because it means you are unaware of possible risks but try to plan for catchall time slots that help you deal with surprises. As a project lead, you should fully understand possible risks and prepare to handle these risks, such as by designing alternative ways to push these tasks out of the critical path and by assigning sufficient resources to investigate possible solutions. Once you gain enough clarity, you shouldn't need a blanket catchall buffer.

When Everything Falls Apart

Sometimes, everything goes south. People react to pressure differently. When your team is under tremendous pressure, some of your team members may snap. And when the negative mood spreads, your team falls apart. In such cases, you are the last defense against a total failure. As an experienced team leader, you would act swiftly but you should never panic, because this is the time when your team looks up to you for leadership.

One thing you should avoid doing in such a case is to analyze why the project is failing. Instead, keep your attention sharply focused on how to make the project work. Especially when your team members start to point fingers, you need to help them refocus on solving problems instead of trying to find who to blame. You should be clear that your team fails as a whole and wins as individuals. When your team succeeds, you should fully acknowledge contributions of individuals. This ensures that your team members continue to make exceptional contributions in your future projects. On the contrary, if your team fails, it doesn't matter who caused the failure. Postmortem should happen only when the project has been wrapped up. And when you do that, focus on what can be done differently next time. It's very rare that someone would intentionally jeopardize a project. Most failures are caused by underestimating risks. And developers are often overoptimistic. One of my manager friends told me that whatever time estimation a developer gives you, you should double that. I don't agree with this rule. But it is true that many developers, especially junior developers, don't fully realize the complexity of problems. Your job is to help keep them truthful to their commitments. Following the trust-and-commit principle, you should have a clear idea of what everyone can deliver and take corrective actions before it's too late to adjust.

In a storm of applause, the executive walks off the stage. The show is a hit. The venue staff is a very efficient team. Everything is torn down quickly in preparation for the next event. My team members have scattered and moved on to other things as well. Yet there is still something left for me to do. First, I need to fully acknowledge contributions from my team members. My records show that for each event, I need to work with around 50 people from different teams, exchange about 300 emails, and hold about 15 meetings. When the event finishes, I send out thank you notes to all of them and their managers to acknowledge their investments. Second, I need to send out postmortem notes to individual team members with my suggestions on what can be done better next time. Third, I replay my interactions with team members, especially those that didn't go as well as expected. I think about what could have been done differently to make the communications more effective. Different people shows distinct characteristics in their email communications. The "forwarders" don't take actual actions. However, they are often well-connected to whoever can provide practical help. They can be helpful to you in finding the right person to work with. The "silent workers" take actions but don't clearly communicate with you what they do. You need to proactively clarify their tasks to avoid surprises down the line. The "empty promisors" are quite dangerous. They are often overly optimistic in emails but often come up short in deliverables. You need to call them out when they can't deliver. And you need to prepare for alternative solutions. In other words, under the trust-and-commitment principle, if someone can't fulfill their commitment, they should not be trusted. The "proposers" are often managers who keep coming up with new ideas to expand the scope of the project. You need to firmly stand your ground in such cases. Although they may offer valuable insights, you have to make sure you control the project scope and reject any irrelevant requirements.

DevOps

DevOps is a new term. The gist of DevOps is a software engineering culture that unifies software developments (dev) and software operations (ops). There are many different interpretations of what this unification really means. Does it mean everyone should be a developer? Does it mean developers are ultimately responsible for continuous operations of the final products? To understand these questions, you need to first understand why DevOps exists.

Development vs. Operations

Traditionally, development and operations define two different skill sets that require different professionals. The two sets of professionals often form conflicting tribes inside a company because they have conflicting priorities. This causes many unnecessary frictions.

Changes vs. Stabilization

Software engineers need to make changes all the time to include new features, bug fixes, and performance optimizations. IT pros need to keep environments stable to maintain continuous operation. To software engineers, not being able to push out updates slows them down. To IT pros, frequent changes disrupt their work. This conflict in priorities seems irreconcilable and causes constant friction between the two teams.

Dev Environment vs. Production Environment

Many conflicts between development and operation are caused by inconsistencies between different environments. Software often works fine in the development environment and breaks only when it's deployed in production. Scalability problems aside, many of the production environment problems are caused by configuration differences, such as different versions of dependency versions, different OS patch levels, different hardware stacks, or simply different configurations.

Caught in the civil war between development and operation is quality assurance (QA). They are often blamed for not finding obvious bugs that have leaked into production. Their challenge is that the QA environment they use is often different from both the development environment and the production environment. This further complicates the situation: some bugs observed in production can't be reproduced by either engineering or QA; some QA reported bugs can't be reproduced by engineering, but surface in production and so on and so forth.

Debugger vs. Logs

Diagnosing product problems is often more convoluted than debugging in a development environment. A developer can use a rich set of debugging tools in a dev environment. However, she's often left with manually reading logs as the only troubleshooting method. In a multi-tenant, distributed system, finding and collecting necessary logs alone is a daunting task. And you can image how unhappy the IT pros are when developers want to connect to production servers to dig around, and how frustrated the developers are when they have to jump through hoops to gain access to log files from production servers.

Developers often need logs with high verbosity levels to capture error details. IT pros often prefer less granular logs to reduce resource consumption on production servers. So even when logs are in place, developers often can't collect information from the production logs. And as data privacy becomes a greater concern, a company often reinforces restrictive policies on logs accesses and usages.

Rise of DevOps

Over the past ten years or so, many tools and techniques have been developed that eventually enabled the DevOps culture. All these tools boil down to one thing: consistency.

Consistent Deployment

As introduced earlier, one of the biggest gaps between development and operation is inconsistency in different environments. Enabling software to be consistently deployed is one of the first problems the industry tries to solve in commercialized software.

Installation packages were an early attempt at providing consistency. An installation package contains not only the application binaries, but also installation scripts that checks and fixes all dependencies on the target machine. However, installation packages have a few shortcomings. First, writing a robust installation package is very difficult, especially for client software. Each client machine is different. Bringing all of them to a consistent state is quite challenging. Second, different installation packages from different vendors may conflict with each other. They may require and install different versions of common libraries and break each other.

The complexity of client installation inspired the browser-server (BS) architecture, which reduces the consistent deployment problem to a few servers instead of millions of clients. However, it doesn't fundamentally solve the consistent deployment problem.

Because configuring machine consistently is so complex, a new breed of systems arose— Desired State Configuration (DSC) systems. Instead of beginning at a starting state and applying deltas toward a final state, DSC systems directly build up the desired states. This greatly simplifies many configuration tasks. And these configuration tasks can be generalized, shared, and reused as reusable recipes.

DSC is a separate system. The knowledge of application configuration is captured by the DSC system, and is often maintained by operations instead of developers. However, DSC doesn't provide a structured way for developers to convey configuration requirements to operations. When such communication gaps exist, the final environment is consistently configured, but is consistently wrong.

To solve this communication issue, people came up with the concept of *Infrastructure as Code*. The idea is to explicitly capture all infrastructural requirements as unambiguous code. Because code is not subject to human interpretations and can be faithfully executed by computers, environment consistency across environments is ensured.

We are getting close to achieving consistency. However, there's still one problem to be solved— to avoid conflicts among different software, or different software versions.

One possible approach is to start over every time you develop a new software version. You'll start a brand new OS installation, and then install your software. Disk utilities such as Ghost (General hardware-oriented system transfer) were quite popular about twenty years ago. They were used by Internet cafes to restore a client PC to its original state when a customer logs in to the system. The problem was that every time the machine rebooted, the machine state was reset. This means you can't persist data across your sessions. And every time you needed to go through an entire system restoration, which is time consuming. Although this works well for Internet cafes, it isn't suitable for all situations, especially when state needs to be preserved across software updates.

Virtual machines present a better solution. You can capture your machine state and boot into a virtual machine image quickly. Furthermore, the captured image can be shared and applied to different environments, providing strong consistency. The problem with virtual machine images is version control. Because virtual machine images are in binary formats (and often fairly large), you can't easily apply version control on top of virtual machine images.

Virtual machines provide perfect isolation, with a high price. Because each application exclusively owns its own copy of the entire system, hosting multiple applications on the same server requires hosting multiple virtual machines. This seriously constrains the application density you can achieve on a single server.

Then comes container. Containers provide a lightweight isolation that allows a system kernel to be reused across application packages, which are isolated by techniques such as *cgroups, namespaces,* and *chroots*. Because launching a container is just starting a process instead of booting an entire system, containers are much faster to be launched and destroyed. And you can achieve very high hosting density using containers. Although container isolation is weaker than virtual machines, it's enough in many hosting scenarios when trusted software shares the same hosting resource. Last but not least, because text files can describe containers, you can apply version control as well as automated build pipelines on your container definitions.

The industry is also working on containers with stronger isolations. For example, Microsoft has created containers running directly on Hyper-V. And there are companies that work on container-oriented operating systems that provide container supports on bare metal servers.

Containers provide a nice solution to consistent deployment of services. However, we need more. We need a way to capture and consistently recreate networking topologies among these services. *Service mesh* is a new concept for providing a networking abstraction layer. Although it's been presented as a middleware that offers advanced networking capabilities such as smart routing, correlated logging, and throttling, its value resides in providing an abstraction language to describe network topologies independent from the actual network implementations.

So as of today, we are quite happy with isolation and consistency provided by containers. A software packaged as a container can be consistently deployed and launched across many different platforms. Because container elegantly resolves a key friction point between development and operation, many consider it a cornerstone technology for modern DevOps practices.

Continuous Workflow

Consistent deployment is a key capability in enabling a continuous workflow from source code to production. Because software packages can be deployed without any human interpretations, the deployment process can be fully automated. Developers no longer need to hand over software packages to operations to be deployed. Instead, they can set up continuous pipelines to automatically deploy new versions through a process called *Continuous Delivery* (CD).

Continuous integration (CI), continuous delivery, and continuous deployment are related terms. Continuous integration is a software development process in which a new build and automated unit tests are automatically triggered whenever a developer checks in new code. This practice enables bugs to be discovered early. In some systems, a code check-in is allowed only when automated tests are passed—this is called *gated check-in*. Continuous delivery pushes the process further by adding automated integration tests and acceptance tests to ensure the software package remains at a production-ready quality all the time. Finally, continuous deployment automates the last step—deploy to production. With continuous deployment, every code check-in automatically goes through the entire pipeline and ends up in production. Having new versions automatically pushed to production may sound dangerous. However, statistics have shown that most deployment problems are caused by human factors. Eliminating human factors allows more frequent and more reliable deployments, which drastically shortens the customer feedback loop because customers always have access to the latest version.

Traditionally, software deployments are incremental, which means the existing environments are upgraded to new versions. This process is error prone because of possible incompatibilities among different versions. A better way of doing deployment is to start fresh every time. This practice is sometimes referred as *immutable infrastructure*, which means a product is not changed after deployment. When a new release arrives, a brand new deployment is created. Immutable infrastructure has a few advantages. First, it allows clean deployment to avoid possible version incompatibilities. Second, it keeps the production environment stable so that when problems occur, you can recreate the exact environment in your development environment to diagnose issues.

Finally, your product goes into production. However, sometimes you are not sure if a new design will work or not. In such cases, you can use *canary deployment* to push the new version to a small set of customers to try it out. Or, you can conduct *A/B testing* by splitting customer traffic to two separate designs to see which one works better.

Regardless of how many tests you do, you still run the risk of something terrible happening and taking your service down. To address this, people use *blue-green* deployment. Blue-green deployment keeps identical production environments (called blue and green). At any time, only one of the systems takes customer traffic. When a new version is deployed, it's deployed to the idle system and goes through all necessary tests before it's switched to become the active environment. Then the previously active environment becomes idle, and the process continuous.

Continuous Improvements

Back in the late 1940s, a small car factory named Toyota was facing a dilemma: how to make cars cheaply for a small market. Traditionally, factories had been using streamlined mass-production to reduce unit cost. However, this wasn't possible because of limited market size. To solve this problem, Taiichi Ohno, the son of Toyota's founding father Sakichi Toyoda, built a Toyota Production System (TPS). The gist of TPS is to create a stream of value. And all activities in TPS revolved around eliminating waste in this stream. The goal was to perfect the flow of this stream so that it could produce value in the most efficient way. This ultimate efficiency, or *lean production*, provided a strategic competitive edge for Toyota, and led the company to becoming one of the largest manufacturers in the world.

The same principles apply to the software industry as well. If you look at the core of the Agile software process, it's all about perfecting the software iteration process. The focus, however, is not to eliminate waste, but to maximize value extraction throughout the process. It's crucial to factor customer feedback into this process so that customer requirements can be satisfied with minimum delays, and new value-added opportunities can be discovered and then fed back into the process to generate additional value.

Neither Agile not the lean movement is about getting things right at the first try. Instead, they both emphasize continuous improvements. You should continuously learn from your continuous workflow, identify parts that can be done with higher efficiency and quality, and incorporate incremental improvements into your workflow. This process is pretty much approximating an optimal function: you might never get to the optimal value, but you can get fairly close. And when you are closer than your competitors, you can secure a winning position.

The software industry has great opportunities to learn, as it offers much more frequent learning cycles than traditional manufacturing industries. For instance, when you manufacture a car, it may take a few years for a new model to be developed, manufactured, and presented to an end consumer. When you make software, on the other hand, new "models" can occur at a much faster pace because you focus on a minimum set of features that deliver a designed customer experience, and start the feedback loop at a very early stage of the product. This initial product with minimum required features is referred as a Minimum Viable Product (MVP). MVP is a great vehicle for jumpstarting the software iteration process. An MVP should contain only the features required to fully present your design to the targeted customer. In other words, MVP should be succinct. This is not the final product you'll deliver. And the code for MVP is likely to be discarded. And as you work with pilot customers, you may even find a completely different direction than you originally anticipated. Even if you discover the concept does not work, it's still a good thing, which helps you avoid wasting additional resources.

The continuous improvements are based on continuous learning. And continuous learning needs a healthy team dynamic that allows team members to freely exchange ideas and learn from each other. There are no fixed ways to achieve this. Some teams try to impose fixed processes, such as *peered coding*, to facilitate learning. However, each developer works and learns in different ways. As a team lead, you need to encourage continuous learning, and allow your team members to learn in the ways with which they feel the comfortable.

Tutorial: Using Azure DevOps

 Next, you'll go through two tutorials that demonstrate two popular CI/CD systems: Azure DevOps and Jenkins. In both tutorials, you'll deploy a simple containerized web application using Nginx.

In case you haven't heard about Azure DevOps—it's essentially Visual Studio Team Services (VSTS) renamed, which was renamed from Visual Studio Online (VSO), which was an extended version of Team Foundation Services (TFS).

Creating an Azure DevOps Project

1. Log in to the Azure DevOps portal (https://dev.azure.com). If you don't already have an account, you can visit https://azure.microsoft.com/en-us/services/devops and apply for a free account.
2. To create a new project, click on the New Project button on the DevOps home page, as shown in Figure 8.2.
3. On the **Create new project** page, enter a name and a brief description of your project.
4. In the **Version control** drop-down list, select the source code repository you want to use (you can pick between Git and Team Foundation Version Control). DevOps supports a few work item processes, including Agile, CMMI, and Scrum. This tutorial uses the Agile process.

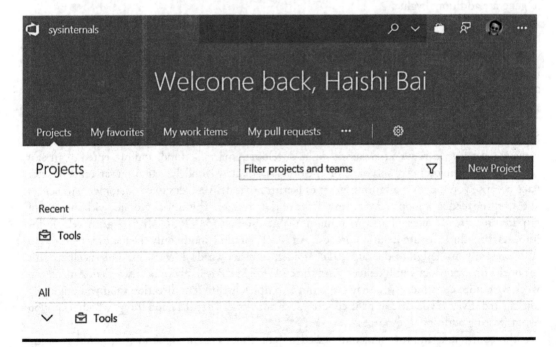

Figure 8.2   Creating a new project

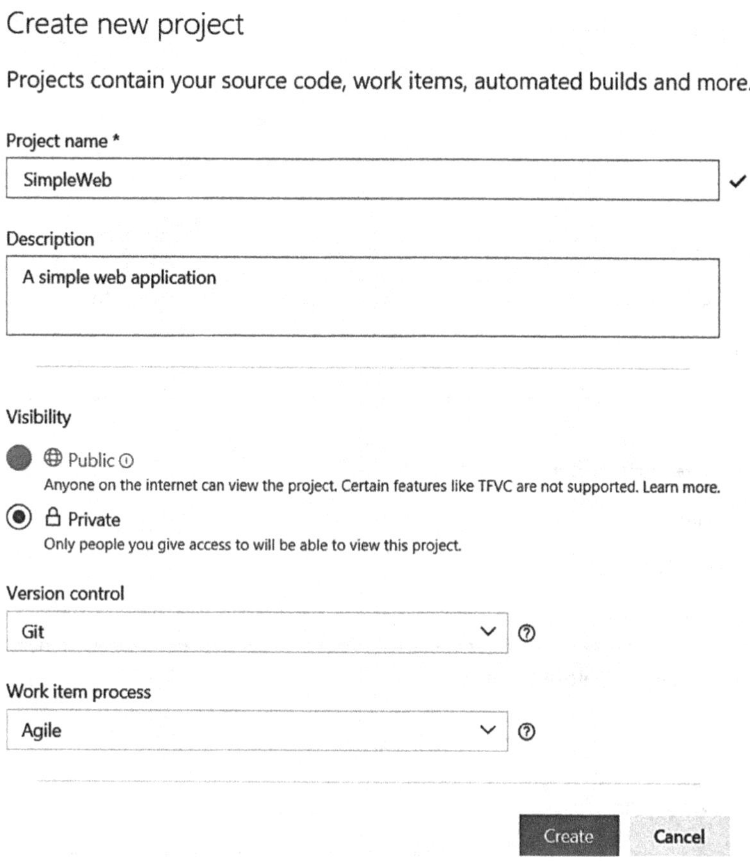

Create new project

Projects contain your source code, work items, automated builds and more.

Project name *

SimpleWeb   ✓

Description

A simple web application

Visibility

⬤ ⊕ Public ⓘ
   Anyone on the internet can view the project. Certain features like TFVC are not supported. Learn more.

◉ 🔒 Private
   Only people you give access to will be able to view this project.

Version control

Git   ∨   ⑦

Work item process

Agile   ∨   ⑦

[Create]   **Cancel**

Figure 8.3   The Create new project page

5. Click on the **Create** button to continue, as shown in Figure 8.3.
6. On the next page, click on the **Generate Git credentials** button (see Figure 8.4) to generate a login credential for the newly created repository.
7. Enter an (optional) alias and password, then click on the Save Git Credentials to save the credential (see Figure 8.5). To get the URL to the git repository, click on the Copy button to the right of the repository address field.

Creating the Application

1. Once you clone the repository to your local folder, create a new **app.html** file under the folder with the following contents:

```
<html>
  <body>
    <h1>My Simple Web App</h1>
  </body>
</html>
```

 **SimpleWeb** ☆

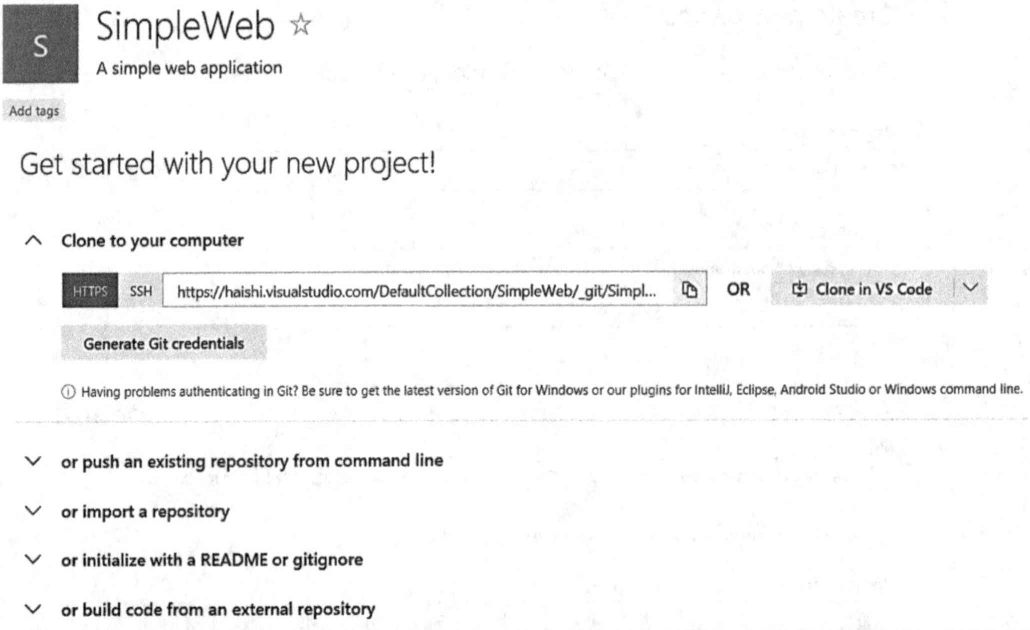

A simple web application

Add tags

Get started with your new project!

∧ **Clone to your computer**

| HTTPS | SSH | https://haishi.visualstudio.com/DefaultCollection/SimpleWeb/_git/Simpl... ⎘ | OR | ⎘ **Clone in VS Code** ∨ |

Generate Git credentials

ⓘ Having problems authenticating in Git? Be sure to get the latest version of Git for Windows or our plugins for IntelliJ, Eclipse, Android Studio or Windows command line.

∨ or push an existing repository from command line

∨ or import a repository

∨ or initialize with a README or gitignore

∨ or build code from an external repository

Figure 8.4   Git repository configurations

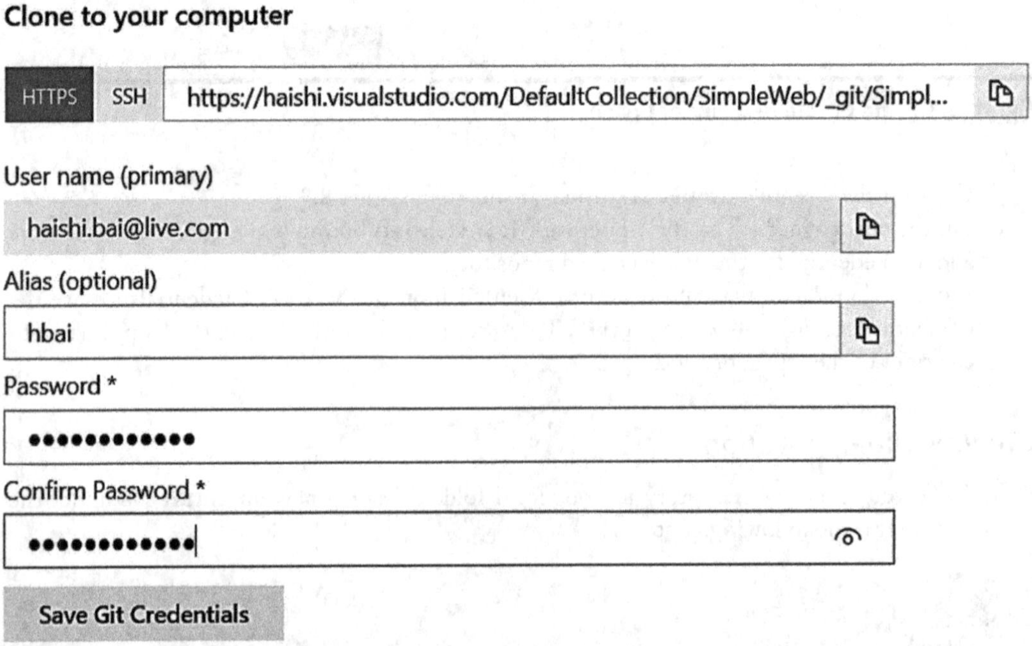

Clone to your computer

| HTTPS | SSH | https://haishi.visualstudio.com/DefaultCollection/SimpleWeb/_git/Simpl... ⎘ |

User name (primary)

haishi.bai@live.com   ⎘

Alias (optional)

hbai   ⎘

Password *

●●●●●●●●●●●●

Confirm Password *

●●●●●●●●●●●●   ⊙

Save Git Credentials

Figure 8.5   Creating new Git credential

2. Then, create a **Dockerfile** that wraps the application as a Docker container based on the public *nginx* image:

```
FROM nginx
COPY . /usr/share/nginx/html
```

3. To quickly test the application, use **docker build** to build the container and then use **docker run** to launch your web app (I used *hbai/simpleweb* as the tag. You should choose your own tag).

```
docker build -t hbai/simpleweb .
docker build -t hbai/simpleweb .
```

Then, you should be able to use curl to retrieve the web page:

```
curl http://localhost:8080/app.html
```

4. Once the application tests out, you can check in your code:

```
git add .
git commit -m "initial commit"
git push
```

Creating a Build Pipeline

1. Return to your Azure DevOps project page and click on the **Pipelines** link at the top of the page. Then click on the **New pipeline** button on the page.
2. On the **Select a source** page, accept all defaults and click on the **Continue** button to continue. You can also pick source repositories on other platforms such as TFVC, Subversion, and Bitbucket Cloud.
3. On the **Select a template** page, select the **Docker container** template and then click on the **Apply** button. The page also shows a list of templates for building various popular project types, including Node.js with Grunt, Xamarin for Android, and ASP.NET Core.
4. The template creates a very simple pipeline, as shown in Figure 8.6. The pipeline contains one build job, which consists of two steps: build a Docker image and push the Docker image to a Docker registry.

    Each pipeline is associated with a build agent pool. When you queue a build with the pipeline, a machine in the pool is selected and configured to carry out the build. Microsoft DevOps provides a cloud-based agent pool. Or you can set up your own build pool (by installing an agent on your machine) and link it to your pipeline. In this tutorial, you'll use the default agent pool provided by Azure DevOps.
5. Click on the **Build an image** step. Change the **Container Registry Type** to **Container Registry**. Then, click on the **New** button besides the **Docker Registry Service Connection**

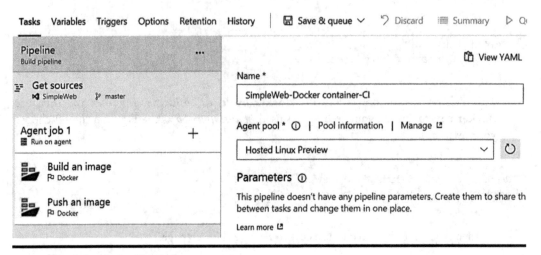

Figure 8.6   Simple build pipeline

field. On the **Add a Docker Registry service connection** dialog, select **Docker Hub** as **Registry type**. Then enter a name for your connection as well as your Docker Hub Credential. Click on the **Verify this connection** link to verify you've entered everything correctly. Then click on the **OK** button, as shown in Figure 8.7.

6. Change the **Image Name** field to *<Your Docker account>/<Image name>*:$(Build.BuildId), for example hbai/simple-web:$(Build.BuildId).

Add a Docker Registry service connection

Registry type	◉ Docker Hub ○ Others
Connection name	Docker Hub
Docker Registry	https://index.docker.io/v1/ ①
Docker ID	hbai
Password	••••••••••••
Email	hbai@Microsoft.com

Connection ✅ Verified   Verify this connection

[OK]   [Close]

Figure 8.7   Add a Docker registry service connection

SimpleWeb-Docker container-CI 20181004.4

◈ SimpleWeb · ⅏ master · ◊ 787456c : initial commit · Manual build

⊘ Add a tag

Logs   Summary   Tests | 🚀 Release   ✎ Edit   Queue ∨   ⋯

Agent job 1 Job	Started: 10/3/2018 11:13:41 PM
Pool: Hosted Linux Preview · Agent: Hosted Agent	⋯ 24.036

✓	Prepare job · succeeded	0.000
✓	Initialize Agent · succeeded	15.870
✓	Initialize job · succeeded	0.524
✓	Checkout · succeeded	3.654
✓	Build an image · succeeded	14.603
✓	Push an image · succeeded	4.477
✓	Post-job: Checkout · succeeded	0.456
✓	Report build status · succeeded	0.267

Figure 8.8   Build result

7. Click on the **Push an image** step. Change **Container Registry Type** to **Container Registry** and change **Docker Registry Service Connection** to the Docker Hub connection you've created in the previous step. Also, change the **Image Name** field to match the image name from the previous step. Then, click on the **Save & queue** button to save the build pipeline and queue a new build.

8. On the **Save build pipeline and queue** dialog, accept all defaults and click on the **Save & queue** button.

9. Once a build is queued, you can switch to the build page to monitor the build process. Figure 8.8 shows an example of a successful build.

10. To enable continuous integration, edit triggers of the build pipeline. Check the **Enable continuous integration** checkbox and save the build definition (see Figure 8.9).

11. Once continuous integration is enabled, a new build will be queued whenever you push a new version to the repository.

Tutorial: Using AWS CodeBuild

AWS CloudBuild is a cloud-based build service for building and testing code on cloud. In this tutorial, you'll set up another build pipeline that builds the same source code you've used in the previous tutorial. Since AWS CodeBuild doesn't support Git

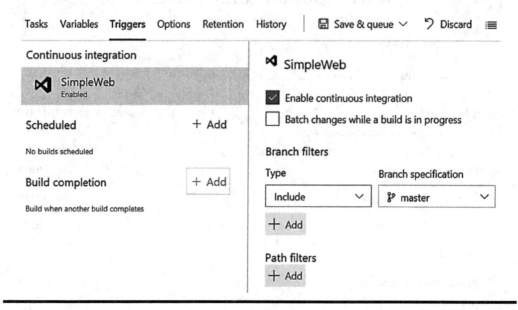

Figure 8.9   Enable continuous integration

repositories hosted by Azure DevOps, I've checked in the above code to a public GitHub repository at http://github.com/Haishi2016/simpleweb.

1. Login to AWS management console's CodeBuild page: https://<region>.console.aws.amazon.com/codebuild.
2. Click on the **Get Started** button.
3. On the **Configure your project** page, configure the following fields:
   - Enter a **Project Name**.
   - Select **GitHub** as **Source provider**.
   - Select **Use a public repository**.
   - Enter **Repository URL**: http://github.com/Haishi2016/simpleweb
   In the **Environment: How to build** section:
   - Select **Use an image managed by AWS CodeBuild** as the **Environment image**.
   - Select **Ubuntu** as the **Operating system**.
   - Select **Docker** as Runtime.
   - Select **aws/codebuild/docker:17.09.0** as **Runtime version**.
   - Select **Insert build commands** for **Build Specification**.
4. Click on the **Switch to editor** link under the **Build commands** field. This opens an online editor that you can use to edit a build specification. Edit the specification file to log in to Docker Hub in the pre-build command, build a Docker image in the build command, and push the Docker image to Docker Hub in the post-build command, as shown in the following code snippet:

```
version: 0.2
phases:
  pre_build:
```

```
    commands:
      - echo Logging in to Docker Hub…
      - docker login -u <user> -p <password>
  build:
    commands:
      - echo Build started on 'date'
      - echo Building the Docker image...
      - docker build -t <user>/simpleweb-aws .
  post_build:
commands:
  - echo Build completed on 'date'
  - echo Pushing the Docker image...
  - docker push <user>/simpleweb-aws
```

5. Click on the **Continue** button and then the **Save** button.
6. To start a new build, click on the **Start build** button. If everything works out as expected, you should see a successful build as shown in Figure 8.10.

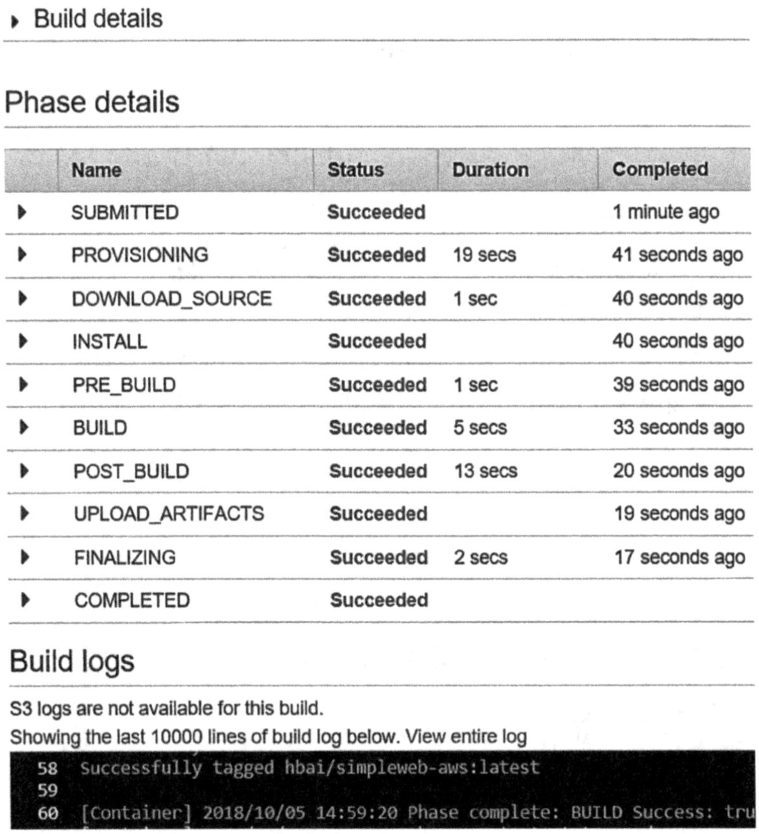

▸ Build details

Phase details

	Name	Status	Duration	Completed
▸	SUBMITTED	Succeeded		1 minute ago
▸	PROVISIONING	Succeeded	19 secs	41 seconds ago
▸	DOWNLOAD_SOURCE	Succeeded	1 sec	40 seconds ago
▸	INSTALL	Succeeded		40 seconds ago
▸	PRE_BUILD	Succeeded	1 sec	39 seconds ago
▸	BUILD	Succeeded	5 secs	33 seconds ago
▸	POST_BUILD	Succeeded	13 secs	20 seconds ago
▸	UPLOAD_ARTIFACTS	Succeeded		19 seconds ago
▸	FINALIZING	Succeeded	2 secs	17 seconds ago
▸	COMPLETED	Succeeded		

Build logs

S3 logs are not available for this build.
Showing the last 10000 lines of build log below. View entire log

```
58  Successfully tagged hbai/simpleweb-aws:latest
59
60  [Container] 2018/10/05 14:59:20 Phase complete: BUILD Success: tru
```

Figure 8.10   A successful build in AWS CodeBuild

Tutorial: Using Jenkins on GCP

Jenkins is an open source automation server that is commonly used for continuous integration and continuous delivery. Jenkins was developed by Sun Microsystem in the early 2000s under a Hudson project. In 2011, the project forked into an Oracle Hudson CI project controlled by Oracle and Jenkins managed by open source community contributors. In this tutorial, you'll set up another build pipeline using Jenkins running on Google Compute Platform (GCP).

Provision a Jenkins Instance

1. Launch a new Jenkins deployment through the GCP Marketplace: https://console.cloud.google.com/marketplace/details/bitnami-launchpad/jenkins

2. Enter a deployment name. Pick the zone, machine type, disk type, size, etc., and click on the **Deploy** button to deploy the Jenkins instance. Once the instance is provisioned, the instance's address, as well as administrator login credential, is displayed (see Figure 8.11).

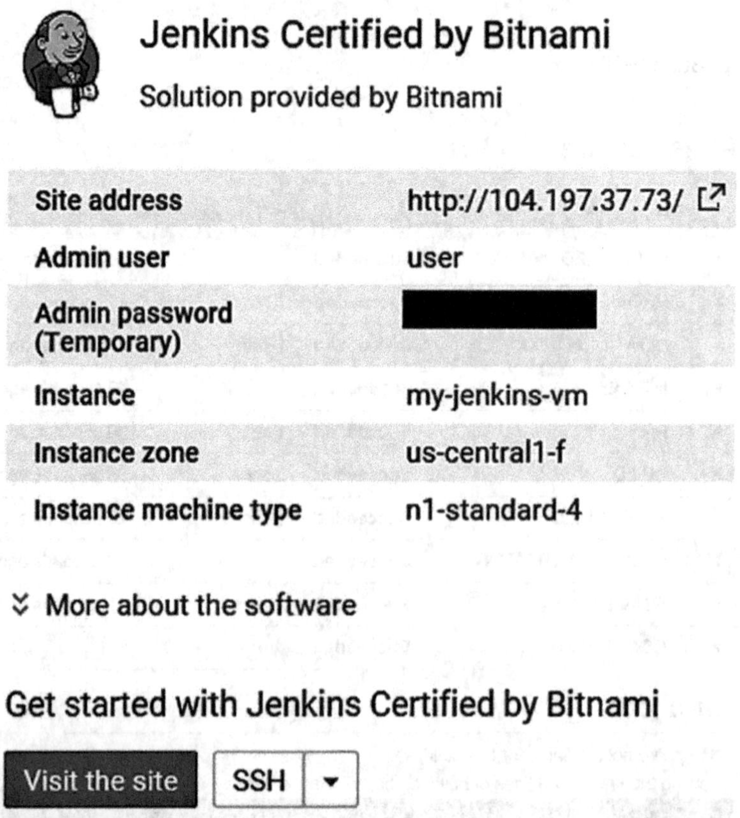

Jenkins Certified by Bitnami

Solution provided by Bitnami

Site address	http://104.197.37.73/
Admin user	user
Admin password (Temporary)	▇▇▇▇▇▇
Instance	my-jenkins-vm
Instance zone	us-central1-f
Instance machine type	n1-standard-4

❯❯ More about the software

Get started with Jenkins Certified by Bitnami

Figure 8.11   Jenkins instance information

3. Because we need to use Docker in our pipeline, we need to add user **tomcat**, under which Jenkins runs, to the **docker** group. To do this, click on the **SSH** button (see Figure 8.10) to connect to the Jenkins host. Then, use the following command to add tomcat to the docker group:

```
sudo usermod -aG docker tomcat
```

4. Back on the page in Figure 8.11, click the site address and use the administrator credential to log in.
5. Click on the **Install Suggested plugins** button.
6. On the **Instance Configuration** page, click on the **Save and Finish** button. Then, click on the **Restart** button.

Define a New Pipeline

1. After Jenkins has restarted, click on the **New Item** link to create a new pipeline.
2. Enter **simpleweb-jenkins** as **item name**. Click on the **Multibranch pipeline** template. Click the **OK** button to continue.
3. Under the **Branch Sources** section, click on the **Add source, Git** menu.
4. Enter **Project Repository**: https://github.com/Haishi2016/simpleweb. Then click the **Save** button, as shown in Figure 8.12.

   I've defined a **Jenkinsfile** in the repository. The fie describes the build pipeline:

```
node {
    def app
    stage('Clone repository') {
        checkout scm
    }
    stage('Build image') {
        app = docker.build("hbai/simpleweb-jenkins")
    }
    stage('Push image') {
        docker.withRegistry('https://registry.hub.docker
.com', 'docker-hub-credentials') {
            app.push("${env.BUILD_NUMBER}")
            app.push("latest")
        }
    }
}
```

   Please note you'll need to use a different image tag (instead of *hbai/simpleweb-jenkins*) in your *Jenkinsfile*. To do this, you can fork the above repository, update the *Jenkinsfile*, and use your own Git repository URL.

5. Click on the **Credentials** link to the left of the page. Then, click on the **global** link beside your pipeline name, as shown in Figure 8.13.

Figure 8.12 Configure branch sources

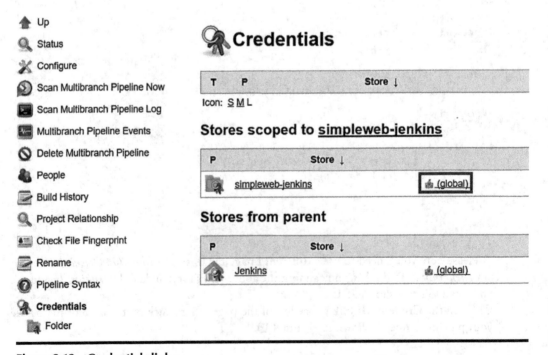

Figure 8.13 Credentials link

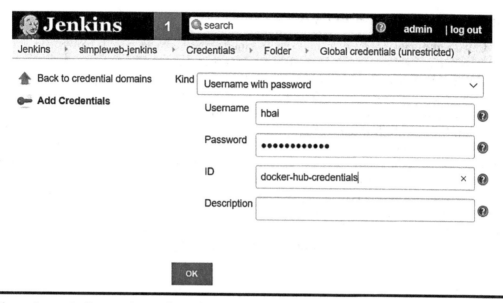

Figure 8.14   Define Docker Hub credential

6. Click on the **Add Credentials** link to the left. Then, enter a user credential for Docker Hub. You'll need this to push the image to Docker Hub. Please note the user ID must match what's specified in your Jenkins file (*docker-hub-credential*). Click then **OK** button to add the credential (Figure 8.14).
7. Back in the pipeline page, click on the **master** branch link. Then click on the **Build Now** link to queue a new build. Figure 8.15 shows a successful build.

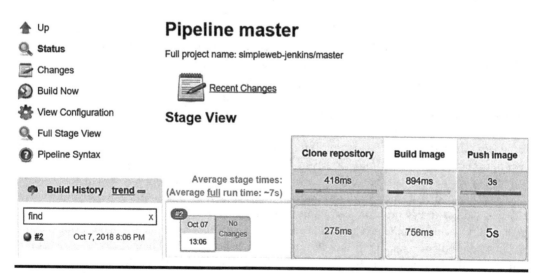

Figure 8.15   A successful build on Jenkins

Useful DevOps Practices

DevOps is not suitable for every team. DevOps requires the entire team to be motivated to make continuous improvements and be focused on reaching a common goal. More than anything else, DevOps is a continuous learning process in which team members seek all opportunities to learn and improve during fast iterations. Unfortunately, not all developers work in this way. I've worked with seasoned developers who insisted on working with their fixed methods, young developers who wanted to do as little as possible, and developers who wanted to follow their own tempo and work toward larger deliverables over an extended period instead of short sprints. Unless you have the choice to change your team members, you need to adjust your strategy to fit your team instead of trying to force a templated process on to the team.

So, instead of introducing an end-to-end methodology, I'll focus this section on practices that have proven useful in my past experiences. I'll try to cover various aspects, ranging from team building, planning, to quality control and automation. I don't believe in fixed processes. Instead, I hope the following discussion can provide you with some ingredients to compose your own workflow.

User Stories

Kicking off a software project is easy—just launch your favorite IDE and start typing, and your project is underway! However, before you do something, you need to be very clear about why you would do it, especially when there are lots of investments at stake.

Some say software is never the end goal. Instead, the end goal is to address problems of your target customers. However, from a developer's perspective your end goal is not to solve your customers' problems. Your goal is to get returns by providing your customers value. Take Google as an example. Google's financial model is based on advertising. And the key to an advertisement solution is user traffic. Before search engines, Internet portals attracted user traffic by curated Internet catalogs. Manually maintaining such catalogs is a very labor-intensive process, and it is hard to keep up with the diversity of ever-growing Internet contents. Google provided a brand new experience that was vastly different from the rich Internet portal experience. It folds the entire Internet behind a single search box. Even today, Google still has the "I'm Feeling Lucky" button on its main page (see Figure 8.15). This button is Google's bold statement of a new experience that takes you quickly to final content. Google's innovation is a tremendous success, leading Google to become one of the top software companies in the world.

Selling advertising has been one of the main financial models for Internet service companies, including various social networks. Obviously, when someone spends money to launch a social network, their goal is never just to provide you a way to connect with your friends or to share funny cat videos. Their goal is to leverage your information to sell targeted advertisements. For these sites, user information is the most important asset. Extracting value from user information while respecting privacy is a delicate balance, which has led to many controversies and scandals in recent years.

Another important category of consumer-facing web service is selling digital content, such as pictures, videos, and games. Although almost all Internet media still relies heavily on advertising, high quality, exclusive content is becoming an increasingly important vehicle for generating income.

So when you come up with a user story, you need to keep in mind how the user story fits into your planned financial model. Then you need to put yourself into your user's shoes and design the story from your user's perspective. This is easy to say but very hard to do. Many developers tend to envision how they are going to implement a feature as they design a feature. As a result, they tend to bend user stories, either intentionally or subconsciously, toward their implementation plans or around their technical limitations. Therefore, it's a good idea for business people instead of developers to come up with user stories.

A good user story should consist of a clear user role, action, and expected results. For example, for Google search, a user story could be "As an Internet user, I should be able to quickly find the most relevant web pages by a keyword search, as shown in Figure 8.16." This user story contains both a functional requirement (keyword search) and non-function requirement (quick response time). You can easily convert this user story into actionable work items. On the other hand, if you find it hard to come up with actionable work items, the user story probably needs to be revised to provide clarity.

A user story is the North star of your development activities. You should focus your effort to deliver the first few user stories as a minimum viable product (MVP), and work with your pilot customers to refine the story and come up new stories. When you work these customers, you should not focus on fixing bugs if the bugs don't affect you delivering the designed experiences. Instead, you should focus on refining user stories and keep an open mind to repivot as necessary.

Running Sprints

Experience tells us that for software projects, a long term plan usually doesn't work well. This is because a software project is not as tangible as physical projects. There are almost guaranteed unforeseen problems surfacing as the project progresses. These problems introduce great variances into the team's productivity. You must use shorter planning cycles to correct your schedule. Furthermore, an agile software process encourages frequent iteration loops to frequently incorporate customer feedback. Shorter planning cycles allow you to adjust your work items based on fresh customer feedback. Last but not least, planning for long periods is complicated. It takes a lot of effort, and the result is likely to be inaccurate anyway. Given all these reasons, modern software projects are conducted in short sprints instead of long marches. The difference between the two approaches is like the difference between a cannon and a guided missile. You need to carefully calculate the trajectory before firing a cannon. Once a cannon shell is launched, corrections aren't possible until another cannon shell is launched. On the contrary, a guided missile keeps adjusting its course as it flies toward the final target.

For an experienced team, two weeks is often an ideal length for a sprint. For a less experienced team, one week sprints can be used. A shorter sprint allows the manager to monitor individual progress more closely and take corrective actions as needed. Mature developers can take on longer tasks because they present less unpredictability in performance. Longer sprints help them remain focused on tougher problems without unnecessary interruptions. Each sprint should have clear

Figure 8.16   Google search experience

deliverables. Everyone on the team should commit to what they plan to deliver at the beginning of the sprint. And their products are checked against their commitments. If you have a difficult problem that can't be solved within a sprint, you should split it into multiple small deliverables across a series of sprints, instead of allowing a problem to stretch over sprints without clear deliverables.

If a user story can't be accurately estimated until some key technical assumptions are verified, you may consider launching a *spike*, which takes one or a few experienced developers out of regular product sprints to investigate the problem in isolation. Spikes should be timeboxed to verify a specific hypothesis. This means the work occurring in spikes doesn't necessarily directly contribute to the final deliverables. As a matter of fact, isolation from product deliverables usually helps the investigators to better focus on the problem itself. For example, when an interactive website team tries to decide on which graphic library to use, a spike can be launched to compare different technologies against key anticipated scenarios and performance metrics. During the investigation, these graphic libraries are compared and benchmarked. The code written in these investigations is not meant to be used in the final product. As the result of the spike, a graphic library is chosen, and general guidance on work item estimation is created based on the library's complexity and the team's experience with the library.

Once team members have some good ideas on workload estimation, they can come together to come up with a sprint plan by using activities such as *planning poker*. In a planning poker game, each developer holds several cards that represent different workload estimates (such as hours needed to complete a work item). As a work item is presented, each player decides on a card individually and all players present their choices at the same time. Then based on some predefined rules such as majority wins or average points, a more accurate estimation is created. For a more experienced team, sprint planning can also be done through a *work item auction*. In a work item auction, each team member holds a certain amount of credits that represent working hours they'll put in the upcoming sprint. Then they start to bid on work items. The developer with the lowest bid wins the work item. Work item auctions combine the process of work planning and work item assignments, so it can shorten the sprint planning process. However, the process assumes all developers are accurate in workload estimations and are motivated to make maximum contributions. If team members are less experienced, the auctioneer can set up a base "price" and allowed maximum variance in bids. The base prices can also be determined by a planning poker game.

As work items are generated, processed, and delivered, it's very useful to have a shared monitoring tool for the whole team. You can certainly pick some software packages for the purpose. However, in many cases, a team Kanban board works very well. A Kanban board has work item states as columns. A work item is written on a Post-it and is placed in the *backlog* column to the far left. Then, it goes across the board through the states from left to right until it's delivered. A Kanban board can have multiple rows as well. The rows can be by developers or teams, by user stories, by functional areas, or by whatever categories that make the most sense to you. Figure 8.17 shows an example of a simple Kanban board with a single row. Work items are generated out of user stories and are added to the backlog column. Then for each sprint, a few work items are selected and placed into the *top priority* column. Once work items are assigned, they are moved to the *in-progress* column. Once a work item is completed, it's fed into automatic or manual test and then released once it passes the tests. At this point, the work item graduates and is removed from the board.

Testing

Testing is an important tool for ensuring your software behaves as expected. There are many types of tests such as unit tests, integration tests, and performance tests. They verify the quality and

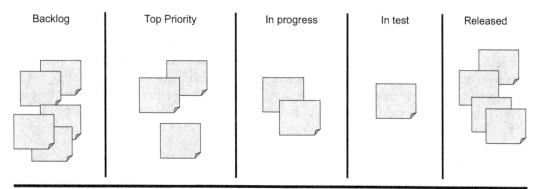

| Backlog | Top Priority | In progress | In test | Released |

Figure 8.17   A simple Kanban board

behavior of software from different angles. I believe most developers agree with the importance of testing. However, not all developers understand how to come up with meaningful tests. I've seen some teams spend lots of time creating many test cases that don't bring much value except for increasing complexity and maintenance cost.

Designing Test Cases

Bad test cases try to verify whether software is correctly written. This may sound a little counterintuitive at first. However, if you think about it, how can you expect a developer to write the correct test cases if they can't implement the code correctly in the first place? For example, to fully test a simple arithmetical *add* function to ensure correctness, you'll need to test many combinations such as adding two positive numbers, adding two negative numbers, adding large numbers that will cause overflow, adding numbers with zeros, adding two malformed numbers, adding decimals, etc. If a developer follows good coding practice, they would have checked input parameters in the first place. This means most of the preceding test cases will just be busy work without generating any value. Instead of spending time creating such test cases, you are better off teaching your developers to write defensive code against invalid and out-of-scope parameters before carrying out business logics.

Good test cases serve as a living specification of your software. As you make changes, you can verify your changes against this living specification by running automated tests. This ensures your implementation will not deviate from your original design. And as the design changes, the updated test cases ensure the new design is landed in the code. Instead of writing specification documents, architects write down their design as test cases. These cases will fail until they are properly implemented. This process is known as a *test-driven development* process. In such a process, test cases are also used as a design tool, especially in API design. The architect will put themselves in the API consumer's shoes and design the API in a way that is clear and easily consumable. They'll create mock implementations that throw *not implemented* exceptions, which cause the test cases to fail. The test cases pass when all designed features are properly implemented.

Testing should be automated as much as possible, because you want to repeat your tests frequently, ideally upon each change. You can also use your CI/CD system to set up *gated check-ins* that stops a developer from checking in breaking changes. In the hands-on lab below, you'll go through the process of setting up such checks.

Load Testing

Conducting load tests used to be hard and expensive before the cloud era. To run a meaningful load test, you need to set up many test agents to drive the workload up because otherwise the test agents themselves become the test bottleneck before they can fully stress the server. To test a global application, you'll need test agents allocated in major geographical regions so that you can properly represent distributed customer groups. When you run multiple rounds of tests, you either need to keep expensive test resources running across multiple iterations or go through complex setup and teardown processes for each of the test iterations.

Cloud-based test platforms have changed the game. With cloud-based test platforms, you can acquire a large number of geographically distributed test agents quickly, run your load tests, and discard the agents once you are done. You can simulate various user workload patterns such as stepped loads and bursting loads with these agents, and you often need to pay only for the test execution minutes without incurring any other management costs. With the rise of containers, you can acquire even more test agents with lower costs. Furthermore, you have greater flexibility to tailor the test agents toward your exact needs by using custom test agent containers.

Hands-On Lab: Automating Pull Request Management with Azure Pipelines

 In this lab, you'll learn the end-to-end steps for setting up an automatic build pipeline using Azure Pipelines (part of Azure DevOps). You'll start with a new repository on GitHub, set up Azure Pipelines integration, enable automatic build and tests, and then perform an automated check on a pull request. And last, you'll add a build status badge to your repository to display the latest build status.

Configure your Azure DevOps Account and GitHub Repository

1. Log in to the Azure DevOps portal (https://dev.azure.com). If you don't already have an account, you can visit https://azure.microsoft.com/en-us/services/devops and apply for a free account.
2. At the time of writing, the new Azure Pipelines experience is still in preview. To enable the preview features, click on your avatar at the upper right corner of the portal page and select **Preview features**. Then toggle all available preview features to **On**.
3. In this lab, you'll create a fork from a https://github.com/calculator-demo/calculator repository, which contains a sample Node.js application that implements a pocket calculator. Log in to your GitHub account and fork the repository.

Azure Pipelines GitHub Integration

1. Click on the **Marketplace** link at the top of your GitHub repository.
2. Search for **azure pipelines** in the **Search Marketplace** search box. Then click on the found **Azure Pipelines** entry.
3. On the **Azure Pipelines** page, click on the **Set up a plan** button. Then click on the **Install it for free** button. At the time of writing, Azure Pipelines offers a generous pricing model—it's essentially free. You can use unlimited build minutes with up to 10 parallel build pipelines on your public repositories.

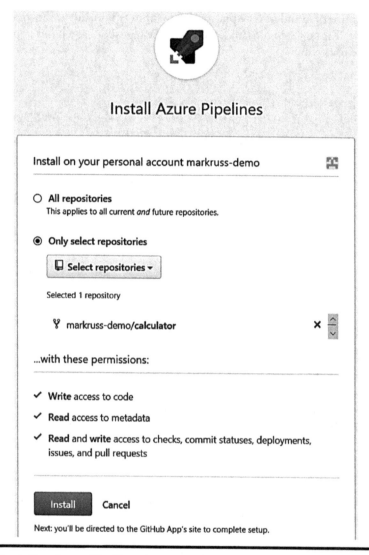

Figure 8.18   Installing Azure Pipelines for a repository

4. On the **Review your order** page, click on the **Complete order and begin installation** button.
5. On the pop-up window, select your calculator repository and click on the **Install** button, as shown in Figure 8.18.
6. This takes you to the Azure DevOps page. Click on the **Create a new project** link below the **Select a project** text box. Then enter **Calculator** as the new project name. Finally, click on the **Continue** button to create the new project.
7. The new pipeline wizard shows up. On the **Select a repository** screen, click on your calculator repository to continue.
8. Azure Pipelines automatically analyzes your repository and generates an appropriate pipeline manifest file. It will detect the project as a Node.js project in this case. Click on the **Node. js tile** to continue.

9. Edit the manifest file and insert **npm test** below **npm run build**, as shown in the following code snippet. The new step runs all test cases in the repository as a build step. The build fails if any of the tests fail.

```
# Node.js
# Build a general Node.js project with npm.
# Add steps that analyze code, save build artifacts, deploy, and
    more:
# https://docs.microsoft.com/azure/devops/pipelines/languages/
    javascript

pool:
  vmImage: 'Ubuntu 16.04'

steps:
- task: NodeTool@0
  inputs:
    versionSpec: '8.x'
  displayName: 'Install Node.js'

- script: |
    npm install
    npm run build
    npm test
  displayName: 'npm install and build'
```

10. Click on the **Save and run** button. On the **Save and run** dialog, click on the **Save and run** button again. This triggers a new build. The build should succeed in about 20 seconds.

Create a Pull Request

1. Navigate back to your GitHub page. Edit the **api/controllers/arithmeticController.js** file using the online editor. Change the line

```
'add':        function(a,b) { return +a + +b },
```

to

```
'add':        function(a,b) { return a + b },
```

2. Scroll down. In the **Commit changes** section, enter a commit comment and select the second option to create a new branch, push your code to the new branch, and create a pull request. Click on the **Propose file changes** to continue, as shown in Figure 8.19.
3. On the **Open a pull request** page, click on the **Create pull request** button. An automatic build is triggered on your new branch and all tests are executed. Seconds later, you'll see the new pull request has failed the tests, as shown in Figure 8.20.
4. Click on the **Details** link in the above box. Then click on the **View more details on Azure Pipelines** link.

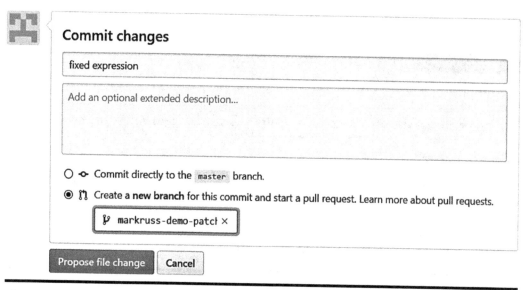

Figure 8.19   Commit changes

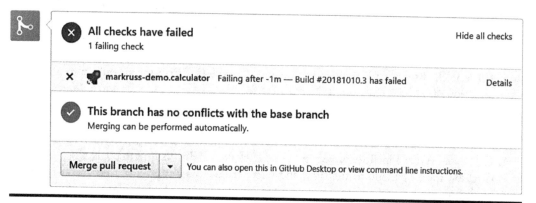

Figure 8.20   Failed tests on a pull request

5. Click on the failed **npm install and build** step. You'll see the error reports on failed test cases, as shown in the following code snippet. What happened is that when you removed the "+" signs before "a" and "b," they were treated as string parameters and concatenated together as a string instead of being added together.

```
1) Arithmetic
 Addition
   adds two positive integers:
 Uncaught AssertionError: expected { result: '2121' } to deeply
equal { result: 42 }
 + expected - actual
 {
 -   "result": "2121"
 +   "result": 42
 }
```

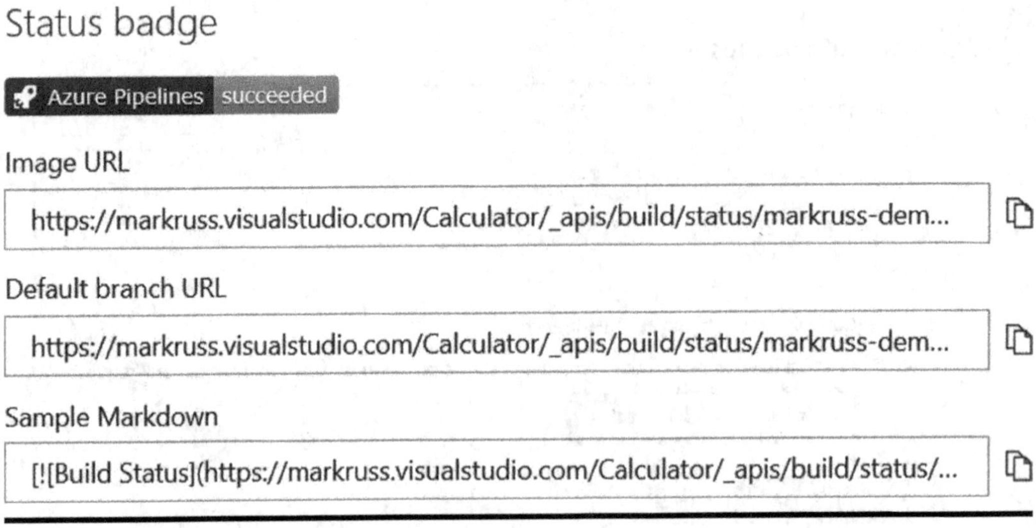

Status badge

🚀 Azure Pipelines succeeded

Image URL

https://markruss.visualstudio.com/Calculator/_apis/build/status/markruss-dem... 📄

Default branch URL

https://markruss.visualstudio.com/Calculator/_apis/build/status/markruss-dem... 📄

Sample Markdown

[![Build Status](https://markruss.visualstudio.com/Calculator/_apis/build/status/... 📄

Figure 8.21   Build badge code snippets

6. To revert your changes, open your pull request and navigate to **Files changed**. Edit the file to restore the original expression and commit to your pull request branch.
7. You'll observe that another automatic build is kicked off, and the pull request passes all tests this time.
8. Click on the **Merge pull request** button and then the **Confirm merge** button to merge the pull request.

Add a Build Status Badge

1. Go to your Azure Pipelines project page and click on the **Builds** link to the left.
2. Click on the (...) menu to the right and select the **Status badge** menu. The **Status badge** blade provides you a few code snippets that you can copy and paste into your pages to display the latest build status (see Figure 8.21).
3. Copy the **Markdown** code snippet and insert it into the **README.md** file under your repository root folder. The badge informs your potential customers whether your code is in a stable state so that they can choose when and which version of your code they should use.

Zen of Cloud

"We place the highest value on actual implementation and taking action. There are many things one doesn't understand and therefore, we ask them why don't you just go ahead and take action; try to do something? You realize how little you know and you face your own failures and you simply can correct those failures and redo it again and at the second trial you realize another mistake or another thing you didn't like so you can redo it once again. So by constant improvement, or, should I say, the improvement based upon action, one can rise to the higher level of practice and knowledge."

Fujio Cho

I volunteer teach Java programming at high schools. I keep telling my students that the best way to learn programming is to program. You should not worry about making mistakes, I tell them, because every single mistake is your opportunity to learn. As an old Chinese saying states, "Be happy when told of one's errors." A smart learner never gets upset with the critics. If what they say is correct, she will think of ways to fix her errors. If what they say is incorrect, she will also learn how people may misunderstand the problem so to avoid repeating their errors in the future.

I've seen may senior developers putting their noses up against junior developers. However, when it comes to learning, seniority doesn't matter. Everyone's knowledge is like a circle. Some circles are bigger and some circles are smaller. Even if your circle is much larger than other circles, unless it completely covers the other circles, any of the non-overlapping parts are the areas you don't know and your opportunity to learn. The knowledge base in computer science is refreshed and expanded rapidly. Your old, big circle keeps eroding, and you must supplement with new knowledge, sometimes from junior developers who have smaller but fresher knowledge circles.

To build a successful DevOps culture, the number one task is to encourage your team members to maintain an open mind to keep learning and improving. Then everything falls in place naturally.

Chapter 9

Blockchain

Distributed Ledger

My wife and I have been happily married for 19 years. As we look back on our journey together, one question often comes up: who noticed the other first? We both claim each other as the one who started the chase. We both have some proof such as letters, pictures, and stories recalled from memory, but neither of us has definitive proof show who was the suitor or pursuer. Of course, such discussions are never meant to have a conclusion. They are just excuses to bring back sweet memories of the past two decades.

Now imagine we had maintained a ledger that recorded every interaction between us—conversations, dates, mail, phone calls, and others. Then we could look at the ledger and trace back the genesis of the story: June 23th, 1998. At 10:15 in the morning, Jing came to Haishi's cubical and asked if he would be interested in going on a trip along the Yangzi River.

Now the problem becomes, how trustworthy is this ledger? Has it recorded everything truthfully? Has it been altered? Has it missed any events? First, having a neutral trusted third-party is not an option. No one wants a third wheel during dates to record every single detail. And no one would be interested in such a job anyway. Second, every record going into the ledger must be consented to by both parties. This means writing in the ledger must be a coordinated process, and all records going into the ledger must be made available to all parties so that they can vote on whether the records should be accepted. All records must be chronologically ordered so that the sequencing of events can be reliably verified (i.e., who came on to whom first). Third, there must be a mechanism to ensure the records are not modified by any party in any way once they are recorded in the ledger.

How would you design such a ledger?

Consensus

Because the goal of maintaining a distributed ledger is to avoid future disputes, log entries written to the ledger must be approved by both of us. When either of us tries to write an entry, instead of writing directly into the ledger, one makes a proposal to make a change. And the entry is officially logged only when all members, or most of the members, approves the proposal.

Reaching consensus in a distributed system with possible faults in network and nodes is much more complicated. Many consensus protocols have been developed over the years, such as *Paxos* and *RAFT.* Paxos defines three roles: *proposers, acceptors,* and *learners.* During a Paxos run, a proposer first get promises from most of the acceptors that they will accept its value. Then it proposes the value. Once the majority of acceptors accepts the value, a consensus is reached. Then learners learn about the agreed value. In a RAFT system, a node can be a *leader* that makes decisions, a passive *follower* that takes decisions, or a *candidate* that is used to elect a new leader. There's only one leader at any given time. When the leader fails, its heart beats messages to followers to stop. This triggers a new election for a new leader. A follower changes itself to a candidate and casts a vote for itself. Then it asks votes from other servers and becomes a leader if it gets a majority of the servers.

Paxos and RAFT represent two different trains of thought: vote-based and leader-based. In a vote-based system, consensus is reached by majority vote. In a leader-based system, the elected leader makes decisions. They both assume the participating servers are cooperative, which means they are honest and try their best to reach consensus as quickly as possible. However, in a more open environment such as the Internet, such assumptions don't hold. The consensus protocol needs to work with some of the participants who are deliberately or incidentally unfaithful. Ideally, it should also work even when some of the participants collaborate to corrupt the system. I'll discuss such protocols in the blockchain section.

Peer-to-Peer Network

Because neither of us wants to involve a third-party in maintaining our ledger, we must coordinate our work directly with each other. When we sit in the same room, we can communicate with each other to reach consensus before committing a log entry. When we are at different locations, it becomes hard to keep away from any third-party—even email messages go through some centralized email server. But, for the sake of discussion in this case, I'll assume email does provide point-to-point communication.

For a distributed ledger system, such assumptions don't hold. To ensure decentralized communication, the traditional client-server architecture won't work. Instead, participating parties need to communicate with each other through a peer-to-peer network.

Most distributed consensus systems require frequent inter-node communications. Because of potential network partitions, nodes need to keep each other up-to-date to ensure both consistency and durability of data. Over time, consensuses are *eventually consistent* but *explicit*, which means any of the nodes will eventually get all consensuses. And all consensuses they see will be final.

When communicating over an open network, all messages need to be encrypted and often signed to ensure authenticity, privacy, and integrity. In addition, consensus systems also have additional message verification mechanisms to detect malformed or outdated messages.

Immutability

Once an entry is written into the ledger, it can't be altered. For a paper ledger, the pages can be laminated to protect from future edits. Each page should also have a sequential page number so that missing pages or inserted pages can be detected. However, this doesn't protect against someone pulling out an entire page, altering it, laminating it, and inserting the page back into the ledger.

One way to protect such an attack is to include a digest of the previous page (such as a hash of the page text) at the top of each page. When a page is replaced, its digest will differ from what's been recorded in the next page, allowing us to detect the fraud. To make a change to an existing

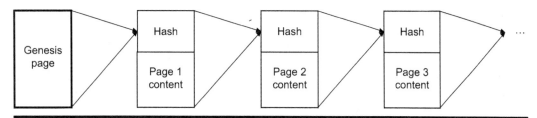

Figure 9.1   A chain of ledger pages

page, the attacker will need to change the page and all pages after it. Figure 9.1 shows how ledger pages are linked together through hashes. Any changes on any of the pages requires changing the page and all subsequent pages.

Because you can't insert new pages into the chain, the ledger is append-only. To make new entries, you must create a new page to append to the last page and then link the page into the chain. In a distributed system, multiple updates from different users may cause collisions. For example, both user A and user B create and append a new page to the ledger at the same time, creating a fork in the chain. Both pages are legit; however, only one should survive.

There are different strategies to solve such collisions. For example, in RAFT, the elected leader pushes its entries to other members, and all conflicting entries on member servers are discarded. Discussion on how RAFT ensures such synchronizations are safe is not in the scope of this book. Essentially, entries that have not been accepted by a majority of members are subject to pruning.

Another way to solve such collisions is to allow members to vote on which branch to keep. When a member wants to create a new page, it picks a longer branch and appends its page to the branch. This mechanism allows members to converge on the longest branch. All other shorter branches are eventually abandoned. However, in this case, there's no clear indication if a branch will be abandoned. The only thing you can tell is that if there's a much longer branch than your current branch, your branch is at high risk to be eliminated, and you should probably merge with the longer branch.

A longer branch is not always a safe bet. If a powerful hacker can control so much compute resources to build up a faux branch faster than the good guys, he will lure members to jump onto his branch and highjack the whole chain in a so-called *51% attack*. Of course, pulling off such an attack is hard in a massive distributed network with hundreds of thousands of compute nodes.

Blockchain

Blockchain was created for Bitcoin, which we'll discuss further in the next chapter. Over the past few years, people has been seeking scenarios to which Blockchain can be applied. This is a very interesting case in computer history—instead of finding a solution to a problem, people are looking for problems that can fit into a solution. This phenomenon was generated by the incredible cryptographic currency hype of the past few years, and it's distorting the importance of Blockchain to a ridiculous scale. Some even claim that Blockchain should be the future platform of all distributed computing.

This is far from the truth. Outside the context of cryptographic currency, Blockchain brings very little new contributions to the table in terms of solving distributed computing problems. It's true that you can implement a distributed ledger or a consensus mechanism using Blockchain. But there have existed other solutions and algorithms to the same problems.

Nevertheless, because Blockchain has attracted much attention, it's worth to examining how Blockchain implements a distributed ledger and a consensus system.

Transactions

Transactions are the basic unit of activity on Blockchain. A transaction is composed of at least one input and output. A typical transaction is to transfer funds from one address to another. A transaction is signed with the sender's private key and is broadcast to the Blockchain network. Blockchain member nodes compete to handle newly submitted transactions through a process of mining, which will be introduced later in this section.

The only way to verify which account initiated a transaction is to check the signature of the transaction using the sender's public key, because only the owner of the corresponding private key can generate the signature. This means the only protection of all your wealth on Blockchain is your private key. If you lose your private key, you lose everything because anyone who gets ahold of your private key can impersonate you and drain your account.

Blocks

A block contains a number of transactions. Each block is identified by a hash in the chain and is linked to a previous block through the hash of the previous block. This structure ensures all transactions in a blockchain are chronologically ordered and immutable. The first block in the chain is called a *genesis block*, which is often hard coded with a fixed value.

Figure 9.2 illustrates the structure of a block and how blocks are linked together. A block contains a header, a transaction counter, and a list of transactions. A block's header contains a hash of the Merkle tree of all transactions in the block (see Merkle tree in the next section). And the next block references the hash of the block's header. This ensures that no transactions can be modified unless the block containing the transaction and all blocks that follow the block are updated. Otherwise the chained references break.

Blockchain relies on a highly available and highly reliable storage, because losing any block means losing all blocks following that block and losing the genesis block means losing the entire chain. A *full node* on a Blockchain keeps a local snapshot of the blockchain state tree and copies of full blocks. A *light node* syncs only header information, which is sufficient for submitting new transactions because to generate a new block, you need only the block header from the latest block.

Mining

Blockchain is a totally distributed system. When a transaction is submitted to the network, there's no centralized processors to handle these transactions. Instead, the transaction is broadcast to the entire network and any member on the network can process the transaction. Once a member

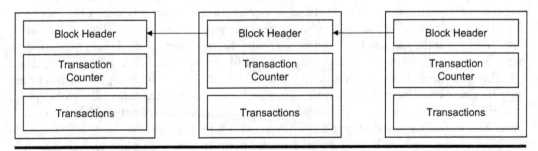

Figure 9.2 Blockchain structure

processes a group of transactions, it records the transactions in a block and submits the block to the network. The block is verified by the members and appended to the chain.

To keep the members motivated, a reward is given to the member who successfully submits a block that's accepted by the chain. To avoid a malicious member generating bogus blocks, certain proof of legality is required. There are many types of proof, including Proof of Work (PoW), Proof of Stake (PoS), Proof of Authority (PoA), and some other forms.

With PoW, a member needs to solve a cryptographic puzzle before it can submit a block. The puzzle is to generate a hash with certain number of leading zeros. Because hashing an algorithm is irreversible, the only way to generate a required hash pattern is to try different nonce values, which are hashed together with transaction hashes to generate the final hash. This is a repetitive, costly, tedious, and wasteful process, which discourages people from spamming the system. On the other hand, if someone investigates resources to do so, it's likely to be more profitable to follow the rules instead of working against the rules.

The following Python 3 code is a simulation of the mining process.

```
import hashlib
import codecs
def solvePuzzle(data,prefix):
    count = 0
    for x in range(0, 0xFFFFFFFF):
        binData = codecs.decode(data+format(x, 'x').zfill(8), 'hex')
        hash = hashlib.sha256(hashlib.sha256(binData).digest()).
          digest()
        rst = codecs.encode(hash[::-1], 'hex_codec')
        count += 1
        if rst.startswith(prefix.encode()):
            print("\nSolved in " + str(count) + ' steps!\n')
            print(rst)
            return
```

To try out the code, import the file to your Python environment call and invoke the *solve-Puzzle* function with an even-digit hexadecimal number and a string of zeros. The length of the second parameter decides the difficulty of the puzzle—the algorithm needs to generate a hash that matches with that many zeros.

I tried the algorithm with "ABCDEF" as the payload and got the results in Table 9.1 (the code accidentally found a solution to a 6-zero puzzle when it was asked to find a

Table 9.1 Sample Mining Results

# of zeros	Steps needed	Result hash
1	4	0529e2ea173f05cc99742a77d0003dc54d2d667eb8c7205e0a8c57ce...
2	101	0096caa545fdb7752e015f5c962fa43efca6df670ac3a8fae91c15bf80...
3	6433	000b828e987b203b22d0120eeba9d3aba4199eb8a88d99b8a9661d9...
4	44999	00003afc9ddf8fecf7ca673b62ccfc0c8ad910086dbcde4fc633a51c28...
5	1007589	0000004a19c00579966b965adf9a9f358135240849548c0e934df8a0...

solution for the 5-zero puzzle). You can observe that as the number of zeros increases, the difficulty of the puzzle exponentially grows.

Many Blockchain networks dynamically adjust the puzzle difficulties to throttle the number of blocks that can be mined during any period. For example, bitcoin adjusts the difficulty so that a block is mined roughly every 10 minutes. This means throwing more compute power into the network doesn't make the chain run faster. It just increases waste.

As multiple members compete to solve the puzzle, multiple members may simultaneously solve it. In such case, multiple valid blocks will be proposed. As the blocks are broadcast to the network, they are likely to be picked up by different members who continue with their own work based on any of these blocks. This causes a fork, or a split, in the chain. As members always pick the longest branch to work with, they will eventually converge on the longest branch, abandoning all blocks in shorter branches.

Because a valid block may be abandoned, you need be careful with the merchant you exchange based on the transactions in the block. Let's say you sold a TV to another person. The transaction is logged in a block, and you deliver the TV to the purchaser. However, minutes later, you found out that the block was abandoned, which cancels his payment. Now, you are out of both TV and money. To remain on the safe side, you should wait for a block to accumulate enough trailing blocks so that it's very unlikely to be abandoned. As a rule of thumb, you should wait for at least four to five blocks to be appended to your block before you release the physical goods. This means your transaction should clear in roughly an hour.

In 2016, an attacker successfully drained tens of millions of dollars worth of digital currency from the Decentralized Autonomous Organization (DAO). To deal with this attack, the Ethereum Foundation decided to manually create a hard fork to roll back transactions since the attack. This decision split the community into one group who is against the split and another group who supports the split.

> (i) Mining is a tremendous waste. And it's the primary reason I'm against bitcoin and PoW-based Blockchain in general. It was estimated that the energy consumed by mining was equivalent to the energy consumption of Denmark in 2017. It's mind-boggling how the world is okay with that. The possibility of financial gain dwarfs the goodwill to preserve energy and to save our planet. This is a dark period in computer history.

Blockchain Technologies

I've touched on a few technologies in the previous section. This section provides introductions to each of the technologies in more detail. The segments below are independent from each other and are presented in no particular order. Feel free to skip through the concepts that you are already familiar with.

Merkle Trees

A Merkle tree (named after Ralph Merkle) is a binary tree in which a non-leaf node's value is a hash of both its children. Initial values are entered to the leaf nodes. And they are hashed in pairs through the tree layers until a final hash is generated at the *Merkle root*. The Merkle root hash is

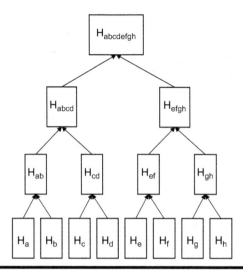

Figure 9.3   A sample Merkle tree

what is saved in the header of a Blockchain block. Figure 9.3 shows a sample Merkle tree with eight leaf nodes and how the hashes are rolled up all the way to the Merkle root.

Because a parent node in a Merkle tree is a hash of all its descendants, a Merkle tree can be pruned to save storage space without losing the holistic view on all nodes. As new transactions are being added as leaf nodes to the right, you can gradually trim the nodes to the left to save space. As you trim, the older transactions are discarded. However, you retain an (increasingly) blurry image of older transactions.

Tutorial: Using OpenSSL to Experiment With Public Key Cryptography

 I've covered how RSA public key cryptography works in chapter 4. It's used extensively in the context of Blockchain, especially for encryption and digital signatures. In this tutorial, you'll use OpenSSL to conduct a series of experiments with various aspects of public key cryptography.

Create an RSA Public and Private Key Pair

1. Use the following command to generate a private key:

```
openssl genpkey -algorithm RSA -out myPrivateKey.pem -pkeyopt
   rsa_keygen_bits:1024
```

2. You can use the ***cat*** command to examine the private key:

```
cat myPrivateKey.pem
```

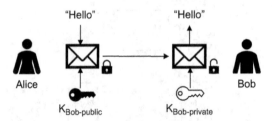

Figure 9.4   Data encryption and decryption using RSA key pair

3. Use the following command to generate the corresponding public key:

```
openssl rsa -pubout -in myPrivateKey.pem -out myPublicKey.pem
```

Encryption and Decryption

Data encrypted by an RSA private key can be decrypted only with the corresponding public key (and vice versa). This characteristic can be used to ensure privacy in communication. For example, when Alice tries to send Bob a message, she uses Bob's public key to encrypt the data and sends the data over the Internet. Because only Bob has the private key, he's the only one who can decrypt the data. So, even if data is passed along the untrusted Internet, privacy is maintained between Alice and Bob, as shown in Figure 9.4.

1. Encrypt a piece of data using the public key you just generated:

```
echo Hello > message.txt
openssl rsautl -encrypt -inkey myPublicKey.pem -pubin -in message.
  txt -out message.dat
```

2. If you try to print the content of message.dat, you'll see the data is scrambled. The only way to decrypt the data is to use the corresponding private key:

```
openssl rsautl -decrypt -inkey myPrivateKey.pem -in message.dat -out
  message-bob.txt
cat message-bob.txt
```

Hash and Digital Signatures

Hash functions create fixed length digests of input data. They are used to ensure data integrity. A sender creating a digital signature of the data to be sent usually does this. First, it calculates the hash of the data to be sent. Then, it signs the hash value using its own private key. When a receiver receives the data, it decrypts the hash value using the sender's public key. Then, it calculates a hash of received data and compares the calculated hash with the decrypted hash. If the hashes match, it knows the data originated from the sender without being tampered by anyone. Several hash function families are commonly used, including MD, SHA-1, SHA-2, SHA-3, and MACs.

1. You can use the following command to create a hash of the **message.txt** file:

```
openssl dgst -sha256 message.txt
```

2. The above command generates the following output:

```
SHA256(message.txt)=
66a045b452102c59d840ec097d59d9467e13a3f34f6494e539ffd32c1bb35f18
```

3. You can also generate the digital signature using a single command:

```
openssl dgst -sha256 -sign myPrivateKey.pem -out signature.bin
  message.txt
```

4. Use the following command to verify the signature:

```
openssl dgst -sha256 -verify myPublicKey.pem -signature signature.
  bin message.txt
```

If the signature checks out okay, you should see the following output:

```
Verified OK
```

Consensus Mechanisms

Distributed nodes on a blockchain network need to establish a means of agreeing to a single version of truth. Earlier in this chapter, I noted that consensuses are often reached through a leader election-based system or a voting system (which is often referred as a traditional Byzantine Fault Tolerance, or BFT, system).

In a closed blockchain network, which is often called a *consortium* or *permissioned* network, consensuses are often achieved by using a *BFT-based* approach. Such systems assume the participating nodes are trustworthy and are generally collaborative. In a public blockchain with participating members from all around the Internet, a *proof-based* system is often used. I introduced Proof of Work (PoW) earlier in this chapter when I introduced mining. There are many other proof-based mechanisms such as Proof of Deposit (PoD), Proof of Importance (PoI), Proof of Elapsed Time (PoET), Proof of Activity (PoA), Proof of Storage (PoS), and many others.

Ethereum

Ethereum was conceptualized by Vitalik Buterin in 2013. The idea was to create a Turing-complete language that can express any business logic as smart contracts. Ethereum blockchain can be viewed as a distributed, transaction-based state machine. A contract starts from an initial state, goes through a series of state transformations, and reaches its final state. Because all transactions are recorded in immutable and chained blocks, all transformations on a contract are auditable and verifiable.

When a transaction is submitted, it is picked up by *miner* nodes to be verified and included in a block. Then the block is proposed to the network. Once the block is accepted, all the transactions in the block are considered committed.

Ethereum Networks

The main Ethereum network is called *Mainnet* with a chain ID of 1. You can use https://etherscan. io to explore the Ethereum blockchain. Figure 9.5 shows a screenshot of the website, which shows the latest blocks and transactions on the network. This should remind you that all transactions

Figure 9.5   A screenshot of etherscan.io

and blocks on the network are visible to everybody. You can also drill into accounts associated with the transactions and see the account balances as well as all transaction histories. Although account address are hash codes without associated personal information, in theory it's possible to infer the account owner from information such as known transactions and specific transaction patterns. The currency on Mainnet is *ether* (ETH), which has actual monetary values. You can purchase ether with fiat or bitcoins. There are a few websites you can use to purchase ether. For example, in the United States, Canada, and Europe, you can use www.coinbase.com or www.gemini.com to purchase ether using a bank account or credit card. Chinese readers can buy ether from www.okcoin and www.btcc.com. At the time of writing, one ETH is worth about $198, with a total market cap around $20 billion.

In addition to the *mainnet*, there exist several test networks such as *Ropsten* (with network ID 3), *Rinkeby* (with network ID 4), *Kovan* (width network ID 42), and *Morden* (with network ID 2, and now deprecated). Testnets use *faucets* to distribute test ether for developers. For example, you can use https://faucet.rinkeby.io/ to acquire test ethers for the Rinkeby network (please see the hands-on lab below for more details).

Developers can also set up private test networks for development purposes. You'll learn how to create a private network in the hands-on lab later in this chapter.

Key Ethereum Components

An Ethereum blockchain consists of several components. The core network is a blockchain running on a number of peer-to-peer networks. On each of the nodes runs an Ethereum client (such as *geth*) that offers functionalities such as account management and mining. The Ethereum client hosts an RPC service that is often consumed through JSONRPC using libraries such as *web3.js*. Figure 9.6 shows a typical topology for a user app connecting to a blockchain through an Ethereum client.

Accounts, Keys, and Addresses

Users or applications interacting with an Ethereum network need to have valid accounts. Each account is associated with a public-private key pair. An account is identified by an address, which is the last 20 bytes of the Keccak256 hash of the public key. Accounts initiate transactions. All transactions are encrypted by the sender's private key. An account has associated balances and nonce, which increments after each transaction to avoid duplicate transactions. In addition to user-controlled accounts, smart contracts, which will be introduced next, have their own accounts. Funds can be transferred between accounts (both user-owned and smart contract accounts) through transactions.

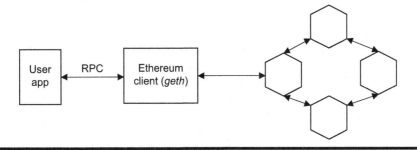

Figure 9.6   Ethereum network, client, and user app

Gas and Gas Price

Each transaction is assigned with a certain amount of *gas*. Each operation (opcode) in a smart contract has an associated *gas fee*. For example, the ADD operation consumes three units of gas, and an SSTORE operation requires 5,000 to 20,000 units of gas. The send of a transaction can specify a *gas price* in the unit of *Wei*. Because transactions are prioritized by gas price, the transactions with higher gas price tend to be processed (mined) faster. The total cost of a transaction is calculated by consumed gas × gas price.

Ethereum Virtual Machine (EVM)

EVM is a simple stack-based execution engine that runs compiled smart contract bytecode instructions. An Ethereum EVM is a Turing-complete machine, which means they can execute any possible business logics expressed in bytecode. The EVM has a word size of 256-bit and its stack size is limited to 1,024 elements. EVM is designed to provide an isolated execution environment that shields the contract code from any external resources. Real world data can be fed to smart contracts through *Oracles*. *Oraclize* is a popular Oracle contract, which you can find more info on at http://www.oraclize.it/.

EVM has both in-memory state and persistent state. In-memory state is cleared before each execution, while persistent state is stored on a hard disk. Saving state is expensive. It's usually advisable to reduce the amount of state you save with your contracts.

Ethereum Clients

Ethereum clients implement the Ethereum protocol. They sync with the connected blockchain, download and verify blocks, verify and execution transactions, and provide basic mining ability. Popular blockchain clients include: *Geth*, which is the official Go implementation of the Ethereum protocol; *TestRPC*, which is a lightweight Ethereum client for running private chains; and *Eth* is the official C++ implementation. For instance, the following command launches *geth* in RPC mode listening to a specific port (8485):

```
geth --rpc --rpcport 8485
```

Smart Contracts

Smart contracts is an old idea that can be traced back to the 1990s, when Nick Szabo envisioned an electronic transaction protocol that executes digital contracts with business logics and conditions encoded as executable routines. The rise of Blockchain has given smart contracts a great boost, leading to considerable adoptions in various industries, especially among financial institutes and banks.

Simply put, a smart contract is a business contract expressed in securable, executable, and verifiable code. Unlike paper contracts, which are subject to human interpretation and variances in execution, smart contracts hold explicit, defined, and autonomous business rules that are always reinforced.

Smart contracts are inheritably required to be deterministic. A smart execution is repeated by many member nodes and only consistent results can lead to a final consensus This means that a contract generally should not be influenced by outside data or logics. In case some external information, such as current stock value and exchange rate, is needed, a trusted *Oracle* can be used to bring data from external data sources into the smart contract.

Solidity Basics

A commonly used language to implement smart contracts is Solidity. Just like any other programming language, you can use variables, structs, functions, control statements, loops, and other constructs to build your smart contract logics. This section serves as a brief introduction to Solidity. In the following hands-on lab, you'll build an actual smart contract and deploy it to a test network.

Data Types

Solidity is a strongly typed language. Every variable is declared with a type descriptor. For instance, the following statement defines a signed 32-byte integer and assigns it to hexadecimal value 1A:

```
int a = 0x1a;
```

Solidity has a series of different integer types, from *int8*/*uint8* through *int256*/*unit256* by multiplies of eight. For example, *uint216* and *int32* are both valid integer types. It also offers a series of fixed size byte arrays, from *byte1* through *byte32*, with each holding a certain number of bytes specified by the postfix. It also defines a *bytes* type, which is a dynamic size byte array that can be initialized with a length parameter. For example, the following statements initialize a 32-byte array and then extend it to 64 bytes by changing its length property:

```
bytes d = new bytes(32);
d.length = 64;
```

Solidity *string* type represents a Unicode-encoded byte array. The type doesn't support any string-specific operations such as concatenation or searches. The following statement defines a simple string:

```
string message = "Hello, World!";
```

You can define enumerable types in Solidity as well. Each enumerable value corresponds to a *unit* value starting with 0. The following code snippet defines and uses an enumerable:

```
enum ShipmentState {Packaged, InTransit, Delivered}
ShipmentState shipment = ShipmentState.Delivered;
uint(shipment); //2
```

A special Solidity data type is *address*, which is a 20-byte Ethereum address. An address has a *balance* property and a *transfer* method for transferring balance.

```
address contract = "0xf12b5dd4ead5f743c6baa640b0216200e89b60da";
```

Arrays and Maps

You can define both fixed-length arrays and dynamic-sized arrays in Solidity. The following code snippet defines and uses two addresses.

```
address[3] candidates; //fix-sized array with three address elements
uint[] numbers; //a dynamic uint array
numbers.push(818);
int size = numbers.length;
numbers.length += 3; //append three zero elements to the array
```

The mapping type in Solidity is a key-value hash map. The following code snippet defines an *address*-to-*uint* map. Solidity doesn't provide methods for checking whether a key exists. When you access a key whose value hasn't been set, you get a zero value back.

```
mapping(address => uint) balances;
balances[msg.sender] += 1000;
```

Statements

Like other high-level programming languages, Solidity allows you to write sequential code, branches, and loops. The following code snippet shows how to use an *if* statement:

```
if (sales <= target[msg.sender])
        bonus[msg.sender] = 0;
else
        bonus[msg.sender] = (sales - target[msg.sender]) * 20;
```

The following code snippet shows how to use a *for* loops:

```
for (uint i = 0; I < players.length; i++) {
        players[i].health = 100;
}
```

Finally, the following code snippet shows an example of using a *while* loop:

```
while (balance > 0) {
    balance -= withdraw();
}
```

Functions

A function declaration in Solidity includes function name, parameter list, access decorators, and return types, for example:

```
function multiply(int a, int b) public pure returns (int) {
    return a * b;
}
```

A function may have a visibility modifier and a state permission modifier. The visibility modifier can be *public* (visible to all), *external* (can be triggered by a transaction or external contract), *internal* (visible to the current contract and child contracts that inherit current contract) or *private* (visible only to the current contract). The state permission modifier can be *view* (read state), *pure* (doesn't interact with state) or *constant* (deprecated, alias to view). A function without a state permission modifier can read and write state. The above example is a function that is callable by anyone. And it doesn't interact with state at all.

There's a special *payable* modifier, which signifies that a function can accept ether. Sending ether to function without the modifier will result in an exception. A contract can also define an unmade function, which serves as the default function when no matching functions can be located in a transaction call, or the function is not specified in the transaction.

Contract

A contract looks like a class in other OOP languages. You can define member variables and functions on a contract. And a contract can inherit from another contract. The following example shows a simple TV contract that supports methods for turning the TV on or off:

```
contract TV {
    bool state = off;
    function turnOn() public pure returns (bool) {
        state = true;
        return true;
    }
    Function turnOff() public pure returns (bool) {
        state =f alse;
        return false;
    }
}
```

Hands-On Lab: Getting Started with Ethereum Smart Contract

This lab guides you through the process of setting up a local development that you can use to author, test, and deploy smart contracts. The instructions below are based on Ubuntu. However, they are fully tested on Windows Subsystem for Linux (WSL, https://docs. microsoft.com/en-us/windows/wsl/install-win10). So if you use a Windows PC, you should be able to run through all the following steps in an Ubuntu WSL.

This lab uses a test network named Rinkeby. We can request test ethers from its faucet site (https://faucet.rinkeby.io). To use the main network, you'll need to purchase real ethers. Other than that, the operations are the same on both the test network and the main network.

Setting Up Dependencies

1. Install Node.js and NPM. We'll use NPM to install other required packages. And you'll need Node.js when you use web3.js.

```
sudo apt-get install nodejs npm
sudo ln -s /usr/bin/nodejs /usr/bin/node
```

To update your node installation to the latest version (you need at least v7), you can use:

```
sudo npm cache clean -f
sudo npm install -g n
sudo n stable
sudo -ln -sf /usr/local/bin/node /usr/bin/node
```

2. Install Solidity:

```
sudo npm install -g solc
```

3. Install Geth:

```
sudo apt-get install software-properties-common
sudo add-apt-repository -y ppa:ethereum/ethereum
sudo apt-get update
sudo apt-get install ethereum
```

4. Install Truffle:

```
sudo npm install -g truffle
```

5. To sync a full node on the Rinkeby *testnet*, run the following command. This process takes a long time. Depending on your network connectivity, it may take several days. This is optional for the purposes of this lab.

```
geth --rinkeby --syncmode=fast --cache=1024
```

Creating Two Test Accounts and Getting Initial Funds

1. Use **geth** to create two accounts. Don't forget your password!

```
geth --rinkeby account new
```

The above command returns a unique address for the new account, in the format of the following example:

```
{7b52c980ce23ea862ff2e5976943f778caf58047}
```

2. Launch **geth** in console model:

```
geth --rinkeby --verbosity 0 console
```

3. In the console, list the accounts and then query balance of each account. Both accounts should have zero balance.

```
eth.accounts
eth.getBalance(eth.accounts[0])
eth.getBalance(eth.accounts[1])
```

4. Now you need to inject some ether to one of the accounts. https://faucet.rinkeby.io/ offers several options for you to request ether through social networks. This lab uses Twitter. Log in to your Twitter account and make a tweet with one of the account addresses as the tweet account. For example, to request ether for account 7b52c980ce23ea862ff2e5976943f-778caf58047, create a tweet with body 0x7b52c980ce23ea862ff2e5976943f778caf58047 (note the 0x prefix). Once the tweet is made, copy the tweet's URL and paste it to the faucet site. Then click on the **Give me Ether** button with any of the options to generate ethers, as shown in Figure 9.7.
5. Once the account is funded, **eth.getBalance()** queries should return the account balance. The balance unit is *wei*, which is 10^{-18} ether. To display the balance in ether, use:

```
eth.getBalance(eth.accounts[0]) / 1e18
```

Figure 9.7   Use Rinkeby faucet site

Submit a Transaction

1. To transfer from account 0 to account 1, you need to first unlock account 0 using its password:

```
personal.unlockAccount(eth.accounts[0], "<account password>")
```

2. Use the following command to transfer 0.1 ether from account 0 to account 1 (simply press Enter to enter multiple lines):

```
eth.sendTransaction({
  from: eth.accounts[0],
  to: eth.accounts[1],
  value: 1e17,
  gas: 90e3,
  gasPrice: 20e9
})
```

3. Once the transaction is submitted, copy the displayed transaction hash and search for it on https://rinkeby.etherscan.io/. You can observe transaction details on the page, including time, value, transaction fee, and transaction status, etc., as shown in Figure 9.8.

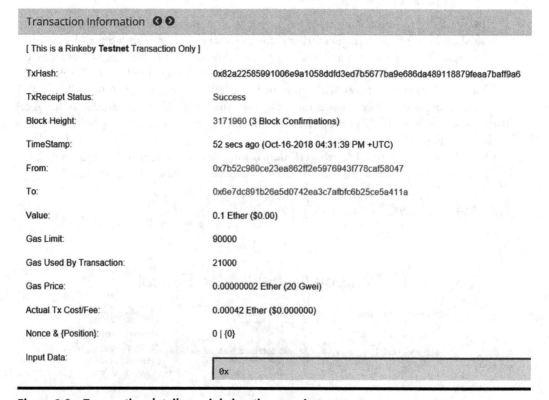

Figure 9.8   Transaction details on rinkeby.etherscan.io

4. Back in the **geth** console, use eth.getBalanc() to query account balances. You should see account balances have been updated accordingly.

Manually Deploy a Smart Contract

1. To create a Hello, World smart contract, use a text editor to create a **HelloWorld.sol** file with the following contents:

```solidity
pragma solidity ^0.4.15;

contract HelloWorld {
        address owner;
        string message = "Hello World";

        constructor() public {
                owner = msg.sender;
        }
        function sayHello() constant public returns (string) {
                return message;
        }
        function kill() public {
                require(owner == msg.sender);
                selfdestruct(owner);
        }
}
```

2. Compile the contract to generate output bytecode and ABI:

```
solcjs --bin --abi -o bin HelloWorld.sol
```

3. Open the bytecode file – **bin\HelloWorld_sol_HelloWorld.bin** and copy all content to the clipboard.
4. In the **geth** console, define a bytecode variable with the file content (please note a 0x prefix is added):

```
bytecode="0x6080604052604080519081…"
```

5. Use the following commands to submit a new transaction with the *to* address omitted and the *data* field filled with the smart contract bytecode. Once this transaction is mined, the smart contract is deployed.

```
Personal.unlockAccount(eth.accounts[0], "<account password>")
tx = eth.sendTransaction({ from: eth.accounts[0], data: bytecode,
   gas: 500e3 })
```

6. Use **web3.eth.getTransactionReceipt(tx)** to get the transaction receipt, as shown in the following example (some values are shortened to save space). The function returns *null* before the transaction is mined. In such case, repeat the command until you get a valid receipt.

```
> tx = eth.sendTransaction({ from: eth.accounts[0], data: bytecode,
  gas: 500e3 })
"0x4daa5bcce2c03fc1634fc1a5428f98e86628df47a9558cb97c7bad75758dde83"
> web3.eth.getTransactionReceipt(tx)
{
  blockHash:
"0x127f054016444bb3e603838a33974b17c7fcdbe7e5fdda7b35f9e
  09debba699d",
  blockNumber: 3175179,
  contractAddress: "0xf130cc8e1fc84fab79ec9c2e6611845bba8c2a39",
  cumulativeGasUsed: 1302893,
  from: "0x7b52c980ce23ea862ff2e5976943f778caf58047",
  gasUsed: 272820,
  logs: [],
  logsBloom: "0x000000…",
  status: "0x1",
  to: null,
  transactionHash:
"0x4daa5bcce2c03fc1634fc1a5428f98e86628df47a9558cb97c7bad
  75758dde83",
  transactionIndex: 4
}
```

7. To get the contract address, use:

```
address = web3.eth.getTransactionReceipt(tx).contractAddress
```

8. To use the compiled ABI, copy the contents in **bin\HelloWorld_sol_HelloWorld.abi** and put them into an **abi** variable, as shown in the following example:

```
abi =
[{"constant":false,"inputs":[],"name":"kill","outputs":[],"payable":fal
se,"stateMutability":"nonpayable","type":"function"},{"constant":true,"
inputs":[],"name":"sayHello","outputs":[{"name":"","type":"string"}],"p
ayable":false,"stateMutability":"view","type":"function"},{"inputs":[],
"payable":false,"stateMutability":"nonpayable","type":"constructor"}]
```

9. Now you are ready to call the smart contract:

```
hw = web3.eth.contract(abi).at(address)
hw.sayHello()
```

You should see a "Hello World" string displayed on the console.

Use Truffle to Deploy to a Private Chain

In this part of exercise, you'll use Truffle to deploy the preceding contract to the private chain.

1. Create a new folder and **cd** into that folder.
2. Initialize a Truffle project:

```
truffle init
```

3. Copy the **HelloWorld.sol** file into the **contracts** subfolder.
4. Create a new 2_HelloWorld.js file under the **migrations** subfolder. This is a *migration file*, which is a deployment spec. A deployment spec defines a callback function that is invoked during the deployment process. Put the following Node.js code into the file:

```
var helloWorld = artifacts.require("./HelloWorld.sol");
module.exports = function(deployer) {
        deployer.deploy(helloWorld);
}
```

5. Use Truffle to deploy to the private chain (not the -f parameter locates the preceding migration file by the prefix "2"):

```
truffle dev
migrate -f 2
```

This will build and deploy the contract (note it's using the "develop" chain):

```
Compiling ./contracts/HelloWorld.sol...
Compiling ./contracts/Migrations.sol...
Writing artifacts to ./build/contracts

Using network 'develop'.

Running migration: 2_HelloWorld.js
  Deploying HelloWorld...
  ... 0x1365b7f92826442c9182096c31589092ce0110be531fba2341fee0025
        b168879
  HelloWorld: 0x8cdaf0cd259887258bc13a92c0a6da92698644c0
Saving artifacts...
```

6. Once the contract is deployed, you can easily invoke it in Truffle:

```
HelloWorld.deployed().then(h=>h.sayHello())
```

Deploy to Rinkeby

This section walks you through the steps to deploy to Rinkeby using Truffle. Deploying to the main Ethereum chain follows the same steps.

1. Launch geth with a connection to Rinkeby (omit --rinkeby to connect to main net).

```
geth --rinkeby --rpc --rpcapi personal,web3,eth,net
```

2. Create a truffle.js file under the Truffle project folder. This is a configuration file that defines Blockchain networks you can connect to, each identified by a network ID. The dev network has an ID of "*," which matches with any ID other than the ids with explicit mappings.

```
module.exports = {
    networks: {
            development: {
                    host: "localhost",
                    port: 8545,
                    netowrk_id: "*"
            },
            main: {
                    host: "localhost",
                    port: 8545,
                    network_id: 1
            },
            rinkeby: {
                    host: "localhost",
                    port: 8545,
                    network_id: 4
            }
    }
};
```

3. Migrate to the Rinkeby network:

```
truffle migrate -f 2 --network rinkeby
```

Calling Smart Contracts

You've seen how to invoke a contract through *Truffle* in the preceding lab. You can invoke smart contracts from *Geth* and other Blockchain tools as well as many programming languages through the web.js API. The following is a list of implementations in common languages:

- Node.js: https://github.com/ethereum/web3.js
- Python: https://github.com/ethereum/web3.py
- Java: https://github.com/web3j/web3j
- PHP: https://github.com/digitaldonkey/ethereum-php

Smart contracts are commonly invoked through JSONRPC (https://www.jsonrpc.org/). The following code snippet shows how you can invoke a read() method on a smart contract at address 0xa43922…

```
HttpClient httpclient("http://localhost:9545");
StubClient c(httpclient, JSONRPC_CLIENT_V2);
try{
        Json::Value request;
        request["to"] = "0xa4392264a2d8c998901d10c154c91725b1bf0158";
        request["data"]="0x57de26a4";
        Json::Value response = c.eth_call(request, "latest");
        std::string str = response.asString();
        strcpy(result, str.c_str());
        *res_length = str.length();
        return result;
}
catch (JsonRpcException &e) {
        return strdup(e.what());
}
```

In the previous example, 0x57de26a4 is the first 4 bytes of the Keccak-256 hash of the function signature, which is "read()" in this case. If you call a method with parameters, you need to include parameter types into the hash as well.

Bitcoin

Bitcoin is said to have been invented by a mysterious Satoshi Nakamoto, which is likely to be a pseudonym. Around 2008, Satoshi published a paper titled "Bitcoin: A Peer-to-Peer Electronic Cash System," which introduces the idea of a fully decentralized digital currency that is not backed or controlled by any government (https://bitcoin.org/bitcoin.pdf).

Digital currency has been an active research area in the past few decades. Many solutions have been proposed, such as David Chaum's *digital cash* and later *e-cash*, Adam Back's *hashcash*, and Wei Dai's *B-money*. Bitcoin was built on top of some of the ideas such as cryptographic currency and Proof of Work (PoW). And it has gained tremendous popularity in the past decade. At the time of writing, the hype is slowly dying off.

Benefits of Bitcoin

I'm not an expert in finance, but I'll nonetheless try to list a few benefits of bitcoin based on common sense (or common misconceptions). I'm sure bitcoin has more significant meanings in the financial world. But for our discussion, the following should suffice.

Bitcoin is completely distributed. This means bitcoin is not controlled by a single country or a single organization. You can spend bitcoin without country boundaries and settle transactions with other peers directly on the bitcoin network without going through any intermediaries or complex settlement processes.

Unlike paper currencies, bitcoins can't be counterfeited. A new bitcoin is released to the network about every 10 minutes. And the total number of bitcoins was capped at 21 million in the year 2014. This makes bitcoin currency deflationary in theory. However, there were more blocks mined than intended in 2017, causing inflation in bitcoin as well.

Traditional digital currencies are cleared by central banks to avoid double spending. Bitcoin transactions are verified in public, making double spending much harder.

Bitcoin Pitfalls

I'm against the idea of bitcoin because it has generated tremendous waste via its mining process. Because a bitcoin is released every 10 minutes regardless of the amount of compute power on the network, as it gains more popularity, tremendous compute power is thrown into the network and most of it is wasted. The waste of the bitcoin network obviously outweighs its benefits. At the time of writing, bitcoin has not become a widely accepted payment method (and some major websites such as Expedia.com have removed bitcoin support). Many bitcoin transactions can be linked to black market sales and money laundering.

Bitcoin operates pretty much like a ponzi or pyramid scheme. Bitcoin has no value by itself. The only reason it gained value was because new investors kept coming in under the bitcoin hype. Figure 9.9 shows the bitcoin price history in the past few years (data source: https://www.worldcoinindex.com/coin/bitcoin). You can see a typical surge in price, reaching an all time high of nearly 20,000 dollars at the end of 2017. The price plummeted to nearly 5,000 dollars one year

 Bitcoin   BTC/USD $ 5,639.20   -1.76 %

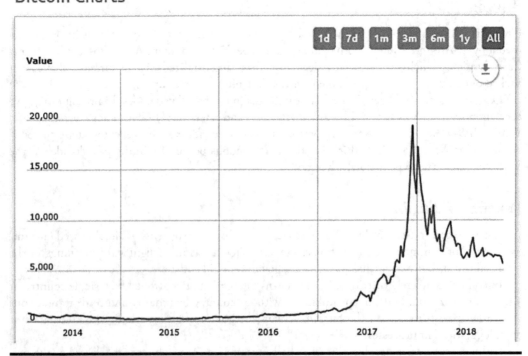

Figure 9.9   Bitcoin price history

later, which is an over 70% drop within a year. It looks like this global party is coming to an end, and bitcoin is on the verge of collapsing. As the bitcoin value vanishes, all the compute hours, hardware investments, power consumptions, derivatives, and literatures (including this one) are fading into history. I don't see bitcoin as a revolution. Instead I view it as the darkest piece of history in computer industry.

Industry and thought leaders such as Bill Gates and Warren Buffett have also voiced their concerns about bitcoin. I'm not against the proposal of a distributed, global digital currency. I simply think the price we've paid to gain the benefits is way too high to be rational. We should search for more efficient and sustainable approaches, instead of continuing to invest in this wasteful approach.

Getting Started

Before you begin, I need to go on record stating that getting into bitcoin trading is probably not a good idea at this point. If you still want to give it a try, you need to get a bitcoin wallet, buy some bitcoin, and start trading.

A bitcoin wallet is a program that you install on your PC or mobile device. It syncs with the bitcoin network and verifies proposed transactions. You can use a wallet program to send or receive bitcoins. There are many different bitcoin wallet programs to choose from. You can get a list of wallet programs here: https://bitcoin.org/en/choose-your-wallet.

Once a wallet is installed, it starts to sync all blocks from the beginning of bitcoin. At the time of writing, it takes about 200G to 300G disk space to sync all bitcoin data to your local computer. Make sure you have enough disk space for the purpose. Figure 9.10 shows the sync progress display after Bitcoin Core Wallet has been installed. As you can see, it takes hours to sync all the data.

You can buy from a bitcoin exchange, a bitcoin ATM, or a friend who already has some bitcoins. There are international and regional as well as peer-to-peer (P2P) exchanges such as Coinbase, Bitstamp, BitQuick, bitFlyer, CoinCorner, and many others. Bitcoin ATM and some bitcoin exchange service providers allow you to exchange bitcoins with cash. And finally, you can simply pay cash to your friends in exchange for bitcoins.

You can send or receive bitcoins using your wallet program. Bitcoin Core Wallet allows you to request a new sender address or a new receiver address for every new transaction. This helps you to remain anonymous.

Your wallet program data is your money, and your passcode is the only gatekeeper of your wealth on bitcoin. You should keep your passcode safe and backup your wallet to avoid losing all your digital currencies.

Zen of Cloud

> *"I think the Internet is going to be one of the major forces for reducing the role of government. The one thing that's missing but that will soon be developed, is a reliable e-cash."*
>
> **Milton Friedman**

An open, free world without boundaries is a very intriguing idea. In such a free world, you have the freedom to acquire and share knowledge, the freedom to acquire and consume resources, and the freedom to move and settle. These may sound like easy goals. However, we are far from it. Internet

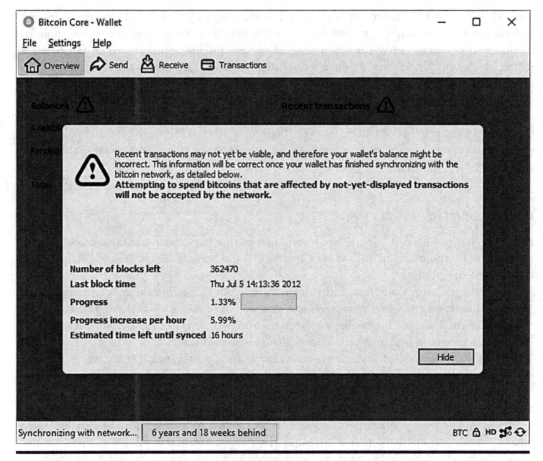

Figure 9.10 Bitcoin Core Wallet sync screen

gives glimpses of this world by granting accesses to information with unprecedented richness and allowing purchasing merchandises and services from remote sellers. Yet it's still a long journey ahead of us to fully realize these freedoms.

Bitcoin is an early attempt. At the time of writing, bitcoin is on the verge of a total collapse. When I was on a few pages back, bitcoin was still trading at $5,000. As of December 4th, 2018, the price has dropped to $3,800. That's an 80% loss from its peak value. It's estimated that the cost to mine one bitcoin is about $5,000. Such a low price is insufficient to keep a strong miner ecosystem, which is critical to bitcoin's survival. As mining machines are being sold as junk, the ecosystem is collapsing in front of our eyes.

If bitcoin disappeared, would Blockchain survive? At the re:Invent 2018 event, Amazon announced a Quantum Ledger Database (QLDB), which was designed to provide a shared ledger among a consortium. This was an important move, as it led more people to reconsider whether Blockchain was appropriate for solving problems such as shared ledgers and distributed consensus.

Chapter 10

Cloud-Native Applications

Cloud-Native Applications

As in 2018, the major way to use cloud is through either IaaS or SaaS. When many enterprises adopt cloud, their first motivation is to migrate their existing on-premises workloads to cloud. IaaS provides a familiar infrastructural environment for them to "lift-and-shift" their legacy applications to cloud. On the other hand, SaaS offers managed, specialized services for scenarios such as high-reliable storage, customer relation management (CRM), office automation, machine learning, and DevOps.

As cloud platforms and cloud users mature, the focus of cloud has been shifting toward PaaS, which hosts cloud-native applications. Cloud-native applications are designed for cloud. They comprise loosely coupled services that are designed for horizontal scaling and self-healing. These services are often developed and hosted independently, and are connected through a networking layer that offers service discovery, traffic routing, event passing, and other communication capabilities.

How do you describe a cloud-native application? Intuitive as it seems, this is a new topic that is just starting to get its deserved attention. I think this is an appropriate topic to discuss in this last chapter of the book, as it tries to peek into the future of cloud application development in the coming years.

Modeling an Application

Although modeling a cloud-native application is new, the concept of application modeling has long existed throughout computer science history. However, because the scope of an "application" is arbitrary, several different terminologies are often used interchangeably although they actually represent different concepts, namely Application Model, Programming Model, and Application Package.

Application Model describes the logical topology of application components. It's not concerned with how components or their interconnections are implemented. Programming Model is used to implement application components and their connectivity. Application Packages wrap application binaries and assets into deployable units. As you can see, each of the three terminologies represents a very distinct concern and should not be confused with one another. Lots of frameworks and tools do provide all three capabilities and don't explicitly distinguish the three concepts. For example, when you create a C# Console application with a dependent class library, the Application Model describes that the application is made up of a console app and a supporting library; the Program Model is object-oriented programming (OOP); and the Application Package is the compiled executable and dynamically linked library (dll). To fit these concepts into Visual Studio artifacts—the project file is your application model; the source code is your programming model; and the compiled binaries is your application package.

A clear understanding of these three concepts is critical to modeling your cloud-native applications. Cloud-native applications are often made of many distributed components. You need to work with the right language at the right abstraction level to keep the complexity in control at different phases of your project. And when we keep the three clearly separated, we gain lots of opportunities to streamline the application development lifecycle without imposing unnecessary lock-ins to specific frameworks or toolsets.

Application Model

Most application models are very opinionated. They are designed to describe specific types of applications. This makes sense because at the end, an application needs to deploy. And if the application model is too abstract, there will be a lot of work to evolve that application model into deployable binaries. However, if the application model is too specific, the application is not portable, and often assumes supports from specific runtimes and frameworks. Most applications we see today use specific application models, making them generally unportable to other platforms.

Intuitively, a high-level, abstract application model can be easily defined: an application is made up of interconnected components. This is indeed a quite powerful model that can be used to describe literally all types of applications. However, this application is apparently too generic to be useful.

Or, is it?

Two emerging technologies have made such a simple model incredibly powerful. These two technologies are container and service mesh. Container provides a powerful abstraction of an application's components. And service mesh provides a powerful abstraction of an application's topology. When combined, they allow the highly abstract application model to be easily materialized into running services without much hassle. This is fantastic news. Now we can model an arbitrary distributed application with a very simple design language. And we can build up consistent development and tooling experiences across many different application types. Later in this chapter, you'll see such an application model in action.

Programming Model

Many programming models have been introduced in the past decades, including procedural programing, OOP, functional programming, reactive, actors, and many others. Among these programming models, OOP is probably the most successful one and has become the pervasive programming model for many modern applications. For distributed systems, reactive programming and actor pattern have achieved great successes in both web services as well as IoT applications.

It's unrealistic to expect the whole coding community to converge on a single programming model. Different programming models are suitable for different types of problems. As a matter of fact, different programming models are opinionated toward solving specific problem domains. The more opinionated a programming model is, the more powerfully it can solve the problem it's designed to solve, but it may become less adaptive in solving other problems.

Application Package

An application package is a pack of artifacts that can be deployed into running applications. An application package format defines the physical layout of application files. This physical layout should not be mistaken as application topology. Application topology is an abstract concept belonging to an application model; it has nothing to do with the physical layout of the final application package.

Manually creating a consistently deployable application is often a punishingly difficult process. You rarely need to do this, because many tools have been created to streamline the process. However, even with these tools, creating packages is still a complex task, especially when you need to create packages for different platforms.

Deploying the application is only the first step in operating a productionized service. So an application package format without a supporting control plane is mostly useless. This is especially true on cloud. In a cloud environment, applications and services often need to be automatically redeployed on different hosting nodes for various reasons such as scaling out and failover. A control plane deploys application packages. It also monitors the health of deployed applications and takes corrective actions to keep the application in operation.

> (i) Discussions in the following sections are theoretical. They don't reflect or suggest any product designs or service offerings.

A Theoretical Application Model

Back in 2015, I started to bounce the idea of a unified application model and a unified control plane with various people. The application model is a highly abstract one, as it describes an application as interconnected components. Most people were skeptical when they heard about the model because it sounded too abstract to be useful. In particular, some of them had already attempted (and failed) to create a generic application model because it was hard to find a perfect balance between simplicity and expressiveness of the model. Many prior attempts failed because they didn't have the right abstraction level. Many of these models aimed at generating runnable code at the end. This made them extremely complex to use. However, the model I propose formally separates the application model from the programming model. This simple separation makes the model simple, flexible, and extensible.

The application model provides a platform-agnostic modeling language for cloud-native applications. This is rather different from opinionated application manifest formats offered by existing PaaS platforms. When you use an existing PaaS platform, you are unavoidably taking a *platform-centric* approach, in which you need to model your application architecture around platform capabilities. The unified application model, on the other hand, allows you to take a *workload-centric* approach, because you are not allowed to make any implicit assumptions on specific platform features. This ensures application portability across platforms without vendor lock-ins.

In theory, a cloud-native application model is quite simple: an application is made up of services sitting on a service mesh. Each service is identified by a name and a type. The most common service type is a containerized service. Services address each other via service names. The service mesh underneath services provides connectivity, and addresses cross-cutting concerns such as tracing, traffic routing, and monitoring.

Because the application is designed for developers, it shall not try to capture operational concerns such as how host environments are provisioned. Instead, such concerns can be captured by satellite models that are specifically designed to express operational concerns such as autoscaling, canary deployment and many others.

Services

A service is a compute unit that offers certain functionalities, such as processing or storage. An application model shouldn't care how a service is implemented. Instead, it should treat all services as compute units with some endpoints that take in requests and send responses back. There are two distinct service types: on-cluster services and managed services. An on-cluster service is a service hosted on cluster nodes. A managed service is hosted off-cluster. It can be a cloud-hosted service or an on-premises service.

An on-cluster service may have multiple replicas. Service mesh puts an internal load balancer in front of the replicas. Traffic is evenly distributed among these replicas. The application control plane monitors the health of these replicas. If the number of replicas drops, the control plane brings up additional replicas to restore the number to the desired level. This mechanism offers both scalability and availability of a service.

A service can be tagged with an arbitrary number of properties, which can be used to influence service scheduling decisions and routing rules. For example, two services that exchange data often can be collocated on the same node to avoid extra network hops. And two memory-hungry services can be kept on separate nodes so that they don't compete.

A service exposes endpoints by listening to selected ports. A service mesh sidecar can serve as a proxy. It exposes the same set of ports, accepts traffic over the mesh, and forwards the traffic to the service replica.

A containerized service is packaged in a container image, which is pulled down to the cluster node before the container is launched. Configurations can be injected into a container through environment variables.

Operational Concerns

A cloud-native application model should separate application developer concerns from operator concerns. The core application model is designed for developers to describe cloud-native applications. On the other hand, an operator can describe various of operation concerns with corresponding operation models. For example:

- Blue-green deployment
  In a blue-green deployment, you have two environments: blue and green. The production version is deployed to the green environment. And you deploy your new version to the blue environment. You perform various tests on the blue environment. And when you are satisfied with the blue environment, you can reroute production traffic to the blue environment. Once the blue environment stabilizes, you can shut down the old green environment and the blue environment becomes the new green environment. To perform blue-green deployment, you can deploy a blue/green policy that allows you to dynamically adjust traffic allocations between the two versions, to automatically promote the blue environment, or to rollback to the green environment.

- A/B testing
  In A/B testing, traffic is split by different percentages to two versions. A/B testing is often used to conduct user tests on specific features to compare the effectiveness of different service designs. To conduct A/B testing, you can deploy a traffic shaping operation model that distributes traffic among different versions.
- Canary deployment
  Canary deployment allows you to perform a controlled rollout after you've tested the new version alongside with the existing version by sending a small portion of user traffic to the new version. The control plane monitors the error rate of both versions. If the newer version has an unsatisfactory level of error rates, you can set up an automatic rollback policy that reverts all service instances to their original versions.
- Dark flighting
  Dark flighting sends a copy of a production service request to a test flight, which runs on a dedicated infrastructure beside the production infrastructure. The idea of dark flighting is to perform A/B testing and canary deployment without splitting live production traffic.

> (i) *Each application has its own public IP with its own ingress configuration. If* an implementation supports deployment slots (such as "production" vs. "staging"), additional routing prefixes might be automatically added to the route. For example, the route to "service-1" under the "production" slot may be "*<application IP>*/production/service-1."

Service Mesh

As introduced earlier, the application model should hide all operational concerns, including networking details as well as many of the cross-cutting concerns, from the service code. A service mesh separates services from all networking concerns. A service can safely make the following assumptions regardless of the underlying mesh configuration:

- It can address other services in the same application by their service names. Although actual access might be refused by the target services or service mesh security policies, service addresses are always stable as specified in the application specification.
- When a service runs multiple replicas, the replicas are automatically load-balanced.

Service replicas are connected to the underlying service mesh through sidecars. For example, when a control plane runs on Kubernetes, it can inject a network sidecar into the service pod. The sidecar intercepts traffic from or to service containers running in the same port. Because the sidecar intercepts all traffic, there's an extra hop in the message pipeline. However, the rich functionalities derived from this extra hop outweigh the slight performance penalty.

The following is not an exhaustive list of service mesh capabilities. However, the list is enough to illustrate the power of service mesh.

- Service discovery. A TCP/IP endpoint requires an IP address and a port. In a hosted environment, a service replica doesn't have a stable IP address. For example, the control plan may choose to launch a new service replica on a new node when the previous replica fails; it may choose to relocate a service replica to a different node to balance resource consumption across the cluster; and it may launch multiple service replicas to scale out the service.

All these activities make addressing service replicas by IP addresses rather difficult. Service mesh tracks such changes (by monitoring the orchestrator, for instance) and automatically reconfigures its routing rules so that service replicas can be addressed by their stable service names.

■ Dynamic traffic routing. As introduced in the previous section, service mesh supports powerful deployment scenarios such as A/B testing and canary deployment. Furthermore, service mesh can offer additional features during service operation. For example, service mesh can be used to improve service reliability by automatically retrying failed messages. A service mesh can also use the *circuit-breaker* pattern to forward requests to a backup service when the primary service fails. It can also be used for service throttling—when a client exceeds a certain request threshold, the service mesh can reject the service request instead of forwarding the request to the downstream server.

■ Cross-cutting concerns. Service mesh also comes in handy when you try to deal with some cross-cutting concerns such as distributed logging. A service mesh can inject a correlation id into the original request, and the correlation id is carried around as the transaction is handed across services. Because such correlation is tagged and maintained by the mesh, individual services don't need to handle the correlation id at all. Service mesh can also collect telemetries on behalf of application code. Many telemetry systems require services installing special agents, or annotating code to insert required metadata to service requests. If two services choose to use different telemetry systems, integrating telemetries from both systems is very problematic. Service mesh takes that burden off the application developer because all the telemetry system integration can be implemented at the service mesh layer in a generic manner.

Service Type Trees

It might be interesting to organize service types in an application model as a tree structure. The nodes on the tree structure follow the following rules:

■ A parent node is a *generalization* of its children. For example, the children nodes for node "postgresql.relational.database" represent different PostgreSQL database hosting platforms, such as "azure," "gc," and "aws."

■ A child node is a *specialization* of its parent.

■ Siblings are alternative implementations of their parent.

Figure 10.1 illustrates the type system. This type system allows some magic to happen. First, it allows you to model your cloud application in a cloud-agnostic way. Second, it allows a control plane to automatically search for alternative services when your primary choice isn't available. Third, it allows a migration plan to be automatically generated when you try to migrate your cloud application to a different platform. Of course, doing this requires the application code is written in such a way that it can accommodate for

Ironically, service type recommendations as well as automated architecture review were proposed before an application model. From my conversations, it seemed that people were not ready to take advantage of these advanced features. However, I remain hopeful that one day people will start to appreciate these values when a control plane accumulates enough data to derive design patterns.

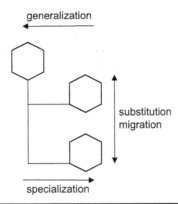

Figure 10.1   Service type system

different service implementation. For instance, if a service is written for a SQL Database, a control plane can use the service type tree to search for on-premises SQL Databases, hosted SQL Databases, or containerized SQL Databases.

An application model can be viewed as a directional graph. This allows a control plane to build up additional intelligence to provide guidance in application design. For example, A control plane can look into existing application models, abstract common application design patterns, and propose that to app designers. It can also perform certain automated architecture reviews to identify common design problems such as SPoF, chatty services, and bottlenecks.

Control Plane

A control plane takes an application model and optionally a group of associated operational models and settings, and deploys the application to the underlying infrastructure. Once an application is deployed, It keeps monitoring the application and takes necessarily actions to maintain the application at the desired state as described by the application specification and operation models.

A control plane should be designed with openness in mind. It should allow different infrastructural components to be plugged into the control plane. It should also be designed to work with different application manifest formats. For instance, in API-first development practice, the development process of an application starts with defining an API specification. A control plane can take the specification and scaffold a skeleton service for each of the defined services. Then, a developer can fill in actual business logic, or map service routes to other existing or new service implementations.

Components

Conceptually, a control plane consists of a few logical *components*.

Service Mesh

A service mesh implements the networking environment for an application. It's implemented as a software-defined network on top of a physical networking infrastructure. Service mesh allows applications sharing the same physical cluster to establish their private, isolated virtual networks. This avoids many potential configuration conflicts in a shared system. It also allows applications to be coded against a stable networking topology without needing to worry about the actual network layouts.

Developers are completely shielded from the complexity of service mesh configuration, which is not an easy endeavor. Instead, all application developers need to do is to assign simple names to their services and to define service endpoints. The control plane handles all the underlying complexities and makes sure all components are annotated with required attributes so that they can be joined to the underlying service mesh correctly.

Most service mesh implementations use a networking sidecar. The control plane should work with the selected service mesh implementation and makes sure the appropriate sidecar is injected and configured with the service container.

Ingress

An ingress provides an entry point to an application. It's configured with a public IP and provides routes to different services within the application.

An application often consists of both public services and private services. Only public services are joined with ingress and governed by ingress rules. Private services, on the other hand, are not accessible through the ingress. They are still addressable by other services within the same application through their names. However, they are inaccessible by Internet users.

Secret Store

Secret stores persist sensitive information, such as passwords and digital certificates, in a secured manner. A control plane should provide built-in support of secret stores so that when you author your application or binding manifests, you can reference these secrets by secret names, instead of embedding sensitive information inside your application specification.

Ideally, the control plane should support different secret store implementations in addition to the default Kubernetes secret store. For example, some Microsoft Azure users may prefer Azure Key Vault over the Kubernetes secret store.

Runtime

The cloud-native application model should be an abstract model. When an application is deployed, it's bound to the underlying infrastructure through a *binding* process. During this binding process, the application model is translated into infrastructural primitives and deployed on the infrastructure. For example, when the control plane runs on Kubernetes, an application is converted to Kubernetes primitives such as deployment specs and service specs during the binding process. When the control plane runs on Azure Resource Manager, an application can be projected into an ARM template and then handed over to Azure Resource Manager for deployment.

This binding process is conducted by a *runtime* component. The responsibility of a runtime is to convert the abstract application model to a deployable format.

Configuration

A configuration objects can be applied to the whole cluster, to applications, and to individual resources. Configuration objects are key-value pairs with values being arbitrary object types.

If a configuration with the same name is found at different levels, the configuration with the most granular scope takes the highest precedence.

Cluster-level configurations are used to define default components to be applied to all applications. Infrastructure operators can use cluster-level configurations to set up default policies to be observed by any applications running on the cluster. Application-level configurations are used to configure application-specific characteristics such as the service mesh framework to be used across services. Last, resource-level configurations control resource behaviors for example if the resource should have a publicly accessible endpoint.

Scheduling

A control plane schedules workload onto the underlying compute plane using a scheduler. In a small-scaled environment, a centralized scheduler using greedy algorithm is usually enough. In a larger environment, a centralized scheduler may become a bottleneck of the system. Systems such as Google Compute Engine use partitioned schedulers with shared state to reach higher scales.

I believe it's interesting to consider getting rid of centralized schedulers altogether. In recent years, especially with the development of quantum inspired algorithms, some traditional software problems can be modeled as physic problems. Scheduling is one of such algorithms. You can imagine a compute plane as a terrain with peaks and valleys. Peaks represent busy nodes and valleys represent idle nodes. When a new workload is to be scheduled, it's simply dropped into (or near) one of the valleys. Then, the workload "rolls down" the hill until it reaches the bottom of the valley.

Because each workload tries to find an optimum position for itself, the calculation can be carried in a fully distributed manner. This essentially forms an adaptive complex system, in which global optimization is achieved by emergent behaviors of the agents.

When multiple workloads pile up at the same location, they create pressure against each other to push them apart. Once a workload starts to take user traffic, it's considered to be attached to the current location with a string. More user traffic makes the string stronger. However, when user traffic lessens, the string becomes weaker and can eventually snap under pressure. This design gives precedence to busy workloads when system tries to balance resource usage.

The workload agent can be modeled to present different behaviors. For example, workloads that are close to each other can "jell" with each other, making more room for future workloads. Such dynamic micro behaviors are the most interesting aspect of the system. The workload agents can be modeled in different ways, and they evolve over time, with the most fitting agents advancing to the next generation. I believe each compute plane faces a unique combination of different workloads; the adaptive workload agents make the whole system adaptable to the observed usage patterns.

A workload agent doesn't have to see the entire terrain. Instead, it can try to find a local optimum based on the limited terrain around its field of view. When a terrain is over-crowed, workloads with weakest attachments are pushed out to neighboring, less busy terrains. The limited field of view can reduce the pressure on shared state store, making the system more scalable. Because a workload is dropped to the least busy terrain, the overall system is likely to be evenly loaded so that such cross-terrain movements should be minimum.

Such distributed scheduling scheme works well with a dynamic compute plane where compute resources come and go at any time. In a serverless platform, especially a serverless platform made up by randomly recruited spot instances, such a scheduling system could work well to schedule workloads on a dynamic compute plane. The same system can be applied to some dynamic edge computing scenarios, in which devices may join and leave the network.

Cloud-Native Programming Model

An application model isn't concerned with how individual services are implemented. A programming model defines an abstraction over the underlying infrastructure. When developers write code following the designed programming model, they are likely to get more returns in terms of performance, productivity and efficiency from the underlying infrastructure. Over the years, many distributed application programming models have been developed and used with varied success.

Lots of these programming models try to allow developers to write distributed systems as if they were writing single-thread, standalone applications. For example, Virtual Actors ensure actor code is invoked in a single-threaded manner. At any given time, only one actor instance is activated. This design shields developers from common challenges in distributed programming such as racing conditions and locking. Some other programming models focus on providing an error-free programming experience, which hides various error conditions such as network failures and process crashes. Because the system automatically preserves call stack states and resumes a program since last failing point when the process is restored, a developer can pretty much assume no such errors can cause any problems.

While many of these programming models are successful, they are often subject to abuse. If a developer is completely oblivious to the nature of distributed computing, she can still make serious mistakes even when she's strictly constrained by the programming model. What I believe is needed is a programming model that can offer simplified calling patterns – such as single-threaded invocations – while still allowing developers to use flexible threading models and concurrency patterns when necessary.

However, I do believe some distributed system concepts should be hidden from developers, such as partitions and primary/secondary replicas. These are implementation details of stateful services. They are used for achieving scale and high-availability. However, they are not well understood by many developers and often misused. Exposing these concepts might provide some flexibility in advanced usages. However, the danger and complexity overshadow the benefits for narrow use cases.

An ideal cloud-native programming model should offer built-in support for state management, message-based integration, instance identity, flexible bindings to various event sources.

State Management

As introduced earlier in this book, many services are inheritably stateful. Hence, state management is a key capability of such a programming model. Centralized state stores such as databases have been widely used in traditional systems. However, due to the distributed nature of microservices, centralized data stores may be unsuitable in some situations. For example, in a geographically distributed system, database servers deployed in different regions may take in write requests from different users at the same time. These databases need to be synchronized for consistency. And conflicting writes must be resolved. Furthermore, if state replication is asynchronous, the states saved in different database copies are *eventually consistent*, which leads to some complexities in application design. Finally, frequent calls to remote storage services may have a negative impact on overall system performance.

On-cluster, distributed stores such as etcd and Service Fabric Reliable Collections can be used as distributed storages. Because these storages are co-located with service components, they offer best availability and performance. Distributed stores also support better microservices isolations, because each service can deploy its own dedicated store without relying on any centralized components. Using distributed stores has its downside, though. First, cross-service state handling is challenging. It's hard to maintain data integrity across multiple scattered services, because they often treat state as their privacy concerns and don't consider coordinated updates or queries with other services. Second, backing up application state across multiple services is also difficult.

A state store is different from a full-scale database. A key-value store is usually enough for saving state, because it's rare for a service to perform complex queries on its own state. The programming model should encourage developers to constrain the size of the state. This is because when service instances are relocated (for load balancing or recovery, for example), its associated state needs to be moved as well. Furthermore, service states often need to be replicated for high availability. Large service state makes such tasks difficult.

Restoring state in user code can be automatic, on-demand, or a mixture of both. In automatic state restoration, service runtime should provide the last saved state to user code whenever it launches a new copy of the user code. The user code can request for states through an on-demand mechanism. This is sometimes referred as *lazy-loading* of states. In a mixed mode, user code is given a minimum state upon launch so that it can function correctly. Then, the user code can request additional states as needed.

Once the state is loaded into user code, it can be cached in memory as local variables in the handling function. Caching state in class properties or global variable may cause problems in multi-threaded environments. A framework may choose to alleviate the risks, but I don't consider that mandatory.

Message-Based Integration

Services in a cloud-native application are architecturally and sometimes operationally independent from each other. A cloud-native programming model should accommodate for the situation that the lifecycles and operational characteristics of these services are not aligned. For example, a service may offer a lower throughput than what the consumers expect. And a service may become offline, affecting all dependent services.

Message-based integration is proven to be a flexible and powerful solution to integrate independent services together without creating hard couplings among them. Message-based integration offers:

■ Loosely coupled service
Services are coupled by messages in message-based integrations. This is a much more relaxed coupling comparing to direct invocations. Direct invocation needs matching communication protocols, matching method signatures as well as matching data schemas. Message-based integration requires only matching data schemas. Many message-based systems also implement versioning on messages, allowing backward compatibility and in some cases forward compatibility across services.

■ Accommodate for performance differences
Message-based integration relies on a highly available messaging backbone. Instead of communicating directly with each other, all participating services send and receive messages through the backbone. This backbone offers many capabilities including reliable messaging, publish/subscription, caching and many others. Once a message is delivered to the backbone, the backbone ensures the message reaches its recipients, eventually. If the recipient is slow in processing messages, the backbone can cache the message and gradually release the messages to the recipient. On the other hand, if the recipient allows autoscaling, the backbone can launch additional recipients to drain the message queue faster.

The message queue also presents another interesting opportunity – the backbone can accept messages on behalf of the recipients when the recipients are not running. Then, it can dispatch the messages when the designated recipients come online.

■ Proven integration patterns

Over the past decades, many proven message-based integration patterns have been designed and successfully applied in many enterprises. For example, the *pub-sub pattern* has been used to publish messages to a topic, to which several subscribers subscribe to get copies of the messages. A *dead letter pattern* puts messages that can't be automatically processed into a dedicated queue so that they can be handled later either manually or by a specialized tool. A *correlation identifier* traces a request across multiple hops across multiple services for diagnose and audit proposes. A *message translator* transforms messages from one format to another so that incompatible services can work together. The set of patterns mentioned here is a just a small subset of many useful integration patterns that you can add to your arsenal.

Different messaging systems provide different message delivery guarantees. Generally speaking, a programming model that supports reliable messaging should support *at-least-once delivery*, which means any messages are guaranteed to be delivered at least once. Some systems can work with *best-attempt*, which means the system make its best effort to deliver a message, but ensured delivery is not guaranteed. Some systems also attempt to guarantee *exact-once delivery*, in which a message is guaranteed to be delivered exactly once. Exact-once delivery is quite hard, and some even says is impossible. Usually a system can guarantee exact-once delivery only within a given time window. This means the consumer code still need to expect in some rare cases, a message may arrive multiple times and implement *idemoptent pattern* to avoid possible state corruptions.

Some programing model also attempts to provide ordered message delivery to developers as well. However, ensuring message orders in a distributed system is hard, and the cost of ensuring ordering could be high. A workaround is to get the consumer program to sort the messages as necessary.

Instance Identity

A service instance usually doesn't have a runtime identity. This is because a service instance maybe dynamically created, destroyed and reallocated. User code that relies on service identities is usually badly designed.

However, service instance identity becomes relevant when it comes to the actor pattern, because each actor instance is uniquely identified by a stable identifier. When an actor client talks to an actor instance, it uses the actor's identifier to locate and invoke the actor. In virtual actor pattern, there's only one actor instance is activated at any given time. This guarantee simplifies user code design as the user code can assume a single entrance at any given time.

There are various possible strategies to activate a new service instance, each with its benefits and limitations. A well-designed programming model should allow different activation policies to be defined and applied.

Per-Message Activation

In this case, a runtime creates a new instance for each request to be forwarded. The instance is torn down once it finishes processing the message. For containerized services, this means a new container instance is created for each request and then torn down when it returns. This is suitable for complex tasks that take a relatively long time to run. If the container crashes before it can return, the control plane will try to launch the container again and wait for a positive answer. A runtime can also activate a process if you supply a launching script that launches a process. This process-launching can happen inside a container as well. Basically, the runtime attaches to the designated container and executes the process-launching script you provide.

Pooled Activation

With pooled activation, a runtime keeps an instance pool and distributes messages among these instances. Logically, this allows the runtime to launch processor instances at a higher density. Furthermore, the runtime can perform additional magic:

- Dynamic scaling, including scaling to zero. A runtime can dynamically adjust the instance pool size as the number of concurrent requests changes. And when there are no requests, it can scale the pool size to zero so that the customer doesn't incur extra costs for keeping idle compute instances around.
- Performance-based routing. Instead of doing round-robin routing, a runtime can monitor the performance of running instances and route messages to the most performant instances.
- Partitioned placement. A runtime can place instances with certain tags inside the same pool node. For instance, in a smart building scenario, it can place digital twins representing sensors on the same floor in the same pool node. Then, as these digital twins try to send telemetries to an aggregator, the runtime sidecar can cache the messages and forward an aggregated message to the aggregator. Aggregation is a very common scenario, and with an actor framework that reinforces single-threaded operations, the aggregator often becomes a bottleneck. The cached delivery avoids such bottlenecks even if the aggregator uses a single-threaded model that doesn't allow re-entrance.

Single Activation

Single activation uses the same service instance for handling all messages. Once a service instance is launched, it's reused for all messages. It's relaunched only if it crashes. If the service is partitioned, a runtime can distribute messages across partitions. If the source event has associated partition annotations, the runtime can use these annotations to pick partitions. Otherwise, the runtime can choose partitions based on hash values of the messages.

An alternate single activation policy allows a secondary service to be appointed. If the runtime fails to activate or re-activates the primary service, it falls back to the secondary service. This is essentially the circuit-breaker pattern or the primary-secondary pattern. When eventual consistent reads are allowed, a runtime can launch additional read-only instances to share the read workload.

The last activation policy is not to activate any new processes. In this case, the runtime assumes the service (such as a managed service on cloud) is always available.

Flexible Bindings

A cloud-native application often needs to work with SaaS services such as AI, authentication and storage. Accessing these services often need specific SDKs, communication protocols, authentication methods and message encoding methods. If a programming model provides an abstraction (through a sidecar, for instance), it can allow user code to be dynamically bound to different event sources without impacting user code, because the sidecar can provide a standardized interface (through JSON payload through HTTP, for instance), as shown in Figure 10.2.

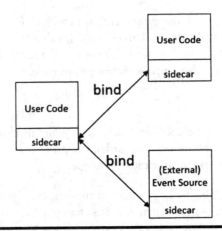

Figure 10.2   Bindings through sidecars

Bindings make application portable across different platforms. When an application is deployed to different platforms, an operator can rebind the services to different event sources. For example, when the application is deployed on AWS, the operator may choose to bind to SQS as a message queue. When the application is deployed to Azure, the same user code can be bound to Service Bus as the queuing service. And when the application is deployed to an edge environment where hosted services are unavailable, service can be bound to local queue implementations, such as containerized RabbitMQ.

Because bindings are supported by sidecars, they can be dynamically reconfigured while the user code is running. For example, the preceding application is bound to a cloud-based service queue by default and rebound to a local queue for business continuity when Internet connection is interrupted.

Additional Services

An application model, a programming model, a control plane with a scalable scheduler provide the foundation for cloud-native application design, deployment and management. This section lists some additional services that bring in other value-added services to the cloud-native application development cycles.

Builders

A builder builds source code into deployable units. For containerized services, building Docker containers using Docker toolchain is an easy task. However, it's quite difficult to build a generic builder for non-containerized applications. Although some systems try to automatically recognize project types of repositories (by using a Machine Learning module, for instance), and then invoke corresponding build scripts to build and package the applications, they've seen limited successes because each project is likely to have some unique requirements that can't be automated.

Of course, asking developers to provide build scripts or build containers is a feasible approach. However, I feel more can be done. Unfortunately, what's "more" remains unclear at this point in time. This is one of those problems that is theoretically easy but tremendously hard to solve with a fully-automated solution.

Package Repositories

A package repository provides a centralized repository for reusable applications. If the applications use a flat resource-based model, it will be easy to merge multiple application models. Each application model is assigned to a namespace (which is named after the application name) to avoid conflicts.

A package repository can creates deep signatures of applications. For example, the signature can be calculated based on all package (such as a Docker image) hashes as well as a hash of the application manifest itself. Then the hash can be signed with the publisher's certificate. This provides the basic building block for code attestation before execution.

Application Designer

In this era of command-line tools, the idea of offering a graphical designer seems irrational. However, I believe a good visualization tool and an AI-aided design system can go a long way in supporting high-quality application designs, especially for complex applications that use tens or even hundreds of services. The intuitive clarity provided by a graphical tool can't be replaced by text-based command-line tools.

As introduced earlier, the cloud-native application model is a directional graph. This allows an application designer to provide intelligent features such as design pattern recommendations, anti-pattern detections, and automatic architecture reviews. I've also created an early prototype that guides a designer through the design process through a chat using natural language between the designer and an automated designer bot.

Service Discovery

Existing container-based service discovery is by host names only. And existing function-level service discovery is by invoking syntax. An established service that allows service discovery by service functionalities doesn't exist. For example, there is no way to locate a service that can add two numbers together. You might be able to find a server that named "add," but you have no guarantee what the function does.

One way to semantically discover services is to use an ontology language to model intentions as well as data structures. The problem with this approach is complexity—developers will need to understand the ontology language to construct service describes and service discovery requests.

Another way to implement semantic service discovery is to use a simple modeling language, such as using a fixed *subject-predicate-object* description sentence structure. And instead of describing arbitrary data structures, the discovery service will limit data structures to flat key-value property bags. Furthermore, a global lexicon can be used to define semantic meanings of property keys and values.

Yet another way to perform semantic discovery is to express your needs using a small but representative set of sample data. The service registry will locate a service that can offer such projection. This really simplifies the service registration and discovery process. When a new service registers with the registry, it doesn't need to provide a semantic description. Instead, the registry automatically categorizes the service by sending some random inputs, collecting outputs, and calculating a category score. And when a service discovery requests (such as a JSON payload with sample requests), the registry tries to find a matching service based on the request data set.

Semantic service discovery can also incorporate other non-functional requirements, such as SLA levels, cost constraints, performance expectations, vendor preferences, and data sovereignty requirements.

Semantic service discovery doesn't replace traditional service discovery. Once the desired service is discovered, the consumer code should use the traditional service discovery mechanism to discover the exact syntax to consume the service.

Skynet

The Terminator is one of my favorite science fiction movies. What fascinates me the most is not the killer robot, but Skynet, a decentralized network that has its own mind. And I believe it can be implemented using the CMR model as introduced in Chapter 1. With the CMR model, all compute resources across the world can participate in workload distribution and collaborate to complete complex tasks. Advances in containerization, container orchestration, event-driven architecture, semantic service discovery, and Machine Learning are paving ways for Skynet to become a reality.

Skynet has its practical application in IoT scenarios. Skynet describes IoT edge infrastructure with three roles: *orchestrator, device representative*, and *device agent*. Orchestrator is responsible in workload distribution. It runs workload auctions to distribute workloads to compute resources. A device representative represents a compute unit. It participates in workload auctions conducted by the orchestrator and works with an on-device agent to distribute workload bits, and it establishes connections between the physical device and the messaging framework. A device agent implements a simple interface that does two things: receives on-device binaries and sends/receives messages from the messaging framework.

Skynet provides a consistent architecture for all IoT deployment topologies. For example, in an IoT scenario that needs to deploy and connect to low-capacity devices, a simple device agent is deployed on a device, and the rest of the system is deployed on a field gateway. On the other hand, if end devices are more capable, device representatives can be deployed on devices as well.

Device representatives can also implement a self-contained orchestrator. This is a much simpler orchestrator because it handles not a generic scheduling problem that may involve scheduling multiple competing workloads to the same infrastructure, but a specific scheduling problem that ensures availability of a single workload.

With semantic discovery, machines can locate necessary functionalities that augment their own capabilities, and they can use Skynet to re-project workloads on to Skynet itself. Although I don't believe this architecture will lead to machine self-awareness, it's close to offering a foundation for a "distributed cloud" that offers limitless compute resources to consumers just like a regular cloud platform.

To encourage community adoption, a financial model based on Blockchain can be established. In such a compute trading system, individuals earn tokens by contributing compute resources to the network.

Furthermore, with multi-party confidential computing, data can be encrypted before is submitted to untrusted parties to process the data in encrypted format. And only the original data owner can decrypt the result.

Zen of Cloud

"Our mission is to empower every person and every organization on the planet to achieve more."

Satya Nadella

Among the leading IT organizations, Microsoft's mission statement is the most precise and the most motivating. As one of the largest technology companies on the world, Microsoft views empowering the world to achieve more as its own core mission. Indeed, Microsoft is one of the few companies who have the technology and resources to influence the world.

Just a decade ago, Microsoft was still a company focused on operation systems and license-based software. Moving to cloud is a bold but necessary move. It has been a very painful process. Microsoft has made many mistakes, but it also has made solid progress in the cloud era. It was not an innovation; it was a rebirth.

AWS started the cloud, and it has been dominating the IaaS world. For years, Microsoft has been trying hard to catch up with AWS to provide a scalable, robust, and efficient cloud infrastructure. This has been a hard journey. However, in the end I believe every cloud platform will figure out efficient ways to operate infrastructure, just like all utility companies have figured out how to efficiently operate the resource infrastructure.

The true innovation, and the core stage for competition, resides in the PaaS world. In this world, Google is coming strong with Kubernetes. Kubernetes has formed not only a vibrant global community, but is also a center of gravity for innovations that attract brain power from not only Google, but also the entire software community, including Microsoft.

I don't believe in converging on a single platform or a framework. This is why I believe the industry should collectively take a workload-centric approach, and allows developers to gain full control of application architectures without locking into a specific platform. I strongly believe this is a value that will be appreciated more over time.

Index

Note: Page numbers in *italics* indicate figures.

365 Main, 38

A

A/B testing, 45, 89, 221, 275
Accelerated networking, 108–109
Accounts, keys and addresses in, Ethereum, 255
Activation. *See specific activation*
Activation layer, 289–290
Active-active model, redundancy, 32–33, *32–33*
Active directories (AD), 29–30
Active-passive model, redundancy, 33–34, *34*
AD. *See* Active directories (AD)
Adleman, Leonard, 103
Agility, 4, 30, 61
AI. *See* Artificial intelligence (AI)
Airbnb, 4
Alpine, 58
American Online (AOL), 48
AOL. *See* American Online (AOL)
API. *See* Application programming interface (API)
Application consistency, 80
Application designer, 285
Application model, 271–272, 273–277
    operational concerns, 274–275
    service mesh, 275–276
    services, 274
    tree structure, 276–277
Application packages, 273
Application programming interface (API), 13
    EndSnapshot, 80–81
    StartSnapshot, 80
Application-specific integrated circuit (ASIC), 108–109
Architecture
    browser/server (BS), 155–156
    client/server (CS), 155
    completeness, 73
    decay, 43–44
    independency, 73
ARM. *See* Azure Resource Manager (ARM)
ARM Template, Azure, 15
Arrays and maps in, Solidity, 258

Artificial intelligence (AI), 123–153
    for agriculture, 178
    on Cloud, 141
    complex systems, 125
    evolutionary computation, 125–126
    machine learning, *See* Machine learning
    neural network, *See* Neural network
    rule-based systems, 124
Artificial neurons. *See* Neural network
ASIC. *See* Application-specific integrated circuit (ASIC)
At-least-once delivery, 161, 282
At-most-once delivery, 161
Attestation, enclave, 119
Authentication, 93–97
Authenticity in data protection, 104–105
Authorization, 93–97
Autoscaling, setting up, tutorial, 51–54
Availability, 1–2, 32, 33
    microservices operation, 74–76
    of multi-component system, 37–38
AWS
    CodeBuild, deployment of CI/CD systems,
        tutorial, 227–229
    Elastic Container Service (ECS), launching a
        container, tutorial, 198–199
    Fargate, launching a container, tutorial, 198–199
    Lambda, creating function, tutorial, 184–188
    virtual private cloud (VPC), creating,
        tutorial, 109–111
Azure, 11–12
    AD, ASP.NET Core web application, authentication,
        tutorial, 97–101
    ARM Template, 15
    Container Instances, launching a container, tutorial,
        196–197
    DDoS Protection Standard, creating, tutorial, 112–114
    DevOps, deployment of CI/CD systems, tutorial,
        222–227
    Functions, Hello-World function, creating, tutorial,
        190–193
    HDInsight, Apache Spark, installation, tutorial,
        173–176
    IoT Hub, 168
    network architecture, *12*